William Wallace Beach

The Indian Miscellany

William Wallace Beach

The Indian Miscellany

ISBN/EAN: 9783337098490

Printed in Europe, USA, Canada, Australia, Japan

Cover: Foto ©ninafisch / pixelio.de

More available books at **www.hansebooks.com**

THE

INDIAN MISCELLANY;

CONTAINING

PAPERS ON THE HISTORY, ANTIQUITIES, ARTS, LANGUAGES, RELIGIONS, TRADITIONS AND SUPERSTITIONS

OF

THE AMERICAN ABORIGINES;

WITH

DESCRIPTIONS OF THEIR DOMESTIC LIFE, MANNERS, CUSTOMS, TRAITS, AMUSEMENTS AND EXPLOITS;

TRAVELS AND ADVENTURES IN THE INDIAN COUNTRY;

Incidents of Border Warfare; Missionary Relations, etc.

EDITED BY W. W. BEACH.

ALBANY:
J. MUNSELL, 82 STATE STREET.
1877.

TO THE MEMORY

OF

SAMUEL GARDNER DRAKE,

WHO THROUGHOUT A LONG AND STUDIOUS LIFE DEVOTED CONSTANT AND UNWEARIED EFFORT TO THE RECOVERY AND PRESERVATION OF WHATEVER RELATED TO THE HISTORY OF A RACE WHOSE ANNALS MUST ERELONG CONSTITUTE THEIR ONLY MONUMENT,

This Volume is Reverently Dedicated.

ADVERTISEMENT.

The purpose of this publication is to preserve, in convenient form, interesting fugitive papers concerning the aborigines of America. Reprinted mainly from reviews, magazines, newspapers, pamphlets and other ephemera, these articles are reproduced in the exact language of the originals; excepting an occasional change of title, the omission of what was deemed irrelevant or redundant, and in the several instances where authors have revised or extended their essays expressly for this work.

CONTENTS.

Historical and Mythological Traditions of the Algonquins; with a Translation of the Walum-Olum, or Bark Record of the Lenni Lenape — By E. G. Squier . . . 9

A Ride with the Apaches — By Herbert C. Dorr . . 43

The Captivity of Christian Fast — By Geo. W. Hill, M.D. . 51

The Esquimaux of Labrador — By A. S. Packard, Jr. . 65

Indian Medicine — By John Mason Browne . 74

Narrative of the Long Walk — By John Watson, Father and Son . 86

The Early Jesuit Missionaries of the North Western Territory — By W. B. O. Peabody 102

Comparative Vocabularies of the Seminole and Makasuke Tongues — By Buckingham Smith 120

A Sioux Vision — Thick-Headed-Horse's Dream — By John Hallam . 127

Joseph Brant, Thayendanegea, and his Posterity — By Wm. C. Bryant 145

Indian Migrations — By Lewis H. Morgan . 158

A Perilous Fossil Hunt — By William C. Wyckoff 258

Indian Affairs Around Detroit in 1706 — By Col. Charles Whittlesey 270

The Aboriginal Inhabitants of Connecticut — By Luzerne Ray . 280

The Indian Reservations of California — By J. Ross Browne . 303

The Dog Sacrifice of the Senecas — By Samuel Crowell . 323

The Spanish Mission Colony on the Rappahannock; The First European Settlement in Virginia — By John Gilmary Shea . . 333

CONTENTS.

ALASKAN MUMMIES — BY W. H. DALL   344

DYEING, SPINNING AND WEAVING, BY THE CAMANCHES, NAVAJOES AND OTHER INDIANS OF NEW MEXICO — BY J. HENRY PETERS 352

A FORTNIGHT AMONG THE CHIPPEWAS OF LAKE SUPERIOR — BY PROF. J. J. DUCATEL 361

THE JANE MC CREA TRAGEDY — BY WILLIAM L. STONE . 379

A VISIT TO THE STANDING ROCK AGENCY — BY DANIEL LEASURE, M.D.   387

AMONG THE GUATUSOS; A NARRATIVE OF ADVENTURE AND DISCOVERY IN CENTRAL AMERICA — BY O. J. PARKER . . . 396

THE REV. JOHN ELIOT, AND HIS INDIAN CONVERTS — BY REV. MARTIN MOORE   405

INDIAN LANGUAGES OF THE PACIFIC STATES AND TERRITORIES — BY ALBERT S. GATSCHET 410

CHASTISEMENT OF THE YAMASEES; AN INCIDENT OF THE EARLY INDIAN WARS IN GEORGIA 448

THE LAST OF THE PEQUODS — BY BENSON J. LOSSING . 452

THE TRADITION OF AN INDIAN ATTACK ON HADLEY, MASS., IN 1675 — BY GEORGE SHELDON 461

THE INDIAN MISCELLANY.

*HISTORICAL AND MYTHOLOGICAL TRADITIONS OF
THE ALGONQUINS.*

WITH A TRANSLATION OF THE WALUM-OLUM, OR BARK RECORD OF THE LENNI
LENAPE.[1]

[Read before the New York Historical Society at its regular meeting in June, 1848.]

BY E. G. SQUIER.

THE discovery of America, in the fifteenth century, constitutes a grand era in the history of the world. From it we may date the rise of that mental energy and physical enterprise, which has since worked such wonderful changes in the condition of the human race. It gave a new and powerful impulse to the nations of Europe, then slowly rousing from the lethargy of centuries. Love of adventure, hope, ambition, avarice — the most powerful incentives to human action — directed the attention of all men to America. Thither flocked the boldest and most adventurous spirits of Europe; and half a century of startling events sufficed to lift the veil of night from a vast continent, unsurpassed in the extent and variety of its productions, abounding in treasures, and teeming with a strange people, divided into numberless families, exhibiting many common points of resemblance, yet differing widely in their condition, manners, customs, and civil and social organizations.

Along the shores of the frozen seas of the north, clothed with the furs of the sea-monsters whose flesh had supplied them with food, burrowing in icy caverns during the long polar nights, were found the dwarfed and squalid Esquimaux. In lower latitudes, skirting the bays and inlets of the Atlantic, pushing their canoes along the shores of the great lakes, or chasing the buffalo on the vast meadows of the west, broken up into numerous families,

[1] Reprinted from *The American Whig Review* (New York), for February, 1849.

subdivided into tribes, warring constantly, and ever struggling for ascendency over each other, were the active and fearless hunters, falling chiefly within the modern extended denominations of the Algonquin and Iroquois families. Still lower down, in the mild and fertile regions bordering the Gulf of Mexico, more fixed in their habits, half hunters, half agriculturists, with a systematized religion, and a more consolidated civil organization, and constituting the connecting link between the gorgeous semi-civilization of Mexico and the nomadic state of the northern families, were the Floridian tribes, in many respects one of the most interesting groups of the continent. Beneath the tropics, around the bases of the volcanic ranges of Mexico, and occupying her high and salubrious plains, Cortez found the Aztecs and their dependencies — nations rivaling in their barbarous magnificence the splendors of the oriental world — far advanced in the arts, living in cities, constructing vast works of public utility, and sustaining an imposing, though bloody religious system. Passing the nations of Central America, whose architectural monuments challenge comparison with the proudest of the old world, and attest the advanced condition and great power of their builders, Pizarro found beneath the equator a vast people, living under a well-organized and consolidated government, attached to a primitive Sabianism, fixed in their habits and customs, and happy in their position and circumstances. Still beyond these to the southward, were the invincible Araucanians, together with numerous other nations, with distinctive features, filling still lower places in the scale of advancement, and finally subsiding into the squalid counterparts of the Esquimaux in Patagonia.

These numerous nations, exhibiting contrasts so striking, and institutions so novel and interesting, it might be supposed, would have at once attracted the attention of the learned of that day, and insured at their hands a full and authentic account of their government, religion, traditions, customs, and modes of life. The men, however, who subverted the empires of Montezuma and the Incas, were bold adventurers, impelled for the most part by an absorbing avarice and unfitted by habit, as incapable, from education and circumstances, of transmitting to us correct or satisfactory information respecting the nations with which they were acquainted. The ecclesiastics who followed in their train, from whom more might have been expected, actuated by a fierce bigotry, and eager only to elevate the symbol of their intolerance over the emblems of a rival priesthood, misrepresented the religious conceptions of the Indians, and exaggerated the bloody observances of the aboriginal ritual, as an apology, if not a justification, for their own barbarism and cruelty. They threw down the high altars of Aztec superstition, and consecrated to their own mummeries the solar symbols of the Peruvian temples. They burned the pictured historical and mythological records of the ancient empire in the public square of Mexico; defaced the sculptures on her monuments, and crushed in pieces the statues of her gods. Yet the next day, with an easy transition, they proclaimed the great impersonation of the female, or productive principle of nature, who in the Mexican, as in every other system of mythology, was the consort of the Sun, to be no other than the Eve of the Mosaic record, or the Mother of Christ; they even tracked the vagrant St. Thomas in the person of the benign Quetzalcoatl, the Mexican counterpart of the Hindoo Buddha and the Egyptian Osiris!

All these circumstances have contributed to throw doubt and uncertainty over the Spanish accounts of the aboriginal nations. Nor were the circumstances attending European adventure and settlements, in other parts of the continent, much more favorable to the preservation of impartial and reliable records. The Puritan of the north and the gold-hunter of Virginia and Carolina, looked with little interest and less complacency upon the "wilde salvages" with which they were surrounded, and of whom Cotton Mather wrote, that "Although we know not *when* nor *how* they first became inhabitants of this mighty continent, yet we may guess the devil decoyed these miserable salvages hither, in hopes that the gospel of the Lord Jesus Christ would never come to destroy his absolute empire over them."

The Jesuits and other enthusiasts, the propagandists of the Catholic faith among the northern tribes, were more observant and correct, but their accounts are very meagre in matters of the most consequence, in researches concerning the history and religion of the aborigines. All treated the religious conceptions and practices and transmitted traditions of the Indians with little regard. Indeed it has been only during the last century, since European communication with the primitive nations of Southern Asia, and a more intimate acquaintance with oriental literature, have given a new direction to researches into the history of mind and man, that the true value of the religious notions and the recorded or transmitted traditions of various nations, in determining their origins and connections, and illustrating their remote history, has been ascertained. And even now there are few who have a just estimation of their importance in these respects. It may however be claimed, in the language of an erudite American, that " of all researches which most effectually aid us to discover the origin of a nation or people, whose history is either unknown, or deeply involved in the obscurity of ancient times, none are perhaps attended with such important results, as the analysis of their theological dogmas, and their religious practices. To such matters mankind adheres with the greatest tenacity, and though both modified and corrupted in the revolutions of ages, they still preserve features of their original construction when language, arts, sciences and political establishments no longer retain distinct lineaments of their ancient constitutions."

The traveler Clarke, maintaining the same position, observes, " that by a proper attention to the vestiges of ancient superstition, we are sometimes enabled to refer a whole people to their original ancestors, with as much if not more certainty, than by observations made upon their languages, because the superstition is engrafted upon the stock, but the language is liable to change." However important is the study of military, civil and political history, the science is incomplete without mythological history, and he is little imbued with the spirit of philosophy, who can perceive in the fables of antiquity nothing but the extravagance of a fervid imagination.[1] It is under this view, in the absence of

---

[1] "The existence of similar religious ideas in remote regions, inhabited by different races, is an interesting subject of study; furnishing as it does, one of the most important links in the great chain of communication which binds together the distant families of nations."— *Prescott's Mexico.*

such information derivable from early writers, as may form the basis of our inquiries into the history of the American race, its origin, and the rank which it is entitled to hold in the scale of human development, that the religious conceptions and observances, and authentic traditions of the aboriginal nations, become invested with new interest and importance. And although the opportunities for collecting them, at this day, are limited, and much care and discrimination is requisite to separate that which is original from what is derivable, still they perhaps afford the safest and surest means of arriving at the results desired. Not that I would be understood as undervaluing physical or philological researches, in their bearings upon these questions; for if the human mind can ever flatter itself with having discovered the truth, it is when many facts, and these facts of different kinds, unite in producing the same result.

Impressed with these views, I have, in pursuing investigations in another but cognate department of research, taken considerable pains to collect from all available sources, such information as seemed authentic, relating not only to the religious ceremonies and conceptions, but also to the mythological and historical traditions of the aborigines of all parts of the continent. An analysis and comparison of these have led to some most extraordinary results, which it would be impossible, in the narrow scope of this paper, to indicate with necessary fullness. It may be said generally, that they exhibit not only a wonderful uniformity and concurrence in their elements and more important particulars, but also an absolute identity, in many essential respects, with those which existed among the primitive nations of the old world, far back in the monumental and traditional periods.

Among the various original manuscripts which, in the course of these investigations, fell into my possession, I received through the hands of the executors of the lamented Nicollet, a series by the late Prof. C. S. Rafinesque—well known as a man of science and of an inquiring mind, but whose energies were not sufficiently concentrated to leave a decided impression in any department of research. A man of unparalleled industry, an earnest and indefatigable collector of facts, he was deficient in that scope of mind joined to severe critical powers, indispensable to correct generalization. While, therefore, it is usually safe to reject his conclusions, we may receive his facts, making proper allowances for the haste with which they were got together.

Among these manuscripts ("*rudis indigestaque moles*"), was one entitled the *Walum Olum*, (literally, *painted sticks*), or painted and engraved traditions of the Lenni-Lenape, comprising five divisions, the first two embodying the traditions referring to the creation and a general flood, and the rest comprising a record of various migrations, with a list of ninety-seven chiefs, in the order of their succession, coming down to the period of the discovery. This manuscript also embraces one hundred and eighty-four compound mnemonic symbols, each accompanied by a sentence or verse in the original language, of which a literal translation is given in English. The only explanation which we have concerning it, is contained in a foot note, in the hand of Rafinesque, in which he states that the manuscript and wooden originals were obtained in Indiana in 1822, and that they were for a long time inexplicable, "until with a deep study of the Delaware, and the aid of Zeisberger's manuscript dictionary in the library of the Philosophical Society, a translation was effected." This translation, it may here be remarked, so far as I have been able to test it, is a faithful one, and there is slight doubt that the original is what it professes to be, a genuine Indian record. The evidence that it is so, is however rather internal and collateral than direct.[1] The traditions which it embodies coincide, in most important respects, with those which are known to have existed, and which still exist, in forms more or less modified, among the various Algonquin tribes, and the mode in which they are recorded is precisely that which was adopted by the Indians of this stock, in recording events, communicating intelligence, etc., and which has not inaptly been denominated *picture-writing*.

The scope of this system of picture-writing, and the extent to

---

[1] Since the above was written, a copy of Rafinesque's *American Nations*, published in 1836, has fallen under my notice. It is a singular jumble of facts and fancies, and it is perhaps unfortunate for the manuscript, spoken of in the text, that it falls in such a connection. The only additional information we have respecting it, is that it was "obtained by the late Dr. Ward of Indiana, of the remnant of the Delawares on the White river."

which it was applied, have not been generally understood nor fully recognized. Without, however, going into an analysis of the system, its principles and elements—an inquiry of much interest—it may be claimed, upon an array of evidence which will admit of no dispute, that under it the Indians were not only able to communicate events and transmit intelligence, but also to record chants and songs, often containing abstract ideas—allusions to the origin of things, the power of nature, and to the elements of their religion. "The Indians," says Heckewelder, "have no alphabet, nor any mode of representing words to the eye, yet they have certain hieroglyphics, by which they describe facts in so plain a manner, that those who are conversant with their marks, can understand them with the greatest ease — as easily, indeed, as they can understand a piece of writing."[1] This writer also asserts that the simple principles of the system are so well recognized, and of so general application, that the members of different tribes could interpret with the greatest facility the drawings of other and remote tribes. Loskiel has recorded his testimony to the same effect. He says: "The Delawares use hieroglyphics on wood, trees and stones, to give caution, for communication, to commemorate events and preserve records. Every Indian understands their meaning, etc."[2] Mr. Schoolcraft also observes of the Ojibwas, that "every path has its blazed and figurated tree, conveying intelligence to all that pass, for all can understand these signs, which," he adds, " are taught to the young as carefully as our alphabet." Testimony might be accumulated upon this point, to an indefinite extent, were it necessary to our present purpose.

Most of the signs used in this system are representations of things: some however were derivative, others symbolical, and still others entirely arbitrary. They however were not capable of doing more than to suggest classes of ideas, which would not be expressed in precisely the same words by different individuals. They were taught in connection with certain forms of expression, by which means they are made essentially *mnemonic* — a simple

---
[1] *Hist. Acct. of the Indian Nations*, p. 118.
[2] *Hist. United Brethren in America*, p. 25.

or compound sign, thus serving to recall to mind an entire sentence or a series of them. A single figure, with its adjuncts, would stand for the verse of a song, or for a circumstance which it would require several sentences to explain.

Thus the famous *Metäi song* of the Chippeways, presented by Mr. Catlin, although embracing but about thirty signs, occupied, in the slow, monotonous chant of the Indians, with their numerous repetitions, nearly an hour in its delivery. James observes, respecting the recorded Indian songs — " They are usually carved on a flat piece of wood, and the figures suggest to the minds of those who have learned the songs, the ideas and the order of their succession. The words are not variable, but must be taught; otherwise, though from an inspection of the figure the idea might be comprehended, no one would know what to sing." Most of the Indian lore being in the hands of the priests or medicine-men, the teaching of these songs was almost entirely monopolized by them. They taught them only to such as had distinguished themselves in war and the chase, and then only upon the payment of large prices. Tanner states that he was occupied more than a year in learning the great song for "medicine hunting," and then obtained his knowledge only at the expense of many beaver skins. After the introduction of Christianity, among some of the Western tribes, prayers were inscribed on pieces of wood, in mnemonic symbols, in the making and teaching of which to their followers, some of the Christian chiefs obtained a profitable monopoly.

Admitting then, as we must do upon this evidence, that the Algonquins had the means of imperfectly recording their traditions, songs, etc., we can readily understand how these might be taught by father to son, and perpetuated in great purity through a succession of priests — the sages of the aboriginal races. The fact that they were recorded, even in the rude way here indicated, would give them a degree of fixedness, and entitle them to a consideration which they would not possess if handed down in a simple oral form.[1]

[1] "Were it not," says Dr. Barton, in his paper on the *Origin of the American Nations*, published in the *Transactions of the Philosophical Society* — "Were it not for the traditions of many of the American nations, we might for ever remain in doubt concerning their real origin. These traditions are entitled to much consideration; for, notwithstanding the rude condition of most of the

TRADITIONS OF THE ALGONQUINS. 17

The manuscript under consideration seems to be a series of Indian traditional songs, in the original mnemonic signs, with the words attached to them, written out from the recitations of the Indians, by some person conversant with the Indian tongue, precisely as we find some of the songs recorded by James, in his Appendix to Tanner's Narrative. As already observed, it has strong internal evidence of being what it purports to be — evidence sufficiently strong, in my estimation, to settle its authenticity. I may however add, that, with a view of leaving no means unemployed to ascertain its true value, I submitted it, without explanation, to an educated Indian chief (Kah-ge-ga-gah-bowh), George Copway, who unhesitatingly pronounced it authentic, in respect not only to the original signs and accompanying explanations in the Delaware dialect, but also in the general ideas and conceptions which it embodies. He also bore testimony to the fidelity of the translation.

In submitting, therefore, the following paraphrase of these singular records, I feel I am not obtruding the coinage of a curious idler, nor an apocryphal record, but presenting matter deserving of attention, and of important bearing upon many interesting questions connected with the history of our aboriginal nations.

It will be readily understood that I have, in numerous instances, been compelled to adopt forms of expression, not common to the Indian languages; so far as practicable, however, the words have been literally rendered, and the Indian form of expression preserved; and I feel some confidence in saying that no violence has been done to the original in the paraphrase.

For the sake of convenience, I have divided the manuscript into two parts; the first embracing the traditions referring to the creation, etc., and the second those which may be regarded as historical. It will be observed that there are various interruptions or pauses in the narrative, which indicate the individual traditions.

In illustration of the manner in which the manuscript is written, the first two songs or chants are presented as they appear in the original. We have first, the original sign; second, the suggested verse or sentence in the Delaware dialect; and third, a literal translation of the same in English.

tribes, they are often perpetuated in great purity, as I have discovered by much attention to their history."

18 THE INDIAN MISCELLANY.

SONG I.—THE CREATION.

1. Sny ewitalli wemiguma wokgetaki.[1]
   At first there all sea-water above land

2. Hackung-kwelik owanaku wakyutali
   Above much water foggy (was) and (or also) there
   Kitanitowitessop.[2]
   Creator he was.

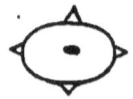
3.[3] Sayewis[4] hallemiwis[5] nolemiwi Kitanitowit-
   First-being, Eternal-being, invisible Creator
   essop.
   he was.

4. Sohalawak kwelik hakik owak
   He causes them much water much land much air (or
   awasagamak.
   clouds) much heaven.

5. Sohalawak gishuk nipanum alankwak.
   He causes them the Sun the moon the stars.

6. Wemi-sohalawak yulik yuch-aan.
   All he causes these well to move.

7. Wich-owagan kshakan moshakwat
   With action (or rapidly) it blows (wind) it clears up
   kwelik kshipelep.
   great waters it ran off.

8. Opeleken mani-menak delsin-epit.
   It looks bright made islands is there at.

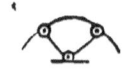
9. Lappinup Kitanitowit manito manitoak.
   Again when Creator he made spirits or makers.

---

[1] The terminal *aki* is a contraction of *hakki*, land, and frequently denotes *place* simply.
[2] Written Ge*tanitowit* by Heckewelder, p. 422.
[3] Figure 3 is a representation of the sun, which was the Algonquin symbol of the Great Spirit.
[4] The termination *wiss* or *iss* makes according to Mr. Schoolcraft, whatever precedes it personal (*Algic Res.*, vol. i, p. 201). The better translation would therefore be, "The First," "The Eternal," &c.
[5] *Allowini*, more, and *wulik*, good, enter into most designations of the Supreme.—Heck., p. 422.

TRADITIONS OF THE ALGONQUINS. 19

10. Owiniwak   Angelatawiwak   chichankwak
    First beings also   and Angels   Souls also
    wemiwak.
    and all.

11. Wtenk-manito 'jinwis¹ lennowak mukom.
    After he made   beings   men and grandfather.

12. Milap   netami-gaho   owini-gaho.
    He gave them   the first mother   first-being's-
    mother.

13. Namesik-milap tulpewik awesik cholensak.
    Fishes he gave him   turtles   beasts   birds.

14. Makimani-shak   sohalawak   makowini
    Bad Spirit but   he causes them   bad beings
    n'akowak   amangamek.
    black snakes   monsters (or large reptiles).

15. Sohalawak uchewak sohalawak pungusak.
    He causes them   flies   he causes them   gnats.

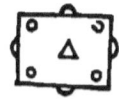
16. Nitisak   wemi-owini   w'delsinewuap.
    Friends   all beings   were then.

---

¹ In the Chippeway, according to McKenzie and Long, *ninnee* or *inini* means *man*. Mr. Schoolcraft states that *ininee* is the diminutive form of the word, signifying *little-men*, as Puck-wudj-*ininee*, "vanishing little men," the fairy-men of Algonquin story. The cognate term of the text seems to have a slightly different meaning: it is translated *beings*, and is written *nijini* or *'jini*, beings; *owini*, first beings, *mako-wini*, evil beings, etc. In the Delaware dialect *lenno* or *lenna* meant man, and is so translated in the text. The true designation of the Delawares was " Lenni-Lenape," which is usually understood to mean " Original" or " True men." It is not impossible that it is compounded of "*nijini*," beings, and *lenno*, men ; literally, men-beings. This compound may have been suggestive of something superior to men in general or collectively.

17. Kiwis, wunand wishi-manitoak essopak.
    Thou being good God good spirits were there.

18. Nijini netami lennowak nigoha netami
    The beings the first men mothers first
    okwewi nantinewak.
    wives little spirits (fairies).

19. Gattamin netami mitzi nijiti
    Fat fruits the first food the beings
    nantiné.
    little spirits.

20. Wemi wingi-namenep wemi-ksin elan-
    All willingly pleased all easy think-
    damep wullatemanuwi.
    ing happy.

21. Shukand eli-kimi mekenikink wakon
    But then while secretly on earth snake-god[1]
    powako init'ako.
    priest-snake worship snake.

22. Mattalugas pallalugas maktatin owagan
    Wickedness crime unhappiness actions.
    payat-chikutali.
    coming there then.

23. Waktapan-payat wihillan mboagan.
    Bad weather coming distempers death.

24. Wonwemi wiwunch-kamik atak-kitahikan
    This all very long aforetime beyond great waters
    netami-epit.
    first land at.

---

[1] The snake among the Algonquins was symbolical of evil or malignant force.

PARAPHRASE OF THE ABOVE SONG.

1. At the first there were great waters above all the land,
2. And above the waters were thick clouds, and there was God the Creator :
3. The first being, eternal, omnipotent, invisible, was God the Creator.
4. He created vast waters, great lands, and much air and heaven ;
5. He created the sun, the moon and the stars ;
6. He caused them all to move well.

7. By his power he made the winds to blow, purifying, and the deep waters to run off :
8. All was made bright and the islands were brought into being.

9. Then again God the Creator made the great Spirits,
10. He made also the first beings, angels and souls :
11. Then made he a man being, the father of men ;
12. He gave him the first mother, the mother of the early born,
13. Fishes gave he him, turtles, beasts and birds.

14. But the Evil Spirit created evil beings, snakes and monsters :
15. He created vermin and annoying insects.
16. Then were all beings friends :
17. There being a good god, all spirits were good —
18. The beings, the first men, mothers, wives, little spirits also.
19. Fat fruits were the food of the beings and the little spirits :
20. All were then happy, easy in mind and pleased.

21. But then came secretly on earth the snake-(evil) god, the snake-priest and snake-worship :
22. Came wickedness, came unhappiness.
23. Came then bad weather, disease and death.

24. This was all very long ago, at our early home.

The grand idea of a Supreme Unity, a Great, Good, Infinite and Eternal Creator, so clearly indicated in the foregoing song, may be regarded by many as the offspring of European intercourse, or as a comparatively late engraftment upon Algonquin tradition. Without denying that the teachings of the early missionaries had the effect of enlarging this conception, and of giving it a more definite form, it may at the same time be unhesitatingly claimed that the idea was an original one with the Indian mind. The testimony of the earliest travelers and of the earliest missionaries themselves, furnishes us abundant evidence of the fact. "Nothing," says Charlevoix, "is more certain than that the Indians of this continent have an idea of a Supreme Being, the First Spirit, the Creator and Governor of the world."[1] And Loskiel, not less explicit in his testimony, observes, "The prevailing opinion of all these nations is, that there is one God, a great and good Spirit, who created the heavens and the earth; who is Almighty; who causes the fruits to grow, grants sunshine and provides his children with food."[2] Says Schoolcraft, "They believe in the existence of a Supreme Being, who created material matter, the earth and heavens, men and animals, and filled space with subordinate spirits, having something of his own nature, to whom he gave part of his power." From this great and good being, it was believed, no evil could come; he was invested with the attribute of universal beneficence, and was symbolized by the sun. He was usually denominated *Kitchi-Manitou* or *Gitchy-Monedo*, literally, Great, Good Spirit. Various other names were employed to designate him under his various aspects, as *Wäskednd*, Maker; *Wāosemigōyan*, Universal Father.

Subordinate to this Supreme, Good Being, was an Evil Spirit, *Mitchi-Manitou*, or *Mudje-Monedo* (Great Bad Spirit), who, according to Mr. Schoolcraft, was a subsequent creation, and not coexistent with the Kitchi-Manitou. This seems implied in the song, where he is first spoken of after the creation of men and beings. Great power was ascribed to him, and he was regarded as the cause and originator of all the evils which befall mankind. Accordingly his favor was desired, and his anger sought to be averted by sacrifices and offerings. The power of the Mitchi-Manitou was not, however, supposed to extend to the future life.[3] He is represented in the text as the creator of flies and gnats,

---

[1] *Canada*, vol. II, p. 141.
[2] *United Brethren in America*, p. 84.
[3] *Carver's Travels*, p. 381.

and other annoying insects, an article of belief not exclusively Indian. While the symbol of the Good Spirit was *the Sun*, that of the chief of the Evil Spirits was *the Serpent*, under which form he appears in the Chippeway tradition of his contest with the demi-god Manabozho.

The idea of a destruction of the world by water seems to have been general amongst the Algonquin nations. The traditionary details vary in almost every instance where they have been recorded, but the traditionary event stands out prominently. The catastrophe is in all cases ascribed to the Evil Spirit; who, as already observed, was symbolized as a great Serpent. He is generally placed in antagonism to Manabozho, a powerful demi-god or intermediate spirit. These two mythological characters have frequent conflicts, and the flood is usually ascribed to the final contest between them. In these cases the destruction of the world is but an incident. As recorded in the *Walum Olum*, it originates in a general conflict between the Good Spirits, " the beings," and the Evil Spirit, *Maskinako*. The variation is, however, unimportant, for in this, as in all the other versions of the tradition, Manabozho appears in the character of Preserver. The concurrence in the essential parts of the several traditions, is worthy of remark.

SONG II.— THE DELUGE.

1. Wulamo   maskan-ako-anup   lennowak
   Long ago powerful snake when men also
   makowini   essopak.
   bad beings had become.

2. Maskanako shingalusit   nijini-essopak
   Strong snake   enemy   beings had become
   shawalendamep   ekin-shingalan.
   became troubled   together hating.

3. Nishawi palliton nishawi machiton, nishawi
   Both   fighting   both   spoiling   both
   matta lungundowin.
   not   peaceful (or keeping peace).

4. Mattapewi   wiki   nihanlowit   mekwazuau.
   Less men   with   dead keeper   fighting.

5. Maskanako gichi penauwelendamep
   Strong snake great   resolved
     lennowak owini palliton.
     men   beings to destroy (fight).

6. N'akowa petonep, amangam petonep
   Black snake he brought, monster   he brought
     akopchella   petonep.
     rushing snake water he brought.

7. Pehella-pehella, pohoka-pohoka, eshohok-
   Much water rushing, much go to hills,   much
     eshohok   palliton-palliton.
     penetrating,   much destroying.

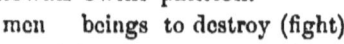

8. Tulapit   menapit Nanaboush,
   At Tula (or turtle land) at that island Nanabush
   maska-boush, owinimokom   linowimokom.
   (strong)   of beings the grandfather of men
   the grandfather.

9. Gishikin-pommixin   tulagishatten-lohxin.
   Being born creeping   at Tula he is ready to
   move and dwell.

10. Owini linowi wemoltin pehella gahani
    Beings men all go forth   flood   water
      pommixin   nahiwi   tatalli
      creeping (floating?) above water   which
      tulapin.
    way (where) turtle-back.

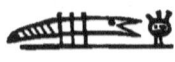
11. Amangamek   makdopamek   alendguwek
    Monsters of the sea they were many   some of
      metzipannek.
    them they did eat.

TRADITIONS OF THE ALGONQUINS. 25

12. Manito-dasin   mokol-wichemass   palpal
    Spirit daughters boat helped   come, come
    payat payat   wemichemap.
    coming coming   all helped.

13. Nanaboush,   Nanaboush,   wemimokom
    Nanabush,   Nanabush,   of all the grandfather,
        winimokom   linnimokom   tula-
    of beings the grandfather, of men the grand-
        mokom.
    father,   of turtles the grandfather.

14. Linapima   tulapima   tulapewi   tapitawi.
    Man then   turtle then turtle they altogether.

15. Wishanem   tulpewi   pataman
    Frightened (startled?) turtle he   praying
        tulpewi   paniton   wuliton.
        turtle he   let it be   to make well.

16. Kshipehelen   penkwihilen   kwamipokho
    Water running off it is drying plain and moun-
        sitwalikho   maskan   wagan
    tain path of cave powerful or dire action
        palliwi.
        elsewhere.

PARAPHRASE.

1. Long ago came the powerful serpent (*Maskanako*), when men had become evil.
2. The strong serpent was the foe of the beings, and they became embroiled, hating each other.
3. Then they fought and despoiled each other, and were not peaceful.
4. And the small men (*Mattapewi*) fought with the keeper of the dead (*Nihanlowit*).
5. Then the strong serpent resolved all men and beings to destroy immediately.
6. The black serpent, monster, brought the snake-water rushing,
7. The wide waters rushing, wide to the hills, everywhere spreading, everywhere destroying.
8. At the island of the turtle (*Tula*) was Manabozho, of men and beings the grandfather —
9. Being born creeping, at turtle land he is ready to move and dwell.

10. Men and beings all go forth on the flood of waters, moving afloat, every way seeking the back of the turtle (*Tulapin*).
11. The monsters of the sea were many, and destroyed some of them.
12. Then the daughter of a spirit helped them in a boat, and all joined, saying, Come help !
13. Manabozho, of all beings, of men and turtles, the grandfather !
14. All together, on the turtle then, the men then, were all together.
15. Much frightened, Manabozho prayed to the turtle that he would make all well again.
16. Then the waters ran off, it was dry on mountain and plain, and the great evil went elsewhere by the path of the cave.

The allusion to the turtle, in the tradition, is not fully understood. The turtle was connected, in various ways, with the mythological notions of the upper Algonquins. According to Charlevoix and Hennepin, the Chippeways had a tradition that the mother of the human race, having been ejected from heaven, was received upon the back of a tortoise, around which matter gradually accumulated, forming the earth.[1] The great turtle, according to Henry, was a chief spirit of the Chippeways, the " spirit that never lied," and was often consulted in reference to various undertakings. An account of one of these ceremonies is given by this author.[2] The island of *Michilimakanak* (literally, great turtle) was sacred to this spirit, for the reason, probably, that a large hill near its centre was supposed to bear some resemblance, in form, to a turtle.[3] The turtle tribe of the Lenape, says Heckewelder, claim a superiority and ascendency, because of their relationship to the great turtle, the Atlas of their mythology, who bears this great island (the earth) on his back.[4]

With these few illustrative observations, which might be greatly extended, I pass to the second or historical portion of the traditional record, with the simple remark that the details of the migrations here recounted, particularly so far as they relate to the passage of the Mississippi and the subsequent contest with the Tallegwi or Allegwi, and the final expulsion of the latter,

---

[1] *Charlevoix*, vol. II., p. 143; *Hennepin*, p. 55.
[2] *Henry's Travels*, p. 168.
[3] *Ib.*, 37, 110.
[4] *Heckewelder*, p. 246.

coincide, generally, with those given by various authors, and well known to have existed among the Delawares.

The traditions, in their order, relate first to a migration from the north to the south, attended by a contest with a people denominated Snakes, or Evil, who are driven to the eastward. One of the migrating families, the *Lowaniwi*, literally northlings, afterwards separate and go to the snow land, whence they subsequently go to the east, towards the island of the retreating Snakes. They cross deep waters, and arrive at *Shinaki*, the Land of Firs. Here the *Wunkenapi*, or Westerners, hesitate, preferring to return.

A hiatus follows, and the tradition resumes, the tribes still remaining at *Shinaki* or the Fir land.

They search for the great and fine island, the land of the Snakes, where they finally arrive, and expel the Snakes. They then multiply and spread towards the south, to the *Akolaki* or beautiful land, which is also called Shore-land, and Big-fir land. Here they tarried long, and for the first time cultivated corn and built towns. In consequence of a great drought, they leave for the *Shillilakiny* or Buffalo land. Here, in consequence of disaffection with their chief, they divide and separate, one party, the *Wetamowi*, or the Wise, tarrying, the others going off. The *Wetamowi* build a town on the *Wisawana* or Yellow river (probably the Missouri), and for a long time are peaceful and happy. War finally breaks out, and a succession of warlike chiefs follow, under whom conquests are made, north, east, south and west. In the end *Opekasit* (literally east-looking) is chief, who, tired with so much warfare, leads his followers towards the sun-rising. They arrive at the *Messussipu*, or Great river (the Mississippi), where, being weary, they stop, and their first chief is *Yagawanend*, or the Hut-maker, under whose chieftaincy it is discovered that a strange people, the *Tallegwi*, possess the rich east land. Some of the *Wetamowi* are slain by the Tallegwi, and then the cry of *palliton! palliton!!* war! war!! is raised, and they go over and attack the *Tallegwi*. The contest is continued during the lives of several chiefs, but finally terminates in the *Tallegwi* being driven southwards. The conquerors then occupy the country on the Ohio below the great lakes — the *Shawanipekis*. To the north are their friends, the *Talamatun*, literally *not-of-themselves*, translated Hurons. The Hurons, however, are not always friends, and they have occasional contests with them.

Another hiatus follows, and then the record resumes by saying that they were strong and peaceful at the land of the Tallegwi. They built towns and planted corn. A long succession of chiefs followed, when war again broke out, and finally a portion under *Linkewinnek*, or the Sharp-looking, went eastward beyond the *Talegachukung* or Alleghany mountains. Here they spread widely, warring against the *Mengwi* or Spring-people, the *Pungelika*, Lynx or Eries, and the *Mohegans* or Wolves. The various tribes into which they became divided, the chiefs of each in their order, with the territories which they occupied, are then named — bringing the record down until the arrival of the Europeans. This latter portion we are able to verify in great part from authentic history.

SONG III.— MIGRATIONS.

1. After the flood the true men (*Lennapewi*) were with the turtle, in the cave house, the dwelling of Talli.
2. It was then cold, it froze and stormed, and
3. From the northern plain, they went to possess milder lands, abounding in game.
4. That they might be strong and rich, the new comers divided the land between the hunters and tillers (*Wikhichik, Elowichik*).
5. The hunters were the strongest, the best, the greatest.
6. They spread north, east, south and west ;
7. In the white or snow country (*Lumowaki*), the north country, the turtle land and the hunting country, were the turtle men or *Linapiwi*.
8. The Snake (evil) people being afraid in their cabins, the Snake priest (*Nakopowa*) said to them, let us go away.
9. Then they went to the east, the Snake land sorrowfully leaving.
10. Thus escaped the Snake people, by the trembling and burned land to their strong island (*Akomenaki*).
11. Free from opposers, and without trouble, the Northlings (*Lowaniwi*) all went forth separating in the land of snow (*Winiaken*),
12. By the waters of the open sea, the sea of fish, tarried the fathers of the White-eagle (tribe ?) and the White-wolf.

13. Our fathers were rich; constantly sailing in their boats, they discovered to the eastward the Snake island.
14. Then said the Head-beaver (*Wihlamok*) and the Great-bird, let us go to the Snake land.
15. All responded, let us go and annihilate the Snakes.
16. All agreed, the northerlings, the easterlings, to pass the frozen waters.
17. Wonderful! They all went over the waters of the hard, stony sea, to the open Snake waters.
18. In vast numbers, in a single night, they went to the eastern or Snake island; all of them marching by night in the darkness.
19. The northerlings, the easterlings, the southerlings (*Shawanapi*), the Beaver-men (*Tamakwapis*), the Wolf-men, the Hunters or best men, the priests (*Powatapi*), the *Wiliwapi*, with their wives and daughters, and their dogs.
20. They all arrived at the land of Firs (*Shinaking*), where they tarried; but the Western men (*Wunkenapi*) hesitating, desired to return to the old Turtle land (*Tulpaking*).

It may be suggested that the account of the second migration, across frozen waters, is so much in accordance with the popular prejudice, as to the mode in which the progenitors of the American race arrived in America, that it throws suspicion upon the entire record. It is not impossible, indeed, that the original tradition may have been slightly modified here, by the dissemination of European notions among the Indians. McKenzie, however, observes of the traditions of the northern Chippeways: "The Indians say that they originally came from another country, inhabited by a wicked people, and had traversed a great lake, which was shallow, narrow and full of islands, where they suffered great hardships and much misery, it being always winter, with ice and deep snows. * * * They describe the deluge when the waters spread over the whole earth, except the highest mountain, on the top of which they were preserved."[1]

The preceding songs have something of a metrical character, and there is in some of the verses an arrangement of homophones which has a very pleasing effect. For instance, the last verse of the above song is as follows:

[1] *McKenzie*, p. 113.

Wemipayat guneunga shinaking
Wunkenapi chanelendam payaking
Allowelendam kowiyey-tulpaking.

How far this system was carried it is difficult to say, but it is not unlikely that most of the transmitted songs or chants had something of this form.

The next song resumes, after the lapse of an indefinite period, as follows:

SONG IV.— THE CHRONICLE.

1. Long ago our fathers were at *Shinaki* or Fir land.
2. The White Eagle (*Wapalanewa*) was the path-leader of all to this place.
3. They searched the great and fine land, the island of the Snakes.
4. The hardy hunters and the friendly spirits met in council.
5. And all said to *Kalawil* (Beautiful-head) be thou chief (*sakima*) here.
6. Being chief he commanded they should go against the Snakes.
7. But the Snakes were weak and hid themselves at the Bear hills.
8. After Kalawil, *Wapagokhas* (White-owl) was sakima at Fir land.
9. After him *Jantowit* (Maker) was chief.
10. And after him *Chilili* (Snow-bird) was sakima. The south, he said
11. To our fathers, they were able, spreading, to possess.
12. To the south went Chilili; to the east went *Tamakwi* (the Beaver).
13. The South land (*Shawanaki*) was beautiful, shore-land, abounding in tall firs.
14. The East land (*Wapanaki*) abounded in fish; it was the lake and buffalo land.
15. After Chilili, *Agamek* (Great warrior) was chief.
16. Then our fathers warred against the robbers, Snakes, bad men, and stony men, *Chikonapi, Akhonapi, Makatapi, Assinapi* (Assiniboins?)
17. After Agamek came ten chiefs, and then were many wars, south, east and west.
18. After them was *Langundowi* (the Peaceful) sakima, at the *Aholaking* (Beautiful land).
19. Following him *Tasukamend* (Never-bad), who was a good or just man.

20. The chief after him was *Pemaholend* (Ever-beloved), who did good.
21. Then *Matemik* (Town-builder), and *Pilwihalen.*
22. And after these, in succession, *Gunokeni*, who was father long, and *Mangipitak* (Big-teeth).
23. Then followed *Olumapi* (Bundler-of-sticks), who taught them pictures (records).
24. Came then *Takwachi* (Who-shivers-with-cold), who went southward to the Corn land (*Minihaking*).
25. Next was *Huminiend* (Corn-eater), who caused corn to be planted.
26. Then *Alko-ohit* (the Preserver), who was useful.
27. Then *Shiwapi* (Salt-man), and afterwards *Penkwonowi* (the Thirsty), when
28. There was no rain, and no corn, and he went to the east, far from the great river or shore.
29. Passing over a hollow mountain (*Oligonunk*) they at last found food at *Shililaking*, the plains of the Buffalo land.
30. After *Penkwonowi*, came *Mekwochella* (the Weary), and *Chingalsawi* (the Stiff).
31. After him *Kwitikwund* (the Reprover), who was disliked and not willingly endured.
32. Being angry, some went to the eastward, and some went secretly afar off.
33. The wise tarried, and made *Makaholend* (the Beloved) chief.
34. By the *Wisawana* (Yellow river) they built towns, and raised corn on the great meadows.
35. All being friends, *Tamenend* (the Amiable, literally *bearer-like*) became the first chief.
36. The best of all, then or since, was *Tamenend*, and all men were his friends.
37. After him was the good chief, *Maskansisil* (Strong-buffalo), and
38. *Machigokhos* (Big-owl), and *Wapikicholen* (White-crane).
39. And then *Wingenund* (the Mindful or Wary), who made feasts.
40. After him came *Lapawin* (the White), and *Wallama* (the Painted), and
41. *Waptiwapit* (White-bird), when there was war again, north and south.
42. Then was *Tumaskan* (Strong-wolf), chief, who was wise in council and
43. Who made war on all, and killed *Maskensini* (Great-stone).

44. *Messissuwi* (the Whole) was next chief, and made war on the Snakes (*Akowini*). .
45. *Chitanwulit* (Strong-and-good) followed, and made war on the northern enemies (*Lowanuski*).
46. *Alkouwi* (the Lean) was next chief, and made war on the Father-snakes (*Towakon*).
47. *Opekasit* (East-looking) being next chief, was sad because of so much warfare,
48. Said, let us go to the sun-rising (*Wapagishek*); and many went east together.
49. The great river (*Messussipu*) divided the land, and being tired, they tarried there.
50. *Yagawanend* (Hut-maker) was next *sakima*, and then the *Tallegwi* were found possessing the east.
51. Followed *Chitanitis* (Strong-friend), who longed for the rich east-land.
52. Some went to the east, but the *Tallegwi* killed a portion.
53. Then all of one mind exclaimed, war, war!
54. The *Talamatan* (Not-of-themselves), and the *Nitilowan*, all go united (to the war).
55. *Kinnehepend* (Sharp-looking) was their leader, and they went over the river.
56. And they took all that was there, and despoiled and slew the *Tallegwi*.
57. *Pimokhasuwi* (Stirring-about) was next chief, and then the *Tallegwi* were much too strong.
58. *Tenchekensit* (Open-path) followed, and many towns were given up to him.
59. *Paganchihilla* was chief, and the *Tallegwi* all went southward.
60. *Hattanwulatou* (the Possessor) was *sakima*, and all the people were pleased.
61. South of the lakes they settled their council-fire, and north of the lakes were their friends the *Talamatan* (Hurons?)
62. They were not always friends, but conspired when *Gunitakan* was chief.
63. Next was *Linniwalamen*, who made war on the *Talamatan*.
64. *Shakagapewi* followed, and then the *Talamatan* trembled.

TRADITIONS OF THE ALGONQUINS.

SONG V.—THE CHRONICLE CONTINUED.

1. All were peaceful, long ago, at the land of the *Tallegwi*.
2. Then was *Tamaganend* (Beaver-leader) chief at the White river (*Wapalaneng*, Wabash).
3. *Wapushuwi* (White-lynx) followed, and much corn was planted.
4. After came *Walichinik*, and the people became very numerous.
5. Next was *Lekhihitin*, and made many records (*walum-olumin*, or painted-sticks).
6. Followed *Kolachuisen* (Blue-bird), at the place of much fruit or food (*Makeliming*).
7. *Pematalli* was chief over many towns.
8. And *Pepomahemen* (Paddler), at many waters (or the great waters).
9. And *Tankawon* (Little-cloud) was chief, and many went away.
10. The *Nentegos* and the *Shawanis* went to the south lands.
11. *Kichitamak* (Big-beaver) was chief at the White lick (*Wapahoning*).
12. The Good-prophet (*Onowatok*) went to the west.
13. He visited those who were abandoned there and at the south-west.
14. *Pawanami* (Water-turtle) was chief at the *Talegahonah* (Ohio) river.
15. *Lakwelend* (Walker) was next chief, and there was much warfare.
16. Against the *Tbwako* (Father Snakes), against the *Sinako* (Stone or Mountain Snakes), and against the *Lowako* (North Snakes).
17. Then was *Mokolmokoni* (Grandfather-of-boats) chief, and he warred against the Snakes in boats.
18. *Winelowich* (Snow-hunter) was chief at the North land (*Lowashkin*).
19. And *Linkwekinuk* (Sharp-seer) was chief at the Alleghany mountains (*Talegachukang*).
20. And *Wapalawikwan* (East-settler) was chief east of the *Tallegwi* land.
21. Large and long was the east land;
22. It had no enemies (snakes), and was a rich and good land.
23. And *Gikenopalat* (Great-warrior) was chief towards the north;
24. And *Hanaholend* (Stream-lover) at the branching stream (*Saskwihanang* or Susquehanna).
25. And *Gattawisi* (the Fat) was sakima at the Sassafras land, (*Winaki*).
26. All were hunters from the big Salt water (*Gishikshapipek*, Chesa-

peake, or literally Salt sea of the sun), to the again (or other) sea.

27. *Makliuawip* (Red-arrow) was chief at tide water (*Lapihaneng*).
28. And *Wolomenap* was chief at the Strong falls (*Maskekitong*, Trenton ?)
29. And the *Wapenend* and the *Tumewand* were to the north.
30. *Walitpallat* (Good-fighter) was chief and set out against the north.
31. Then trembled the *Mahongwi* (the Iroquois ?) and the *Pungelika* (Lynx-like, or Eries).
32. Then the second *Tamenend* (Beaver) was chief, and he made peace with all.
33. And all were friends, all united under this great chief.
34. After him was *Kichitamak* (Great-good-beaver) chief in the Sassafras land.
35. *Wapahakey* (White-body) was chief at the Sea shore (*Sheyabi*).
36. *Elangonel* (the Friendly) was chief, and much good was done.
37. And *Pitenumen* was chief, and people came from somewhere.
38. At this time from the east sea came that which was white (vessels ?)
39. *Makelomush* was chief and made all happy.
40. *Wulakeningus* was next chief, and was a warrior at the south.
41. He made war on the *Otaliwako* (Cherokee snakes or enemies), and upon the *Akowetako* (Coweta ? snakes).
42. *Wapagamoski* (White-otter) was next chief, and made the *Talamatans* (Hurons) friends.
43. *Wapashum* followed, and visited the land of *Tallegwi* at the west.[1]
44. There were the *Hiliniki* (Illinois), the *Shawanis* (Shawanoes), and the *Kenowiki* (Kenhawas ?)
45. *Nitispayat* was also chief, and went to the great lakes.
46. And he visited the *Wemiamik* (Beaver-children, or Miamis), and made them friends.
47. Then came *Packimitzin* (Cranberry-eater), who made the *Tawa* (Ottawas) friends.
48. *Lowaponskan* was chief, and visited the Noisy place (*Ganshowenik*).
49. And *Tashawinso* was chief at the Sea shore (*Shayabing*).
50. Then the children divided into three parts, the *Unamini* (Turtle tribe), the *Minsimini* (Wolf tribe), the *Chikimini* (Turkey tribe).

[1] "At present," says Loskiel, "the Delawares call the whole country as far as the entrance of the river Wabash into the Ohio, *Alligewi-nengk*, that is, a land into which they came from distant parts." — *Hist. United Brethren*, p. 127.

51. *Epallahchund* was chief, and fought the *Mahongwi*, but failed.
52. *Laugomuwi* was chief, and the *Mahongwi* trembled.
53. *Wangomend* was chief, yonder between. (?)
54. The *Otaliwi* and *Wasiotowi* were his enemies.
55. *Wapachikis* (White-crab) was chief, and a friend of the Shore people.
56. *Nenachipat* was chief towards the sea.
57. Now from north and south came the *Wapayachik* (White-comers).
58. Professing to be friends, in big-birds (ships). Who are they?

Here stop the pictured records. There is, however, a fragment in the original manuscripts, which may be taken as a continuation, and concerning which Rafinesque says nothing more than that it " was translated from the Lenape by John Burns." The references, so far as I am able to verify them, are historically correct. It is here given in its original form, with no attempt at paraphrase. It resumes with an answer to the question which concludes the last song, " who are these *Wapsinis?*"

SONG IV.— THE MODERN CHRONICLE.

1. Alas, alas! we now know who they are, these *Wapsinis* (East-people), who came out of the sea to rob us of our lands. Starving wretches! they came with smiles, but soon became snakes (or enemies).
2. The *Walumolum* was made by *Lekhibit* (the writer), to record our glory. Shall I write another to record our fall? No! Our foes have taken care to do that; but I speak what they know not or conceal.
3. We have had many other chiefs since that unhappy time. There were three before the friendly *Mikwon* (*Miquon* or Penn) came. *Mattanikum*[1] (Not-strong) was chief when the *Winakoli* (Swedes) came to *Winaki; Nahumen* (Raccoon) when the *Sinalwi* (Dutch) came, and *Ikwahon* (Fond-of-women) when the *Yankwis* (English) came. *Miquon* (Penn) and his friends came soon after.
4. They were all received and fed with corn; but no land was ever sold to them: we never sold any land. They were allowed to

[1] *Note by Rafinesque.* "*Mattanikum* was chief in 1645. He is called *Matta-horn* by Holm, who by a blunder, has made his name half Swedish. *Horn* is not Lenapi. *Mattawikum* means *Not-horned*, without horns, emblem of having little strength."

dwell with us, to build houses and plant corn, as friends and allies. Because they were hungry and we thought them children of *Gishaki* (or Sun-land), and not serpents and children of serpents.

5. And they were traders, bringing fine new tools, and weapons, and cloth, and beads, for which we gave them skins and shells and corn. And we liked them and the things they brought, for we thought them good and made by the children of *Gishaki*.

6. But they brought also fire-guns, and fire-waters, which burned and killed; also baubles and trinkets of no use, for we had better ones before.

7. After Mikwon, came the sons of *Dolojo-sakima* (King George), who said, more land, more land we must have, and no limit could be put to their steps.

8. But in the north were the children of *Lowi-sakima* (King Louis), who were our good friends, friends of our friends, foes of our foes; yet with *Dolojo* wished always to war.

9. We had three chiefs after Mikwon came — *Skalichi*, who was another *Tamenend*, and *Sasunam-Wikwikhon* (Our-uncle-the-builder), and *Tutami* (Beaver-taker), who was killed by a *Yank-wako* (English-snake), and then we vowed revenge.

10. *Netatawis* (First-new-being) became chief of all the nations in the west. Again at *Talligewink* (Ohio, or place of Tallegwi) on the river Cuyahoga, near our old friends the *Talamatans*. And he called on all them of the east (to go to war).

11. But *Tadeskung* was chief in the east at *Mahoning*, and was bribed by *Yankwis*; then he was burnt in his cabin, and many of our people were killed at *Hickory* (Lancaster) by the land-robber *Yankwis*.

12. Then we joined *Lowi* in war against the *Yankwis*; but they were strong, and they took *Lowanaki* (North-land, Canada) from *Lowi*, and came to us in *Talegawink*, when peace was made, and we called them *Kichikani* (Big-knives).

13. Then *Alimi* (White-eyes) and *Gelelenund* (Buck-killer) were chiefs, and all the nations near us were friends, and our grand-children again.

14. When the Eastern-fires began to resist *Dolojo*, they said we should be another fire with them. But they killed our chief *Unamiwi* (the Turtle) and our brothers on the Muskingum. Then *Hopo-*

kan (Strong-pipe) of the Wolf tribe was made chief, and he made war on the *Kichikani-Yankwis*, and became the friend of *Dolojo*, who was then very strong.

15. But the Eastern-fires were stronger; they did not take *Lowinaki*, but became free from *Dolojo*. We went to *Wapahani* (White river) to be further from them; but they followed us everywhere, and we made war on them, till they sent *Makhiakho* (Blacksnake, General Wayne), who made strong war.

16. We next made peace and settled limits, and our chief was *Hackingpouskan* (Hard-walker), who was good and peaceful. He would not join our brothers, the *Shawanis* and *Ottawas*, nor *Dolojo* in the next war.

17. Yet after the last peace, the *Kichikani-Yankwis* came in swarms all around us, and they desired also our lands of *Wapahani*. It was useless to resist, because they were getting stronger and stronger by joining fires.

18. *Kithtilkand* and *Lapanibit* were the chiefs of our two tribes when we resolved to exchange our lands, and return at last beyond the *Masispek*, near to our old country.

19. We shall be near our foes the *Wakon* (Osages), but they are not worse than the *Yankwisakon* (English snakes) who want to possess the whole Big-island.

20. Shall we be free and happy, then, at the new *Wapahani?* We want rest, and peace, and wisdom.

So terminate these singular records. It is unfortunate that they lack that kind of authentication, which depends upon a full and explicit account of the circumstances under which they were found, transcribed and translated. Rafinesque was not particular in these matters, and his carelessness and often extravagant assumptions, have rendered his name of little weight in matters of research. Still, upon neither of these grounds may we reject these records. As already observed, they have the internal evidence of genuineness, and are well supported by collateral circumstances. Some of these circumstances were presented at the outset, and need not be recapitulated. Rafinesque himself has anticipated, and thus disposes of one objection, not among the least formidable: "That so many generations and names can be remembered, may appear doubtful to some; but when symbolical signs and paintings are accompanied with songs, and carefully taught from generation to generation, their retention and perpetuation is not so remarkable." To this may with propriety be added the subjoined observations of Loskiel: " The Delawares delight in describing their genealogies, and are so well versed in them, that they mark every branch of the family with the greatest precision. They also add the character of their forefathers: such an one was a wise and intelligent counsellor; a renowned warrior, or a rich man, etc. But though they are indifferent about the history of former times, and ignorant of the art of reading and writing, yet their ancestors were well aware that they stood in need of something to enable them to convey their ideas to a distant nation, or preserve the memory of remarkable events. To this end they invented something like hierogylphics, and also strings and belts of wampum, etc."[1]

I have alluded to the general identity of the mythological traditions here recorded, with those which are known to have been, and which are still current among the nations of the Algonquin stock. The same may be observed of the traditions which are of a historical character, and particularly that which relates to the contest with the people denominated the *Tallegwi*. The name of this people is still perpetuated in the word *Alleghany*, the original significance of which is more apparent, when it is written in an unabbreviated form, *Tallegwi-henna*, or *Tallegwi-hanna* literally river of the Tallegwi. It was applied to the Ohio (the present name is Iroquois, and literally rendered by the French *La Belle Rivière*), and is still retained as the designation of its northern or principal tributary. The traditionary contest between the Lenape and the Tallegwi is given by Heckewelder, and is adduced in further illustration of the general concurrence above mentioned. The details vary in some points, but I am inclined to give the first position to the tradition as presented in the *Walumolum*; it being altogether the most simple and consistent. It must be observed, that Mr. Heckewelder's diffuse account is much condensed in the following quotations, and that part which refers to the wars with the Cherokees, etc., is entirely omitted:

[1] *United Brethren in America*, p. 24.

"The Lenni-Lenape (according to the traditions handed down to them from their ancestors) resided many hundred years ago, in a very distant country, in the western part of the American continent. For some reason, which I do not find accounted for, they determined on migrating to the eastward, and accordingly set out together in a body. After a very long journey, and many nights' encampment ('night's encampment' is a halt of a year in a place), they at length arrived on the *Namaesi-sipu*,[1] where they fell in with the Mengwi (Iroquois), who had likewise emigrated from a distant country, and had struck upon this river higher up. Their object was the same with that of the Delawares; they were proceeding to the eastward, until they should find a country that pleased them. The spies which the Lenape had sent forward for the purpose of reconnoitering, had long before their arrival discovered that the country east of the Mississippi was inhabited by a very powerful nation, who had many large towns built on the great rivers flowing through the land. These people (as I was told) called themselves *Tallegwi* or *Tallegewi*. Col. John Gibson, however, a gentleman who has a thorough knowledge of the Indians, and speaks several of their languages, is often of opinion that they were called *Alligewi*." * *

"Many wonderful things are told of this famous people. They are said to have been remarkably tall and stout, and there are traditions that there were giants among them. It is related, that they had built to themselves regular fortifications or entrenchments, from whence they would sally out, but were generally repulsed. * * * When the Lenape arrived on the banks of the Mississippi, they sent a message to the *Alligewi*, to request permission to settle themselves in their neighborhood. This was refused them; but they obtained leave to pass through the country, and seek a settlement further to the eastward. They accordingly commenced passing the Mississippi, when the *Alligewi* discovering their great numbers became alarmed, and made a furious attack upon those who had crossed. Fired at their treachery, the Lenape consulted on what was to be done; whether to retreat, or try their strength against their oppressors. While this was going on the Mengwi, who had contented themselves with looking on from a distance, offered to join the Lenape, upon condition that they should be entitled to a share of the country, in case the combination was successful.

---

[1] This differs from the foregoing record, and is undoubtedly incorrect. It is difficult to derive Mississippi from *namaesi-sipu*, which is made up of *namaesi*, a fish, and *sipu*, river. The etymology is clearly *messu*, *messi*, or *michi*, signifying *great*, or as Mr. Gallatin suggests, the *whole* and *sipu*, river.

Their proposal was accepted, and the confederates were able, after many severe conflicts, to drive the Alligewi down the Mississippi river. The conquerors divided the country between themselves; the Mengwi selecting the lands in the vicinity of the great lakes, and on their tributary streams, while the Lenape took possession of the country below them. For a long period of time, some say many hundreds of years, the two nations lived peaceably, and increased their numbers with great rapidity. Ultimately some of the most adventurous among them crossed the mountains towards the rising sun, and falling on streams running to the eastward, followed them to the great Bay river (Susquehanna), and thence to the bay (Chesapeake) itself. As they pursued their travels, partly by land and partly by water, sometimes near and sometimes on the great-salt-water lake (as they call the sea), they discovered the great river which we call the Delaware; and still further to the eastward, the *Sheyicbbi* country, now called New Jersey. Afterwards they reached the stream now called the Hudson. The reports of the adventurers caused large bodies to follow them, who settled upon the four great rivers, the Delaware, Hudson, Susquehanna and Potomac, making the Delaware, which they call *Lenapewihittuck* (the river of the Lenape) the centre of their possessions.

"They add that a portion of their people remained beyond the Mississippi, and still another portion tarried between the Mississippi and the mountains. The largest portion, they supposed, settled on the Atlantic. The latter were divided into three tribes, two of which were distinguished as *Unâmis*, or Turtle, and *Wnalachtgo*, or Turkey. These chose the lands lying nearest the coast. Their settlements extended from the *Mohicanittuck* (river of the *Mohicans* or Hudson) to beyond the Potomac. * * * The third great tribe, the *Minsi* (which we have corrupted into *Monseys*), or tribe of the wolf, lived back of the others, forming a kind of bulwark, and watching the nations of the *Mengwi*. They were considered the most active and warlike of all the tribes. They extended their settlements from the *Minisink*, where they had their council-fire, quite to the Hudson on the east, and westward beyond the Susquehanna, and northward to the head waters of that stream and the Delaware. * * * From the above three divisions or tribes, comprising together the body of the people called Delawares, sprung many others, who, having for their own convenience chosen distinct spots to settle in, and increasing in numbers, gave themselves names, or received them from others. * * * * Meanwhile trouble ensued with the *Mengwi*, who occupied the southern shores of the lakes, and re sulted in fierce and sanguinary wars. The reverses of the *Mengwi* induced them to confederate, after which time the contests with the Lenape were carried on with vigor until the arrival of the French in Canada."

It will be seen that there is a difference between the traditions, as given by Heckewelder, and the *Walum-olum* in respect to the name of the confederates against the *Tallegwi*. In the latter the allies are called *Talamatan*, literally Not-of-themselves, and which, in one or two cases, is translated *Hurons*, with what correctness I am not prepared to say.[1] Heckewelder calls them *Mengwi*, Iroquois. This must be a mistake, as the *Mengwi* are subsequently and very clearly alluded to in the *Walum-olum*, as distinct from the *Talamatan*.

It is remarkable that the traditions of almost all the tribes, on the eastern shore of the continent, refer, with more or less distinctness, to a migration from the westward. "When you ask them," says Lawson, speaking of the Carolina Indians, " whence their fathers came, that first inhabited the country, they will point to the westward and say, ' Where the sun sleeps, our fathers came thence.' "[2] Most of the nations speak of the passage of the Mississippi river. The Natchez, who assimilated more nearly to the central American and Peruvian stocks (the *Toltecan* family), informed Du Pratz that they once dwelt at the south-west, " under the sun."[3] The Muscogulges or Creeks, according to Bartram's manuscript, assert that they formerly lived beyond the Mississippi, and that they relinquished that country in obedience to a dream in which they were directed to go to the country where the sun rises. They claim that they crossed the river in their progress eastward, about the period that De Soto visited Florida. The Cherokees (a cognate tribe) have a similar tradition. They assert that "a long time ago all the Indians traveled a great distance and came to a great water. Upon arriving there, and

---

[1] In Heckewelder we find the Hurons sometimes called *Delamattenos*, which is probably but another mode of writing *Talamatan*. Although speaking a dialect of the Iroquois language, the Hurons seem to have generally maintained friendly relations with the Lenape.
[2] *Lawson's Carolina*, p. 170.
[3] *Louisiana*, p. 292.

immediately before or immediately after crossing, it is not remembered which, a part went north and another part south. Those who went northwards settled in two towns called *Ka-no-wo-gi* and *Nu-ta-gi;* the others at *Ka-ga-li-u,* or old town, and because they took the lead in the journey were considered the grandfathers of the Indians." [1] Roger Williams informs us that the south-west, or *Sawaniwa,* was constantly referred to by the Indians of New England. "From thence, according to their traditions, they came. There is the court of their great god, *Cawtantowit;* there are all their ancestors' souls; there they also go when they die, and from thence came their corn and beans, out of *Cantantowit's* field." [2]

It will thus be seen that the general tenor and some of the more important details of the traditions of the Indians of the Algonquin stock, as they have been presented to us by various authorities, are the same with those of the foregoing remarkable records. These records are peculiar, chiefly as giving us a greater number of details than we before possessed. Whatever their historical value, they possess the highest interest, as coming to us through the medium of a rude system of representation, which may be taken as the first advance beyond a simple oral transmission of ideas, and from which we may trace upwards the progress of human invention to its highest and noblest achievement, the present perfected form of written language.

[1] J. H. Payne, manuscripts.
[2] *Key to the Indian Languages of America, &c.*

A RIDE WITH THE APACHES.[1]

By HERBERT C. DORR.

[The following sketch has been prepared from the unpublished Narrative of José Mendivil, who was a captive of the Apaches, and became by adoption one of the tribe, remaining with them seven years.]

The Apaches are in the habit of making, about once a year, a grand visit to the Zuñi Indians, for the purpose of trade and talk; to hear and tell stories; occasionally, to get wives, or see a sweetheart secretly. This visit to the Zuñis is an event in the Apache calendar — like a journey to some renowned city or great natural wonder — and for it they make much preparation. Their horses are fattened in advance until their coats are glossy and sleek, and they are trained daily, like racers for the racetrack, with the utmost care. Each Indian strives to make the greatest impression on his Zuñi friends, by the quality of his horse, his fleetness and strength, the splendor of his trappings, and the magnificence of his rider, as well as by the value and beauty of the presents he carries with him.

The trappings of a single horse sometimes have the value of hundreds of dollars. If they can obtain them, by theft or purchase, they have the richest Mexican saddles embossed with silver, and sometimes even set with gems, their bridles of the finest wrought leather, resplendent with silver ornaments, and all the adornments which the Mexican, in his luxurious taste, lavishes upon a favorite horse.

A half-dozen horses are sometimes killed in the training, before one is found of sufficient bottom and fleetness to satisfy the fastidious savage. The horse is shod with rawhide, and many extra pairs of shoes are carried along, lest the hoofs of the favorite should become tender before the home-journey. The Indian himself dresses in the best style that his circumstances will permit. He wears the garments of any nation, or of any class of Mexicans or Americans that he may have recently robbed

[1] Reprinted from *The Overland Monthly* (San Francisco), for April, 1871.

and murdered on the highways of travel. The Mexican garb, with pants open at the sides and garnished with silver bells, pleases him the best; but, if all else fail, a red or gray shirt taken from a murdered soldier will do, in addition to his national costume of paint and the *thchlacah* (waistcloth, worn around the loins), which constitutes their only raiment in warm weather.

Every body in the encampment manifests the greatest interest in the intended expedition. Nothing else is talked about. They no longer speak of the *gente* (the generic term applied to all civilized people, their hereditary enemies); no one goes out to see whether there is a distant cloud of dust — the sign of an immigrant train; all interest is lost in deer, antelopes, wild turkeys, or bears: they talk of Zuñis only — of what presents they shall take, what articles of barter, what presents they probably will get in return, etc. A list of the articles desired is talked over until it is impossible to forget it. An Apache, however, never forgets what his wife, or sister, or sweetheart, and especially his mother, tells him to do. He first remembers and obeys the latter.

There is no duty more binding on the Apache warrior, or more willingly performed, than that of pleasing and providing for his mother. The longest life does not release him from the duty of obedience and respect to her. For her all else must give place; she takes the precedence of all other relations; her wants are paramount to those of self, or wife, or child. If she commands it, even an enemy is spared for the time, though when she is out of sight vengeance again takes its course. These bloody and remorseless savages possess singular virtues, in contrast with their extreme cruelties.

At length, the long-looked-for morning of departure arrives. The day has hardly dawned before the encampment is all awake, and out of its lodges. Old and young, women and children, are standing around, and all talking. The children are playing all sorts of pranks, to catch the last glance of the departing braves: they run foot-races, play leap-frog, stand on their heads. All is mirth and hilarity. All prophesy success and a speedy return. They supply themselves with an abundance of the choicest provisions, such as dried meats, wheaten bread, and sweet-cakes made of flour and sugar. The wheat is of their own raising, as they often grow large crops in various places remote from their dwellings; and it is ground into flour by their women, in the same mode used by the Mexicans. They carry, on this journey, no water or beverage, but only gourd-cups to drink from; also, no one accompanies them a part of the way and then comes back, as in their hunting and marauding expeditions. They take extra horses for presents to their Zuñi friends, and others for barter. They also take with them presents and goods for exchange: Mexican saddles and bridles, finely wrought *lomillos* (*lomillo*, is the crouper-cloth or bear-skin attached to the saddle behind), *lariatas* of excellent make, and splendid *serapes Saltilleros* — a kind of blanket, in which are interwoven gold and silver threads, so fine and soft that one can be put in the coat-pocket. These *serapes* are made in the city of Saltillo, Mexico, and bought or stolen by the Apaches in their forays.

They also take with them fine swords and curiously wrought javelins and daggers, which have been stolen from Mexico, or stripped from travelers. In short, all curious or remarkable things, for which they have no use themselves, they carry to their æsthetic friends, the Zuñis, who have boundless tastes for articles of luxury and ornamentation. Finally, having applied the last touches of paint to their faces, until they are so masked that their friends will hardly recognize them, the journey begins; first at a gallop, amid shouts and cheers, and, after they are out of sight, slackening to a slow pace, and making the pilgrimage in an easy, leisurely manner, resting at every spot where there is good grass for their horses.

The distance from the place occupied by the Apaches to the Zuñi villages is about three hundred miles, over a country diversified with mountains, low hills, broad valleys, and some desert spots. One comes suddenly upon an island of trees, in the midst of a plain or valley verdant with waving grass. Again, a narrow belt of cotton-wood and willows, winding along for miles, indicates the place of a water-course, which, however, contains running water only during the rainy months of the year. A tuft of green willows and rushes, intermingled with flowering grasses, marks the site of a spring low down on the mountain side. Around these verdant places the painted savages gather, and while one runs to the nearest eminence to keep a lookout against a surprise from some lurking foe, the others tether their horses in the grass, and then throw themselves on the ground for a moment's sleep. The more restless young men practice shooting arrows at small game, or engage in a game of cards with a well-worn pack, saved from the sack of an immigrant's baggage, or purchased in the town of Chihuahua. In this manner the five or six days' journey is passed. When within a few miles of the Zuñi villages, a final halt is made. The horses are fed and rubbed; the gallants paint themselves anew; packs are seen to; presents are talked over and arranged in the most attractive manner. Now comes the full-dress charge of this barbaric cavalcade. Their long, plaited hair streaming in the wind as they gallop in full career toward the entrance to the Zuñi towns; their plumes and gay-colored *serapes*, jingling spurs, and the gaudy trappings of their glistening steeds, with the crowds of Zuñis running to meet them, and shouting their welcome after an absence of a year; the lofty mountains of the Sierra Madre in the near distance; the quaint, immemorial architecture of the Zuñi buildings, and their strange occupants — sole remnant of the ancient races who lived in the golden age of centuries past — all unite in making a panorama, which for natural, scenic splendor is rarely surpassed.

The Apaches now dismount, and mingle with their hereditary friends — friends with whom, for a thousand years, they have never broken faith; and who, in their turn, through the ages have been friendly with the Apaches. Their language being the same, differing only in accent, intonation, and cadence, they understand each other without difficulty. The Zuñi, or Apache, language is very flexible and *suave*, and may at some time have been the court language of the ancient races. It is often as expressive of fine shades of distinction as even the Greek itself. It preserves — in the *adyta* of its wonderful radicals — the traditional duality of the human race: its dual, as well as singular and plural, forms of speech.

Groups of Apaches and Zuñis may now be seen in different places in front of the houses, and in the public places under the trees. Meat is brought, and bread with wild fruits is spread in profusion before the hungry guests. The children gather round to see the painted strangers, and the beautiful horses, with their gaudy trappings. After the eating, which is always in the morning (that being the time the Apaches select for entering the Zuñi city), the packs are opened and presents distributed with grave solemnity to the principal men of the city; for the Zuñis have high and low, rich and poor. They have judges and justices of the peace, as well as a sort of high-court of appeal, in which all questions of equity are settled; they have also policemen and officers like our constables, to arrest offenders and bring them before the judges. To these men of influence presents are given, without any definite expectation of an equivalent. If the Zuñis give presents in return, it is well; if not, the Apaches are equally well satisfied. If the Zuñi presents are more or less in value, it is all the same: no questions are asked, no remarks made either to their friends or to each other.

Next comes the trading. This is carried on with much spirit, and with mutual concessions. When it is over, both parties are satisfied: they never accuse each other of cheating or attempting to cheat, and there is no manifestation of anger on either side. It is not uncommon for them to decide a question of value by a wager. The Apache and the Zuñi agree that the one who can run and jump a longer distance at a single leap, shall have the price he has asked. In such wagers the Apache is almost always the winner, owing to his greater agility from long training, as well as from the difference in modes of life.

It sometimes happens that an Apache becomes stricken with one of the Zuñi beauties. In that case, if the woman is unmarried, unengaged, and willing to marry him, the arrangement of details with the Zuñi chiefs is not impossible. The Apache names the number of horses, or the amount and kind of other goods, he will give for the damsel; and, if the patriarchs are willing, she returns with her husband. If it should afterward happen that she is treated cruelly, or that he neglects her, then by the terms of the contract she is free, and may return unmolested to the home of her ancestors, who receive her back with tenderness and love. It is, however, very rare that a woman ever leaves her Apache husband. Even Mexican female prisoners, who have become wives and mothers, would not accept of liberty, were it offered to them. José Mendivil, who narrates these things, says that he has seen many of them refuse to escape when it was perfectly easy. He has known them, while in the neighborhood of Mexican towns, when all the Indians were away hunting, to refuse to walk into the towns and ask protection, preferring the life of a savage to the affection and affluence of the homes of their girlhood.

When at length the trading, feasting, and perhaps love-making are ended; when the sports and story-telling are finished, then the Indians begin to prepare for their return to their mountain fastnesses. In an instant, all is haste and enthusiasm. Like children, hurrying and talking of their return, they immediately forget every thing but their families waiting for them hundreds of miles away. Slowly and cautiously they had made the outward journey, so as not to weary their horses, in order that they might be fresh and fleet, to excite the admiration of the Zuñis. But now, even the horses seem to know that they are expected to go like the wind on the return career. The Apaches being mounted, a score or more of young Zuñis, on their fleetest horses, escort their friends out of the great gate of their walled town, and also many miles on their homeward way. Not unfrequently horses are exchanged, in token of friendship, in the last moments of parting; but the generous Zuñi will never exchange unless he is quite certain his horse has more speed and bottom than the other, lest his friend should fall behind in that terrible homeward race.

This race soon begins in earnest. There is no more quarter for horse or rider; the three hundred miles must be made in two days and nights. On dash the cavalcade, each far from the other, the wild horses snuffing the clear air of the mountains; on — on — swifter and swifter, increasing their speed constantly. The ruins of Aztec cities and fields seem to fly past like clouds driven by the blast. There are deserts of sand and salt, along the green margin of which these demon-steeds sweep with the clatter and noise of a thousand charging horses. The lips of the Apache are firm-set; his limbs almost encircle his horse; he leans forward nearly to his neck; his hair streams out, like a sheet of darkness, above his painted, swelling shoulders. The eyes of rider and horse are like fire, and their mouths dry as ashes; but no water is allowed to wet their lips until more than a hundred miles have been passed over at this terrible speed. Herds of antelopes see the demon-chase, snuff the air, turn to run, wheel and gaze again, while the whole band of savages have passed like meteors out of sight down some precipitous wall of rocks. In a moment their tossing manes and streaming masses of black braids are seen waving, still at a gallop, as they mount up the opposite cliffs and along the crest of the mountain summit, that seems a dark line drawn against the morning sky. A yell and a wild shout, and down they go into the depths of the forest, whose dim paths only they and the wild beasts have ever known. Streams are passed like dry land, even while the horse and rider are famishing with thirst: they dare not stop and taste, lest their terrible energy for one moment should diminish. On — on — thunder these weird wanderers, looking not to right nor to left, but ever onward toward the turrets and domes of those distant mountains, in whose shaded vales their swarthy wives and kindred are watching for their return.

And now the savages take a few hours of sleep while their horses are grazing; again they mount, and for a few leagues ride slowly; then is heard a yell and a scream that echo among the hills, and away they dash in full career. The pebbles and stones fly behind them, the plains sweep round them as the horizon around a flying train, and the mountains echo with their screams. Their horses are spotted with foam, like waves in a storm; their nostrils are wide and red as blood: if they should halt now, they could never start again. One more hill, and one more plain, and the curling smoke of their lodge-fires will be seen against the distant sky. But what is that thick cloud of dust coming directly toward them? Higher and higher it rises: now the line of horsemen can be seen, rising and falling like a far-off bark on the waves; nearer the coming horsemen speed, but the home-bound Apaches stop not, nor turn to right or left: they ride, as if to the charge, right into the faces of the approaching band. They had seen and recognized each other long ago; their keen vision discerned the riders as friends when first they rose, a faint black line, on the horizon. They, too, are Apaches from the camp, mounted on fresh horses, and come to meet their friends for fifty miles, well knowing their reckless speed, and that their horses will drop dead if not exchanged at the end of the race. All cast themselves from their panting steeds, as if by word of command; and sooner than it can be told, horses are exchanged, the tired ones released from their loads and driven at speed in advance, while on they go toward the distant smoke in the aisles of the hills. At last appear the well-known paths; and now old men, women, and children are seen grouped among the lodges of the tribe. The braves dash wildly in, and leaping to the ground, stretch themselves upon the sward. Their horses are unladen by willing hands, meat is brought to the famishing men, and water is offered. Then the whole story of the journey is told. They boast their own superiority over the Zuñis in all athletic games, in the speed of their horses, and the utility of their women for getting food and cultivating the fields. This pleases their women, and, if no husband has returned with a Zuñi wife, all are happy.

The presents — of inestimable value to the Indians — are distributed as impartially as possible. Soon may be seen Apache women clad in the shell trinkets and the gaudy sashes of the Zuñis. Savages walk proudly folded in the splendidly colored blankets of the friendly dwellers in the walled towns, although but Indians like themselves. Thus a day or two is passed, and then all return to the usual routine of hunting, eating, starving, feasting, stealing, and passing life away in savage indifference.

THE CAPTIVITY OF CHRISTIAN FAST.[1]

By Geo. W. Hill, M.D.

In the month of June, 1780, an expedition composed of Indians and Canadians, destined to invade Kentucky, moved from their places of rendezvous at Detroit, the Sandusky, the Miami and the Wabash. The salient point of the campaign was the falls of the Ohio, or Louisville, then containing only a few cabins, and a station for soldiers to protect the scattered settlements of Kentucky against Indian invasion.

Col. George Rogers Clark, the hero of Kaskaskia and St. Vincent, learning that the British and Indians were about to invade that region, stationed a small body of troops at the village of Louisville, to intercept the passage of war parties on their way to the interior of Kentucky. His command was soon increased by the arrival of one hundred and fifty Pennsylvanians and Virginians under the command of Col. Slaughter.

For reasons never fully explained, the British expedition commanded by Col. Byrd, on reaching the mouth of the Great Miami, changed its destination; and when the boats conveying his troops, cannon and military stores arrived on the Ohio river, instead of descending its rapid current, turned up the stream, and ascended the Licking to its forks, where he landed his men and munitions of war. It is probable the destination of Col. Byrd was changed in consequence of his advanced Indian spies and scouts coming in contact with the forces of Col. Slaughter in their descent of the Ohio.

Some thirty-five or forty miles above the falls, the boats of Col. Slaughter, which were conveying horses and a few soldiers, became separated from the main body of the expedition in the night. At day-light the advanced boats drove an occasional stake near the shore, and attached written directions thereto, to guide the boats in the rear. The boats thus abandoned, being deprived

---
[1] Reprinted from the *Ashland (O.) Press*, for November 26, 1874.

of proper rations for the soldiers, had no alternative but to supply themselves with such game as could be obtained from the forest. Perceiving a buffalo heifer leisurely feeding a short distance from shore, the larger boat was shoved to a shoal and the heifer shot. It was hastily skinned, a fire was built, and the soldiers proceeded to prepare breakfast. While in the act of cooking the flesh of the heifer, the party was attacked by Indians, who were probably drawn to the spot by the sound of the guns. The frightened soldiers, who had neglected to station pickets, fled to the boat which had been stranded on the shoal, just as the smaller boats were making toward the shore for breakfast. They were unable to shove the boat to the current, and the Indians rushed down the shore firing into the boat, wounding and killing several of the men and horses. All was consternation. Many of the soldiers endeavored to save themselves by leaping overboard and attempting to swim to the opposite side of the river; but on reaching it, were again fired upon.

Among those who fled to the opposite shore was Christian Fast, a youth of about seventeen years of age, who had volunteered as a cavalry-man, from what is now Fayette county, Pennsylvania, then a part of Westmoreland county. Young Fast was an expert swimmer. As the Indians rushed upon the men, he leaped over the opposite side of the horse-boat, and struck out boldly for the Kentucky shore, which he reached in safety. Just as he was about to rise from the water and ascend the bank, two or three Indians approached him saying: "Come on, brother, we will use you well," at the same time reaching out their hands in token of friendship.

Knowing the savage character of the red man, he doubted their pacific intentions; and speedily turning about, started for the middle of the river. He had scarcely got in motion, when they commenced to fire after him, a ball passing so near his head that it stunned him by its concussion in the water, for a moment, while another ball passed through the fleshy part of his thigh, making a painful wound, notwithstanding which, he succeeded in reaching the centre of the river. The boats having floated some distance below the stranded one from which he had fled,

THE CAPTIVITY OF CHRISTIAN FAST. 53

he resolved to swim after and overtake a small horse boat which was a few rods in the rear of the rest. After a vigorous exertion, aided by the current, and a shower of bullets from shore, he reached the boat just as it surrendered. The Indians boarded it at once; and the prisoners were taken on shore, and the plunder secured.

After the prisoners had been deprived of all means of defense, the savages next proceeded to strip them of such wearing apparel as they desired. In fact, the majority of the captives were left almost nude. The military suits with which the soldiers were clothed were deemed a God-send to these children of the forest. The appearance of the captives was most distressing; nevertheless resistance would have been rewarded with a cruel, lingering death by torture. When the exulting savages had secured such plunder as they could carry away, it was put up in bundles, and their new prisoners were compelled to pack it. The whole party proceeded on their way through the forest in the direction of Upper Sandusky. The level lands along the Ohio and the Miami, at that season, abounded in rank, almost impenetrable weeds, briars and nettles. The journey was a severe ordeal.

Fast was small, had hair as black as a raven, dark eyes, and a swarthy skin; was exceedingly agile, and very slim and straight. His appearance pleased the Indians; and an old Delaware warrior claimed him as his prisoner. The leader of the band was old Thomas Lyon. On the route to Upper Sandusky, which was principally up the Great Miami until they reached the portage, the poor prisoners endured many hardships and cruelties. Having been deprived of their clothing, the nettles, briars, weeds and undergrowth made fearful havoc with their uncovered bodies, so much so, that on one occasion, after they had been some hours in the forest, young Fast put down his head and refused to proceed, telling his Indian master to tomahawk him! The old warrior took pity on him and returned most of his clothing. His wound was becoming quite painful. The old warrior assisted in dressing it until it healed.

After the war party had been two or three days in the forest, the Indians built a camp-fire and cleared a spot for a dance. The prisoners were all tied so as to prevent their escape. The savages engaged in the dance with much spirit, singing, hopping, leaping, brandishing their tomahawks and scalping knives, and grimacing in a most frightful manner. Their music was a sort of wail, between a shout and a moan, while a kind of time was beaten on a brass kettle by a warrior. When the Indian dance had ended, the prisoners, one by one, were untied and requested to give an exhibition of their agility. With bodies torn and bruised, half famished for want of food, wearied with the journey, and almost nude, they endeavored to comply, knowing that a refusal would incur the hate and severity of their savage masters. When the time came for Fast to dance, he felt it impossible to do so, in consequence of his painful wound; but fearing to incur the censure and vengeance of the warriors, he said to his comrades: "Boys, I can't dance and run on my feet, but I can run on my hands." So, limping into the ring, when the Indian music began, he proceeded a few steps, and then springing upon his hands, he elevated his feet, and commenced a sort of bear dance, accompanied by sundry singular maneuvres on his hands, turning an occasional somersault, and yelling like an Indian!

At first the savages seemed amazed at his performances, but soon began to applaud by the most uproarious laughter and shouts, some of them actually rolling on the ground in their merriment. After he had passed around the ring in this gymnastic manner, several of the warriors who had been most delighted with his antics, put their hands on the ground and desired him to "do so more." He pointed to his wound and refused, saying, he was "too lame." His singular vivacity and good nature captivated the Indians, and from that time on, he was the hero of the party; and was no longer tied at night.

On reaching the Shawnee towns on the Great Miami, the prisoners were compelled to run the gauntlet for the amusement of the old Shawnees, the squaws and youth. Several of the prisoners were severely beaten. A man by the name of Baker, a silversmith by trade, from Westmoreland county, Pennsylvania, was beaten almost to death. In his desperation, he ran past the council-house two or three times, being blinded by the blows and fright, and was about to sink, when a friendly voice directed him to enter the door. He did so and was spared. While this performance was going on, the old warrior who had Fast in charge, shoved him back among the Indians, and he did not have to undergo the punishment of the gauntlet.

When the party arrived at Upper Sandusky, the prisoners were again compelled to undergo the ordeal of running the gauntlet. They were all handled very severely; but none of them were killed. Fast was again excused from the gauntlet by his Indian master. His wound by this time had nearly healed. The surviving prisoners soon recruited from their fatigue and were exchanged at Pittsburg and on the Muskingum.

Fast was retained and adopted into an old Delaware family in lieu of a son who had lost his life in a border skirmish. His hair was plucked out in the usual manner, leaving a small scalp-lock about the crown — his white blood was all washed away — his ears and the cartilage of his nose perforated and brooches placed therein. After this he was dressed in Indian costume, his hair roached up and filled with feathers of gaudy colors. Being taken to the council house he was regularly indoctrinated as a son of the tribe. He received the name of *Mo-lun-the*, and was taken to the cabin or wigwam of his new parents. Fast resided on the banks of the Tymochtee about two years. He was treated very kindly by his Indian mother. He had an Indian brother by the name of *Ke-was-sa*, to whom he became much attached. They often hunted coon and other game.

On one occasion, Kewassa invited Fast to accompany him to hunt bear. After traveling some distance in the forest, they discovered evidences of the ascent of a bear up a large elm, which was hollow near the top. After trying sometime in vain to rouse the bear from its retreat, it was proposed that a tree, which stood at a proper distance from the elm, should be felled in such a manner as to lean against the elm to enable Fast to climb to the hole and smoke Bruin out with punk and rotten wood. The tree was cut, and fell against the elm. Fast, being expert in climbing, ascended it to the proposed point, and commenced operations with a view of smoking Bruin into a surrender. Kewassa placed himself in a position, gun in hand, where he could welcome the bear on its appearance to a smell of powder. Fast lighted the dry tinder and threw it into the hole; but Bruin failed to make his appearance! While engaged in this fruitless enterprise, a strong breeze struck the leaning tree and it fell to the ground! Here was a dilemma. Fast was some forty feet from the ground on a large elm! He could not grasp his arms about it, so as to safely descend. Kewassa was alarmed for his safety. There could be no help; for the only tree in the vicinity had been cut. After gazing at Fast for some time, without being able to offer assistance, he hastened to the camp several miles away, expecting that his new brother would be dashed to pieces. Taking in the situation at a glance, Fast concluded that he only hazarded his life by remaining where he was; and the attempt to descend could result in nothing more than death, but might terminate in safety. Summoning all his strength, he grasped the rough bark with his hands, at the same time making good use of his feet and legs, and commenced the descent, moving cautiously until he came within fifteen or eighteen feet of the ground, when his strength so far failed him, that he was compelled to relax his grip and slid down mangling his hands, the inside of his arms and legs badly. On reaching the ground, he was considerably stunned, but soon revived and started for the camp, where he arrived amidst the grief of his Indian mother and brother, who had given him up as lost.

On one occasion, after he had been a captive over a year, when all the warriors were absent from the village, his Indian mother having also left the camp for a short time, he became very melancholy. Thoughts of home stole upon him. He left the wigwam and proceeded a short distance into the forest, and seating himself upon a log, soon became absorbed in meditation. While thus musing, he was interrupted by a stranger who suddenly appeared and confronted him. Discovering his embarrassment and dejection, the stranger said in the Delaware language:

"Ah young man what are you thinking about?"

Fast. "I am alone, and have no company, and feel very lonesome."

Stranger. " That is not it, you are thinking of home. Be a good boy and you shall see your home again."

After some further conversation, he learned that the stranger was none other than that terror of the pioneers, the renegade, Simon Girty! Fast afterward became well acquainted with Girty, and was the recipient of many favors at his hands. In fact, Girty's assurance that he would again see his home in Pennsylvania, greatly revived his drooping spirits and led him to believe that Girty, though often denounced by the pioneers as a villain, a demon in human shape, was not destitute of sympathy and kindness, though associating with the fierce red men of the northwest.

During the campaign of Colonel William Crawford, which ended so disastrously, Mr. Fast was with the Delawares on the Tymochtee. Capt. Pipe and Wingemund, leading Delaware chiefs, resided, when in their villages, in that region of Ohio. After the rout of Crawford's army, when the colonel was brought back a prisoner, Fast was present and saw him. He was in hearing distance when the Delawares tortured the colonel, and could hear his groans. He was so much affected that he left the spot in company with his Indian brother and mother. Fast, in his lifetime, often related incidents connected with the unfortunate expedition of poor Crawford. As they have been repeated by Dr. Knight, Slover and Heckewelder, it is unnecessary to narrate them here.

Shortly after the execution of Crawford, Fast was urged to marry a young squaw, a daughter of an Indian family of some distinction. He was then about nineteen years of age. It was a question of much delicacy, and required a good deal of tact to repel the proposal in such manner as to avoid offense. When the subject was again seriously pressed upon his attention, he intimated he was only a boy, and was too young to marry! The Delawares were greatly amused at his modesty, and his reason for refusing. He added, as a further objection, that no man should marry until he had become a good hunter, and could provide meat. Not being the owner of a gun, it would be impossible for him to supply the quantity of game required for food. Moreover, he thought he could not get along without a cow, an essential to every person designing to marry. As soon as these could be procured he would gladly consent. He professed much admiration for the young squaws, and intimated he could easily select a wife from among them, if his terms could be met. It was agreed that his ideas were correct, and that he should accompany the first expedition to the settlements along the Ohio, and the first gun captured should be his, and on returning he should be permitted to bring back a cow.

In August, 1782, there was a grand council at Chilicothe, on or near the Great Miami, in which the Wyandots, Delawares, Ottawas, Mingoes, Shawnees, Miamies and Pottawatomies participated. Simon Girty, Elliott and McKee were present and addressed the assembled warriors. The council resolved to raise two armies, one of six hundred men, and the other of three hundred and fifty, the larger to march into Kentucky, and the smaller into Western Virginia and Pennsylvania. By the last of August, the greater army appeared under the lead of Simon Girty, at Bryant's Station in the territory of Kentucky. The story is narrated in all the histories of Kentucky.

The Indian forces destined to operate against the border settlements of Virginia and Pennsylvania, delayed their march until a runner brought tidings of success from Kentucky. Some four hundred fierce warriors assembled on the Sandusky, and were armed and equipped by the agents of the British. The warriors were dressed and painted in the most fantastic manner, their hair being gathered in a sort of cue and drawn through a tin tube, was ornamented by colored hawk or eagle quills. With scalping knives, tomahawks and guns, they presented a formidable appearance. For many days and nights before the expedition started, their wild orgies echoed through the forests. Speeches, dances and the like, accompanied by threats of extermination against the white race, were common. Fast was painted in true warrior style, and was furnished a tomahawk, scalping knife and bow, and told he might accompany the expedition. Before departing, he buried, in a secure place, his fancy brooches and other ornaments of silver, so that if he ever returned, he could reclaim them.

The expedition passed down the old Wyandot trail through

what are now Crawford, Richland and Ashland counties, Ohio, by Mohican — Johnstown; thence, near the ruins of the Moravian towns on the Tuscarawas. Arriving at that point, a difference of opinion arose as to the exact destination of the expedition. After some consultation in council, as the expedition to Kentucky was proving successful, it was decided that the Indian army should proceed to and attack the small fort or block house at what is now the city of Wheeling, West Virginia. On the approach of the Indian army, the expedition was discovered by John Lynn, a noted spy and frontier hunter, who was scouting through the forests and watching the Indian paths west of the Ohio. He hastened to the stockade and gave the alarm. The stockade had no regular garrison, and had to be defended exclusively by the settlers who sought security within its walls. On the arrival of Lynn, all retired within the stockade, except a family of Zanes; and when the attack began, there were but about twenty efficient men to oppose nearly four hundred savages led on by James Girty !

The Indian army soon crossed the Ohio river and approached the stockade waving British colors ! An immediate surrender was demanded. Col. Silas Zane responded by firing at the flag borne by the savages. The assault commenced by the Indians and was kept up briskly for three days and nights, but each attack was successfully repelled by the little garrison. While the men within were constantly engaged in firing at the enemy, the women moulded bullets, loaded and handed guns to the men, and by this means every assault was repulsed. The galling fire poured upon the savages exasperated them to madness. In the night they attempted to burn Zane's house, from which they had suffered most; but through the vigilance of Sam, a colored man, their intentions were thwarted.

On the return of light on the second day, the savages, after some delay, renewed the siege. A wooden cannon loaded with balls captured from a small boat on its way to the falls of the Ohio, was pointed towards the stockade and amid the yells of the infuriated Indians discharged. They expected to see a section of the stockade blown to splinters, and an opening for the warriors created. It exploded, and the fragments flew in every direction. Several of the warriors were wounded and a number killed, and all were appalled at the result. Recovering from their dismay, and being furious from disappointment, they again pressed to the assault with renewed energy. They were as often repelled by the deadly aim of the little garrison, and forced to retire.

The achievements of Elizabeth Zane, on this occasion, are matters of history, and too well known to require repetition in this article.

The third day the siege was renewed with terrible ferocity; but every attempt to storm the fort was successfully resisted. In the afternoon, despairing of success, the Indians resolved to change their programme. About one hundred warriors remained to annoy the stockade, lay waste the country, and scour the neighboring settlements. The balance of the army crossed the Ohio, and made a feint of returning to Sandusky; but the next morning recrossed the river above the stockade, and divided into two parties, and hastened towards the settlements about Fort Rice, some forty miles away, in what is now Washington county, Pennsylvania.

On the third night of the siege, learning of the departure of a part of the Indian army and presuming the savages were about to invade his old home, Fast resolved, if possible, to effect his escape. Late in the night, while reposing beside his Indian brother on his blanket, on the ground, the memory of his home and dear friends came fresh to his recollection, and knowing the whole settlement was imperiled by the approach of his savage companions, intent on revenge and blood, he could not sleep. Kawassa, his Indian brother, wearied with the exertions of a three days' seige, slept soundly. Knowing the nature of an Indian, when profoundly slumbering, Fast attempted to awaken his brother, stating that he was very thirsty and desired him to go with him to the river for water. He refused to rise, telling Molunthe to wait until morning. Permitting his brother to return to his state of stupor for some time, he again made an effort to arouse him, insisting that he could not wait, but must have water.

The Indian, having full confidence in Fast, told him to go himself, as no one would harm him. He was but too happy to comply. Taking a small copper kettle, he hastened to the river bank and placed the kettle in a position that might imply that he had fallen into the stream, been drowned and floated down the current. Then carefully wending his way through the Indian lines, he proceeded across the hills and valleys in the direction of Fort Rice, on Buffalo creek, some fifteen or twenty miles from his old home. He groped his way among rocks, down declivities and across small streams, sometimes falling headlong down the embankments, and about day-light, became exhausted from fatigue and want of food, and was compelled to seek repose at the base of a steep bluff, in a thicket of undergrowth; and while resting there, could distinctly hear the passing warriors conversing. A short distance hence the trail divided.

Carefully concealing himself until all the warriors passed, he again proceeded in the direction of the fort, taking a ridge midway between the trails. By a vigorous exertion he got in advance of the savages, and when within about two miles of the fort, he discovered a white man approaching with a bridle and halter in his hand. Springing behind a large tree, he waited until the settler arrived within a few feet of his concealment, when he stepped into the path and confronted him. The white man was taken by surprise and trembled with fear, and was about to flee for life, when the supposed warrior addressed him in English, briefly informing him who he was, where he was going, the approach of the warriors and the danger that environed the settlement. Calmed by the assurances of present safety, the white man caught his horses, which were near, and he and Fast mounted and hastened to the fort and spread the alarm, and succeeded in gathering the settlers, in the vicinity, into it before the savages appeared. The fort consisted of a strong block-house, surrounded by several cabins of the settlers. When all the men were gathered in there were only six.

The savages approached with much assurance, and offering to spare all the prisoners, if the little band would surrender. Fast assured the inmates that the cold steel of the tomahawk would be the price of such an indiscretion. Their proffers of safety were not accepted. A fierce assault at once commenced. The siege was kept up all day and night; but the little fort held out. Several of the savages were wounded, and the warriors, finally despairing of success, suddenly withdrew and spread among the scattered settlements in detached parties, burning houses, and shooting cattle and hogs. They had probably learned the approach of Colonel Swearinger with relief for Wheeling, that was yet beleaguered by the red fiends.

After the retirement of the savages, Fast hastened to his old home, painted and dressed as an Indian warrior. On arriving at the cabin of his parents in what is now Fayette county, he so nearly resembled a wild Indian warrior of the wilderness, that his parents were unable to distinguish him. Indeed, they were much alarmed at his presence, fearing he was a genuine savage acting as a decoy. He attempted to calm their fears by assuring them, in their own tongue, that his name was Fast, and that he was really their own son! At length his mother recalling some peculiarity about the pupils of his eyes, and some spots on his breast, recognized him, and rushing forward to embrace him in her arms, was told not to do so, as he was covered with vermin from the Indian camp. The tube in which his scalp-lock was enclosed was removed, and he repaired to an out building where his infected garments were taken off and burned. Soap and water soon removed the encrusted paint and soil from his person, when he was presented with a clean suit of clothes, which restored him to his status as a white man. The joy of his parents on his safe return home, scarcely knew bounds. A full detail of his adventures was given, and often repeated to enquiring friends.

On arriving at manhood, Mr. Fast located in Dunker township, Greene county, Pennsylvania, where he married, and remained until the spring of 1815, when he removed with his family, to what is now Orange township, Ashland county, Ohio, and settled about half a mile south-east of the Vermillion lakes. When Mr. Fast and family arrived at the lakes, he found a number of Indians encamped near where he subsequently erected a cabin. He built a fire and his wife proceeded to prepare supper, surrounded by a dense forest. While in the act of cooking, their little company was alarmed by the appearance of eight or ten Indians, headed by an old warrior who was extremely ugly, shriveled in flesh, and ferocious in appearance. They had just discovered their new neighbors and came to see who they were. On approaching within a few feet of Mr. Fast, and his children, who were seated on a log near where Mrs. Fast was preparing supper, the old Indian looked steadfastly at Mr. Fast for a moment, and then rushing forward exclaimed, Molunthe! at the same time offering his hand in token of friendship.

The old warrior was Thomas Lyon, who was present at the capture of Fast on the Ohio, some thirty-five years prior to that time, and was along with the expedition to Wheeling, when his favorite young warrior, Molunthe, made his escape. The Indians had never suspected him for desertion, but had always believed he had, in the darkness, fallen into the river and drowned. On finding him here, alive, *old Tom* manifested much gratification and gave many tokens of a friendship that remained very cordial up to 1822, the last appearance of the Delawares in this region. During the ensuing seven years, the Delawares often encamped in the vicinity, regarding Mr. Fast and family as of their tribe. They frequently went into his cabin, in the evening, and danced after the Delaware manner, making rude music by pounding on a stool and singing, while the dancers hopped about the room, flourishing their scalping-knives, shouting and keeping time to the music.

In the fall of 1819 old Thomas Lyon and a party of Delawares had a feast on what is now known as the John Freeborn farm, south-west of Savannah, to which Mr. Fast and his sons were invited. Being unable to be present, his sons Nicholas and Francis, aged respectively twenty-five and fifteen, attended. The feast was in their camp. There were present some fifty or sixty Indians, and no whites, except the Fasts. A large black bear had been roasted and boiled. The body being roasted, was cut into small slices and handed around on new bark plates. The head and feet, unskinned, were boiled in a copper kettle, and a sort of soup made therefrom, which was passed around in wooden ladles.

Nicholas and Francis partook, courteously with the Indians. The roast was elegant, but the soup was not relished. At the conclusion of the feast, Lyon insisted on painting Francis Indian fashion. The boy readily submitted, for the fun of the thing.

Old Tom laid on a good coat of vermillion, which gave him the appearance of a young Indian. The paint was so adhesive that when he returned home, he was unable to remove it for a long time; and was afterwards known as Indian Frank. Billy Montour, Jim Jirk, Monos, Jonacake George and Jim Lyon, Buckwheat, Billy Dowdy, Capt. George, and other well known Delawares were at the feast.

Christian Fast had nine sons, Jacob, Martin, William, Nicholas, David, Francis, George, Christian and John; and four daughters, Margaret, Barbara, Isabel and Christena.

Christian Fast senior died at his farm in Ashland county, Ohio, in 1849.

THE ESQUIMAUX OF LABRADOR.[1]

By A. S. Packard, Jr.

In the summer of 1864 the writer had a rare opportunity of visiting the coast of Labrador, in company with William Bradford, the well-known marine artist. * * *

For a month our fleet-winged schooner, ill adapted for the dangers of arctic navigation, had been held ice-bound, for several days at Belles-Amours, in the straits of Belle-Isle; also at Henley harbor, a noble fiord nearly opposite Belle-Isle; and for a fortnight at a little box of a harbor in Square island, south of the entrance of Hamilton inlet, or, as it was earlier named, Invuctoke bay, where the floe-ice crowded and almost jammed in the sides of our vessel, and for many days formed a natural bridge for us to pass ashore. From the mountains above us we watched, day by day, the ceaseless march of icebergs and cakes, large and small, composing an ice-pack, extending probably a thousand miles or more from the banks of Newfoundland up to the arctic regions, and perhaps a hundred miles in width (sometimes vessels coming from London strike it two hundred miles off shore), the ice-king occasionally forcing into his ranks a Newfoundland or Nova Scotia fishing-smack, which was either carried far to the southward, or exposed to the danger of being crushed between immense masses of floe-ice, or foundering, should a storm arise. We had escaped these perils; a fresh westerly breeze forced the ice-pack off shore, leaving a channel, studded with small lumps of ice, between the shore and the ice-floe. Two or three days previous, on the 25th of July, while laid up in a harbor, so very snug and narrow that we had not room to swing by our cable, a snow storm visited us, leaving drifts a foot deep on the hills rising five hundred to eight hundred feet above us.

Our sail to Hopedale, under these auspices, reminded us of the experiences of arctic voyagers. As we glided along the snow-

[1] Reprinted from *Appleton's Journal* (New York), for December 9, 1871. Revised by the author for *The Indian Miscellany*.

clad coast, our reveries were often rudely disturbed by a shock and start, as a hard lump of the clearest fresh-water ice jarred our craft from stem to stern. But the sail was a rare one for our yachtmen. The ice-floe, with its prospective dangers of closing in upon us, should the wind veer around to its favorite quarter — the northeast — walled us in from the open sea beyond. We scud along with two reefs in our main-sail, our vessel under the guidance of an Esquimaux pilot, a boy in the employ of a Norwegian, himself once a subordinate in the Hudson Bay Company. He knows the courses by which to steer, and some of the dangerous rocks in the way; for the rest we trust to luck, since there are no charts of this rock-and-reef-studded coast. As we sail on, the islands and main-land rise higher and bolder from the water, and their outline against the clear northern sky is ragged and broken in the extreme. This wild coast-scenery culminates in the strange, volcano-like, glacier-streaked, jagged mountains of Cape Chudleigh, which we had longed and designed to see, but ice and ignorance of the coast forbade.

As we ran into Hopedale harbor, situated at the head of a deep, broad bay, we nearly overhauled the Moravian supply ship Harmony, just in from London, having made her annual summer trip, bearing supplies to the three Moravian stations, Hopedale, Nain and Okkak. She is a bark of three hundred tons, American measurement, and as neatly kept as a naval vessel. For ninety years the London agent of the Moravian society has sent a Harmony to this dangerous coast, losing but a couple of men during the whole period, one of these having been upset in a *kayak*. As our predecessor in these waters nears the station, and before our eyes had fairly distinguished the red roofs of the mission houses, she fired a salute from two nine-pounders; and we observed her flag drooping at half-mast, conveying the intelligence of the death during the past year of the London secretary, Latrobe. The boom of the mission gun answered reply, with an irregular, rattling volley from the fowling-pieces of the Esquimaux. We noticed the mission flag also at half-mast, as the station had recently lost by death Superintendent Kruth.

We secured good anchorage near the Harmony. A clumsy

row-boat, native-built, accompanied by a kayak, brought from the shore the three missionaries and their wives. The Harmony had brought out a missionary, who had been absent two years in the fatherland, and Mr. Linklater, the agent of the Labrador missions. The meeting partook of all the heartiness of the Germans, the brethren greeting one another with a kiss.

The harbor now seemed alive with kayaks, hastening to the bark, and then flying over to our craft. Up they scrambled, swarming over our decks — nothing of the stolidity and apparent self-absorption of the Indian in their faces. These intelligent Esquimaux were fully alive to the beauty of our model and spars, the neatness of our decks, the comforts of our cabin, even to the interior of our swill buckets; and soon, in the course of the trade that sprung up, our old clothes found their way to their backs and limbs, that seemed lost in them. The tallest Esquimaux just came up to the shoulders of a medium-sized Yankee, and these diminutive folk seemed better fitted for their kayaks and *iglooks* than for the luxuries of vessels and storied houses.

An exodus of sea-worn Caucasians was the result of this *impromptu* visit. We returned the polite attentions of our newly-made friends of the kayaks and iglooks, and novel enough were the scenes of that afternoon. Some of us, with intentions of trade in furs and articles of Esquimaux *vertu*, at once, with strings of beads and other stock in trade, struck off for the huts of the natives, and found their match in shrewdness and skill in trade. Others — myself among the number — preferred to take a bird's-eye view of this century-old town. We sauntered through the rows of huts, picking our way through the accumulated filth of decades, and the ancient mud-puddles and quagmires interspersed among the streets, gazing upon the various forms of hideousness which, in a curious mixture of seal skins, woollen jumpers, duck jackets, red-bordered swallow-tails, and dirty calico gowns, stared and grinned at the new comers. Aged Esquimaux are not fair to look upon. The patriarch of the place was a woman of seventy years; for old age creeps rapidly on the Innuit matron, and she does not grow graceful or beautiful with age. There were in this colony three women sixty years old. A man forty-five years old is considered aged, as the autumnal seal-fisheries with all their hardships make them prematurely old. The young women and girls, with black hair, coal-black, shining eyes, stuck like beads between their huge, high, plump cheeks, nearly effacing their snub noses, giggled and grinned a welcome. The natives were at first a little shy of us, but gradually a brisk trade sprung up. We gave them fishhooks, beads, tobacco and pipes, old clothes, and letter-paper, taking in return seal-skin boots and mittens, skin suits, and ivory models of kayaks, while the naturalists of the party took birds'eggs and other curiosities.

The native huts were thirty-five in number, and a description of one will answer for all, as the dirt, squalor, and architecture, are a characteristic of each and all. They are made of upright logs, turfed on the outside, with cross logs forming a low roof, pierced for two windows, one in the roof, and of five or six panes each, glazed with the intestines of the seal, while in some the panes were filled with pieces of glass. The interior forms a single room, sometimes tenanted by two families, the tenements separated by a slight partition. At the farther end of the small, low room, which in the better sort of houses is floored over, and was not high enough for us to stand erect in, is a sort of divan or seat, on which materfamilias reclines. We make her a bow, rendered low both from courtesy and the height of the door-way of the low, narrow portico, pick onr way among two or three sleeping dogs, give a wide berth to a Scylla of a seal's carcass with more than "an ancient and fish-like smell," steer by a strange sort of vesicular Charybdis, in whose urinary contents lies soaking a seal-skin which is destined to be chewed between the grinders of our hostess, as she may design making a pair of seal-skin boots, and the leather has to be thus softened to be easily sewed. Our spectacled hostess is, however, as we enter, engaged in making a basket of dried rushes, colored blue and red. A shelf within her reach contains a soapstone lamp of the pattern described by Dr. Kane, needles, and other articles of housewifery, together with a well-thumbed Bible printed in the Esquimaux tongue. Indeed, we noticed one in each house, with the name of the owner written in a neat, regular hand; for it must be remembered that these natives are Christianized and taught to read and write. After all, upon reflection, considering their antecedents, their mode of life, and the freedom of arctic regions from noisome exhalations, our dusky friends were passably neat, and their houses perhaps orderly enough. After a three days' acquaintance, we found the natives quiet and well-behaved, honest in their dealings, of mild, gentle manners, always ready with a smile and a nod. They are remarkably intelligent, quick to learn, and far above the Indians in aptness and industry. They are taught to make boats, and there lay in the harbor a schooner of fifty tons, built and manned by Esquimaux. They also learn to read and write and sing. They seem to be good church-goers, and are probably as free from vice, even of the grosser sorts, as their fellow-Christians in more favored lands, who probably make greater pretensions to piety. But these people, so interesting to the students of fossil tribes, whose remains are found in the shell-heaps and caves of the old world, and to the anthropologist generally, are rapidly passing away, and, before another century goes by, Labrador will probably be depopulated of its Esquimaux. They are even now partly dependent for their supplies on the kindness of their German friends, who in their care for their souls do not neglect the outer man. Consumption sweeps them away, about seventy having perished in the previous March from the three colonies of Hopedale, Nain, and Okkak — twenty-one alone having died at Hopedale, which numbers about two hundred souls. The wars between the Indians and Esquimaux have now ceased. Formerly, the latter extended down to the straits of Belle-Isle, and four summers previous we saw the last full blooded Esquimaux on the straits — the wife of an Englishman at Salmon bay, at the mouth of Esquimaux river. She was a bold and skilful hunter, even more successful in shooting seals than the hunters in the neighborhood, and withal a neat, capable housewife.

During the winter they go on lumbering trips, fifty miles up the rivers, bringing down logs fifty feet in length, and twenty inches in diameter at the butt, a number of which were lying by the mission house. The girls and young women were, in some cases, quite pretty, with a neatly turned foot, and an instep a queen would be proud of. All seemed industrious, some filling orders for skin suits our party had given, or rubbing up their toys and other salable articles for barter. The men do little more than hunt and fish; but I found that they were very observing, and, through a young man that spoke English, learned some important facts regarding the distribution of arctic animals. He said that the white bear was not unfrequently brought down from the north on the floe-ice, and was seen about the shore during the summer, while the black bear is common in-shore.

Indeed, the flora and the fauna were here intensely arctic. On the hills and rocks about us was the little white sandwort, familiar to those rambling among the rocks of the summit of Mount Washington, with many other truly arctic forms, and the butterflies, moths, and beetles that hovered over them, or ran among their leaves, were the most typical arctic insects.

On showing our interpreter a book with figures of the narwhal and walrus, we learned that one of the older men, when a boy, saw a narwhal off the harbor, indicating that that strange animal, now exclusively confined to the arctic seas, formerly ranged far to the southward, and may, during the glacial period, have been a New Englander. He also said that the walrus was never seen here. A century ago, however, the walrus lived along the Labrador shore, and our fishermen and whalers exterminated it from the Magdalen islands, in the Gulf of St. Lawrence. On showing him a picture of the lobster, he declared that both it and the common shore crab were not found north of Hamilton inlet, where he had observed them. The sea trout is taken here abundantly with the net. This seems to be a truly arctic fish. It was much more abundant than the salmon. The wolverine is not uncommon here. Indeed, this was the border land between the arctic and boreal flora and fauna, the white bear disputing the proprietorship of the soil with the black, the arctic foxes outnumbering the red, and all the humbler forms of animal life being almost purely arctic, with a small percentage of more southern types. The climate is like that of Greenland, the scenic features of the land are thoroughly arctic, and the ice laden sea, of a temperature bordering on the freezing point, is frozen up fully six months in the year.

A voyage of two weeks from Boston or New York will bring one into these Arctic surroundings. The summer days, when the sky is clear, are warm and delightful, the air is wonderfully invigorating, and a voyage to this coast often does wonders in restoring those afflicted with pulmonary diseases, as well as dyspeptics. When the summers are tolerably pleasant, and the coast free from fogs, yachting in these waters, though somewhat dangerous from the want of charts and pilots, is delightful, and our pleasure boats will doubtless often push their way up into these hyperborean regions. Curlew shooting, reindeer hunts, a possible white bear, salmon fishing, duck shooting, and bird's nesting, will entice them to explore the deep, awe-inspiring fiords, the rapid rivers, and the rugged mountains of this picturesque and deserted coast.

But the chapel bell tolls the hour of evening prayers. We have chatted by the language of fingers and signs, with occasional *eilars na-mes, aps,* and other interjections, having had no difficulty in conveying our meaning, nor in understanding our host's, and now wend our way to the church. The surroundings about the huts are peculiar. A kayak or two recline on a framework of poles, a bear-skin swings in the breeze on one side of the hut, and, in front of the porch, a string of cut and drying codfish perfume the air. We allow our feminine friends to walk on before us, and their gait, originally awkward enough, is intensified by the swinging tails to their jumpers, and the loosely-setting, low-waisted trousers, when the form of the wearer is not fortunate enough to be concealed by a cast-off calico gown. With them, waddling is reduced to a fine art.

Entering the chapel, a wooden one-storied building, we find the native portion of the audience already seated, the sexes separately, even having entered by a separate door, and the youngest seated in the front row of unpainted benches. Soon file in the missionaries and their wives, and they sit, the sexes apart, on a stoop next the wall, directly facing the native audience, with the pulpit, or reading-desk, dividing the seat. They sit with grave, composed countenances, and among the Esquimaux the utmost reverence for the place and attention to the exercises prevail. The minister makes a short invocation in the Esquimaux language. The organ strikes up, played by an Esquimaux boy, and the minister gives out the number of the hymn in German; the people rise, and the quaint melody of an old-fashioned, droning German hymn, composed, for aught we know, in Luther's time, though set to Esquimaux words, fills the church. All stand up reverently during the singing, and the music is not unpleasant, soothing the senses, and doubtless most beneficent in its effects on these untutored minds. Hymn after hymn is thus chanted for perhaps twenty minutes, all the congregation joining; a short prayer completes the service, and thus ends the day. The audience quietly disperse, retiring in quiet to their homes; the sun has set, the shades of night gather about the hamlet, and, if the inquisitive traveler should in a few minutes perambulate the deserted streets, he would meet only the silence of the midnight, as all are abed and asleep.

The first day of August was a lovely one; the thermometer rose to perhaps 70°, the warm rays of the sun encouraging the mosquitoes unduly, which hovered in swarms about our deserted vessel. Groups of Esquimaux accompanied them, clambering up the sides of the vessel, coming off from shore in boats and kayaks. Kayak races and other aquatic sports were now the order of the day, a plug of tobacco being the highest prize. They handled their kayaks in the most approved style. A favorite sport seemed to be for one to paddle his kayak over the bows or stern of another lying still across his track. Our crew and passengers borrowed the kayaks freely, and some soon learned the use of this frail skiff, so as to paddle ashore and back, a distance of nearly a mile. These kayaks had wooden frames, over which seal-skins were stretched, but they seemed broader and clumsier than those from Greenland. We ventured to paddle about in one, and found it very easy to manage, the principal difficulty being to keep the head steadily pointed in the desired course, as a too powerful stroke would make her veer from one side to the other. Of course, if one capsizes, he is in a dangerous predicament, as the hole in which he sits closely fits his body, and a tall man could not extricate himself while head downward in the water. The spears and bladder floats are like those of Greenland.

In fishing, the Hopedale Esquimaux use small nets, with which they take the sea trout, a fish with large scales, being a compound of the ordinary river and lake trout and the salmon. They catch codfish with the jigger. Though the missionaries have set them an admirable example in pleasantly arranged and highly cultivated gardens, in which quite a number of vegetables were raised with more or less success in this rigorous climate, yet the Esquimaux is no farmer. His sole occupation consists in keeping his family supplied with animal food. The Esquimaux are flesh-eaters, *par excellence*, and a Grahamite would scarcely be tolerated among them. During the summer, if unusually enterprising, he takes his family and travels about with a skin tent, fishing and shooting birds, and occasionally killing a seal or bear. In the autumn and spring, seal-hunting is his exclusive care, though water fowl and a deer or two may sometimes enliven his monotonous seal diet, while in the long winter, when the seals are not to be had, and starvation stares him and his family in the face, the kindly aid of his Moravian brethren is invoked.

His family is not usually a large one; the good wife is not blessed with many children in that cold, bleak, harsh climate. Indeed, the days of the Esquimaux in Labrador are numbered. They are rapidly disappearing, victims of desolating wars between themselves and the Indians, of consumption and severe colds, and their own shiftlessness and improvidence. Before another century has passed, the few stragglers living upon this coast will be chiefly interesting to the student of mankind, as relics of a semi-fossil people who figure largely in books on prehistoric times.

INDIAN MEDICINE.[1]

By John Mason Browne.

Every one who has fed his boyish fancy with the stories of pioneers and hunters has heard of the character known among Indians as the *medicine man*. But it may very likely be the case that few of those familiar with the term really know the import of the word. A somewhat protracted residence among the Blackfoot tribe of Indians, and an extensive observation of men and manners as they appear in the wilder parts of the Rocky mountains and British America, have enabled the writer to give some facts which may not prove wholly uninteresting.

By the term *medicine*, much more is implied than mere curative drugs, or a system of curative practice. Among all the tribes of American Indians, the word is used with a double signification, a literal and narrow meaning, and a general and rather undefined application. It signifies not only physical remedies and the art of using them, but second sight, prophecy, and preternatural power. As an adjective, it embraces the idea of supernatural as well as remedial.

As an example of the use of the word in its mystic signification, the following may be given. The *horse*, as is well known, was to the Indian, on his first importation, a strange and terrible beast. Having no native word by which to designate this hitherto unknown creature, the Indians contrived a name by combining the name of some familiar animal, most nearly resembling the horse, with the medicine term denoting astonishment or awe. Consequently the Blackfeet, adding to the word elk (*pounika*) the adjective medicine (*tōs*), called the horse *pounika-ma-ta*, i. e. medicine elk. This word is still their designation for a horse.

With this idea of medicine, and recollecting that the word is used to express two classes of thoughts very different, and separated

[1] Reprinted from *The Atlantic Monthly* (Boston), for July, 1866.

by civilization, though confounded by the savage, it will not surprise one to find that the medicine men are conjurers as well as doctors, and that their conjurations partake as much of medical quackery as does their medical practice of affected incantation. As physicians, the medicine men are below contempt, and, but for the savage cruelty of their ignorance, undeserving of notice. The writer has known a man to have his uvula and palate torn out by a medicine man. In that case the disease was a hacking cough caused by an elongation of the uvula; and the remedy adopted (after preparatory singing, dancing, burning buffalo hair, and other conjurations) was to seize the uvula with a pair of bullet-moulds, and tear from the poor wretch every tissue that would give way. Death of course ensued in a short time. The unfortunate man had, however, died in "able hands," and according to the "highest principles of [Indian] medical art."

Were I to tell how barbarously I have seen men mutilated, simply to extract an arrow head from a wound, the story would scarce be credited. Common sense has no place in the system of Indian medicine men, nor do they appear to have gained an idea, beyond the rudest, from experience.

In their quality of seers, however, they are more important, and frequently more successful persons, attaining, of course, various degrees of proficiency and reputation. An accomplished dreamer has a sure competency in that gift. He is reverently consulted, handsomely paid, and, in general, strictly obeyed. His influence, when once established, is more potent even than that of a war chief. The dignity and profit of the position are baits sufficient to command the attention and ambition of the ablest men; yet it is not unfrequently the case that persons otherwise undistinguished are noted for clear and strong power of *medicine*.

Of the three most distinguished medicine men known to the writer, but one was a man of powerful intellect. Even this person preferred a somewhat sedentary, and what might be called a strictly professional life, to the usual active habits of the hunting and warring tribes. He dwelt almost alone on a far northern branch of the Saskatchewan river, revered for his gifts, feared for his power, and always approached with something of reluctance by the Indians, who firmly believed the spirit of the gods to dwell within him. He was an austere and taciturn man, difficult of access, and as vain and ambitious as he was haughty and contemptuous. Those who professed to have witnsssed the scene told of a trial of power between this man — the Black Snake, as he was called — and a renowned medicine man of a neighboring tribe. The contest, from what the Indians said, must have occurred about 1855.

The rival medicine men, each furnished with his medicine bag, his amulets, and other professional paraphernalia, arrayed in full dress, and covered with war paint, met in the presence of a great concourse. Both had prepared for the encounter by long fasting and conjurations. After the pipe, which precedes all important councils, the medicine men sat down opposite to each other, a few feet apart. The trial of power seems to have been conducted on principles of animal magnetism, and lasted a long while without decided advantage on either side; until the Black Snake, concentrating all his power, or "gathering his medicine," in a loud voice commanded his opponent to die. The unfortunate conjurer succumbed, and in a few minutes "his spirit," as my informant said, "went beyond the sand buttes." The only charm or amulet ever used by the Black Snake is said to have been a small bean-shaped pebble suspended round his neck by a cord of moose sinew. He had his books, it is true, but they were rarely exhibited.[1]

The death of his rival, by means so purely non-mechanical or physical, gave the Black Snake a preëminence in *medicine*, which he has ever since maintained. It was useless to suggest poison, deception, or collusion, to explain the occurrence. The firm belief was that the spiritual power of the Black Snake had alone secured his triumph.

I mentioned this story to a highly educated and deeply religious

---

[1] The Mountain Assinaboins, of which tribe the Black Snake is (if living) a distinguished ornament, were visited more than a hundred years since by an English clergyman named Wolsey, who devised an alphabet for their use. The alphabet is still used by them, and they keep their memoranda on dressed skins. With the exception of the Cherokees, they are, perhaps, the only tribe possessing a written language. They have no other civilization.

man of my acquaintance. He was a priest of the Jesuit order, a European by birth, formerly a professor in a continental university of high repute, and beyond doubt a guileless and pious man. His acquaintance with Indian life extended over more than twenty years of missionary labor in the wildest parts of the west slope of the Rocky mountains. To my surprise (for I was then a novice in the country), I found him neither astonished, nor shocked, nor amused, by what seemed to me so gross a superstition.

"I have seen," said he, "many exhibitions of power, which my philosophy cannot explain. I have known predictions of events far in the future to be literally fulfilled, and have seen medicine tested in the most conclusive ways. I once saw a Kootenai Indian (known generally as Skookum-tamaherewos, from his extraordinary power) command a mountain sheep to fall dead, and the animal, then leaping among the rocks of the mountainside, fell instantly lifeless. This I saw with my own eyes, and I ate of the animal afterwards. It was unwounded, healthy, and perfectly wild. Ah!" continued he, crossing himself and looking upwards, "Mary protect us! the medicine men have power from Sathanas."[1]

This statement, made by so responsible a person, attracted my attention to what before seemed but a clumsy species of juggling. During many months of intimate knowledge of Indian life, as an adopted member of a tribe, as a resident in their camps, and their companion on hunts and war-parties, I lost no opportunity of gathering information concerning their religious belief and traditions, and the system of *medicine,* as it prevails in its purity. It would be foreign to the design of this desultory paper to enter at large upon the history of creation as preserved by the Indians in their traditions, the conflicts of the beneficent spirit with the adversary, and the Indian idea of a future state. With all these,

[1] I do not feel at liberty to give the name of this excellent man, now perhaps no more. In 1861, he lived and labored, with a gentleness and zeal worthy of the cause he heralded, as a missionary among the Kalispelm Indians, on the west slope of the Rocky mountains. Such devotion to missionary labor as was his may well challenge admiration even from those who think him in fatal error. His memory will long be cherished by those who knew the purity of his character, his generous catholicity of spirit, and the native and acquired graces of mind which made him a companion at once charming and instructive.

the present sketch has no further concern than a mere statement that *medicine* is based upon the idea of an overruling and all-powerful Providence, who acts at His good pleasure, through human instruments. Those among Christians who entertain the doctrine of special providences may find in the untutored Indian a faith as firm as theirs — not sharply defined, or understood by the Indian himself, but inborn and ineradicable.

The Indian, being thoroughly ignorant of all things not connected with war or the chase, is necessarily superstitious. His imagination is active — generally more so than are his reasoning powers — and fits him for a ready belief in the powers of any able mediciner. On one occasion, Meldram, a white man in the employ of the American Fur Company, found himself suddenly elevated to high rank as a seer by a foolish or petulant remark. He was engaged in making a rude press for baling furs, and had got a heavy lever in position. A large party of Crow Indians who were near at hand, considering his press a marvel of mechanical ingenuity, were very inquisitive as to its uses. Meldram, with an assumption of severity, told them the machine was snow medicine, and that it would make snow to fall until it reached the end of a cord that dangled from the lever and reached within a yard of the ground. The fame of so potent a medicine spread rapidly through the Crow nation. The machine was visited by hundreds, and the fall of snow anxiously looked for by the entire tribe. To the awe of every Indian, and the astonishment of the few trappers then at the mouth of the Yellowstone, the snow actually reached the end of the rope, and did not during the winter attain any greater depth. Meldram found greatness thrust upon him. He has lived for more than forty years among the Crows, and when I knew him was much consulted as a medicine man. His chief charms, or amulets, were a large bull's-eye silver watch, and a copy of *Ayer's Family Almanac*, in which was displayed the human body encircled by the signs of the zodiac.

The position and case attendant upon a reputation for medicine power cause many unsuccessful pretenders to embrace the profession; and it would seem strange that their failures should not have brought medicine into disrepute. In looking closely into this, a well marked distinction will always be found between *medicine* and the *medicine-men* — quite as broad as is made with us between religion and the preacher. I have seen would-be medicine men laughed at through the camp — men of reputation as warriors, and respected in council, but whose *forte* was not the reading of dreams or the prediction of events. On the other hand, I have seen persons of inferior intellect, without courage on the warpath or wisdom in the council, revered as the channels through which, in some unexplained manner, the Great Spirit warned or advised his creatures.

Of course it is no purpose of this paper to uphold or attack these peculiar ideas. A meagre presentation of a few facts not generally known is all that is aimed at. Whether the system of Indian medicine be a variety of mesmerism, magnetism, spiritualism, or what not, others may inquire and determine. One bred a Calvinist, as was the writer, may be supposed to have viewed with suspicion the exhibitions of medicine power that almost daily presented themselves. And while, in very numerous instances, they proved to be but the impudent pretensions of charlatans, it must be conceded, if credible witnesses are to be believed, that sometimes there is a power of second-sight, or something of a kindred nature, which defies investigation. Instances of this kind are of frequent occurrence, and easily recalled, I venture to say, by every one familiar with the Indian in his native state. The higher powers claimed for medicine are, in general, doubtfully spoken of by the Indians. Not that they deny the possibility of the power, but they question the probability of so signal a mark of favor being bestowed on a mere mortal. Powers and medicine privileges of a lower degree are more readily acknowledged. An aged Indian of the Assinaboin tribe is very generally admitted, by his own and neighboring tribes, to have been shown the happy hunting-grounds, and conducted through them and returned safely to the camp of his tribe, by special favor of the Great Spirit. He once drew a map of the Indian paradise for me, and described its pleasant prairies and crystal rivers, its countless herds of fat buffalo and horses, its perennial and luxuriant grass, and other charms dear to an Indian's heart, in a rhapsody that was almost poetry. Another, an obscure man of the Cathead Sioux, is believed to have seen the hole through which issue the herds of buffalo which the Great Spirit calls forth from the centre of the earth to feed his children.

Medicine of this degree is not unfavorably regarded by the masses; but instances of the highest grades are extremely rare, and the claimants of such powers few in number. The Black Snake and the Kootenai, before referred to, are, if still alive, the only instances with which I am acquainted of admitted and well-authenticated powers so great and incredible. The common use of medicine is in affairs of war and the chase. Here the medicine man will be found, in many cases, to exhibit a prescience truly astounding. Without attempting a theory to account for this, a suggestion may be ventured. The Indian passes a life that knows no repose. His vigilance is ever on the alert. No hour of day or night is to him an hour of assured safety. In the course of years, his perceptions and apprehensions become so acute, in the presence of constant danger, as to render him keenly and delicately sensitive to impressions that a civilized man could scarce recognize. The Indian, in other words, has a development almost like the instinct of the fox or beaver. Upon this delicate barometer, whose basis is physical fear, impressions (moral or physical, who shall say?) act with surprising power. How this occurs, no Indian will attempt to explain. Certain conjurations will, they maintain, aid the medicine man to receive impressions; but how or wherefore, no one pretends to know. This view of *minor medicine* is the one which will account for many of its manifestations. Whether sound or defective, we will not contend.

The medicine man whom I knew best was *Ma-què-a-pos* (the wolf's word), an ignorant and unintellectual person. I knew him perfectly well. His nature was simple, innocent, and harmless, devoid of cunning, and wanting in those fierce traits that make up the Indian character. His predictions were sometimes absolutely astounding. He has, beyond question, accurately described the persons, horses, arms, and destination of a party three hundred miles distant, not one of whom he had ever seen, and of whose very existence neither he, nor any one in his camp, was before apprised.

INDIAN MEDICINE. 81

On one occasion, a party of ten voyageurs set out from Fort Benton, the remotest post of the American Fur Company, for the purpose of finding the Kaimè, or Blood Band of the Northern Blackfeet. Their route lay almost due north, crossing the British line near the Chief mountain (Nee-na-stà-ko) and the great Lake O-màx-een (two of the grandest features of Rocky mountain scenery, but scarce ever seen by whites), and extending indefinitely beyond the Saskatchewan and towards the tributaries of the Coppermine and Mackenzie rivers. The expedition was perilous from its commencement, and the danger increased with each day's journey. The war-paths, war-party fires, and similar indications of the vicinity of hostile bands, were each day found in greater abundance.

It should be borne in mind that an experienced trapper can, at a glance, pronounce what tribe made a war-trail or a camp-fire. Indications which would convey no meaning to the inexperienced are conclusive proofs to the keen-eyed mountaineer. The track of a foot, by a greater or less turning out of the toes, demonstrates from which side of the mountains a party has come. The print of a moccasin in soft earth indicates the tribe of the wearer. An arrow-head or a feather from a war-bonnet, a scrap of dressed deer-skin, or even a chance fragment of jerked buffalo-meat, furnishes data from which unerring conclusions are deduced with marvellous facility.

The party of adventurers soon found that they were in the thickest of the Cree war-party operations, and so full of danger was every day's travel that a council was called, and seven of the ten turned back. The remaining three, more through foolhardiness than for any good reason, continued their journey, until their resolution failed them, and they too determined that, after another day's travel northward, they would hasten back to their comrades.

On the afternoon of the last day, four young Indians were seen, who, after a cautious approach, made the sign of peace, laid down their arms, and came forward, announcing themselves to be Blackfeet of the Blood Band. They were sent out, they said, by Ma-què-a-pos, to find three whites mounted on horses of a peculiar color, dressed in garments accurately described to them, and armed with weapons which they, without seeing them, minutely described. The whole history of the expedition had been detailed to them by Ma-què-a-pos. The purpose of the journey, the *personnel* of the party, the exact locality at which to find the three who persevered, had been detailed by him with as much fidelity as could have been done by one of the whites themselves. And so convinced were the Indians of the truth of the old man's medicine, that the four young men were sent to appoint a rendezvous, for four days later, at a spot a hundred miles distant. On arriving there, accompanied by the young Indians, the whites found the entire camp of Rising Head, a noted war-chief, awaiting them. The objects of the expedition were speedily accomplished; and the whites, after a few days' rest, returned to safer haunts. The writer of this paper was at the head of the party of whites, and himself met the Indian messengers.

Upon questioning the chief men of the Indian camp, many of whom afterwards became my warm personal friends, and one of them my adopted brother, no suspicion of the facts, as narrated, could be sustained. Ma-què-a-pos could give no explanation beyond the general one, that he " saw us coming, and heard us talk on our journey." He had not, during that time, been absent from the Indian camp.

A subsequent intimate acquaintance with Ma-què-a-pos disclosed a remarkable medicine faculty as accurate as it was inexplicable. He was tested in every way, and almost always stood the ordeal successfully. Yet he never claimed that the gift entitled him to any peculiar regard, except as the instrument of a power whose operations he did not pretend to understand. He had an imperfect knowledge of the Catholic worship, distorted and intermixed with the wild theogony of the red man. He would talk with passionate devotion of the Mother of God, and in the same breath tell how the Great Spirit restrains the rain spirits from drowning the world, by tying them with the rainbow. I have often seen him make the sign of the cross, while he recounted, in all the soberness of implicit belief, how the old man (the god of the Blackfeet) formed the human race from the mud of the Missouri — how he experimented before he adopted the human frame, as we now have it — how he placed his creatures in an isolated park far to the north, and there taught them the rude arts of Indian life — how he staked the Indians on a desperate game of chance with the spirit of evil — and how the whites are now his peculiar care. Ma-què-a-pos's faith could hardly stand the test of any religious creed. Yet it must be said for him, that his simplicity and innocence of life might be a model for many, better instructed than he.

The wilder tribes are accustomed to certain observances which are generally termed the tribe-medicine. Their leading men inculcate them with great care — perhaps to perpetuate unity of tradition and purpose. In the arrangement of tribe-medicine, trivial observances are frequently intermixed with very serious doctrines. Thus, the grand war-council of the Dakotah confederacy, comprising thirteen tribes of Sioux, and more than seventeen thousand warriors, many years since promulgated a national medicine, prescribing a red stone pipe with an ashen stem for all council purposes, and (herein was the true point) an eternal hostility to the whites. The prediction may be safely ventured, that every Sioux will preserve this medicine until the nation shall cease to exist. To it may be traced the recent Indian war that devastated Minnesota; and there cannot, in the nature of things, and of the American Indian especially, be a peace kept in good faith until the confederacy of the Dakotah is in effect destroyed.

The Crows, or Upsàraukas, will not smoke in council, unless the pipe is lighted with a coal of buffalo chip, and the bowl rested on a fragment of the same substance. Their chief men have for a great while endeavored to engraft teetotalism upon their national medicine, and have succeeded better than the Indian character would have seemed to promise.

Among the Flat-Heads female chastity is a national medicine. With the Mandans, friendship for the whites is supposed to be the source of national and individual advantage.

Besides the varieties of medicine already alluded to, there are in use charms of almost every kind. When game is scarce, medicine is made to call back the buffalo. The man in the sun is invoked for fair weather, for success in war or chase, and for a cure of wounds. The spirits of the dead are appeased by medicine songs and offerings. The curiosity of some may be attracted by the following rude and literal translation of the song of a Blackfoot woman to the spirit of her son, who was killed on his first war-party. The words were written down at the time, and are not in any respect changed or smoothed.

> "O my son, farewell !
> You have gone beyond the great river,
> Your spirit is on the other side of the sand buttes,
> I will not see you for a hundred winters ;
> You will scalp the enemy in the green prairie,
> Beyond the great river.
> When the warriors of the Blackfeet meet,
> When they smoke the medicine-pipe and dance the war-dance,
> They will ask, ' Where is Isthumaka ?—
> Where is the bravest of the Mannikappi ?'
> He fell on the war-path.
>   Mai-ram-bo, mai-ram-bo.
>
> " Many scalps will be taken for your death ;
> The Crows will lose many horses :
> Their women weep for their braves,
> They will curse the spirit of Isthumaka.
> Oh my son ! I will come to you
> And make moccasins for the war-path,
> As I did when you struck the lodge
> Of the Horse Guard with the tomahawk.
> Farewell, my son ! I will see you
> Beyond the broad river.
>   Mai-ram-bo, mai-rambo," etc., etc.

Sung in a plaintive minor key, and in a wild, irregular rhythm, the dirge was far more impressive than the words would indicate.

It cannot be denied that the whites, who consort much with the ruder tribes of Indians, imbibe, to a considerable degree, their veneration for medicine. The old trappers and voyageurs are, almost without exception, observers of omens and dreamers of dreams. They claim that medicine is a faculty which can in some degree be cultivated, and aspire to its possession as eagerly as does the Indian. Sometimes they acquire a reputation that is in many ways beneficial to them.

As before said, it is no object of this paper to defend or combat the Indian notion of medicine. Such a system exists as a fact; and whoever writes upon American Demonology will find many fruitful topics of investigation in the daily life of the uncontaminated Indian. There may be nothing of truth in the supposed prediction by Tecumseh, that Tuckabatchee would be destroyed by an earthquake on a day which he named; the gifts of the *prophet* may be overstated in the traditions that yet linger in Kentucky and Indiana; the descent of the Mandans from Prince Madoc and his adventurous Welchmen, and the consideration accorded them on that account, may very possibly be altogether fanciful; but whoever will take the trouble to investigate will find in the *real* Indian a faith, and occasionally a power, that quite equal the faculties claimed by our civilized clairvoyants, and will approach an untrodden path of curious, if not altogether useful research.

NARRATIVE OF THE LONG WALK.[1]

BY JOHN WATSON, FATHER AND SON.

[Communicated to the Historical Committee of the American Philosophical Society, Philadelphia, in 1822.]

William Penn with a number of settlers came to Pennsylvania in the year 1682. His first care was to establish a good understanding with the natives by personal sociability and friendly acts of hospitality and generosity, and regarding them as men, whose rights were not to be invaded either by force or fraud. He therefore purchased of them a tract of land, for a price agreed upon, of the following description, taken from the original deed:

"Beginning at a white oak in the land now in the tenure of John Wood, and by him called the Grey Stones, over against the falls of Delaware river, and from thence up the river side to a corner spruce tree, marked with the letter P, at the foot of the mountains (this tree stood 140 perches above the mouth of Baker's creek)—and from the said tree along by the ledge or foot of the mountains west southwest to a corner white oak, marked with the letter P (on land now Benjamin Hampton's)—standing by the Indian path that leads to an Indian town called Playwicky and near the head of a creek called Towsisnick, and from thence westward to the creek called Neshaminah (this line crosses where the Newtown road now is), at the old chestnut tree below Doctor Isaac Chapman's lane end and along by the said Neshaminah to the river Delaware, alias Makerickhickon, and so bounded by the said main river, to the first mentioned white oak in John Wood's land (above Morrisville) with the several islands in the river," etc. Dated 15th July, 1682.

This purchase was limited by previous agreement to extend as far up the river from the mouth of Neshaminah as a man might walk in a day and a half—which tradition has said to have been executed by William Penn himself, on foot, with several of his

---

[1] Reprinted from *Hazard's Register of Pennsylvania* (Philadelphia), for October 2, 1830.

friends, and a number of Indian chiefs. It was said by the old people that they walked leisurely, after the Indian manner, sitting down sometimes to smoke their pipes, to eat biscuit and cheese, and drink a bottle of wine. It is certain they arrived at the spruce tree in a day and a half, the whole distance rather less than thirty miles; and the northwest boundary being traced out and marked on many trees with the letter P, for Penn; and all parties being well satisfied, the above deed was signed by the Indian sachems with their respective hieroglyphics.

It is certain that William Penn did not arrive in Pennsylvania for several months after the date of the above deed. We are therefore left to conjecture to account for the inconsistency; the business might have been done in the next year, and the deed dated back for some reason not now known, perhaps to cover some settlement already made; there might be an error in the date of the original deed or in taking the copy.

Four years after another purchase was made of the natives, the description of which is contained in the following extract from the deed: "Beginning at the before mentioned spruce tree (says the grant) about Makerickhitton (Baker's creek) from thence running along the ledge or foot of the mountains west southwest to a corner white oak marked with the letter P, standing by an Indian path that leadeth to an Indian town called Playwicky; and from thence extending westward to Neshaminah creek, from which line the said tract or tracts hereby granted doth extend itself as far into the woods as a man can go in a day and a half; bounded on the westerly side by the creek called Neshaminah or the most westerly branch thereof as far as the said branch doth extend, and from thence by a line to the utmost extent of the one and a half day's journey, and from thence by a line to the aforesaid river Delaware, and from thence down the several courses of the said river to the first mentioned spruce tree." Dated the 28th of August, 1686.

The deed was executed by the parties, and as the Delaware and the Neshaminah were to be the northeast and southwest bounds, most of the lands in Buckingham, Solebury, etc., were located, and as the proprietary was much engaged in other business, the walk was not made when he went to England, and although it is evident from the deed that the place of beginning must be the west corner of the first purchase on the Neshaminah, yet the Indians always insisted on going up the Delaware from the spruce tree — and probably for this reason, nothing was done in the business for six years.

In the year 1692 a white man living at Newtown and Cornelius Spring, a Delaware Indian, accompanied by several Indians and white people, undertook and performed the walk in the Indian manner; but by what authority or by whose direction is not now known. They started from the spruce tree, and walked up the river; the Indians jumped over all the streams of water until they came to the Tohickon, which they positively refused to cross, and therefore they proceeded up the creek on the south side to its source, and then turning to the left, they fell in with the Swamp creek, and going down it a small distance, it was noon on the second day, or a day and a half from the time of setting out. To close the survey it was proposed to go from there to the source of the west branch of Neshaminah (so called), thence down the creek to the west corner of the first purchase, and thence to the spruce tree, the place of beginning. These bounds would have included a tract of land rather larger than the first purchase, and no doubt would have been satisfactory to the Indians. It does not appear to have been a final settlement, or that any thing was done relative to the subject except talk about it, for forty-three years, in which time a large tract was sold to a company at Durham, a furnace and forges were erected there, and numerous scattered settlements made on the frontiers as far back as the Lehigh hills. The chief settlements of the Indians at the time were in the forks of the Delaware and Lehigh, below and beyond the Blue mountains. But in the summer season many families migrated in their way, and cabined among the white people in different places, as far down as Pennsbury manor, where they long retained a permanent residence on sufferance, and although a general harmony subsisted between the natives and the white people, yet they showed a dislike to the surveys and settlements that were every year extending further back in the woods, and as *they* presumed far beyond the proper limits of the land they had sold.

In the spring of the year 1735, a surveyor, employed for the purpose, run and measured a line beginning where the northwest boundary of the first purchase crossed the Durham road, and thence northwesterly on the said road to somewhere about the Haycock, and then turned more to the left through the woods to the Lehigh gap in the Blue mountain, blazing the southeast side of the trees and saplings in the woods within sight of each other. At some time before this period, a treaty or conference had been held with some of the Indians, who Teedyuscung at the treaty of 1756 called *pretenders*, and said, as there was no king presumed to do national business without proper authority. At this conference (perhaps in 1784) both parties agreed, by compromise, to alter the *day* and an *half's* walk to *one* day, and to go a northwest course. The Indians probably presuming that at twenty miles a day, the average of the preceding walks, it would not extend further back than the hills below Durham; accordingly a new instrument, called a release, was made probably for a trifling additional present of a few goods. Preparation was then made for a walk to be performed under the direction of the sheriff of Bucks county, two men of uncommon abilities for fast walking were employed for the purpose at five pounds each, or an equivalent in land; and the Indians being notified, a number of them attended, also the sheriff with his sutlers, and several white men on horseback. About the 12th of September, 1735, at sunrise, the whole company started from the old chestnut tree above mentioned, below Wrightstown meeting house, or near there. The men walked moderately at first, but soon quickened their march, but the Indians called to them to *walk*, and not *run;* and the remonstrances being frequently repeated without effect, the Indians and a number of white people who had collected to see them set off, left them in ill humor at such conduct, except one Indian who continued with them during the day. The two walkers pursued their course, first on the Durham road and then by the line of marked trees, to the Blue mountain, and going through the gap on a level road, they pursued their way up the river, and at sunset the walkers arrived on a spur of the second, or Broad mountain, upwards of sixty miles from where they had set out in the morning, where they piled up a large heap of stones, and marked a number of trees around it. They passed the night in serious apprehensions, as their Indian companion left them and went to an Indian *cantico* not far off, perhaps the same company that had left them in the morning, who shouted and hallooed a great part of the night. But they were happily favored to return the next day in safety to their respective homes. The northwest boundary was afterwards run on the Pocony, and to the river at the short bend, and down the courses of the Delaware, by a measurement then made more than one hundred miles to the spruce tree.

This scandalous transaction was the subject of much conversation, and an apprehension prevailed, that it would sometime produce serious consequences.

Surveyors were sent for six years successively to locate large tracts of land in the forks, even among the Indian towns. They therefore procured letters to be sent to Jeremiah Langhorne and the governor, advising them to remove the settlers or they would take up the hatchet against them. The affair was now become serious, and therefore a deep laid scheme was contrived and carried into execution.

The chiefs and warriors of the Six Nations were to attend a treaty at Philadelphia in June, 1742. The Delawares, etc., were also invited to attend at the same time, which they did, making nearly one hundred Indians in the whole. And as there was at that time a prospect of a war between England and France, the Six Nations were courted to join in the contest on the side of the English. The record says that handsome dinners were provided, and the health of King George, the proprietaries, the governor, etc., were drank in high good humor, and at a certain time, at one of these sociable canticoes, the subject of the walk was introduced, and the several deeds and writings shown and explained by way of appeal to the high authority of the Six Nations, against the conduct of their cousins the Delawares, etc. In a private council among themselves, these mighty Cæsars of the lakes and woods determined to chastise and humble their dependents, which they did in the following decisive manner, at a council at Philadelphia. Present the governor and his council, Canassatigo, Schickcalamy and sundry chiefs of the Six Nations, Sassoonan, and Delawares, Nuttimus and Fork Indians; Conrad Weiser, Pisquitoman, and Cornelius Spring, interpreters.

Canassatigo, on behalf of the Six Nations, said: "Brethren, the governor and council. The other day you informed us of the misbehavior of our brethren the Delawares, with respect to their continuing to claim, and refusing to remove from some land on the river Delaware, notwithstanding their ancestors had sold it by a deed under their hands and seals to the proprietaries, for a valuable consideration upwards of fifty years ago; and notwithstanding that they themselves had —— years ago, after a long and full examination, ratified that deed of their ancestors, and given a fresh one under their hands and seals; and then you requested us to remove them, enforcing your request with a string of wampum; afterwards you laid on the table our own letters by Conrad Weiser, some of our cousin's letters, and the several writings, with a draft of the land in dispute to prove the charge against our cousins. We now tell you, we have perused all these several papers, we see with our own eyes that they have been a very unruly people, and are altogether in the wrong in their dealings with you. We have concluded to remove them, and oblige them to go over the river Delaware, and quit all claim to any lands on this side for the future, since they have received pay for them, and it has gone through their guts long ago. To confirm you that we will see your request executed, we lay down this string of wampum in return for yours."

Then turning to the Delawares, holding a belt of wampum in his hand, spoke to them as follows: "*Cousins* — let this belt of wampum serve to chastise you; you ought to be taken by the hair of the head, and shaken severely till you recover your senses and become sober. You don't know what ground you stand on, nor what you are doing. Our brother Onas's cause is very just and plain, and his intentions to preserve friendship. On the other hand, your cause is bad; your hearts are far from being upright, and you are maliciously bent to break the chain of friendship with our brother Onas and his people. We have seen with our own eyes a deed signed by nine of your ancestors, above fifty years ago, for this very land, and a *release* signed not many years ago by some of yourselves and chiefs, now living, to the number of fifteen or upwards. But how came you, to take upon you to sell land at all? We conquered you, we made women of you — you know you are women, and can no more sell land than women. Nor is it fit you should have the power to sell land, since you abuse it. This land that you claim is gone through your guts; you have been furnished with clothes, meat and drink, by the goods paid you for it, and now you want it again like children, as you are. But what makes you sell land in the dark? Did you ever tell us you had sold this land? Did we ever receive any part, even the value of a pipe shank, from you for it? You have told us a blind story, that you sent a messenger to us, to inform us of the sale; but he never came among us, nor we never heard any thing about it. This is acting in the dark; and very different from the conduct of our Six Nations on such occasions. They give public notice, and invite all the Indians of their united nations, and give them all a share of the presents they receive for their lands; this is the behavior of the wise, united nations; but we find you are none of our blood, you act a dishonest part, not only in this, but in other matters, your ears are ever open to slanderous reports about our brethren; you receive them with greediness, and for all these reasons we charge you to remove instantly. We don't give you the liberty to think about it, you are women. Take the advice of a wise man and remove immediately; you may return to the other side of the Delaware, where you came from (Minisinks). But we do not know whether, considering how you have demeaned yourselves, you will be permitted to live there or whether you have not swallowed that land down your throats, as well as the land on this side; we therefore assign you two places to go, Wyoming or Shamokin; you may go to either of those places, and then we shall have you more under our eye, and shall see how you behave, and deliberate, but remove away and take this belt of wampum."

This being interpreted by Conrad Weiser into English, and by Cornelius Spring into the Delaware language, Canassatigo, taking a string of wampum, added further.

"After our reproof and absolute order to depart from the land, you are to take notice what we have further to say: this string of wampum serves to forbid you, your children and grand children to the latest posterity, for ever meddling in land affairs; neither you, nor any that shall descend from you are ever hereafter to presume to sell any lands, for which purpose you are to preserve this string in memory of what your uncles have this day given you in charge. We have some other business to transact with our brethren, therefore depart the council, and consider what has been said to you."

When this terrible sentence was ended, it is said that the unfeeling political philosopher walked forward, and taking strong hold of the long hair of the king of the Delawares, he led him to the door, and forcibly sent him out of the room, and stood there, while all the trembling inferiors followed him: he then walked back again to his place like another Cato, and calmly proceeded to another subject, as if nothing of the kind had happened. The poor fellows, in great and silent grief, went directly home, collected their families and goods, and burning their cabins, to signify they were never to return, marched reluctantly to their new home beyond the Susquehanna.

This shameful imposition was equally reprobated by all distinguished and candid men in the province, and it was seriously apprehended that mischief would sometime grow out of it. But no doubt there were some land speculators, and those who had conducted the business to such an issue, who enjoyed the triumph with unfeeling satisfaction. Some families of those Indians continued to come down every summer and cabin in the woods among their former friends, and go back in the fall. But when war began between England and France in 1754, and Washington and Braddock were successively defeated, there can be no doubt, that aggressions upon Indian rights by force and fraud, and in general the extension of settlements by the whites, became popular subjects of inquiry and explanation, at their great council fires;

even the history of the running walk might then be patiently listened to. And it is said that leave was given by the Six Nations, to their cousins the Delawares, Shawanees, etc., to strike the white people living on the lands they had been wronged out of. Therefore they immediately fell upon the back inhabitants of Northampton county, in all the inhuman and cruel manner of Indian warfare, burning houses and barns, killing, scalping, and taking many women and children into captivity; and these terrible depredations continued for about eighteen months. And strange as it may now appear to many in retrospect, notwithstanding the evident cause and origin of the war, a reward of £100 was offered by the governor in the public papers, for the head of Captain Jacobs, and £50 for the head of Captain Shingask, two Indian warriors. In this time of great public distress, there was much conversation on the subject; and as there could be no doubt but that it was occasioned by the imposition of the walk, it was proposed to try by way of experiment, how far it would have extended if executed according to the deed. Therefore in the month called June, 1756, John Heston and Joseph Smith (tavern keeper) began to walk at the high rocks on the Neshaminah creek in Wrightstown, about a mile below the bridge, thence up the branch north of John Wilkinson's and up the several courses of the creek to the head at Richard Thomas's; thence followed the county line to Mayer's mill on Perkioming, then crossing the Swamp creek, four miles from the swamp, continued west to Jacob Bonduman's by the main branch of Perkioming, then west three miles into Philadelphia county, and from thence continued their course into the new Coshoppen about three miles into Berks county, and four from Bucks county, on the west side of a hill, near a heap of rocks.

Some friendly Indians visited Philadelphia and on conversing freely with them, and the supposed cause of the war being explained, a prospect opened that a peace might be obtained, if proper measures were pursued for that purpose. Therefore a number of Friends or Quakers united in friendly association for regaining and preserving peace with the Indians by pacific measures. Many of the members of this association, with the free concurrence of the governors, Morris and Denny, attended divers conferences and treaties at Philadelphia and Easton, in which their presence, and the remembrance of the fair dealings of William Penn with their forefathers were of essential service towards procuring a cessation of hostilities, and finally the settlement of peace. Governor Hardy of New York and Sir William Johnson, and Christian Frederick Post, one of the Moravian brethren, afforded their advice and assistance, in favor of peace.

Through the interposition of some persons in Philadelphia, also of General Johnson and others, conferences were held at Philadelphia and Easton with the Indians; and at the latter place, November 13th, 1756, Governor Denny enquired of Teedyuscung, king of the Delawares, and agent of the Six Nations, why the Indians struck the white people, and what grievances they had suffered, he answered:

"Brother — You have not so much knowledge of things done in this country, as others who have lived longer in it, being lately come over to us. I have not far to go for an instance; this very land that is under me (stamping his foot on the floor) was my land and inheritance, and is taken from me by fraud; when I say this ground I mean all the land lying between Tohickon creek and Wyoming on the Susquehanna. When I have sold lands fairly I look upon them as fairly sold. A bargain is a bargain. Though I have had nothing for the land I have sold, but broken pipes and such trifles, yet when I have sold them, even for such trifles, I look upon the bargain to be good. Yet I think I should not be ill used on that account by those very people who have had the advantage in their purchases nor be called a fool for it. Indians are not such fools as not to know when they are imposed upon or not to bear it in remembrance."

The governor asked him what he meant by fraud in relation to the sale of lands? He answered: "All the land, extending from Tohickon over the great mountains to Wyoming has been taken from me by fraud; for when I had agreed to sell the land to the old proprietary by the course of the river, the young proprietary came and got it run by a straight course, by the compass, and by that means took in double (he might have said five times) the quantity intended to be sold."

Conrad Weiser, the interpreter, and Richard Peters, Esq., being asked what they knew about the subject, they agreed in substance, that they had heard of the Indians' uneasiness, but referred to the final settlement made of the dispute by the judgment of the Six Nations at the treaty at Philadelphia in 1742; but when Peters came out of the council he said the walk was dishonorable, and could not be defended, and therefore it was agreed to make the Indians a present speedily, on that account, which was afterwards done accordingly, which in common acceptation goes to prove which of the parties had been in the wrong.

In consequence of Teedyuscung's complaint, that the Indians had been cheated out of their land by the walk, some of the members of the Friendly Association above mentioned applied to the governor's secretary for leave to search the Provincial Records relative to the subject, which he refused to admit, although they were immediately interested in the Indian claim being extinguished on land they had purchased agreeably to the proprietary's agreement with the first settlers.

There may be some small errors in the foregoing narrative, but it is presumed the principal facts are correctly stated as they have been taken from original Indian treaties and from copies and notes, made by John Watson, surveyor, and in some minor parts derived by oral tradition, directly received from persons who were living at the time of the *long walk*, and such as had the best opportunities of being acquainted with the particulars of that unhappy affair.

It may be proper to remark, that William Penn went to England in 1701 and died in 1718; that those who succeeded him in managing the executive business of the province, especially about the year 1742, were not governed by those principles of generosity and justice that the Indians so highly respected in the conduct of the first worthy proprietary of Pennsylvania, or otherwise there might not have been any disturbance with the natives during the administration of the Penn family, a period of more than ninety years.

(Signed) JOHN WATSON.

Buckingham, Pa., 1815.

The preceding narrative was written by my father about seven years ago, and was then published in the *Pennsylvania Correspondent*, printed at Doylestown, from which I have copied it; but apprehending it to be incorrect in some particulars, I visited Moses Marshall who in his eightieth year is yet in the full possession of his faculties, and from his general character through life may safely be relied on. He informed me that his father was one of the persons employed to walk out the purchase made by William Penn of the Delaware Indians, that he has frequently heard him relate the particulars which he well remembers, and gave me the following account which I took down as he related it.

That he always understood from his father that William Penn, soon after his arrival in this country, purchased a tract of land of the Indians, to be bounded by the river Delaware on the northeast and the Neshaminy on the northwest, and to extend as far back as a man could walk in *three* days; that he and the Indians began to walk out this land at the mouth of the Neshaminy, and walked up the Delaware; that in *one* day and a *half* they got to a spruce tree near the mouth of Baker's creek when Penn concluding this would include as much land as he would then want, a line was run and marked from the spruce tree to Neshaminy, and the remainder left to be walked out when it should be wanted for settlement.

That in the year 1733, notice was given in the public papers that the remaining day and a half walk was to be made, and offering 500 acres of land any where in the purchase and £5 in money to the person who should attend, and walk the furthest in the given time.

By previous agreement the governor was to select three white persons and the Indians a like number of their own nation. The persons employed by the governor were Edward Marshall,

James Yates, and Solomon Jennings; one of the Indians was called Combush, but he had forgotten the names of the other two.

That about the 20th of September (or when the days and nights are equal), in the year aforesaid, they met before sunrise, at the old chestnut tree below Wrightstown meeting house, together with a great number of persons as spectators. The walkers all stood with one hand against the tree until the sun rose, and then started. In two hours and a half they arrived at Red Hill in Bedminster, where Jennings and two of the Indians gave out. The other Indian (Combush) continued with them, to near where the road forks at Easton, where he laid down a short time to rest, but on getting up was unable to proceed further. Marshall and Yates went on and arrived, at sun down, on the north side of the Blue mountain. They started again next morning at sun rise; while crossing a stream of water at the foot of the mountain Yates became faint and fell; Marshall turned back and supported him until others came to his relief, and then continued the walk alone, and arrived at noon on a spur of the second or Broad mountain, estimated to be eighty-six miles from the place of starting, at the chestnut tree below Wrightstown meeting house.

He says they walked from sunrise to sunset without stopping, provisions and refreshments having been previously provided at different places along the road and line that had been run and marked for them to walk by to the top of the Blue mountain, and persons also attended on horseback by relays with liquors of several kinds.

When they arrived at the Blue mountain they found a great number of Indians collected expecting the walk would there end, but when they found it was to go half a day further, they were very angry, and said they were cheated. Penn had got all their good land, but that in the spring every Indian was to bring him a buck skin and they would have their land again, and Penn might go to the devil with his poor land. An old Indian said "no sit down to smoke, no shoot a squirrel, but lun, lun, lun all day long."

He says his father never received any reward for the walk, although the governor frequently promised to have the 500 acres of land run out for him, and to which he was justly entitled.

Some time after a man came to their house having a summons for his father to appear before the Lord Loudon in Philadelphia. His father went with him, and was very particularly examined respecting the walk, his account taken down in writing, in order to be sent home to England. While in Philadelphia he was strictly guarded by two grenadiers, and not suffered to talk to any other person respecting the walk or his present business. When he was about to return home James Logan made him a present of £10, as a compensation for his time and expenses.

In 1754, his father lived about eighteen miles above Easton. In the next year two hundred Indians, headed by their chief or King Teedyuscung, made an attack on the white inhabitants; they fired on a company attending a funeral, but killed none; these fled and gave the alarm, and they all got off. His father's family went back in the year 1756, but lived until the fall of the next year on the Jersey side of the river, when they returned to the farm. Soon after about sixteen Indians attacked the house in the absence of his father of whom they always appeared afraid. One of them threw his match coat on a bee hive by the side of the garden, the bees came out and stung them, by which means five small children that were playing in the garden got away. They shot one of his sisters as she was running, the ball entered her right shoulder and came out below the left breast, yet she got away and recovered. They took his mother, who was not in a condition to escape them, some miles and then killed her. There were five guns in the house all loaded, which they never touched, and took nothing away, except a coat with £3 in money in the pocket, belonging to Matthew Hughes who boarded with the Marshalls.

In 1758, the people having forted together, the Indians came and turned the creatures into the wheat field; five young men went out of the fort to turn them out again. The Indians waylaid them and shot two, one of whom was his brother.

His father said the Indians always insisted that the walks should have been up the river, along the nearest path, which was also *his* opinion, and that they had been improperly dealt with, and cheated out of their land, but would have quietly submitted if the walk had not extended beyond the Blue mountain.

From the foregoing statement of Moses Marshall, as well as from what I remember to have heard from a few old people when I was young, I am inclined to believe my father must have been mistaken in a few particulars, first with respect to the original purchase made by William Penn. I believe it was *three* days' walk, but when one and a half days were measured out, the grant or deed was made and executed for so much, and the other deed four years after for the remainder, for it appears the first walk was made by William Penn and the Indians themselves, *up the river*, and they always insisted that the remainder should be in like manner measured out by walking *up the river* and to begin where the former had ended.

Again my father says the day and a half was changed by agreement to one day, and to go a northwest course. Mr. Marshall is positive that his father walked a day and a half, and so I have always understood it. He says two persons of uncommon abilities for fast walking were employed for the purpose, at £5 each or an equivalent in land. Mr. M. says there were three and gives their names, and says they were offered 500 acres of land and £5 in money. Perhaps my father may have been led into the first mistake, from the circumstance of there being two deeds or grants of different dates — the extracts from which used by him I have now in my possession among the papers left by John Watson, surveyor — the others probably from wrong information received about the time the narrative was written, as I remember he took considerable pains and called on several old persons to assist him.

I have for several years past been anxious that a correct history should be written of the first settlement of the United States, as that settlement was connected with the history of, and interested the Indian nations, the true original cause and consequence to them of the wars that ensued between them and the white people, not as they have been related by interested or prejudiced historians, professing to live under the dispensation of the gospel of peace, and proud of the advantages of civilization, but as they would be narrated by intelligent Indians; and I have been the most anxious to see such a history written, as I apprehend many important facts necessary thereto, even now only linger in the recollection of a few old men, and in a short time, unless collected at present, will be lost for ever.

A prominent fact of this description in my view is what has been called the long walk, and the foregoing contains perhaps as true an account of it as it is now possible to collect. It is important as being the cause of the first uneasiness of the Indians in Pennsylvania, and the first murder committed by them in the province, being on the very land they believed themselves thus cheated out of; and it appears this is yet remembered as one of the wrongs committed on them by the white men of which they complain.

(Signed)   JOHN WATSON.

Greenville 9th of 9th mo., 1822.

THE EARLY JESUIT MISSIONARIES OF THE NORTH WESTERN TERRITORY.[1]

BY W. B. O. PEABODY.

THERE is no one subject which presents to the mind of the antiquarian and the scholar, a finer field for investigation, than the early settlement of that region once known as the North Western Territory — now comprehending within its limits an empire embracing the three great states of Indiana, Illinois, and Michigan, and the present territory of *Ouisconsin ;* for such was, and such should now be, the name of the territory alluded to, and known on the modern maps, as *Wisconsin.* When a portion of this territory was first discovered, is unknown. The Jesuit father, no doubt, was the first white man who " paddled his light canoe" over those inland seas, extending from the St. Lawrence to the further limits of Lake Superior ; and long before civilization or empire had extended their star westward, he had unfurled the banner of the cross on the shores of Lakes Huron, Michigan and Superior ; and the missions of St. François Xavier at Green Bay, of St. Ignace at Mackina, of St. Mary at the straits, in the latter part of the seventeenth century, show conclusively, with what zeal and ardor these heralds of the cross pushed their "tabernacles in the wilderness," and made known to these wandering Arabs of the prairies the symbols of the Christian's faith, and the mysteries of their holy religion. But it was not simply as stationed preachers, that these good and great men attempted the conversion of the innumerable multitude who then swarmed the shores of the lakes, and spread from Lake Erie to the Ohio — from the Miami to the Father of Waters. They followed the Indian to his hunting ground, threaded forests, swam rivers, bivouacked with their troupe in the immense natural meadows which abound in that region ; endured hunger, thirst, cold, suffering, disease, death. The supposed conversion of a single

[1] Reprinted from *The Democratic Review* (New York), for May, 1844.

Indian to the doctrines of the Catholic faith, the baptism of a single infant, seems to have been to them an ample reward for all their labor, for all their toil, and for all their suffering. From the slight memorials which have come down to us, of the labors of love of these venerable, intellectual and devoted sons of the church, it is evident no sacrifice was too great, no suffering too severe, no enterprise too hazardous, no toil unendurable, which led to the accomplishment of the great object upon the success of which they had periled their all in this life, and sought that crown of glory in the next, which they felt sanguine would be the reward of their apostolic labors here. "I have been most amply rewarded for all my trials and suffering," says one of the lowly followers of Jesus, after having, for six days, lived on *tripe de roche* and a part of an Indian moccasin given him by a squaw, "I have this day rescued from the burning an infant who died from hunger, its mother's resources, in the general famine, having failed her; I administered to the dying infant the sacred rites of baptism: and thank God, it is now safe from that dreadful destiny which befalls those who die without the pale of our most holy church."

With us in the latter days, differing, as most of us do, in our religious opinions, from this school of ecclesiastics, it is almost impossible to do them justice. As a whole, their history has been little studied, and less understood. They have neither had their Livy, nor their Polybius; and if the history of these men, of their exertions, of their influence, of their actions, for good or evil, ever is to be written with candor, *it must be in this country* — the scene of many of their labors, and we might well add, of their sufferings and their death. No subject would form a more imposing theme for the historian; none demands higher qualifications, more laborious research, and above all, the most dignified superiority to all the prepossessions of age, of country and of creed. The individual who has closely examined the colonial history of the North Western Territory cannot but be struck with the truth of the remark, that "neither commercial enterprise nor royal ambition, carried the power of France into the heart of our continent; *the motive was religion.*" The same religious feeling which prompted our pilgrim fathers to plant the banner of the cross on the sterile rocks of Plymouth, carried it to the borders of the Mississippi: and while the influence of Calvin is felt in the worship and schools of New England, the no less powerful impulses of Loyola and his followers have left their marks upon the whole Algonquin race, who dwelt on the borders of the Illinois and the Wabash. The morning matin and the evening vespers were heard amidst the war-whoop of the Indian, and the symbol of the Christian's faith to this day hangs in bold relief above the girdle which suspends his tomahawk. The history of the Jesuit's labors is connected with every tribe from the waters of the *Lac Tracy* to where *La Belle Rivière* flows into the *Michasippd* — "not a cape was turned, nor a river entered but a Jesuit led the way." From the period when Charles Raymbault and Isaac Jogues accepted the invitation of the Chippewas to visit their tribe at the Sault St. Marie in 1641, down to the middle of the eighteenth century, there was a succession of missions, not only along the borders of the lakes, but at St. Joseph, now Vincennes, on the Wabash, among the Mascontins, the Pottawotamies, the Miamis; at Peoria, among the Illinois; at Cahokia among the Tamarois or Cahokias; at Kaskaskia, and along the shores of the Mississippi; from the mouth of the Wisconsin to the mouth of the Ohio; down the whole valley of the Mississippi to the Arkansas, and the Natchez. Wherever the *fleur de lys* was hoisted, and the power of the *grand monarque* made known to the Aborigines of the west, the humble but no less powerful influence of that sign by which the Jesuit conquered the stubborn hearts and pagan superstitions of these powerful nations, was displayed; and the Manitou of the Christian was acknowledged and worshiped as the only true God. The influence of their exertions is felt even in the nineteenth century, among the remnants of those tribes which once lorded it over this Western Barbary; and it was no idle boast of Le Jeune when he said, "The Mohawk and the feebler Algonquin shall make their home together; the wolf shall lie down with the lamb, and a little child shall lead them." Their bows have indeed been broken, and their tomahawks turned into ploughshares; but whether their condition has been bettered by the progress of civilization, is a problem yet to be solved.

There were three routes taken by the Jesuit fathers, on their pilgrimage to the tribes bordering the Mississippi — all three passing out of Lake Michigan. The first up the St. Joseph's and thence into the Wabash; the second up the Chicago river, thence by a portage across into the Kankiki (called on the old maps Teakiki) and thence into the Illinois; the third the route taken by Marquette and Joliet, ascending the Fox, and descending the Wisconsin to the Mississippi. That one or more of these routes had been traversed by the Jesuit fathers, years before Marquette and Joliet launched their frail bark, in 1673, on the waters of the Mississippi, is susceptible of proof; and that the Mississippi had been known, and the tribes inhabiting it visited, and missions established before Marquette even coasted its borders, is now well understood. As early as the year 1653, twenty years before Marquette and Joliet started on their voyage of discovery to the "great river Mechasippi," Father Jean Dequerre, Jesuit, went from the mission on the Superior to the Illinois, and established a flourishing mission, probably the mission of St. Louis where Peoria is now situated. He visited various Indian nations on the borders of the Mississippi, and was slain in the midst of his apostolical labors in 1661.

In 1657, Father Jean Charles Drocoux, Jesuit, went to the Illinois, and returned to Quebec the same year.

In 1670, Father Hugues Pinet, Jesuit, went to the Illinois, and established a mission among the Tamarois, or Cahokias, at or near the present site of the village of Cahokia, on the borders of the Mississippi. He remained there until the year 1686, and was at that mission when Marquette and Joliet went down the Mississippi. In the same year M. Bergier, priest of the Seminary of Quebec, succeeded him in the mission to the Tamarois or Cahokias; and Father Pinet returned to the mission of St. Louis (Peoria), where he remained until he died, the 16th of July, 1704, at the age of seventy-nine.

In 1663, Father Claude Jean Allonez, was appointed vicar general of the north and west, including Illinois. He preached to the Pottawotamies and Miamis about Green Bay; in 1665, he returned to Quebec, and went to the Illinois in 1668, and visited the missions on the Mississippi.

In 1670, M. Augustine Meulan de Circe, priest of the Seminary of Quebec, went to Illinois. He left the mission there in 1675, returned to France, was sent missionary to Siam, made bishop in 1708, nominated vicar apostolical of China, and in 1713 was in Japan. Thus it will be seen that for *twenty years*, to wit, from 1653 to 1673, anterior to the discovery of Marquette and Joliet, there was a succession of missions in the Illinois, and one of them, that of Cahokia, established on the very banks of the Mississippi. There are no other memorials of these missions now extant, as known to us, except those preserved in the Seminary of Quebec; from a copy of which the above notices are taken. The only object is to show, that for years before Marquette and Joliet visited the country, the Mississippi had been discovered, and missions actually established on its borders. That these good fathers made notes of their travels, and rendered an account of the various Indian tribes, which they visited along the Father of Waters, to their superior, there can be no doubt. What have become of these memorials of early western adventure and discovery now it is impossible to say. That they would throw much light on the early history of the west, there can be no doubt.

It will be remembered, by all who have taken any interest in the settlement of la Nouvelle France, that in the year 1628, the government of Canada, civil and military, was confided by Louis XIII to one hundred associates; at the head of whom was the celebrated Cardinal Richelieu. Hostilities commenced the same year between England and France, and the first vessels sent out by the company of New France were captured by the English. M. de Champlain commanded at Quebec. The inhabitants, reduced to seven ounces of bread per diem, and the garrison with but five hundred pounds of powder in the magazine, were summoned to a surrender. Champlain, although at the greatest extremity, refused to do so.

To add to the misfortunes of the colony, the French squadron, under command of M. de Roquemont, one of the associates, and bringing relief to the colony, was captured by the English in the St. Lawrence. The savage allies of the French, since the approach of the English, became alienated; and all the firmness of Champlain could not arrest the disorders daily accruing in this new settlement. The necessary consequence was, the surrender of the garrison with the honors of war to the English. The French were permitted to retire without molestation; but the greater part of the inhabitants chose to remain in the province. The capture of Quebec is attributed by Charlevoix to the perfidy of some *French Calvinists*, among whom the most conspicuous was Jacques Michel; and who, according to Charlevoix, was acting on board the English squadron in the capacity of vice-admiral. Whether this was so or not, it is now too late to determine. Suffice it to say, that Canada, in the year 1632, was again ceded to the French crown by the treaty of St. Germain. In 1633, the company of New France was restored to all its rights; and M. de Champlain being appointed governor general of Canada, sailed from France with a squadron to take possession of it, carrying with him the Jesuit fathers Brebeuf and Evremond Massé. Precise orders were given by Louis XIII that no Protestant should settle in Canada, and no other religion than the Catholic should be tolerated. Among the great number of Indian tribes which were found in the country, and which opened to the missionaries a vast field for the exercise of their functions, none seemed to claim their attention more than the Hurons. Champlain had for a long time formed the design of making an establishment in their country. Inhabiting the immense region between the Lakes Ontario, Erie, and Huron, mostly along the northern and eastern borders of the two last, a nation numerous, amounting to 40 or 50,000 souls, when first known to the French, whose true name was Yendats, but to whom the French had given the name of Hurons, from the French word *hure*, owing to the peculiar manner in which they wore their hair. "Quelles Hures?" said the French, when they first saw them; hence the word Hurons.[1] The object of Champlain was to make this country the centre of the missionary labors of the Jesuits, from whence,

---

[1] Charlevoix, i, 184.

as a starting point, they might spread the Catholic religion among the vast tribes supposed to inhabit the country south and west. The Fathers Brebeuf and Daniel were the first missionaries. In 1834, after great delay, owing to the unwillingness of the Hurons to take them, they departed from Quebec, and with great difficulty and danger, arrived at their mission, and built a small chapel, which they dedicated to St. Joseph. The fruit of their labors was small. Some five or six adults were baptized: but they consoled themselves with the fact "of having assured the eternal safety of a great number of infants, who expired immediately after having received the rites of baptism." The Indians listened to the relations of these good fathers, relative to the mysteries of their most holy religion; but it must be acknowledged the results were but indifferent; and even when they exhibited the marks of entire conviction, "it was evident they had not paid the least attention to what was said, nor comprehended it if they had."

"I saw you had no person to keep you company," said one of the Huron chiefs to the missionary, whom, from the attention, modesty and reverence manifested, the good father hoped to convert — "I saw you had no person to keep you company, and pray with you. I had compassion on your solitude, I therefore remained with you. As others now wish to render you the same service, I will retire."

Even some who went so far as to demand and receive baptism, and performed, for some time, all the outward duties of a convert, acknowledged they had done it with a view of pleasing the *robe noire* who had persuaded them to change their religion.

"You preach well," said a Huron chief to Father Brebeuf, "and there is nothing in all you teach us, but what is probably true enough, and will answer for those beyond the sea, from whence you came; but do you not see we inhabit a world entirely different from yours, and should have another heaven, and by consequence another way to get there?"

Such were the unsophisticated notions of these sons of the forest.

"These savages," says one of these reverend fathers, "have proposed for our consideration, all the objections to our faith, ever made by the wisest of the Greeks and Romans, to the earliest apostles."

This was the first mission established west of Lake Erie, yet, before the end of the year 1636, there were counted six Jesuit missionaries in the different Huron villages, besides many Frenchmen who had followed them. In the year 1642, the Jesuits established their mission at Sault St. Marie. A deputation of the tribe dwelling there came to St. Joseph, and Fathers Isaac Jogues and Charles Raymbault were sent with the deputation to the sault. They were soon, however, recalled. This is the same Father Jogues, who, on his return from the Huron mission to Quebec, was taken prisoner by the Iroquois, suffered the greatest indignities, was mutilated in his hands, scourged in three villages, and finally redeemed by a Dutch officer from Fort Orange, now Albany. He returned to France, and demanded from the pope the liberty of celebrating mass with his mutilated hands. Consent was given in these words: "*Indignum esset Christi martyrem Christi non bibere sanguinem.*" He returned from France to Canada, established a mission among the Iroquois, and was slain by them in 1646.

The fate of the Hurons was truly pitiable. Of their various villages, those which were not destroyed by pestilence and famine, were attacked by their old enemies, the Iroquois; and as no quarter was given by these modern Goths, they were butchered *en masse*. Weak, powerless, overcome, the very name of an Iroquois alarmed them. Two whole villages voluntarily surrendered themselves, and were adopted into the Six Nations; others fled to the tribes south and west, others joined the English, and some established themselves in what is now the state of Pennsylvania. Not only the country of the Hurons, but the whole borders of the Ottawas, were abandoned, and three hundred Hurons, accompanied by their missionary, Father Raguenaw, were in 1650 led back by him from the mission of St. Joseph to the very walls of Quebec, where, under the guns of the fort and the protection of their "great father Ononthio," they were induced to believe they could find safety from the exterminating enemies of their tribe and kindred, the fierce and bloody Iroquois. The entire destruction, in 1655, by the Iroquois, of the *Nation du Chat, ou Heries*, who inhabited the southern borders of Lake Erie, and whose very existence as a nation is known at the present day only by the name given by them to the lake (Erie) on which they dwelt, is a sad memorial of what would have been the fate of the Huron, had he not deserted his hunting grounds, and the graves of his ancestors, and sought protection from his more warlike neighbors. But even there he was not safe. Many a Huron scalp has been carried as a trophy to his tribe, by the fearless Onondaga, who has sought his victim under the bastions of Fort Levi, or on the plains of Sylleri.

In the years 1687-9, Father Maret and another Jesuit established a mission among the Sioux. In 1663, the Marquis de Tracy, lieutenant general in the French armies, was named viceroy of *la Nouvelle France*, M. de Courcelles, governor, and the celebrated Talon, intendant. Affairs then presented a new aspect. The regiment de Carignan (in which François Morgan Vincennes, the founder of Vincennes on the Wabash, was an officer), arrived in the colony in 1665, accompanied by M. de Tracy. An expedition was undertaken against the Iroquois; many of their settlements destroyed, and this formidable enemy of New France humiliated. It was a primary object with the viceroy, to endeavor, if possible, to induce the red men to adopt the language, habits and manners of their conquerors; but this, like every other experiment of the same kind for upwards of a century, entirely failed. In 1667, M. de Tracy returned to France. M. de Talon was left as his successor. In the meantime, new missions were established in the west. The Ottawas, who had their villages on the east side of the straits connecting Lakes Erie and St. Clair, in the Bay of Sagamon, and the western end of Lake Huron, sent a deputation to Quebec; and the Father Claude Allonez, at their solicitation, was sent as a missionary to their tribe. The sufferings endured in the same mission, but a few years before, by the Fathers Garreau and Mesnard, did not deter this holy man from the performance of what he conceived his duty to his God and his fellow men. He arrived at the sault the first of September, 1668, but he did not stop there. He employed the whole month of September in coasting the southern portion of Lake Superior, where he met many Christians baptized by Father Mesnard. "I had the pleasure," says this venerable man, " of assuring by baptism the eternal salvation of many a dying infant." His success with the adults seems to have been less. At Chagouamigon or St. Michael, on the southwestern side of Lake Superior, there were gathered eight hundred warriors of different nations; a chapel was built; among them were several tribes who understood the Algonquin language. So fine an occasion for exercising his zeal could not be overlooked. "I spoke in the Algonquin language," says he, " for a long time, on the subject of the Christian religion, in an earnest and powerful manner, but in language suited to the capacity of my audience. I was greatly applauded, but this was the only fruit of my labors." Among the number assembled were three hundred Pottawattamies, two hundred Sauks, eighty Illinoians.

In the year 1668, peace having been established between the French and the Six Nations, many discoveries were made, and many new missions established. In this year Father Dablon and Marquette went to the mission of Sault St. Marie. In the same year, Father Nicholas, who was on the mission with Allonez, conducted a deputation of Nez Percés, an Algonquin tribe, to Quebec; and Father Allonez went to the mission at Green Bay. Sault St. Marie was made the centre of their missionary labors among the Algonquin tribes. In the year 1671, Nicholas Perrot was sent by M. Courcelles, intendant in the province in the absence of M. Talon who had gone to France, on a special mission to the Algonquin tribes, to induce them to send deputies to the Sault St. Marie for the purpose of entering into an alliance with the French visiting the tribes north, with whom the French had commerce; he left the straits and went to visit the Miamis at *Chicago*. Tetenchoua was the head chief of the nation, and could bring into the field four or five thousand combatants. He himself seems to have preserved the dignity and state of royalty, as he never, according to Perrot, moved "without a guard of forty warriors, who kept watch day and night about his cabin."

His reception was in accordance with the dignity of the chief, and the rank of the ambassador. Perrot remained among the Miamis some days. The chief would have accompanied him, but was, owing to his age, dissuaded from doing so by his subjects. He gave full power, however, to the deputation of the Pottawattamies, who accompanied Perrot, to act for him at the conference at the sault. Perrot was unable to visit the Mascoutins or the Kickapoos, but returned to the straits. / The conference took place in the month of May, 1671. Father Allonez made them a speech; deputies were in attendance from all the tribes north as far as Hudson's bay. The deputies acknowledged subjection to the French monarch, and declared they would have no king but the Grand Ononthio of the French. Two cedar posts were placed in the ground, and to these were attached the cross and the arms of France; and the envoy, M. de St. Lusson, declared, through Father Allonez as his interpreter, that he took possession of the whole country in the name of the French monarch, and placed all the inhabitants under his protection. The whole ceremony finished with a Te Deum and a discharge of fire-arms. /

In 1671, Louis de Buade Conte de Frotignac became the successor of M. de Courcelles in the government of New France. In the short space of time that the talented and enterprising M. de Talon was employed as intendant in New France, he established the authority of his master in the extreme north, and far in the west he had already undertaken new discoveries. Not only by the report of the tribes who dwell along the further end of Lake Superior, but of those who occupied the country in the southern bend of Lake Michigan, as well as from the relation of the Jesuit fathers, it was known that to the west of Nouvelle France, there was a great river, supposed to run south, and most probably emptying into the gulf of Mexico, if it ran that course, or that of California if it ran west. This river was called Mechassippi by some, by others Micisippi. The spirited and enterprising Talon was unwilling to leave the province until he had made some arrangement for its exploration. He charged the Father Marquette with the expedition, and gave him for his companion the Sieur Joliet, a citizen of Quebec, a man active and enterprising, and fully capable of sustaining the fatigues of such an enterprise. No individual could have been better fitted for such an undertaking than the Father Marquette. In 1663 he was established at the mission of St. Joseph, on the river which bears that name, in the northern part of the present state of Indiana, and labored among the Pottawattamies located there. In 1668, we have seen he was engaged with Father Dablon, at Sault St. Marie, to which place he accompanied Father Dablon, with the Ottawas. He had traversed the great lakes, had intercourse with the various tribes who inhabited there, spoke several of the Algonquin languages, and no doubt had heard not only from the Pottawattamies, but from the Sacs, the Sioux, and more particularly from the Illinois, who attended the conference at Chagouamigon, of the existence of the river, and its general course, of the tribes who dwelt on its borders, and all the particulars necessary to be known to one who contemplated, as he says he did, its discovery. The difficulties of communication between these remote points — Quebec and the banks of the Mississippi — had probably prevented any communication between the missionaries who had preceded him and their superior, at the time Marquette embarked on his voyage; though it is to be presumed, that Marquette was not ignorant as late as 1673, when he left Green Bay, that missions had been already established in the Illinois, some years before; and the éclat attending the discovery might have induced him to withhold all the sources of information, which as a *discoverer* alone, and not as a *missionary*, might have been in his possession.

I feel no disposition to detract at all from the Father Marquette any portion of the merit which properly belongs to him. It is certain, that to his journal we owe our first knowledge of the Father of Waters. With Joliet as his companion, he entered the Mechasippi, in his bark canoe, on the 17th of June, 1673; having ascended the Fox from Green Bay, and crossing the portage, descended the Ouisconsin until its confluence with the Mississippi. Leaving their frail bark to the guidance of the swift current of the river, they descended to the mouth of the Illinois. Three leagues below the junction of the Missouri (called by

Marquette, Pekitanoni) with the Mississippi, they found three villages of the Illinois. They remained here some days, and again embarking, descended the Mississippi as far as the Arkansas. Their provisions and munitions beginning to fail them, and believing it imprudent to advance further into a country whose inhabitants were unknown, and feeling perfectly satisfied from the course of the river that it discharged itself into the Gulf of Mexico and not into the Gulf of California, they retraced their steps to the mouth of the Illinois, ascended that river to the portage, and thence into Lake Michigan. Marquette remained at the mission of the Miamis, at Chicago, and alternately attended this and the mission of the Pottawattamies, on the St. Joseph. Joliet returned to Quebec, to render an account of their voyage to Talon, but found he had returned to France. Father Marquette remained at the mission for two years after his voyage, of which he gave a relation, published in 1687, under the modest title of *Découverte de quelques Pays et Nations de l' Amerique Septentrionale."*

When on his voyage from Chicago to the Isle of Mackinaw, he entered, the 18th day of May, 1675, the mouth of a small river on the western shore of Lake Michigan, known on the old maps as Rivière du P. Marquette,[1] erected his altar, for the purpose of saying mass at some little distance from the companions of his voyage, having first requested the two men who were his *voyageurs* to leave him alone for the space of half an hour. This time having expired, his companions went in search of him, and were astonished to find him dead. The soul of this good and great man had taken its flight to another and better world; and in accordance with a presentiment, no doubt entertained by him as he remarked to his companions when landing: "Here will be the end of my voyage." As it was too far from Mackinaw to remove his body there, it was buried on the bank of the river, which, according to Charlevoix, who visited it in 1721, had, since the burial of Marquette, "receded little by little from the grave, as if respecting the burial place." The following year, one of

[1] According to the map of Charlevoix, accompanying his *Histoire de la Nouvelle France*, 1734, the location of the Rivière du P. Marquette is placed further north than it is on the recent maps of Michigan; and it is the third river south of Bay du Travers, known on the modern maps as Rivière au Betsies.

the two voyageurs who had accompanied him, and assisted in performing the last duties to this enterprising and devoted son of the church, returned to the place where he had been interred, and carried his remains to Mackinaw. The Indians, after his death, gave to the stream on which he was buried the name of Rivière de la Robe Noire; the French, that of P. Marquette; and these voyageurs of the inland sea of Michigan, for years, did not fail to invoke the spirit of the sainted man, as their frail barks braved the tempest of the lake, on their annual voyages to Mackinaw; and the Algonquin, as he coasted its borders, or hunted along its banks, cast his votive offering on the resting place of one, whose amenity of manners, goodness of heart, and kindness of feeling, had endeared him to every tribe from the mouth of the Huron to Sault St. Marie — from Chicago to Michilimackinac. Yet at this time, not a cross marks the place of his death; not a stone shows that of his grave; and the traveler, as he is carried by the genius of Fulton, with all the appliances of comfort and luxury, through the waters of Michigan, may inquire in vain, where he died, or where he was buried.

In the prairies to the west of the southern part of Lake Michigan, between the country occupied by the Foxes and the Illinois river, dwelt a tribe in the latter part of the seventeenth century, of whom, so far as we know, not a vestige now remains. They were known on the old maps as the Mascontins, or *Nation de Feu*. Charlevoix states, that the true name was Mascontenec, signifying an open country. The Pottawattamies pronouncing it Masconten, from them the French had taken the name; and as the word in the Pottawattamie language, or a word similar to it, was translated fire, the name of Nation de Feu was given to them. The Kickapoos were their neighbors, and in interest were united with the Mascontens. Whether this last tribe were amalgamated with the first, and lost their original name, it is impossible to say. They were visited by the Jesuit missionaries; and Fathers Allonez and Dablon, in 1674, met the chief of the Miamis, Tetenchoua, with three thousand braves, at their village. The fear of the Sioux and the Iroquois had united those two tribes against their common enemy. The relation attributed to Tonti, however, mentions Mansolia, a secret emissary of the Iroquois of the neighboring nation of Mascontens, as having made his appearance in 1678 in the Illinois; but we conceive very little credit is to be attached to the work itself, as Tonti, who was lieutenant of La Salle, and accompanied him to Illinois, where he was left in charge in the absence of La Salle, denies the authorship. Be this as it may, we have no knowledge of the existence of such a nation, except the relations of the Jesuit fathers, and the name given to them on the early maps; though they appear to have been a very numerous tribe. It is possible they may have been entirely destroyed, like the Ileries by the Iroquois, who waged a war of extermination against them, as well as their neighbors the Miamis, the Kickapoos, the Sioux and the Illinois. We shall not follow La Salle in his discoveries, nor Hennepin, nor Tonti's account of them. The last is now known to be fabulous; and the first was writen by the author, with great prejudice existing towards La Salle. Hennepin was the subject of the king of Spain; and his *amor patriæ* was by no means agreeable to the courtly, polished, and French La Salle. The French were at war with the Spaniards; and one of the vessels of his squadron had been captured at St. Domingo by two Spanish pirogues. This circumstance by no means helped to conciliate these subjects of two rival nations; and it is evident from reading "Le voyage on un pays, plus grand que l'Europe, entre la mer glaciale et le Nouveau Mexique," that the prejudices of Father Hennepin, even the unfortunate and untimely death of the Sieur La Salle had not mitigated. His works, therefore, must be taken with some grains of allowance; though in the main, furnishing some important particulars in reference to the early discoveries in the northwest. He accompanied La Salle on his expedition to the Illinois, and gives a very lively, but very romantic picture of this *nouvel pays*. In the midst of much chaff, there are some grains of wheat to be gathered in the works of the reverend father; and after nearly two centuries, we must be thankful even for the few details which, in the *relations*, the works of Marquette, Allonez, Hennepin, Tonti, Hontan and Charlevoix, have come down to us. That, in the archives of the French government, in those of the superior of the Jesuits, in the records in Quebec, much interesting matter might be found connected with this subject, is beyond a doubt. The historian of the northwest will have a task in collecting the materials; the collating of them when gathered would be a work of but little labor. Two centuries have elapsed since the Jesuit fathers launched their bark canoes on the waters of the Illinois. Where now are the rude temples which these pious men dedicated in the wilderness to the service of the ever living God? Where the fathers themselves? Where the memorials of their worship?[1] Where their neophytes? Where the red men of the forest who lingered around the symbols of the Christian's faith, and bending before the sign by which they were spiritually conquered, worshiped the Manitou of the stranger, and yielded obedience to the heralds of the cross? Echo answers — Where? The monuments of their piety are broken down. Each succeeding winter's gale, each summer's sun, for a century and a half, has but made their destruction more certain. So that now, " even the places which once knew them, know them no more for ever." The hiss of the snake may now be heard, where once ascended the *Te Deum Laudamus.* The harsh cry of the raven and the melancholy whoop of the owl answer now, where once responded the aborigines of the forest to the morning matin and evening vesper. But the untutored yet faithful worshiper is gone. The grass of the prairie, long and coarse, waves over the graves of the curate and his flock. And where once ascended the notes of praise and thanksgiving, the thistle rears its tall head in triumph; the nettle and the foxglove, and the deadly night-shade thrive undisturbed; or perhaps the sturdy settler, as " he drives his team a-field," runs his furrows over the bones of the accomplished, learned, enterprising and zealous Jesuit fathers, who, nearly two centuries since, left the cloisters of Paris, or the Seminary of Quebec, to carry the banner of the cross to the tribes who dwelt on the Father of Waters.

Fallen obelisks, broken head-stones, and mossy tombs, nowhere

---

[1] The newspapers state, that in digging a cellar for a house lately at Green Bay, where the first Catholic church was erected by the Jesuits, a silver plate — evidently a part of the communion service — was found, with an inscription in French, dated 1681.

mark the resting places of these great and good men — the pioneers of civilization and Christianity in the western wilds; and as the antiquarian searches for some slight memorial of these holy men — of the places which they once inhabited on the borders of the lake, the shores of the Illinois or the Mississippi — the modern preëmptioner looks with jealousy at the stranger, and imagines that the corners of sections, quarter sections, and forty acre tracts, excite his curiosity, or awaken the avarice of the speculating land hunter — a melancholy but certain lesson relative to those changes which are constantly going on with empires as with men. Time, in its resistless course, as it sweeps on to eternity, whispers of the one, as well as the other, " THEY WHO SLEEP HERE, ARE SOON FORGOTTEN ! "

Note.— It may not be uninteresting to know the successors of Father Marquette in the Illinois mission, down to the commencement of the 18th century, and their fate. It is a melancholy tale of suffering and death ; and an evidence of the warmth, zeal, and piety of these faithful followers of the cross — a zeal and piety, which might put to shame many of their Protestant successors.

Father Gabriel Lambronde, Jesuit, went missionary to the Illinois in 1678; was slain at his mission in 1680.

Father Maxime Le Clerc went to the Illinois in 1678; was killed by the Indians in 1687.

Father Zenobe Mambré, Recollet, went to the Illinois in 1678; and returned in 1680, employed in visiting the tribes on the Mississippi.

Father Louis Hennepin went to the Illinois in 1678 with La Salle; occupied in making discoveries on the Mississippi; returned in 1680.

M. Jean Bergier, mentioned as the successor of Father Pinet, priest of the Seminary of Quebec, went to the Illinois in 1686; was at the Tamarois or Cahokia mission, died there in 1699; was buried by Father Marest, who was in the mission to the Kaskaskias.

M. Philip Beucher, priest of the Seminary of Quebec, was sent to the Tamarois or Cahokia mission, to assist M. Bergier; remained with him until 1696, when he went to visit the Arkansas and other Indian tribes on the lower Mississippi; returned and died at Peoria in 1719.

In 1692, Father Louis Hyacinth Simon, went as missionary to St. Louis, Peoria; went from there in 1694 to visit the different establishments and posts on the Mississippi; returned to Quebec in 1699.

Father Florentin Flavré, Jesuit priest, went to the Illinois in 1694; established a mission on the Mississippi; descended that stream in 1708 to Natchez; returned to Illinois in 1709; remained there until his death in 1713.

Father Julien Benettau, Jesuit priest, went to the Illinois in 1696; labored at the mission of St. Louis with great success; died there in 1709.

M. François Joliet de Montigney, priest, in 1696 was sent to Louisiana in the character of vicar-general, by the bishop of Quebec. He visited the missions in Illinois, St. Louis, the Tamarois or Tahokias, while M. Bergier was there, traversed the whole country, and returned to Quebec in 1718.

M. Michael Antoine Gamelin, priest of the Seminary of Quebec, accompanied him. They descended the Mississippi, and went as far as Mobile.

Father Gabriel Marest, Jesuit, went to the Illinois in 1699; fixed his residence at Kaskaskia; died there in 1727.

Father Antoine Darion, priest, went in 1700 on a mission to the Tunicas, a tribe living on the Mississippi; and adjoining the Natchez. He went from Quebec.

COMPARATIVE VOCABULARIES OF THE SEMINOLE AND MIKASUKE TONGUES.[1]

By BUCKINGHAM SMITH.

These words were recently taken down in Washington from the mouth of a Seminole delegation from Arkansas — Foos-harjo, an educated Indian, and Johnson, a black, speaking the Mvskoke, and Chocot-harjo, the Mikasuke, the last communicating through the Mvskoke, and sometimes himself writing out the words in his own tongue. The Indians were born in Florida, the negro in Alabama.

Major Caleb Swan, U. S. A., in a report to the department of war respecting the Seminoles in the year 1790-1, states that they were inhabiting country in Alabama, Florida and the state of Georgia; and, according to tradition, that they came originally in roving bands from the northwest with the name Seminole; that subsequently they conquered the Alabamas, and, according to their policy, united that people to their own nation, called Mvskoke; that later, the Apalaches were added, and, at the time of writing, he speaks of their having *Mikasuka* and some other permanent villages on the Apalachicola river. The language had then undergone so great change among the wandering hordes, still called Seminoles, that it was hardly understood by the Creeks (Mvskokes inhabiting fixed settlements), or, in general, even by themselves. It must be remembered, that, at the time he writes the nation had already added to their number the remnants of the Alabamas or Coosadas, Uchees, Natches, Hitchitis and Shauanos, with their several languages, six constituting the number spoken by the members of the confederacy.

The Hitchitis resided on the Flint and Chatahooche rivers. They are near of kin to the Mikasukes, to judge from the words of a small vocabulary taken by Mr. Gallatin from a Chelaqui, reprinted here with numerals taken at Tampa by Capt. Casey,

---

[1] Reprinted from *The Historical Magazine* (Morrisania, N. Y.), for August, 1866.

and entitled: "Hitchittee or Chel-o-kee Dialect, spoken by several tribes of the great Muskokee Race." Those speaking the Mikasuke in Florida probably went from Georgia with the Mvskoke family, and some of them, at the time of the cession of the province to the United States by Spain, were living at a well-known lake bearing their name. From names borne by geographical objects, they appear to have widely extended their wanderings over the peninsula.

Whatever may be the theoretic history of the early migration of the Seminoles or Mvskokes, this much seems certain: the meaning of the word. *seminole* is *wanderer, strayed off*, and is applied to the nomadic Mvskoke; that, while traditions among an unlettered people become vague and uncertain in less than three generations from the time of the event they would commemorate, names preserved in the narratives of the march of Hernando de Soto, attest that the Mvskoke language was in use among the Indians of Georgia, over three centuries since.

ENGLISH.	SEMINOLE.	MIKASUKE.	HITCHITEE.
Sound of the vowels: *a* as in far, *e* as in they, *i* as in marine, *o* as in go, *v* as in gun.			
man	hvnvnwa	nakvni	nuckenih
woman	hokte	taikee	hohlagih
old woman		konchaka	
boy	chipane	ahlehloee	auchebanotche
girl	choktoche	taikoche	autech auchee
infant	istoche, hipoachee	iatoche	
my father (said by son)	chalskee	tate	ilgih
my father (said by daughter)	"	chalhke	
my mother (said by son)	chvtskee	hoache	ahgih
my mother (said by daughter)	"	"	
my husband	chahee	vnnvk'ne	enukenih
my wife	chahaiua	chahvlke	chahulgih
my son (said by father)	chvpuchee	achóche	auchee
my son (said by mother)	chvtshusua	"	
my daughter (said by father)	chvtshuste	achostaike	auchooouhgtda
my daughter (said by mother)	chvtshusua	"	
my elder brother	chvtslaha	chachaie	
my younger brother	chachose	chaiapose	
sister	chauanua	hamóchaca	
my elder sister	hoktala	chafvnke	
my younger sister	chauunua manitka	chafvn ochapaca	
an Indian	iste chate	iatketesché	

ENGLISH.	SEMINOLE.	MIKASUKE.	HITCHITEE.
people	iste	iaton	
head	icá	iose	
hair	ica isé	ios hiske	
face	itothlofá	tafokee	
forehead	icahoma iuinha	thlafeele	
ear (his)	ihustsko	hakehobe	
eye (his)	itolhuá	eté	
nose	iupo	ebé	
mouth	ichukua	eichi	
tongue	tolasua	cholase	
teeth	inútee	enote	
beard	chukhisse	choske	
neck	nvkua	nokbe	
arm	sakpa	thlokfe	
hand	inke	elbe	
fingers	uisaka	ilbe uisake	
thumb	inkitski	ilbeke	
nails	inkikosusua	ilbakose	
body	ina	achakná	
chest	ohokpe	chonoke	
belly	nulhke	lvmpé	
female breasts	ipisi	monche	
leg	ele	ecie	
foot	ile	elepalase	
toes	ileuasaka	cuesake	
bone	fane	cfone	
heart	chafike	chonosbé	chifegaut
blood	chata	pechekche	bitchikchee
town, village	talofa	oelé	ochgiliohgih
chief	micko	mikei	mickee
warrior	tusikya*vlge* (*all*)	tusikiahlhe	tustenuggee
friend	anhise	achame	ahchormih
house	choko	chiki	chickee
bread	tvklaike	pvlvste	
kettle	chalkvs hvtke	leckhahatkee	
bow	ichokotakse	iftchekotokbi	
arrow	thí	slakee	
axe, hatchet	pochusun	chiafe	
knife	islafka	eskvlvfkee	
canoe	pithlochee	pithlochee	
moccasins	*chuse* iste libika	*chuse* neléé (*buckskin*)	
pipe	iche pakua	taloobe	
tobacco	ichí	akchvmó	
sky	aholoche	hossóte	
sun	hasse	haase	hahsohdih
moon	hoslibu	haso tale	hahsodalih
star	cochochompa	oache ke	ohwohchikee
day	nitta	nihtaki	uhbuksee
night	nihli	nihthlaki	mohsoostee
morning	huthijutki	hampole	
evening	iatké	opivs	
spring	tasahchi	lvkhachoslas	
summer	miske	lvkhache	
autumn			
winter	slafo	sláfi	
wind	hotali	fapliche	
thunder	tinitkí	tonohkahche	toknoukkee
lightning	atoiohattí	lamalecheeche	
rain	oské	okóbache	

COMPARATIVE VOCABULARIES.

ENGLISH.	SEMINOLE.	MIKASUKE.	HITCHITEE.
snow	etotc	eptivelc	
fire	tootka	été	edih
water	oiva	ohkc	okkee
ice	etotc	epte	
earth, land	icána	iaknc	
sea	oihatka	okatkc	
river	oislako	okichobc	
lake	okhasse	aiopc, okelose	
valley	oihossi, panofa	ponatké	
prairie	hiakpo	hiatlé	
hill, mountain	ican haluc	iacncbeké	
island	otí, houitska	okantaklc	
stone, rock	cható	talé	
salt	okchanva	okchahni	ochchahnih
iron		kochone	
forest	ituvlkatc	pahayókc	
tree, wood	itú	ahí	ahlce
leaf	tuisí	ahihískc	
bark	itohulhpc	ahehnlbc	
grass	pahe	pahe	
pine	chole	choie	
maize	ache	aspe	usppc
squash	tahaia	chicoie	
flesh, meat	apesua	akné	
dog	ita	efé	
buffalo	ianasa	ianasé	
bear	noposé	iansé	nognsaut
wolf	iahá	oba hosé	ohboorhoosc
fox	cholá	cholé	
deer	echo	eché	cchee
elk	chopieká	cichhokc	
beaver	eichhasua	posafc	
rabbit, hare	chofc	chokfé	
tortoise	locña	iokchc	
horse	cholako	cauaie	
fly	chana	choane	
mosquito	okieha	hoskotonc	
snake	chittoo	chinté	
rattlesnake	chittoo miko	chintmikc	
bird	fosua	foosé	
egg	itshostake	onase	
feathers	tafa	hiské	
wings	italhpa	tolokbé	
goose	sasakua	hoshalé	
duck (mallard)	fochó	fooché	
turkey	pínuá	faiti	
pigeon	pachí	pachi	
fish	thathlo	thlathle	
name	ochifka	ochilké	
white	hvtké	hvtké	
black	lvstc	loóchc	
red	chatc	ketesché	
light blue	holatte	onotbé	
yellow	lané	[*like*] lakvnc	
light green	pahi *lanomt* (*looks*	pahetalukchome	
great, large	slakkc	choobe	
small, little	chukki	uikchosis	
strong	yikchi	uante	
old	achuli	naknosi	
young	mvniti	ojahbí	
good	héintle	heintlos	

ENGLISH.	SEMINOLE.	MIKASUKE.	HITCHITEE.
bad	holouak	humpíkos	
dead	ilí	eie	
alive	uinaki	fisahke	
cold	kasuppi	kabalekosche	
warm, hot	haye	haieche	
I	aní	aní	
thou	chiimi	chihni	
he	imi	inihni	
we	pomi	pohni	
ye	chintaki	chénoche	
they	imetahke	inenohche	
this	hiamá	iyale	
that	ma	mamé	
all	omulka	laapké	
many, much	anachome	anakapen	
who	istahnut	nohlotó	
far	opaie	opvnke	
near	ahole	auelosis	
here	yama	yalé	
there	ma	mamí	
to-day	mochanetta	emanetaki	
yesterday	paksangke	opiahchama	
to-morrow	pakse	paksaka	
yes	encá	hó	
no	ecosche	mates	
one	hvmkin	thlamen	thlah' hai
two	hokolen	toklan	to kai
three	totchínen	tochínan	to chay
four	oosten	citaken	see tah
five	chaskepen	cháskepvn	chah kee
six	ipaken	ípaken	ee pak
seven	colapaken	colapaken	ko lapah
eight	chinapaken	tosnapaken	tos nap pah
nine	ostapaken	ostapaken	os ta pah
ten	palen	pokolen	po kolin
eleven	hvmkon talaken	tklaunikvn	po thlah' wai kan
twelve	hokolokaken	toklauaican	
twenty	pale hokolen	poco toklan	po ko to ko lin
thirty	" totchinen	" totchinan	
forty	" osten	" sitaken	
fifty	" chaskepen	" cháskepen	
sixty	" ipaken	" lepaken	
seventy	" kola paquen	" kolapaken	
eighty	" chinapaken	" tosnapaken	
ninety	" ostapaken	" lostapaken	
one hundred	chokpi hvmkin [kin	chokpi thlamen	chok pee thlah' min
one thousand	chokpi thloko hvm-	" chobí thlamen	
to eat	hvmpita	empike	
to drink	iskita	iskeke	
to run	litkita	isthnitkikí	
to dan	litkita	isthnitkikí	
to sing	iahaikita	hopvnke	
to sleep	nochita	nocheke	
to speak	opoonaita	apvnke	
to see	hechita	hechéke	
to love	anokichita	anokachike	
to kill	ille ichita	illi chike	
to sit	laikita	chokoliki	
to stand	hoythlita	hachaleke	

COMPARATIVE VOCABULARIES.

ENGLISH.	SEMINOLE.	MIKASUKE.	HITCHITEE.
to go	ayeta	athicki	
to come	atita	onteke	
to walk	yakapita	chaiake	
to work	atotketá	tukalskake	
to steal	holskopita	okepeke	
to lie	laksitá	olaske	
to give	emeta	emekeke	
to laugh	apilita	haiakeki	
to cry	hacaihkita	hilaihkiki	
alligator	hvlpata	hvlpati	
slave	salvfki	anope	
cane	coha	othlane	
pumpkin	chase	chokse	
turtle	olakaa	ilakue	
wildcat	coaki	koosi	
ravine	panasofki		
brier-root flour	kuntí	kantiki	
high	hvlui	abvntí	
low	kunchapí	iakne	
flute	fíhpa	conbokachichiki	
gourd	iphipi	iphipi	
ghost		solope	
opossum	sokha hatka	sokeasikeni	
raccoon	uulko	shaue	
persimmon	sata	othkofé	
hawk	aiú	akale	
owl	opá	opaké	
tiger	kacha	koachobe	
bean	taláko	shalale	

PROPER NAMES, WITH THEIR SIGNIFICATIONS.

Istopoga, *iste atepogo*, person drowned. Sem.
Okichobe, *oki chobe*, water big. Mik.
Halpatioka, *hvlpati oka*, alligator many. Mik.
Wekiwa, water spring. Sem.
Pilatka, *waca ak pilatka*, driving many cows across. Sem.
Pithlo-chokco, boat house (ship). Sem.
Oclawaha, water muddy in there. Mik.
Tohopkilige, *tohopki laiki*, fort site. Sem.
Locktshapopka, *locktsha popka*, acorn to eat. Sem.
Hichepoksasa, *hihepok sassa*, pipe many. Sem.
Wekiwache, *oiva vche*, water. Sem.
Homosasa, *homo sassa*, pepper many. Sem.

Echashotee, *echas hotee*, beaver his house. Sem.
Choko-chate, house red. Sem.
Choko-liska, house old. Sem.
Panasoffke, *pane sofke*, valley deep. Sem.
Withlacooche, *oiva slakke uche*, water long, narrow. Sem.
Chase-howi ska, pumpkin kay. Sem.
Alaqua (hiliqua ?) sweet gum. Sem.
Fenholloway, *fenholoue*, young turkey. Sem.
Oklokne, *okeloknee*, much bent. Sem.
Etawa, one polling (a boat). Sem.
Etenaiuh, scrub. Sem.
Econholloway, *icana halue*, earth high. Sem.

THE LORD'S PRAYER IN MIKASUKE.[1]

In the last number of *The Historical Magazine* was published some vocabularies of the Indian languages, to which is now added the Lord's Prayer, given by one of the chiefs. As he did not speak English, and as the letters did not appear to be the same

[1] From *The Historical Magazine* for September, 1866.

as ours, and perhaps, if identical, not sounded the same, it was sent to Washington to be verified, and is now printed as it comes, rewritten by the competent ability of George Gibbs, Esq., who says, beyond this : " I tried to get something approaching a literal " translation, but it was beyond either the comprehension of Indian, negro, or white man." B.S.

Má-minn   a-ká-minn   mi-ko-sá-pits   pokhlki   a-bun-ti
And   now   pray   our father high
tcho-kó-lits   ka-kat   tché-ho-tchif-kôt   hol-lat-tish.
sits   there   thy name [be praised]   great
Má-minn tche-hai-at-lektchót   e lá-tish mónti   a-búnti
And   thy glory   be it   heaven
na-ki   á-ke-lets-ka-ká   ó-me-kat   má-mi-tchá-lot yá-léh
         as thou wishest   like
yak-a-nún'   o-makh-me-tish.

Nikh'-tak-a-lamp'-un pa-las'h-té et-lé-ché-ka-ka ó-men hé-mané-tak'-e po-me gis.

Ma-mik'h ná-ki po-má-ta-kun pun'-ka-pa-ye-cha-chish na-ki pó-má-tukh e-lengh-káp pa-yé-chan-chi'-ka-ka o-me-cha lún.

Shát-o-pakh-ki'-kun pó-ba nah sho-ná-ba-kun shi-po ná-litsh kish ma-mish-ka hám-pa-kun po-tla-nas-chish me-kí-kót tche-nákósh wan'-té-e-kot tche-ná-kósh má-minn tchobe-é kót tche-náke e-mong kot óm-mish.

A SIOUX VISION— THICK-HEADED-HORSE'S DREAM.[1]

By John Hallam.

In May, 1845, Calvin Jones, one of the most remarkable hunters and trappers our frontier has produced, went on a trading expedition to Whirlwind's village,[2] in the southeastern part of what is now known as Dakota territory. Whilst there, he met Thick-Headed-Horse, a Sioux Indian, whom he describes as one of the most intelligent of his race, possessed of poetic fancy, a remarkable command of language and withal the best orator he ever heard amongst the aboriginal tribes. He delighted to be in the society of intelligent white men, and never tired in relating to them his experience and observations. During this visit, he related the following strange dream to Mr. Jones, to whom the writer is indebted for it.

I went out alone with my gun, bow and knife, to hunt buffaloes in the rich meadows and valleys, towards the land of the Dakotas. I stood in the midst of a vast plain, covered with waving grasses and smiling flowers. The air was freighted with sweet incense, and laughing waters sung to the flowers as they rushed on through the wild meadows. My heart was filled with sunshine, and I loved the God who created and gave this land to the Sioux.

Whilst I stood wrapped in meditation, in the midst of this enchanted scene, I looked across the plain and discovered what I conceived to be a buffalo approaching me, and secreted myself to await its approach. Presently it drew near, but I could see nothing but its head and part of its forelegs which supported it. The tall grass concealed the body from view. In my effort to discover the body, I could see nothing but the grass waving, for

---

[1] Reprinted from *The Inland Magazine* (St. Louis), for June, 1870. Revised by the author for *The Indian Miscellany*.

[2] Whirlwind was a noted Sioux chief.

four hundred yards to the rear. This surprised and aroused my Indian suspicion and curiosity to their utmost capacity, and I was tempted to run, but my curiosity proved stronger than my fear, and I stood still.

The animal continued to advance, and I soon discovered that it was a monster snake, with the head and forelegs of a buffalo. I was now greatly alarmed, and my gun and bow fell to the ground, whilst I stood paralyzed, and involuntarily suffered the monster to enclose me within its coil. In this condition, for a few moments, I stood speechless and motionless, whilst the monster darted its tongue out thirty feet. I gazed into its brilliant eyes, that glistened like a mirror in the sun, until I was seized with a potent charm, which dispelled all fear, supplanted the normal state of my nature and transfused a new existence into my body. An irresistible inclination then seized me to mount and ride the animal, and I threw myself astride its neck and seized its horns for support.

The animal then lengthened itself out and started at the velocity of one hundred miles an hour, towards the rising sun, and carried me at this high rate of speed near two thousand miles without halting. Rivers, mountains, plains and forests whirled around in a ceaseless circuit, and I was filled with delight, infused with undefined fear. The excitement supported my strength for a much greater period than the normal state of the body could sustain, but this acquired strength began gradually to wane, with the curiosity which imparted it, and the physical powers began to assert their claims to repose.

At this crisis, the neck of the animal distended and assumed the shape of a beautiful carriage, and the scales widened into oval-shaped windows, as transparent as the clearest crystal. In the left hand corner of the apartment thus created, hung a snow-white curtain, made of the downy skin of a swan, which concealed a small apartment.

Curiosity impelled me to draw this curtain aside, and I beheld the uncooked saddle of an antelope lying on a wickerwork of willow twigs and beside it the white skull of Wanawanda (a great Sioux war-chief, who had died a thousand years before), filled with a crystal liquid. Hunger and thirst, which I had not felt until now, attacked and impelled me to partake of the enchanted feast before me. I seized the meat and drew it forth, but it fell from my grasp, on the cushion before me, and a fire, covered with strange wickerwork, instantly appeared under it and commenced roasting the meat. Above the fire a square chimney, beautifully checkered with figures of red, yellow, purple and white diamonds, pierced the roof, and conducted the smoke away. When the meat was roasted, I took it off the fire, and the spit dissolved and disappeared in a white mist. The meat surpassed in flavor and excellence anything the imagination can picture to mortals. I then picked up the skull of Wanawanda and drank from it a nectar sweeter and more delicious than fiction ever pictured for an Indian god. When I set the skull down, it dissolved and was transformed into a fairy picture representing a beautiful landscape, covered with many thousand young Sioux warriors arrayed in costumes of great beauty and brilliancy, mounted on horses of surpassing beauty and speed.

My Buffalo-snake-horse was still traveling to the east, with unabated celerity. We were now passing through the cañon of a mighty range of mountains, and I looked out on them for a moment, but when I turned to gaze on the picture again, it had vanished. It was now far into the night; the full moon was marching through a cloudless sky, the stars glittered with renewed beauty, and lent all of their glory to brighten every corner of the heavens. Again I looked out through the crystal windows, and saw that we approached a range of mountains twenty miles high, with almost perpendicular sides and no pass through or over them. Here I thought nature planted a barrier to further progress, and that my destiny would soon be made known, the mysterious unfolding of which I dreaded; the nearer it approached, the further off I wished it to be. I felt a keen desire and curiosity to know it, but was not yet prepared to accept or embrace it. My heart thumped against its walls of flesh, and, much against my Indian training and instincts, told me that I was a coward.

As we neared the mountain, my steed halted for the first time, and stood upon its tail in front of an immense cliff, and mounted to the top. In this way it ascended to the summit and coiled its way down to an immense plain below, and again proceeded towards the rising sun, with unabated vigor. Day was now beginning to break in the east, and I fell asleep from physical exhaustion. This slumber closed the gate against the enchanted scenes around me, and let in another vision more true to nature, to delight and yet disturb my weary brain.

This apparition came in the form of Omarinta (my wife), and three little hungry children, whom I much loved, and had left in our lodge on the banks of the Wapka Schicha, in the land of the Sioux. They implored me to return home and not desert them in their hunger and destitution. I swore by all the gods of the Sioux, to disenthrall myself and break away from the power of the monster. For a moment my courage rose to a height worthy of the greatest warriors of my tribe. I drew my knife, which was yet in my belt, and attempted to cut off the head of the monster, but it fell harmlessly from my hand. The courage inspired by the suffering condition and appeal of Omarinta was but momentary and soon vanished, to give way to the contemplation of my own helplessness and the scenes around me. At this stage of the wonderful journey, I heard a mighty roaring of waters, which woke me. I looked out, and beheld my steed struggling in the roaring waters of a mighty river, the waves of which rose and lashed each other high over its body, but it kept head and neck high above the foaming billows and sped its onward course. In an hour it reached the shore, and gained a woodland country, varying in every respect from all the countries we had passed through. The peoplé, fields, rivers, mountains and animals were much larger, but all animate nature fled at the appearance of the monster, and the high rate of velocity which it continued to maintain prevented closer observation.

The sun was again high in the heavens; the animal kept on, and I wondered when it would stop. The next moment a peal of thunder leaped from its stormy throne in the heavens and rent an immense chasm in the earth, into which the monster entered, and descended into the earth with the same velocity it had maintained in passing over its surface. For awhile all was darkness, and sickening despair overwhelmed me; but after awhile my sense began to return, and with it a dark and shadowy light to quicken my vision. This let in a ray of hope, which is more tenacious than any faculty which animates the soul, and I yet indulged the idea of escape and deliverance, but I had no defined idea of the agency which was to accomplish my desires, and I felt no power within myself to do it. The only rational idea of escape which I could indulge was, that chance had made me the victim of a weird wizard, as strong as the elements and swifter than the wind, and that the same agency could release me. Reason began to assert its sway, as time and contact with the monster lessened my terror and told me that my present destruction was not sought, because that, if desired, was the easiest of all things.

At sunrise the next day, we emerged into a new and beautiful world, with rivers, meadows, flowers, fine horses and an abundance of game. At the tenth hour of the morning, I looked ahead and saw we were approaching an immense black lodge, with a hole in the basement story large enough to admit my steed, into which it went, and dragged me off. At this I felt a sense of great relief, but was far from feeling either happy or secure from danger in this new world, into which I had been so unceremoniously and involuntarily thrust.

I immediately faced the west and started off, but had proceeded but a few paces until I heard a voice cry out, "Stop!" I looked up to the eave of the lodge from whence the voice proceeded, and saw twelve round apartments finely constructed and lined with furs, in each one of which stood a small black man, looking and laughing at me. This omen, or seeming mockery of my misfortune, portended no good, and I started off again, at increased speed.

I proceeded but a few paces, before a large, fine looking man opened a door in the basement of the lodge and told me to come back and get my horse. He spoke good Sioux, and I obeyed him, through fear, but I bitterly denied having any horse, to which the man replied, "You dog, you rode one here and you shall take him away. You can't leave such an animal on my premises."

After collecting my scattered and distorted faculties as well as I could, I told him that I was no designing or voluntary intruder into this world; that I had not come by choice, but by chance, over which I had no control; and that I would make my escape as soon as possible, to which he replied in a modified tone, indicating that his harsh feelings were giving way a little.

"No matter how you came or what agency brought you; if you came by chance, you can employ the same agency to conduct you away." And he continued: "That animal, sir, is the devil, in his own proper person, I have seen him before. The people in this happy hunting ground have no use for him, or any person who is as intimate with him as you appear to be."

At this speech I was overpowered with fear, trembled in every limb and spoke in half intelligible sentences. My worst fears were realized. I was with the devil, who seemed willing for me to escape, but another agency had appeared and commanded me to continue with him. When the good old Sioux discovered this, his heart softened and he took pity on me and said, "Don't be alarmed, my friend, I see you are from the land of the Sioux, in the other world. I am from that tribe myself; come into my lodge, I will give you food." I gladly obeyed him now, and he gave me a fat roast of buffalo, and told me I was in the spirit land and happy hunting ground of the Sioux; that his name was Spotted Wolf, the great medicine man of the Sioux, who was shot on the Missouri river three hundred years ago, by the Rhea Indians, with a round stone cut out of a white buffalo, the only thing against which his life on earth was not charmed.

"You have often heard of Spotted Wolf," he said, and I assented to the supposed knowledge and feigned great delight at meeting him in the happy hunting ground, which pleased him very much. I then asked him who the little black men were in the upper story or apartments of his lodge, and he said, "They are my little medicine men. I have trained them to attend the game here. When game is wanted, I send them after it. They possess a potent charm over all game in the happy hunting ground."

He was very communicative and seemed desirous of imparting

to me his whole stock of information, before questioning me. With other things, he said, "I am a strong man, and can run that devil horse of yours out of the happy hunting ground, and will show you how to do it yourself, when you sit and rest yourself; but you must go with him — we have no use for you here." After I had finished my repast and rested a little, he commanded me to take a large branding iron, heat it to a white heat and apply it to the belly of the beast, and mount him. To this I dissented and told him that if I had to go off with the devil, that I had better keep on good terms with him and not make him mad by applying a hot iron to him. This angered Spotted Wolf; he stamped his foot imperiously on the ground and ordered me to immediately execute his orders. I obeyed him through fear, but determined, in my own mind, not to mount the devil's back after burning him with a hot iron. I much preferred to encounter the displeasure and rage of Spotted Wolf to that of the devil. In the execution of the strategy designed, I was left no alternative but apparently to obey the order; so I opened the door leading to the beast, and applied the hot iron as gently as possible. At the touch of the iron, he darted away as quick as lightning and prevented, by the celerity of his movement, any attempt to mount his back, and this relieved me from any apparent design to disobey my order. Spotted Wolf looked on, and saw that it was almost an impossibility to mount the animal after applying the iron, and though angry, gave me the benefit of the doubt in his mind.

I now thought myself rid of any further trouble with the devil, and only thought of devising means to enable me to return home. Spotted Wolf, after the first pangs of disappointment passed away, invited me to remain all night with him, and suggested that I could take an early start next morning. I gladly accepted the proffered hospitality, and hoped that the interval might profitably be employed in devising means to return to my own world. My host gave me a good and bountiful repast of roast deer, boiled corn and broiled fish. Then he told one of his children to hand the pipes and tobacco; he took one made out of the thigh-bone of a Pawnee warrior and gave me one made out of the arm-bone of a Blackfeet Indian. These, he said, were buried with his body after he was killed by the Rhea Indians, and were brought by him to the happy hunting ground, as reminders of his worth and valor on earth. He talked long and late into the night, and gave me little opportunity to relate my own history and importance. When he perceived that I was weary and sleepy, he gave me a fine robe and told me to go to sleep. The mental and physical exhaustion and torture which I had now undergone, capacitated me to enjoy a profound slumber. I awoke early in the morning, and Spotted Wolf immediately resumed conversation, and gave vent to his curiosity by inquiring into all the details of my journey to the Spirit Land.

I told it to him as it is related to the reader, and he listened with profound attention. But he was master of the emotions which stirred his soul within and suffered no movement of the facial muscles to betray his thoughts. In this, he proved himself master of that Indian philosophy which teaches subjection and control of the passions and emotions in the face of danger, as a means of avoiding it. Whilst relating my wonderful adventures, I eyed him intently, to discover if possible the influence it had upon him and the corresponding influence his action might exert on my destiny, and in this I exerted all my faculties in the full strength of their normal force, but was foiled, and discovered no index.

For some moments after my story was ended, he held me in painful suspense and doubt, and hung his head as if in profound meditation, revolving the ominous meaning of my strange visit.

The first question he asked me after breaking the deep silence was, whether I had died before leaving the world from which I came. On being answered that I had not, he exclaimed, "It is impossible; no Sioux ever came to this hunting ground before dying on earth."

A moment of silence and profound agony to me then ensued. An issue was thus raised which I was wholly incapacitated to meet; my integrity was flatly disputed by one whom I regarded as superior in authority and power over me, by one whose fiat would determine my destiny. Hope died within me, apparently to rise no more, when Spotted Wolf cried out, in a commanding voice, to his attendants, bidding them to seize and bind me. This command was instantly executed and a council was called to dispose of me. As soon as it assembled, an eagle appeared hovering on its wings over the assembly of wise men, and cried out in a loud voice, in the language of the Sioux, "Turn him loose and let him go, turn him loose and let him go." Consternation seized every member of the assembly, and they all dispersed, leaving me free to follow my own volition. I then proceeded on my journey five miles to the west, and met a great war chief from the Sioux country, who halted and spoke to me in an angry tone. He asked me what I was doing in the happy hunting ground, and I told him that I had not come by choice but by chance, and that I was leaving as fast as I could. To which he replied, "You must get out of here quickly, sir. I am the great war chief of the Sioux. I was killed on Medicine Bow river, by the Pawnees, two hundred years ago. Come with me, get your horse and leave at once."

I told him that I had no horse, and he said, "why do you speak falsely, like a cowardly dog; your horse has your brand on him, and is now at my lodge; he came there yesterday."

I was again stricken with fear and amazement, and dared not dispute anything he said, or refuse to obey his orders. I wondered how, or through what agency he knew all this. I obeyed, and followed along after him like a dog. We soon arrived at his lodge, which was the largest I had ever seen. It was made out of lion skins, finely dressed and painted. When we arrived in front of his lodge, he did not ask me in, but said, " Your horse is in that rock lodge, go and mount him, and leave this country at once."

After this speech, his squaw presented herself and said, "Big Lion, don't send the poor man away on that horse; he wants to go back to the world he came from; you know that horse will never take him back there. Have pity on him, for the sake of his wife and children; they are hungry and in distress on the banks of the Wapka Schicha, in the land of the Sioux, and have no one to provide for them."

At this speech, hope revived in my bosom, and I began to feel joy in my heart. I had found one who espoused my cause, in the land of spirits. But my hopes were again crushed, when Big Lion replied, " I know the horse will never return to the land of the Sioux, and for this reason I make Thick-Headed-Horse mount him; I want him to ride into the land of the Pawnees and slay them; they are the enemies of my people.

Big Lion and his wife had a maiden child born unto them in the happy hunting ground; she was then ten years old, and was dressed in a white swan skin. Her mother, after her father's speech, called her and told her to bridle the poor man's horse. The little maiden came at her mother's bidding, all radiant with smiles and ran into an apartment of the lodge and returned with a bridle, wrought of white buffalo hair, with silver bit and gold rings, and beckoned me to follow her. I obeyed, feeling powerless to resist. She opened the door and walked up to the animal, devoid of fear and unconscious of danger. After bridling the animal, she led it out and held the reins until I mounted. She then waved her hand to the north, and it started at a high rate of speed, spreading its neck and folding the skin so as to seat me comfortably. I was conducted a distance of two thousand miles, through this happy hunting ground. We next entered a burnt forest, where everything was scorched and blackened with fire. This burnt forest was five hundred miles in width. We emerged from it into an open, rolling, prairie country, covered with vast herds of game, fine horses, beautiful rivers and Indian lodges, but our speed was so great that I could not tell what tribe inhabited this beautiful country. On the same evening of this journey, we approached a vast mountain range, covered with snow. As we neared the foot-hills, a peal of thunder rent a great chasm in the earth, into which the monster entered.

I had now settled in the conviction that I was a child of destiny, and was, for some purpose unknown to me, being driven and conducted through a vast network of worlds, by the God who created them all. The fear which every living creature possesses, began to be exhausted in me, and the greatest source of anxiety which I now felt, was at the loss and sorrow of Omarinta and the children. I was now conscious that I was passing through one world into another, where a great battle was to be fought with the Pawnees, the hereditary enemy of the Sioux. This much I divined, when Big Lion rejected the entreaties of his squaw in my behalf.

Nature now asserted her dominion over the physical body, and I was soon wrapped in sound, tranquil slumber, from which I awoke as we were emerging into a world of surpassing beauty. I saw hills, valleys, streams, plains and meadows, and great quantities of game, fine horses, birds of rich plumage, and many beautiful Indian villages.

At the tenth hour in the day, I saw a vast army. My steed drew near, halted, and awaited its approach. The army spread out on the plains and enclosed the monster in a circle, which gradually diminished as they cautiously approached. They were all young Pawnee warriors, dressed in brilliant armor, and mounted on fine horses. When they drew near, the monster sprang forward, threw its tail around, and repeated the movement until the army, amounting to one hundred thousand, was destroyed. After this, the beast moved off a few miles at a slow pace, and halted. Then, to my great amazement, it spoke to me in good Sioux, and said: "The god of the Sioux has chosen you above all others of your tribe to lead them. I am the enchanted war-chief of the Sioux in the happy hunting ground. I was killed eight hundred years ago on Snake river, by the Pawnees and Blackfeet Indians in a great battle. My name is Big Snake. The god of the Sioux commanded me to assume this shape, and conduct you through the worlds as I have done, that you might see all things and become wise and brave and the great chief of a mighty tribe. All the game, horses, birds and people which you have seen, once lived on earth, their spirits have been brought hither to people and populate all the worlds you have seen. The great country we passed through, after crossing the mighty river, is occupied exclusively by Indian gods and their squaws. Each chief, after serving as such in a spirit land for one thousand years, becomes a god, and settles on the margin of the mighty river. You have seen the happy hunting grounds of the Sioux. Arapahoes, Cheyennes, and Pawnees, the Blackfeet and Crows, live in worlds similar to those you have seen. Henceforth you will be invincible in battle, and will raise your tribe to the greatest height of power. You will conquer all the nations who oppose you. From hence you are to return to your tribe in a few hours. Dismount — take your knife, go to the end of my tail and rip open the skin, under the border of hair there, and you will find an enchanted whistle and medicine bow made by the god of the Sioux, for you. With that bow, you will slay thousands of enemies, and will always be victorious. When you blow the whistle, all your desires at that moment will be instantly accomplished. My mission is now performed. I am no longer your guardian; you possess now as much favor and power as I do."

At this marvelous speech, I was amazed and bewildered, and doubted my own senses. I dismounted, obeyed the order, and found the enchanted bow and whistle. This gave me a degree of confidence, but I was still not satisfied that all these marvelous things would prove to be true. The transition from utter dependence and helplessness to power so transcendent was too great, and proved more than my mind could embrace in so short a time. The first thing I did, after possessing myself of the bow and whistle, was to tell the war chief that I wanted a fine spotted war horse, before he left me. I still felt dependent and far from possessing the power his discourse indicated. He rebuked me sharply, for making such a request of him, and said: "Did I not tell you to will and blow your whistle, and your desires would be gratified?"

I am of a sensitive nature, and keenly felt the rebuke. I had suddenly found myself the possessor of vast power without that consummate wisdom which is necessary to direct it in attainment of desirable and worthy ends, and this vision admonishes me that, whenever mortals attempt to assimilate the power and character of the gods, they are to be pitied for their weakness rather than censured for their arrogance.

The rebuke of the great war chief recalled my senses, and I blew my enchanted whistle. Instantly one of the finest spotted war horses I ever beheld appeared before me, caparisoned in all the attractive insignia of war. Up to this period, the enchanted chief had maintained his assumed form. He now said, "My labors with you are finished; I am going to dissolve and return to my own happy hunting ground, in my natural body."

The animal then dropped down instantly and assumed the shape of an old dried snake-skin and skeleton on the plain, and the chief appeared before me clothed in a fine war dress, and mounted on a snow-white horse. He then called out an army of young Sioux warriors to appear and conduct him home, and five thousand made their appearance, clad in bright armor and mounted on white horses. They saluted him with songs and ravishing music, and all started off in one grand cavalcade.

I stood motionless and gazed at them until they disappeared. The reverie which enthralled me at the sight of this grand pageant, caused me to forget my own consequence, and for a few moments I contemplated what to do. The first great pleasure which my new situation imparted was derived from a sense of being freed from danger. That rapturous sensation of delight which is supposed to spring from the possession of power was slow in possessing my soul to the exclusion of more rational ideas. The first sensation of pain which I felt, grew out of a sense of utter loneliness. Man is eminently a social being, and both the rude and refined elements of his nature lie dormant in the presence of solitude. After being alone a short time, the first practical idea which presented itself to my mind was to try the speed of my horse. This I did, and found him as swift as the wind. Next, I tried my enchanted bow in a chase after deer and elk, and found it a weapon which I could use with unerring aim and perfection. Next, I desired to try the merits of my enchanted whistle, and meditated for some time as to the character of the test to be applied.

I remembered two Blackfeet Indians who had chased me on Okoboga creek, near the land of the Dakotas, and came near catching me. They were mortal enemies, and I thirsted for revenge. I wished for them to present themselves before me, blew my enchanted whistle, and they appeared immediately. Their sudden appearance at first startled and alarmed me, as when I first saw them armed and seeking my life, and my first impulse was to run, as I had done before. They stared me fully in the face, and appeared to be wholly unconscious of fear or danger. I gazed at them for a full minute before I again thought of my enchanted bow; then I fired two shots, and each one fell dead. I scalped them. My confidence was now very great in all that Big Snake had told me. The day was now spent, the sun was sinking behind the western plains, the birds in the spirit land were hurrying to their nightly shelter, and I thought of Omarinta and the children. So ecstatic was the thought of seeing them in a few moments that it overpowered me, and nearly took my breath away.

As soon as I collected myself a little, I fathered a convulsive wish to be in their presence, blew my whistle, and found myself standing at the door of my lodge. Omarinta seized me by the neck and wept tears of joy as she hung her confiding head on my bosom, and the children seized me by the hands and legs and pulled me down to their level and share of domestic joy. After the first spasm of domestic greeting, Omarinta looked embarrassed, as she began to excuse herself for not being able to set a repast before me. For four days she and the children had had nothing to eat but bark and twigs. This imparted a strange confusion of sorrow and joy, and I cried out:

"Oh, Omarinta, I am now the strongest medicine man the Sioux ever saw. I will call a buffalo to the door in a moment, and we will have a great feast. I am possessed of a potent charm, which gives me control of the world." She involuntarily drew back and looked at me with amazement, evidently thinking me delirious or insane.

This conviction of my wife for a moment forestalled the pleasure I had anticipated, and gave me pain when it was least expected. In the pride and intoxication of supernatural power, I had forgotten the strongest instincts and prejudices of my race. After a little reflection, I recognized the folly of trying to convince her by mere oral declaration of the wonderful powers of which I was master. All the powers of speech of which I was possessed would have been thrown away in an effort to convince her, without occular demonstration, of the powers asserted. I seized my bow and whistle and stepped out on the banks of the Wapka Schicha, and told her to follow me in the light of the moon. She obeyed, but gave me a look of incredulity, which told more forcibly than words could express of the subdued pity which reigned in her bosom. In my eagerness to remove her doubts and vindicate myself, I hurriedly asked her what species of game she preferred, buffalo, deer, elk, antelope or bear. She hesitated for a moment, and seemed unwilling to say, because she dreaded the disappointment which she felt sure would react on me. I urged her to speak, and she said; "There is no game near here, but I prefer elk to any other species." I blew my whistle, and a large elk stood before me. I drew my magical bow and sped an arrow through its chest; it bounded in the air, floundered on the ground, and died in a few moments.

Omarinta screamed with joy, called the half-famished children, cut out the liver, and all of them fell to devouring it. After we had dressed the meat and stowed it away, the children, with their bellies distended, went to sleep, Omarinta picked up the half burned chunks, and we sat down on a robe. I then related my story to her. Tears came to her eyes, alternate joy and amazement asserted their sway; then incredulity would drive each away from her beautiful face and painfully assert its control; then love and confidence would assume the mastery of the contending passions, but beneath it all, doubt lingered and asked for further confirmation.

I had been a man of some parts, and was respected by my tribe, so I had but little trouble in assembling the tribe to hear my wonderful story. I went to the chief and influenced him to assemble the tribe, and a large concourse attended, not knowing the object for which they were called together. All listened with profound attention until the conclusion, an omen which I regarded as highly favorable. But as soon as I concluded, Old Fox, the cunning medicine man of the tribe, rose, and gravely asserted that all I had said was a lie; that it was evidently a cunningly devised scheme to supersede him, and become the medicine man of the tribe. When he took his seat, twenty of his friends rose and all desired to speak at once. After order was restored, each in turn pronounced me a humbug of the first class, and some went so far as to suggest that such a dangerous character ought to be disposed of at once. These were succeeded by others more moderate in their criticism, but all concurred in declaring their disbelief in all of my statements. After all had spoken who desired, the chief rose and stated that he concurred in the general verdict, but that he was opposed to resorting to extreme measures in my case, in consideration of my former good standing in the tribe; that he would consult with Old Fox, and devise a test which would be satisfactory to all.

With this conclusion, I was well satisfied, and resolved not to make a too sudden display of the extraordinary powers with which I was clothed. My experience with Omarinta had set me to reflecting, and had imparted a valuable lesson. Old Fox said that he would take me to Fox mountain, three miles distant, and test my capacity to catch wild foxes; that if I could catch as many foxes[1] as he could, he would agree that I was a very strong man; and that if I could even catch one fox, he would agree that no penalty should be inflicted for the imposition I had attempted on the tribe. This test was to be immediately applied.

When we arrived at the foot of the mountain, Old Fox went to the right and I to the left. We were to meet on the opposite side. After he passed out of sight, I blew my whistle, and one thousand foxes, as large as buffalo bulls, appeared before Old Fox, and gnashed their teeth at him. I stood still to await the result. He came running to me, and fell, terror stricken, at my feet. After he had collected himself a little, he stated that he had been menaced by a thousand foxes, as large as buffalo bulls, and that he could not catch one of them; that, in his opinion, the devil had turned them loose to destroy the Sioux.

Presently the foxes approached us. I lassoed one and tied it to a tree; caught another and mounted its back. Then I struck Old Fox dumb and bade him follow me to the village.

---

[1] The Sioux regard the tongue of a fox as an infallible remedy for any wound inflicted with an arrow, or any puncture of the flesh. They believe that it will draw out a nail, needle, poisonous or virus matter or foreign substance. Old Fox was master of this school, and always kept a cage of foxes in Fox mountain, ready for any emergency. When he wanted a fox, he pretended to go and catch the wild animal, and had thus acquired great reputation with the Sioux.

I then told the chief what had transpired, and that Old Fox had habitually imposed upon the tribe, by keeping a cage of foxes in Fox mountain. This did not convince the tribe that I was the mighty man I claimed to be, but it for the moment diverted inquiry and criticism from myself to Old Fox. He was severely questioned, and condemned by some, but stood mute. One-half of the tribe was for executing him on the spot, but he had many friends, and the other half seized their weapons to defend him. Civil war was thus imminent, and it required judgment to avert its calamities.

To avert this, I ordered the chief and all of his principal men to go to the mountain and bring in the fox I had tied. When we arrived there, I commanded the fox to lie down and the chief to mount it. The order was obeyed with much reluctance and fear. He rode back to the village, and I ordered the foxes re-released.

In this exhibition, I was mistaken as to the effect it would produce on the tribe. My powers were generally conceded, but it greatly embittered both the friends and opponents of Old Fox, who again rushed to arms, and necessitated another diversion to prevent civil war. My experience thus far in the exercise of that unlimited power with which I was so unexpectedly invested, convinced me that unrestrained power ought never to be separated from consummate wisdom and that goodness of heart which is the attribute of the gods.

At this juncture, I blew my whistle, and instantly five hundred Pawnee and Blackfeet warriors appeared and offered battle. They dashed through the village, and captured large booty, embracing the greater portion of the horses belonging to the tribe. This healed all dissension in the tribe. After the enemy had departed with their booty, I commanded them to halt, and summoned an army of Sioux warriors from the spirit land, and put the enemy to death. The tribe did not participate in this slaughter. Many looked on as awe stricken spectators; others fled in dismay, and took shelter in the mountains.

I dismissed my warriors to the spirit land, collected the scattered Sioux, and was hailed as their mighty chief. They made a litter, and carried me in triumphal march through the village.

All the maidens of the tribe assembled, anointed me with sweet incense and sung songs of praise to the mighty warrior of the Sioux. Under my leadership, the Sioux conquered all the surrounding nations, and became the rulers of the earth; but my knowledge was not commensurate with my power, and I often experienced the most perplexing difficulties. I often planned the accomplishment of great ends, which could not be attained without great injustice to my fellow mortals. These difficulties ever attended me in the execution of the minor as well as that of the most important affairs of my government. In my elevation to power, my conscience suffered many rude blasts, and as declining years advanced, it continually admonished me that my glory rested on the broken columns which attested the ruin of multitudes of my fellow mortals. In the evening of a long life, my conscience developed a sound growth and photographed on the walls of my soul all the follies, errors and crimes of my life. Then, could I have done it, I would have gladly exchanged all the pomp and splendor which power had conferred, for the simple, unheralded virtues of my humblest subject.

JOSEPH BRANT, THAYENDANEGEA, AND HIS POSTERITY.[1]

By Wm. C. Bryant.

BRANT HOUSE.

More than a generation has passed away since Col. Stone's elaborate biography of the great Mohawk chieftain was issued from the press. The book, once a thumbed and dog-eared favorite in every district school and circulating library, was eagerly devoured by a class of young readers whose imaginations revelled in its romantic and thrilling pictures of border warfare and forest life, and whose sympathies were irresistibly drawn out toward the central figure in that picturesque group of actors.

That Brant and his Mohawks cast their fortunes with the British in the war for independence, did not materially lessen the admiration of that ardent and generous class of readers. It

---

[1] Reprinted from *The American Historical Record* (Philadelphia), for July, 1873. With a supplementary note written by the author for the *Indian Miscellany*.

was the crowning act of that grand fidelity to the flag of our British ancestors which this loyal race had illustrated in the long and doubtful contest with the French, which they were ready to seal with their blood and which involved the sorrows of expatriation, the sacrifice of home and country.

In Col. Stone's volumes, Brant is depicted as a brave and consummate warrior, a statesman of rare forecast and sagacity, an adroit diplomat and accomplished courtier, a magnanimous foe, a faithful and chivalrous friend. Since then, the iconoclastic tendencies of the age have conspired to cast down Col. Stone's hero from the high pedestal on which that enthusiastic writer had placed him. His success and consequence are held by some writers to have been purely adventitious and largely overestimated. In fact, Brant, divested of the glamour which Col. Stone had thrown around him, has been described as a prosaic and altogether commonplace personage, not superior to, if indeed he were not surpassed in native scope and vigor of intellect, and all heroic qualities, by many less prominent cotemporaries of his race.

Allowing all reasonable deductions for Col. Stone's enthusiasm and partiality, there is abundant evidence in his pages to show that Brant was a great man — in many respects the most extraordinary his race has produced, since the advent of the white man on this continent. There is no contesting the facts that his influence over his own people was controlling; that he was no mean strategist and won the praise of trained tacticians for the manner in which some of his military enterprises were conducted; and that he was the pet of the British government which spared no pains to conciliate and retain him in its interests. His humanity toward a captive or fallen foe is too well established to admit of controversy.

Brant was never, in any sense, the willing tool of the British government. He possessed the barbarian jealousy without its capriciousness. His letters reveal a proud and sensitive spirit, jealous of its dignity and which could not brook the slightest imputation of dishonor; an irritable though generous temper that involved his correspondents in endless explanations, and which it was their constant effort to soothe and allay. The extent and amplitude of his mental vision were as remarkable as were his courage, energy of character and resolute will. Nothing eluded his observation, whether it transpired in the cabinets of ministers or in the forest-senates of the far south and west. He would not yield to the persuasions of Lord Dorchester, and other agents of the British crown in 1787, and precipitate a general Indian war against the infant republic because he clearly saw what escaped their sagacity, that such a war would sweep away in a torrent of patriotic fervor the murmurs of popular discontent which so elated the British, and would end in irretrievable disaster to the red man and further humiliation to the British arms. Captain Brant was born to no titles or dignities. He was created a chief by the popular voice, and his influence far outweighed that of the higher class of rulers, the hereditary sachems.[1] This influence was not, as has been suggested by some writers, the result of his English education — his superior fitness for being the organ or medium of communication between a cultivated nation and its barbarous allies. He was an illiterate man. There were other Indians, attached to the British interests, who enjoyed superior opportunities for becoming acquainted with the English language and the learning taught in English schools. The following letter, printed for the first time, reveals his imperfect acquaintance with the idiom and grammar of our language — a few years later, when he had abandoned the war path and devoted himself to promoting the moral and material interests of his people, the work of self-education commenced and in its rapid progress developed an astonishing capacity for mental acquisition and development.

Cataraqui, Jan. 13, 1785.

Sir:

Mindfull my promise to you I now take the opportunity to inquire after your health which I hope this letter will find you in good state of health and hope you will be able to answer me this, without any delay

---

[1] The sachemships of the Iroquois descend through the female line. John Brant inherited the office of *tekarihogea* from his mother. He himself could not have transmitted the title to a son. The family tomb at Brantford publishes the error that John Brant "succeeded his father as tekarihogea." The monument was built and the inscription written by white men not versed in the Indian laws and customs.

and be agreeable your promise to me likewise. I have nothing any particular to inform alone you concerning the public affairs because I live here. I been away from the five nations very near three months. Shortly after I parted with you at F. I was as far as Quebec my way to England but hearing there that Capt. Aaron Hill a Mohoc chief was detained and kept as hostage by the commissioners of Congress which alarmed me made me turn back from there to this place and shall winter myself here.

I have wrote letters to his Excellency governor Clinton & to my friend Major Peter Schuyler the time I left at Niagara, but I had no answer, neither of them since. So in short I am at present in the dark as to many points of business. Even I had no true account the manner Capt Hill is kept & where he is I dont know. The conclusion of that council at Fort Stanwix by the Commissioners I have had no account at all. Therefore I hope you will please explain me some of the heads of that council. I hope those commissioners did not oversett all what you & me have settled there. I intend to be at Montreal the 10th of February. I think it would not be of miss if one of you should be there the same time to talk over of those agreements made at our meeting at Fort Stanwix. If it should be so, I think it would be for the interest of both parties, that is if our minds are not changed allready of what we agreed there. I wish Major Peter Schuyler should be the person that would meet me at Montreal. Sir I remain your most
Humbl servant
Jos. Brant.

To Matthew Visscher, Esq.

This letter, brief and clumsily phrased as it is, reveals the secret of Brant's greatness — his enterprising and dauntless spirit, his calm self-reliance and steadiness of purpose, his anxiety to thoroughly interpret and fathom every event and measure affecting his people, or the honor of the flag that sheltered them, and that rare fidelity which led him to abandon a voyage to Europe when on a point of embarkation, and after a journey weary and formidable in those days, and all because an obscure chief was detained as a hostage for causes or upon a pretext with which Brant had not been made acquainted.[1]

---

[1] Captain Brant was a staunch churchman and it was mainly through his exertions that his people, on being transplanted to Canada, were provided with a house of worship. For years afterward he labored unsuccessfully to secure the services of a resident missionary. In this long interval of

Republics, if not ungrateful, seldom take much interest in the posterity of their heroes, but I have thought that the boys of the last generation, whose massy locks have grown scant and silvery since they followed the fortunes of Thayendanegea through Col. Stone's bulky volumes, might care to learn a few particulars concerning the latter and less eventful history of the family.

The gallant and lamented Col. John Brant, Ahyouwaeghs,[1] son of Capt. Brant, as all of Stone's readers are aware, fell a victim to the Asiatic cholera in 1832. He left a will devising all his property to his sister Elizabeth who became the sole proprietress of an estate of baronial proportions. Although she adhered in part to the costume of her poeple, her beauty, intelligence, her queenly grace and refinement of manners, as well as the heroic blood that tinged her cheeks, caused her society to be courted by the most fashionable and aristocratic.

Some years after her brother's death Miss Brant married her cousin, William Johnson Kerr, of Niagara, and who could boast that the blood of a long line of forest kings which coursed in his veins was mingled with that of the most ancient of the Scottish nobility. His father, a first cousin of the Duke of Roxboro, was a surgeon in the British army, and soon after the revolutionary war, married a daughter of Sir William Johnson and the famous Mollie Brant. Mr. Kerr was one of three brothers, the fruit of this marriage.

This gentleman died at the old Brant mansion, at Wellington

---

neglect and spiritual destitution the church service was read in the Mohawk tongue every sabbath morning to a large and devout congregation. Captain Aaron Hill, aforementioned, was the reader. In honor of the day ho was wont to put an extra touch of vermillion on his cheeks, and discharged his sacred office with a dignity and an aspect of sanctity highly edifying. After the service the youth of the nation would assemble on the neighboring common and engage in the Indian game of ball, to which Captain Aaron would lend the encouragement of his presence. He is remembered as a very grave and worthy man.

When Elizabeth Brant's youngest daughter, who afterwards became Mrs. Kerr, was thirteen years old she chanced to wander far into the forest in pursuit of blackberries. While engaged in plucking this fruit a large and venomous snake, vulgarly known as the mlesissanga, fastened his fangs upon her finger. Child as she was, after shaking the reptile off, she had the presence of mind to apply a ligature to the member and then hurried home for succor. Capt. Aaron Hill happened to be the only male person at her father's house and seeing her peril he applied his lips to the wound to extract the virus by suction, following this remedy with a lotion of herbs which in a few hours completed the cure.

[1] Pronounced Ah-ü-waca. The engraved portraits of the chief, and the painting in the state library at Albany, are unlike the original picture at Brant house, and do him great injustice.

square, C. W., in 1842. His devoted wife, Elizabeth Brant Kerr, survived the loss of her husband but a few hours.

About half a mile west of the old historic mansion, known as the Brant house, stands a beautiful little chapel connected with the church of England, and which is a fitting monument to the piety and Christian zeal of the daughter of Thayendanegea. It is approached from the street through a long avenue lined with stately forest trees of her own planting. At the end of this avenue, and under the shadow of this chapel which they reared, and in which they long worshiped, are the graves of Colonel and Elizabeth Kerr. Captain Brant and his son sleep in the burying ground attached to the old Mohawk church near Brantford. Mr. and Mrs. Kerr left four little children, Walter Butler, Joseph Brant, Catharine Elizabeth and John William Simcoe. The eldest, Walter, inherited the principal chieftainship of the Six Nations. Of him Col. Stone wrote, "The infant chief is a fine looking lad, three-quarters Mohawk, with an eye piercing as the eagle's." These children were carefully nurtured and educated by their testamentary guardians. Of the four, however, only the younger two survive. Walter and Joseph were both cut off in early manhood; the former died in July, 1860, the latter in February, 1870. Walter was a rarely gifted young man, and his untimely death blasted many fond hopes and sent a pang to many sympathizing hearts. Joseph, without the brilliancy of his eldest brother, possessed sterling traits, and his amiability and gentle manners won the affections of all who knew him.

After the death of Walter Butler Kerr, his aunt, Catharine Brant Johns, who was of the blood royal of the Mohawks, and who according to their customs, had the right of conferring the title of tekarihogea, or principal sachem, nominated her son William Johns to fill the vacant office. The writer remembers this chief well. He was a tall, handsome young man with gentle manners and a voice and smile of winning sweetness. Unfortunately he became dissipated and met his death in a tragical manner about fifteen years ago. The office of tekarihogea thus made vacant was again filled by the nomination of the daughter

JOSEPH BRANT, THAYENDANEGEA, AND HIS POSTERITY. 151

of Brant. Her nephew Isaac Lewis, son of her sister Mary, was the fortunate candidate. Lewis was a sober, exemplary man, but in nowise remarkable. He died suddenly in 1863. The venerable daughter of Brant was again called upon to exercise her prerogative and her choice fell upon her nephew, W. J. Simcoe Kerr, the son of Col. and Mrs. Kerr, and who is probably the last tekarihogea of the Iroquois. The expanding intelligence of his people, and the infectious example of the Senecas of New York, threaten the overthrow of their ancient form of government and the adoption of another more compatible with progress.

W. J. SIMCOE KERR.[1]

Catharine E., the sister of the chief and a most lovely and accomplished woman, is a teacher among the Mohawks and has consecrated her life to the mental and moral elevation of her people.

About seven hundred of the Mohawks reside on the Grand river near Brantford, and the residue, about three hundred, live on the bay of Quinté. They have made considerable advancement in husbandry and the mechanic arts, and are believed to be slowly increasing in numbers. They have always been noted for their indomitable pride, pluming themselves upon the fact of their being the head of the famous league of the Iroquois or Six Nations and accustomed to look down with something like scorn upon other tribes. This pride has stood in the way of their progress. The more tractable Chippewas of Canada, willing to turn their

---

[1] Hereditary chief of the Wolf tribe of the Mohawks.

backs upon the past, bid fair to outstrip their ancient enemies, the Iroquois, in the race of civilization.

"They were always a haughty people," remarked an educated Chippewa to the writer not long since, " but," he added with a slight tone of exultation, " their day is almost gone."

While most of the Mohawks are of mixed blood they are more unalterably Indian in their feelings than any other tribe whom I have met. It is their boast that there has never been an instance of marriage or cohabitation between individuals of Mohawk and African descent, while the Tuscaroras and Senecas furnish many such examples. A few years ago a Mohawk lad, on his way to matriculate at Kenyon college, called on the writer. He was a remarkably handsome youth with a refined Indian cast of features; clustering hair; full, lustrous eyes; skin of the color of gold alloyed with copper but melting into carmine on the cheeks; dazzling white and regular teeth, and limbs rounded and symmetrical as an antique statue, obviously the choice fruit of grafting a scion of our race upon native stock. I asked him if he was not of mixed Caucasian and Indian parentage. He replied, with some confusion, that his people were of fairer complexion than other tribes, adding proudly that the Mohawk blood in his veins was unmingled with that of any other race. "But," persisted the writer, "Burning, one of your chiefs whom I have met, is of a deep copper color, the traditional hue of an Indian." "True," he rejoined, with a curl of his handsome lips, "but Burning is half Oneida." "Did not the Oneidas, Mohawks and the other members of the Six Nations spring from one common stock?" "Yes," he answered quickly, "and so did the blond Germans and swarthy Hindoos whom you class together as Caucasians. Besides, the Mohawks have been Christianized for over a hundred years. The smoke of the pagan wigwams deepens the color on an Indian's cheek." This lad had the blood of Sir Wm. Johnson in his veins, but had it been the blood of the proudest duke in the British realm, it would have afforded him no consolation. At the instance of the Prince of Wales this young man was afterwards taken to England to complete his studies at Oxford.

The present chief, W. J. Simcoe Kerr, has received a liberal education, and his manners, naturally engaging, have been softened and refined by European travel and intercourse with the best society. In person he is tall, upwards of six feet in stature, straight as an arrow, with a piercing black eye, raven locks and olive complexion. He married, a few years ago, a daughter of the late Dr. Hunter of Hamilton, Canada, who was one of the executors of Mrs. Kerr's will and testamentary guardian of one of her children, Catharine Elizabeth; the other executors being Mr. Beasly, her legal adviser, and the Rev. Dr. McMurray. The young chief resides at Brant house, the old ancestral mansion, where he dispenses the same elegant hospitality for which it has long been noted.[1] This venerable structure presents nearly the same appearance it did eighty years ago when Captain Brant, with a retinue of thirty negro servants, and surrounded by gay soldiers, cavaliers in powdered wigs and scarlet coats, and all the motley assemblage of that picturesque era, held his barbaric court within its walls.

To visit this quaint old mansion and find it untenanted for the moment, as chanced to the writer one sunny day last June, is like stepping backward from the nineteenth century into the last quarter of the eighteenth. You enter a spacious hall and turning to the right find yourself in a large, old fashioned drawing room whose front windows look out upon the blue expanse of Burlington bay. On the opposite side of the room is a grate surmounted by an absurdly tall mantel and flanked on each side by a curious, arched recess. Life-size oil portraits of Brant in his paint and war dress, of John Brant the ideal of an Indian hero; of Sir William Johnson and members of his family, in stiff wigs, and scarlet coats richly laced, stare down upon you

---

[1] The writer saw this chief sitting in council last autumn with the grandsons of Red Jacket, Cornplanter, Gov. Blacksnake, Mary Jemison and other personages associated with the revolutionary epoch. Mr. Kerr was attired in the full war dress of his people and looked every inch a chief. This was the first time that a Mohawk chief had met the Senecas in council since the days of Brant. On his late visit to Canada, Prince Alfred spent a day among the Mohawks of Grand river and was complimented by being chosen to a chieftainship second in rank to that of Mr. Kerr. The ceremonies were impressive and were followed by merrymakings and joyous festivities. In the event of war his royal highness will be the lieutenant of tekarihogea, and in council he pledged the honor of a prince that he would be found at the side of that chief when the summons came.

from the walls. Upon the mantel lies Brant's dagger which drank the blood of his ruffianly son Isaac; carelessly disposed upon a table are a pair of richly ornamented duelling pistols, the gift of the Duke of Northumberland; there lies his tomahawk; yonder hangs the queer conch-shell medal which he wore, and in the corner is flung his small sword, its ivory handle studded with gems, a testimonial from his sacred majesty, George the Third, to his gallant and faithful ally.

So carelessly are these and other relics strewn about the room as to lend encouragement to the fancy that the old chief had hurriedly thrown them down expecting momentarily to return and reclaim them. A dreamy atmosphere pervades the apartment disposing the mind to revery and rendering it hospitable to visions of the past. The writer, on the occasion mentioned, instinctively cast a look toward the door, expecting to hear the tread of moccasined feet, to catch a glimpse of those swarthy features and be transfixed by a glance of the basilisk eyes which are reproduced in the portrait over the mantel. But the spell was broken by the hum of approaching voices, and a peal of childish laughter, proceeding from three bright little elves, descendants in the fourth generation from Joseph Brant.[1]

I can readily credit the rumor, reported to me in good faith by a neighboring farmer, that Brant house is haunted.

Before his departure from home on the eve of the battle of Stony creek, fought near Hamilton during the last war with England, the young chief, John Brant, warned his aged mother that the Brant house would be likely to receive a hostile visit from the invaders and promised to send a runner in time to insure the escape of its inmates. The warning came and the family and the servants sought the shelter of the neighboring woods. Returning the next day they found the house in great disorder

---

[1] Among the oil portraits at Brant house is one of Peter Johnson of whom Gov. Tryon, in a letter addressed to the Earl of Dartmouth, under date of Feb. 8, 1776, wrote as follows: "The Indians have chosen Peter Johnson, the natural son of Sir William Johnson (by an Indian woman), to be their chief. He is intrepid and active and took with his own hand Ethan Allen in a barn, after his detachment was routed before Montreal. The Indian department demands all possible attention, and a commission of general to Peter would be politic." The portrait is of a handsome young man with no preceptible trace of Indian blood. He fell by the hand of a rival suitor for a young lady's affections in a duel fought soon after the close of the revolutionary war. Peter's mother was the celebrated Mollie Brant.

JOSEPH BRANT, THAYENDANEGEA, AND HIS POSTERITY. 155

but no irreparable damage done to the buildings. The Americans had evidently taken alarm and retired before their work of destruction was complete. Of the booty carried away with them the loss of nothing was so much deplored as a small pipe tomahawk, inlaid with silver, which the enemy had found under the pillow of Mrs. Brant's bed, where, in the hurry of her departure, she had left it. It was the gift of her husband and she had a fancy for sleeping with it under her pillow.

This remarkable woman survived her husband just thirty years. A short time before his death she had the misfortune to drop from her finger, when strolling about the grounds, a gold ring, the wedding gift of her husband. Earnest and repeated search failed to find it. Twenty-six years afterwards a plowman turned up the jewel with his furrow and restored it to the delighted owner. I lately saw it on the finger of the grand-daughter of Brant from whom I learned this incident. The ring bears the inscription in deeply traced characters, "Thayendanegea to Catharine." Catharine Johns, the last survivor of Brant's children, died after a brief illness at Brant house in January, 1867, aged sixty-seven years. Mrs. Johns was a very intelligent and interesting woman. In her youth she was noted for her great personal beauty. When the writer last saw her, in her old age, her carriage was still erect, her person tall and commanding and her aspect one of mingled dignity and benevolence. She told me she

JOSEPH BRANT, AGE 43.[1]

---

[1] This is from the miniature mentioned in the text, exquisitely painted on ivory, from life, whilst Brant was in London in 1785-'86. It is in the possession of the Brant family, and has ever been considered the best likeness of him, ever painted. While he was in England, Brant sat for his portrait for Lord Percy (afterwards the Duke of Northumberland) as he had done for the Earl of Warwick and Dr. Johnson's friend Boswell, when he was there ten years before.—*Lossing*.

could readily recall her father's tones and features — remembered sitting on his knee and receiving his caresses. She wore a gold locket containing an exquisite miniature likeness of her father painted in London. This, she said, was the most faithful likeness of Capt. Brant extant.

Mrs. Johns adhered to the dress and many of the customs of her people. Her feelings were warmly enlisted in their welfare, and the only shadow that dimmed her cheerfulness in her last hours was regret that she must die away from the people she loved so well. Her last request was that she should be buried near the old mission church on the Grand river. It is needless to say this wish was piously fulfilled.

Father and daughter, surrounded by kindred dust, sleep on the banks of the river where the remnant of their people linger, and where the echoes still repeat the music of the Mohawk tongue, so soon to be numbered with those lost, mysterious languages in which Pocahontas pleaded for the English adventurer's life and King Philip roused his warriors to battle.

BUFFALO, N. Y., Nov. 2, 1876.

Since the foregoing article was written the two grand children of Thayendanegea have passed from earth. Wm. John Simcoe Kerr died suddenly of heart disease on the 17th day of February, 1875. The brother and sister were tenderly attached to each other. They were still young, the only survivors of a large and interesting family, and were frequently spoken of as "The last of the Brants" by their acquaintances.

Under date of March 15, 1875, the sister wrote : " My dear brother's death was indeed a very great shock to me. It was not wholly unexpected, owing to his precarious state of health during the past year. I tried to prepare myself for the announcement but only one placed in a like position can comprehend the utter misery of such tidings. Yes, my friend, I feel very much alone now, were it not for the loving sympathy of friends I would be more wretched still."

The sister died on the 25th day of February, 1876, on the Mohawk reservation, Grand river, Canada. I violate no confidence in publishing the following extract from a letter written by one who long sought to sustain the relation of mother to these orphaned children: "The first intimation I had of my poor Kate's illness was a telegram such as you received. We started at once for Onondaga — all was over. On Sunday she had attended church and returned on the ice with several friends who remarked that they had never seen her look more blooming and lovely or in better spirits. On the following day she felt that she had taken cold, but did not think much of it until Tuesday when she had a chill and fever. Inflammation of the lungs followed. The doctor felt no alarm until Thursday following. On Friday morning he thought her better, when a sudden change came. She had, she said, 'no fear of death, trusting only in her Saviour.' She was quite conscious to the last, and made all arrangements, requesting to be laid beside her aunt, Mrs. Johns, near the old Mohawk church. So ended this most precious and beautiful life.

INDIAN MIGRATIONS.[1]

By Lewis H. Morgan.

In this article I intend to present such evidence bearing upon the migrations of the North American Indians as may be drawn from a consideration of physical conditions, especially the influence of abundant means of subsistence; and such other evidence upon the same subject as may be derived from their systems of consanguinity, their relative positions, languages, and traditions, and in addition, notices of such actual migrations as are known to have occurred. A determination of the probable source of the aboriginal inhabitants of South America will be involved in the general conclusions I seek to establish.

Since the materials we now possess are insufficient for a conclusive discussion of this subject, some of the views presented will be necessarily conjectural. But as philosophical speculations precede systems of philosophy, so historical speculations often lead the way to veritable history. In the present state of our knowledge, the great movements of the American aborigines in prehistoric ages still lie within the domain of speculation. A probable hypothesis with respect to the initial point of these migrations is the utmost we may hope at present to reach.

It will be my principal object to bring together a body of facts, bearing upon these migrations, which tend to establish their starting-point in the valley of the Columbia river, and at the outset three propositions will be assumed to be true: First, that there was a time, in the past, when North and South America were destitute of human inhabitants. Second, that at the period of the discovery of their several parts a people were found thinly scattered over their vast areas, who agreed so minutely in physical and mental characteristics, that they all received a common name, and were regarded, whether correctly or incorrectly, as a common stock. And third, that the epoch of their first occupation was of very ancient date.

---

[1] Reprinted from *The North American Review* (Boston), for October, 1869, and January, 1870.

With respect to the first proposition, no discussion is necessary. The second, though of limited significance, is nevertheless important. From New Mexico to Patagonia, including the West India islands, the Spanish navigators and explorers found this singular people universally distributed, and bestowed upon them, all alike, the name of *Indians*. They observed no difference in type, but, on the contrary, abundant evidence of a common type. The English and French met the aborigines from near the confines of the Arctic sea to New Mexico, and from the Atlantic to the Pacific, and pronounced them, without distinction, *American Indians*. This uniform testimony of the first discoverers, the general truthfulness of which has been confirmed by all subsequent observers, tends to establish one of two alternative conclusions :— either that all these aboriginal nations were of immediately common descent, or that this uniformity in physical characteristics was the result of a continuous intermingling of blood.

Upon the third proposition, it may be observed that the occupation of America by the ancestors of the present Indians extends backward to a remote age, covering a period of many thousand years. If the unity of their origin is assumed, the lapse of many ages would be requisite to break an original language into the several existing stock languages, of which there are forty, more or less, in North America alone — the number which have perished being unknown — and to allow these in turn to pass into the multitude of dialects which are now spoken. On the contrary, if a diverse origin is assumed, it would still require several thousand years for two or more families genetically unconnected, and occupying such immense areas, to have intermingled so completely as to create a typical stock, such as the Indian stock has become. The hypothesis of a diverse origin would seem further to require that these families should have been restricted, for mutual accessibility, either to North or to South America, and to a limited portion of one of these areas, until the coalescence had become complete; since the inhabitants of the two continents and of the islands were entirely isolated from, and ignorant of, the existence of each other at the epoch of their discovery.

Barbarians, ignorant of agriculture and depending upon fish

and game for subsistence, spread over large areas with great rapidity. Under the operation of purely physical causes, they would reach in their migrations the remotest boundaries of a continent in a much shorter time than a civilized people with all the appliances of civilization. This important and well-established fact should be kept constantly in view. A narrow sea or treeless plain might arrest their progress for centuries; but wherever their feet could carry them, with subsistence accessible upon the way, they would be certain to go, until a continent as vast as the American in both its divisions had been traversed in all its parts. Agriculture tends to localize nations and wed them to the soil, thus arresting their dispersion or confining it to contiguous areas. Abundant means of subsistence tend to the same result; but when there is a surplus population which becomes emigrant, it seeks similar areas, without much regard to distance.

Whether the ancestors of the American aborigines were first planted in North or South America remains a question.[1] Our knowledge of the aboriginal inhabitants of South America, except of those upon the Andes, is still very imperfect. Descriptive notices of the people, with some classification of dialects into stock languages, exist, but the aggregate of information fails to meet the requirements of systematic ethnology. The inhabitants of the Andes, who in material progress and in the importance of their position far surpassed all the other aborigines

[1] Dr. Daniel Wilson, in his *Prehistoric Man*, advances the hypothesis of a peopling of South America from the Polynesian Islands, and of North America from South America. It is with reluctance that I am compelled to dissent from the views of this eminent scholar, who has done such excellent work for American ethnology. He remarks: "From some one of the early centres of South American population planted on the Pacific coasts by Polynesian and other migrations, nursed in the neighboring valleys of the Andes in remote prehistoric times, the predominant southern race diffused itself, or extended its influence through many ramifications. It spread northward beyond the Isthmus, expanded throughout the peninsular region of Central America, and, after occupying for a time the Mexican plateau, it overflowed along either side of the great mountain chain, reaching towards the northern latitudes of the Pacific, and extending inland to the east of the Rocky mountains through the great valley watered by the Mississippi and its tributaries. It is not, however, to be supposed that such a hypothesis of migration implies the literal diffusion of a single people from one geographical centre" (p. 595). Farther on he observes: "But independent of all real or hypothetical ramification from southern or insular offsets of oceanic migration, some analogies confirm the probability of a portion of the North American stock having entered the continent from Asia by Behring's straits or the Aleutian islands, and more probably by the latter than the former, for it is the climate that constitutes the real barrier" (*Ibid.*, p. 597).

of South America, were an insulated people. This great chain, with its table-lands, mountains, valleys, lakes, and rivers, forms a continent within itself; and however satisfactory the information we possess with respect to the Village Indians of this secondary continent might be regarded, as a guide to trustworthy conclusions concerning their original derivation, some knowledge of the great movements of the remaining nations would be necessary. The facts with respect to the movements and relations of the North American Indians are much better understood, and may contain sufficient evidence for a settlement of the question in favor of an original home in North America. It is with an impression of the controlling character of this evidence that I shall treat the migrations of the North American Indians independently.

At the period of their discovery the American aborigines were ignorant of the use of iron, and, consequently, of the arts which require this metal; but they had undoubtedly made great progress, as compared with their primitive state. They were found in two dissimilar conditions. First were the Roving Indians, depending for subsistence upon fish and game. Second, the Village Indians, depending chiefly upon agriculture. Between these, and connecting the extremes by insensible gradations, were the partially Roving and partially Village Indians.[1] The first class had developed many useful arts. They possessed the art of striking fire; of making the bow, with the string of sinew, and the arrow-head, both of flint and bone; of making vessels of pottery; of curing and tanning skins; of making moccasins and wearing apparel, together with various implements and utensils of stone, wood, and bone; of rope and net making from filaments of bark; of finger-weaving, with warp and woof, the same materials into sashes, burden-straps, and other useful fabrics; of basket-making with osier, cane, and splints; of canoe-making — the skin, birch-bark, and dug-out; of constructing timber-frame lodges and skin tents; of shaping stone mauls, hammers, and chisels; of making fish-spears, nets, and bone hooks, implements

---

[1] Vide *North American Review*, April, 1869, p. 494.

for athletic games, musical instruments, such as the flute and the drum, weapons, and personal ornaments of shell, bone, and stone. They had invented the art of picture writing, and had also developed a language of signs, which became the common medium of communication between nations speaking languages mutually unintelligible. They possessed a form of government, and clearly defined domestic institutions, which served to regulate their political affairs. When the extent of their progress in these several respects is fully appreciated, the differences between them and the Village Indians will be found much less in degree than is usually supposed.

Whilst the Village Indians possessed the same arts, implements, and utensils, as well as institutions and forms of government, they had obtained native copper, had formed copper implements, and, in certain areas, implements and utensils of bronze, and had also worked native gold and silver into various forms. But a knowledge of the use of these metals was limited chiefly to the Village Indians of Mexico and Peru. Even among these, little progress had been made in the employment of them in the practical arts of life. In addition to these means of advancement, they had learned the art of cultivating the ground, which established them in villages, and thus gave them a new impulse forward. It is plain that village life, upon the stable basis of agricultural subsistence, stimulated in a remarkable manner the development of their primitive arts. A decrease in the severity of the struggle for existence, and an increase of numbers in a small area, would necessarily be favorable to this progress; which is conspicuously shown in their architecture and stone sculptures; and, perhaps more decisively, in the Maya and Aztec calendars to measure annual time, and in the solstitial stone of the Peruvians.[1] Ages upon ages of experience, with vicissitudes of lapse and recovery, were required, to produce the progress they had made at the epoch of European discovery.

[1] In the lunar months the Iroquois and other northern Indians, we find an early stage of the same thought. In like manner we find in the language of signs of the Roving Indians the incipient forms out of which sprung, probably, the picture writings of the Aztecs, and ultimately the still higher ideographs upon the Copan monuments. If either of these forms is ever read, it is not improbable that the key will be found in this language of signs, which is still in constant use among the western nations. It is a very ingenious and very expressive language.

Measured from the stand-point of their primitive condition — could the extremity of its rudeness be known — the progress of the Roving Indians was probably much more remarkable in degree than that of the Village Indians after the change from a roving to a stationary life. The stages of progress in the ages of barbarism were as measured and real as the stages of progress in ages of civilization. Notwithstanding their knowledge of agriculture, the Village as well as the Roving Indians, were still in the age of stone. They were found using stone implements and utensils, which had not been abandoned even among the more advanced of the former class. Agriculture, however, performed an important part in the elevation of the Indian family, although it never reached a sufficient development to give to the Village Indians the mastery of the continent, or to emancipate them from the superior power of the Roving and partially Village Indians, from whose ranks issued the migrating bands which peopled the continent. The principal nations of Village Indians in Mexico, if their traditions can be trusted, were themselves emigrants from the north but three or four centuries prior to the Spanish conquest. Natural subsistence was contending with agricultural for supremacy when European colonization commenced. It will be seen in the sequel that the former appeared to hold the mastery.

The American aborigines undoubtedly commenced their career as fishermen and hunters, but chiefly as fishermen; and the mass of them remained substantially in that condition down to the period of European discovery. The exceptions were the Village Indians, who, if not a minority of the whole population of both North and South America, were not much superior in numbers to the less advanced nations.[1] It will be perceived at once that the hunt is a precarious source of human subsistence. Without the horse to follow the larger animals of the chase upon the plains, it was entirely impossible for nations of men to maintain themselves from this source exclusively, or even principally.

---

[1] This opinion is expressed conjecturally. The Village Indians occupied but a small portion of the continent. They were confronted with Roving and partially Village Indians on every side, and their numbers, there are strong reasons for believing, have been grossly exaggerated.

Increased numbers increased the diligence of the hunt in the same ratio, and this tended, in turn, to diminish the supply of game. Nations would rapidly perish if dependent upon so uncertain a source of maintenance. With the supply of fish the rule is different. In the ocean and in the lakes, which are the nurseries of fish, they are found in unlimited abundance. From these, as they enter the bays and rivers, they are taken in all seasons of the year with facility, and at certain seasons in the largest quantities. There is no doubt whatever that the principal reliance of the American aborigines for subsistence, with the exception at a later day of the Village Indians, was upon fish. This fact will be found to have an important bearing upon the formation of their centres of populations and upon their primary and secondary migrations. They were in reality, from first to last, nations of fishermen, who eked out their scanty sustenance with game, natural fruits, and bread roots, and afterwards — a portion of them — with the products of a limited agriculture. They were found in all the intermediate conditions, from those who subsisted principally upon fish, as the Athapascans and Ojibwas, to those who subsisted principally upon vegetable food, as the Aztecs and Tlascalans, and with no definite boundary line to separate one class from the other. A comparison of the principal facts bearing upon the point tends to show that *fish was the basis of subsistence* of the Indian tribes, to which their increase in numbers and diffusion over North America is to be ascribed. It was by the abundance of this article of food that certain centres of population were created, which first supplied, and afterward replenished, the continent with inhabitants.

It should also be observed that the migrations of men are not fortuitous. They are deliberate movements, under the government of law. The influences by which they are immediately brought about are much less important than the physical conditions of climate and subsistence under which they are accomplished. An initial point of migrations does not become such by accident, but has of necessity a material basis in its natural advantages; and it may be remote from the place where the first ancestors of a family were planted, and reached only after several changes of location, and the lapse of centuries of time. Our first inquiry, therefore, should be, whether in fact there was any one region or district of country in North America which possessed advantages for Indian occupation so far superior to all others as to render it a natural centre of population, and consequently an initial point of migrations. If any such region existed upon an uninhabited continent, it would, when occupied, stand in a superior and commanding relation to every other portion of its area until this was peopled in all its parts, or until these advantages were neutralized by a change of conditions — such, for example, as might result from the development of agriculture as a substitute for fishing and hunting.

Leaving certain other preliminary considerations which would naturally suggest themselves, I intend, in the remainder of this article, to examine, first, the geographical features of North America with reference to its natural highways or lines of migration; secondly, to compare its several regions with regard to the amount of subsistence which they respectively afforded to a people living as fishermen and hunters; thirdly, to test the results thus obtained by the statistics of Indian population in these several areas; and lastly, to consider the nature and distribution of Indian agriculture in other areas, as a means of counterbalancing these advantages. In this manner the fact can be ascertained whether any one region existed in North America possessed of such advantages in furnishing spontaneously means of subsistence as to make it the natural nursery of the aboriginal inhabitants of the continent.

1. *Geographical Features of North America.*— These features may be considered under the threefold division of the prairie, the mountain, and the forest areas; the first being the least, and the last the most, desirable territory for Indian occupation.

First, the prairie areas. The great central prairies occupy the interior of the northern continent. In the vastness of their continuous expanse, and in the exuberance of their vegetation, they are without a parallel in any portion of the earth. They extend from latitude 29°, and south of it, to the north of Peace river in the Hudson-Bay territory, in latitude 60° north. In their greatest lateral expansion they extend from the western part of the state of Indiana, in longitude 9°, to the eastern base of the Rocky mountain chain, in longitude 28° west of Washington. From this line of their greatest width from east to west, they contract gradually as they stretch both northward and southward, forming a vast inland plain, carpeted with grass, watered by great rivers, and encompassed by forests. The boundaries of this central prairie region will be made familiar by tracing briefly their circuit. Commencing upon the Rio Grande, which forms, in part, the southern boundary of the United States, and following the general line that separates the forest from the prairie northeasterly, a narrow belt of forest is found in Texas, bordering the gulf of Mexico, but penetrated here and there by the prairie, which reaches the gulf at several points, as at the mouth of the Nueces [1] and at Matagorda bay.[2] Louisiana, the eastern part of Arkansas, and the southeastern part of Missouri, were originally forest; while all west of this line was prairie, with the exception of narrow fringes of forest along the rivers and water-courses, and of small and irregular belts of timber upon the lowlands. Crossing the Mississippi above the mouth of the Ohio, the prairies follow the wide belt of woodlands along the northern bank of the Ohio, until they reach and penetrate the state of Indiana, where their eastern limit is found with the exception of prairie openings in central and eastern Indiana and in western Ohio. Turning thence in a northwesterly direction, the prairie touches the foot of Lake Michigan at Chicago, from which point northward the belt of forest along the western shore of Lake Michigan widens, so that the dividing line passes a number of miles west of the head of Lake Superior, whence it continues near the chain of small lakes to Lake Winnipeg. Keeping to the west of this lake and of Lake Manitobar, which is also bordered with forest, the boundary line of the prairies runs northwesterly to near the west end of Athapasca lake, where it crosses Peace river, and extends beyond, to Hay river, near the sixtieth parallel, after which it bears southwesterly

---

[1] Bartlett's *Personal Narrative*, II, 529.
[2] Bancroft's *History of the United States*, III, 171.

to the slopes at the foot of the Rocky mountains. East, north, and northwest of this line there is forest, whilst all within is prairie.[1] Upon the plateau of Peace river, in the far north, are found the northern limits of these magnificent and verdant fields, upon which no eye can rest without wonder and admiration. Southward, along the base of the Rocky mountain chain, the lower slopes of which are wooded to the edge of the plains, the prairies spread uninterruptedly to our starting-point on the Rio Grande.

This vast area, which traverses thirty-one parallels of latitude and nineteen parallels of longitude, in its greatest continuous expanse, measures more than seventeen hundred miles from north to south, more than a thousand miles from east to west, and embraces upwards of eight hundred thousand square miles. It is not entirely a treeless region, neither is it separated from the surrounding forests by a sharply defined line. East of the Mississippi river the prairie area is a combination of forest and prairies, the latter greatly predominating. There are margins of forest along the rivers and water-courses, upon the hills, and in numerous districts of lowlands. Besides these there are irregular belts of forest, which run for miles independently of rivers and streams. Climate is an efficient cause of the production of forest in the prairie area east of this river. The humidity of the atmosphere from the prevalence of winds from the gulf of Mexico, which determines the climate of the region, tends constantly though slowly, to extend the forest over the prairie and to increase the extent of its development upon the borders of the rivers. After crossing the Mississippi, in going westward, one finds a gradual diminution of the relative extent of forest, and this change becomes more rapid and marked beyond the Missouri, in Kansas and Nebraska.[2] As we recede from the influence of the gulf winds and come in contact with the true climate of the prairies, it becomes constantly drier, since the remaining region is now shut in upon the west by the double barrier of the Rocky moun-

---

[1] There are patches of prairie northwest of Hay river, in which the timber buffalo, so called, is found. This animal is smaller than the ordinary buffalo, but believed to be the same species. Having traversed the intermediate forests, he has remained permanently in this far northern region.

[2] Ne-blas-ka, name of Platte river in the Kaw dialect, "overspreading flats with shallow water."

tains and the Sierra Nevada, which deprive the winds of their moisture on their passage from the Pacific eastward. After traversing about one hundred and fifty miles of Kansas, to the twenty-second meridian west of Washington, the western limit of arable land in the prairie area under consideration[1] is reached. Westward of this line the dryness of the climate continues to increase, the trees diminish in number and decrease in size, and finally disappear from the margins of the rivers. The grasses, yielding to the same influences, become less and less luxuriant, until the prairies, long before they reach the base of the mountains, degenerate under the summer sun into arid plains. Northward, on the Upper Missouri, the grasses never attain the luxuriance which they display in Eastern Kansas and Nebraska, by reason of the western trend of this river, but on the Upper Mississippi and along the Red river of the north to Lake Winnepeg they maintain a vigorous growth.

The most perfect display of the prairies is found in the eastern parts of Kansas and Nebraska. It is no exaggeration to pronounce this region, as left by the hand of nature, the most beautiful country in its landscape upon the face of the earth. Here the forest is restricted to narrow fringes along the rivers and streams, the courses of which are thus defined as far as the eye can reach, whilst all between is a broad expanse of meadowlands, carpeted with the richest verdure and wearing the appearance of artistically graded lawns. They are familiarly called the rolling prairies, because the land rises and falls in gentle swells, which attain an elevation of thirty feet, more or less, and descend again to the original level, within the distance of one or more miles. The crest-lines of these motionless waves of land intersect each other at every conceivable angle, the effect of which is to bring into view the most extended landscape, and to show the dark green foliage of the forest trees skirting the streams in pleasing contrast with the light green of the prairie grasses. In their spring covering of vegetation these prairies wear the semblance of an old and once highly cultivated country, from the soil of which every inequality of surface, every stone

---

[1] *Explorations for a Railroad Route, etc., to the Pacific*, I, 25.

and every bush has been carefully removed and the surface rolled down into absolute uniformity. The marvel is suggested how Nature could have kept these verdant fields in such luxuriance after man had apparently abandoned them to waste. This striking display is limited to about one hundred and thirty miles in the eastern part of Kansas and a narrower belt in Eastern Nebraska.

The great extent and peculiar features of the central prairie area have been brought thus prominently forward for the purpose of calling attention to two facts. In the first place, that this region interposed a serious, if not insuperable, barrier to free communication between the Pacific and Atlantic sides of North America. Between the thirty-second and fifty-fifth parallels, that is, from the southern boundary of New Mexico to the regions north of the Saskatchewan river, there are but three or possibly four routes of migration from one side of the continent to the other — by the Saskatchewan to Lake Winnipeg, and thence by the chain of lakes to the valley of the St. Lawrence; by the Missouri to the Mississippi, the least probable of the four; by the Platte to the Missouri and thence to the Mississippi; and by the Arkansas to the Mississippi. On either route eight hundred miles of prairie, more or less, must be traversed in dependence upon the limited supply of game which the fringe of forest upon these rivers and the open prairies might be able to furnish, and over which American emigrants, aided by the appliances of civilization, have been barely able to pass. In the second place, that the greater part of this area west of the Mississippi, and nearly all of it west of the Missouri, was a solitude at the period of European discovery. It is perfectly evident from the nature of these prairies that they were never occupied by Indian nations, except in districts of very limited extent along the wooded margins of the great rivers by which they are traversed. A region more inviting to nomadic nations possessed of flocks and herds can scarcely be found upon any continent; but inasmuch as the American aborigines were fishermen and hunters, and could not lead a nomadic life upon these plains until they had obtained the horse, these vast pastures were to them a waste, except as the nurseries of the antelope, the elk, and the buffalo. America, generous in every other respect, had denied to her primitive inhabitants all useful animals capable of domestication, except the llama of the Andes.

West of the Rocky mountains there are large expanses of prairie, in Colorado, Utah, Idaho, Nevada, and Arizona; in California, Oregon, and Washington; and also in British Columbia. Southward, in Mexico, the spread and boundaries of the prairies have not been so definitely ascertained. Chihuahua, Sonora, and Zacatecas have broad prairies within their limits, and patches of prairie land are said to be found, here and there, southward to the valley of Mexico.

2. *Mountain Areas.*— The mountain regions of North America are extensive, from the great length and lateral expansion of the Rocky mountain chain, which, under different names, extends in substantial continuity from the isthmus of Panama to the Arctic sea. In its central part it sends off spurs and transverse ranges to such an extent, that, when to these are added the parallel ranges of the Sierra Nevada and Cascade mountains, a large portion of the continent, west of the central prairies, is so broken up as to render it substantially a mountain country. Below the snow-line the declivities of most of these mountains are wooded, as well as their lower slopes for considerable distances outward. Portions of these ranges are sterile, from the dryness of the atmosphere, yet the greater part of them are not only habitable for man, but were in the main well stocked with game, and their valleys with bread roots.[1] These great ranges furnished, as well as suggested, highways of migration. They also gave to these movements a general direction from north to

---

[1] Among the peculiarities of the Rocky mountains are the parks. "The parks of Colorado are elevated bowls in the mountain country, having the appearance of beds of inland seas upheaved and emptied of their waters by volcanic agency. They present to the eye scenery magnificent beyond description, made up of far-reaching forests, fertile meadows, and beautiful streams, surrounded by the lofty peaks of the great Rocky range. The principal of these parks are the North park, ... Middle park, ... South park, ... Huerfano park, ... and the grand San Luis park in the southern part of Colorado, having an area of 18,000 square miles, watered by thirty-five streams — sixteen of them emptying into the Rio Grande del Norte, which flows through its southern limits, and nineteen into San Luis lake, which extends sixty miles from north to south in the centre of the park, and apparently without an outlet. This park is remarkable for its natural scenery, the grandeur of its forests, the fertility of its soil, the purity of its waters, and the vast deposits of peat in the vicinity of San Luis lake."—*Report of the Commissioner of General Land Office for* 1866, p. 51.

south, or the reverse. It is not only probable, but it can be proved with reasonable certainty, that the migrations upon the Pacific side of the continent followed these mountain chains, rather than the prairies or the sea-coast. With respect to the method of these movements, it is not to be supposed that they were a series of flights of tribes or nations under the impulse of fear, seeking a distant habitation by the most convenient route, and leaving not a trace behind; they were rather a gradual spread from an original centre, preserving the continuity of the people over a large area, for the possession of which it was con. tending with bordering nations as it advanced outward. Such movements would result from the displacement from within of unsuccessful competitors for the occupation of an overstocked area.

It is another singular feature of the northern division of the continent, that no mountain chain occurs east of the Rocky mountains until the confines of the Atlantic are reached, where the moderately elevated Alleghanies are found, with more than fifteen hundred miles of prairie and forest between. The last named range possesses but little importance with reference to the migrations of the Indian nations, as it was encompassed on all sides by the great American forests. The same is true of the mountain districts in the British provinces.

3. *The Forest Area.*— The remaining, which is much the largest, part of North America, was covered with forests at the epoch of European discovery. To the American aborigines, as fishermen and hunters, they afforded a not inhospitable home. They offered every advantage which could render the lives of men in their condition capable of maintenance. But the vigorous and overmastering growth of forest vegetation, against which they had no power to contend, must have constantly retarded their advance in civilization. It is impossible to conceive of a region more unfavorable to the progress of nations out of a state of barbarism. And when, in course of time, the Indians obtained corn and the art of tilling the ground, the sturdy forces of nature first resisted and then tended to overwhelm their feeble appliances in husbandry. Notwithstanding these hin-

drances, and the oppressive burdens of forest life, the finest specimens of the Indian, north of Mexico, were found in strictly forest nations. The progress they had actually made, under such immense disadvantages, although small, must heighten our appreciation of their natural capacities.

There are two sections of country not included in the areas already considered — the Barren grounds, and the Colorado basin. The former occupy the northeastern corner of the continent, west of Hudson's bay. They are bounded by a line drawn from the shore of this bay in latitude 61° north to the east end of Great-Slave lake, and thence northeasterly to the Arctic sea. North and east of this line the entire region is destitute of trees and of every species of vegetation except the lichen. It is utterly barren, and more dreary than the ordinary desert, from its arctic climate.[1] The Colorado basin is a district of considerable extent, traversing several parallels of latitude and meridians of longitude, situated south of the Humboldt mountains and between the Colorado river and the Sierra Nevada. Later explorations show that this area is not probably a basin. There is a series of seven basins around and within the rim of the Great basin, above which the lowest parts of the central area rise more than a thousand feet. The central portion, which forms much the larger part of the area, is broken up into mountain ranges running north and south, and having an average altitude of five thousand feet.[2] The sterility of the basin is explained by the dryness of the climate, the annual precipitation being estimated at five inches.[3] Notwithstanding its inhospitable character, this region still sustains a considerable Indian population, but of the lowest grade.

By the distribution of the prairie, the forest, and the moun-

---

[1] *Richardson's Journal of a Boat Voyage through Rupert's Land*, London ed, 1851, I, 151.

[2] *The Shortest Route to California across the Great Basin of Utah*, by Brevet Brig-Gen. T. H. Simpson, 1869.

[3] "This great arid region may be said to embrace ten degrees of longitude and seventeen of latitude, drained only by the Columbia and Great Colorado rivers in any outlet to the sea. Fully half of it is the Great basin of the interior, which does not receive sufficient water to require any external drainage. Taking the basin as nearly eight degrees of latitude and seven of longitude, we have ten hundred thousand square miles, so deficient in rain as to send out no rivers and to accumulate no considerable lakes."— *Blodgett's Climatology of the United States*, p. 352; and *Hyetal Chart*, p. 354.

tain areas of North America, both the primary and the secondary lines of migration are clearly revealed. The principal line, upon the western half, is north and south. It was a great central route furnished and suggested by the Rocky mountain chain. Parallel with this, and nearer to the Pacific, was a second highway along the continuous chains of the Cascade and Sierra Nevade mountains, which extend from a point opposite Queen Charlotte's sound to near the head of the gulf of California. A third was the sea-coast. Between the Rocky mountains on the west, and the Mississippi and St. Lawrence valleys on the east, the natural lines of migration were the great rivers, which were secondary in attractiveness and importance. North of Athapasca lake the forest offered a free communication between the mountains and Hudson's bay, although the principal rivers run northward. From this high northern region to the southern limits of New Mexico, the central prairie area could be traversed only on the lines of the rivers which flowed through them eastward. Of these there are but three, perhaps four, possible lines, as before stated. First, that of the Saskatchewan, which furnished the most feasible route; second, that of the Arkansas, possessing nearly equal advantages; third, that of the Platte, which is more difficult than either; and lastly, that of the Missouri, which is substantially an impracticable route, since the river runs for twenty-five hundred miles through open prairies. For the first four hundred miles east of the Rocky mountains these rivers flow through dry and substantially treeless regions, and for the next four hundred through lands not much more inviting to fishermen and hunters. These obstacles presented a formidable barrier, as before remarked, to all communication between the Pacific and Atlantic sides of the continent. It is not improbable that an original family of mankind, planted in and overflowing from the valley of the Columbia as a nursery land, would reach Patagonia sooner than Florida, migrating under the influence exclusively of physical causes. The influence upon Indian migrations produced by the comparative facilities afforded by these several routes will be referred to again.

4. *Means of Subsistence and Centres of Population.*— The abun-

dance or scarcity of food, in different parts of the continent, must have exercised a decisive influence upon the course of Indian migrations, both as to stock families and individual nations. The people would necessarily be drawn towards the regions where subsistence was most easily procured. In such places the largest development of numbers would naturally be found. These movements would be gradual, and represent long periods of time, as well as a series of struggles for the possession of the most desirable areas. It is difficult to form even a vague conception of the actual condition of the American aborigines in the early periods of their existence. They were thinly scattered over the greater part of the continent, and held together in small bands as fishermen and hunters, by the slender ties of Indian national life. With neither metallic implements with which to cultivate the soil, nor domestic animals for pastoral purposes, they were disunited, belligerent, and mutually destructive. One of the chief marvels connected with their history is the simple fact that so many of them, as we have reason to believe existed, were able to maintain life upon resources so limited and so fluctuating. It serves to demonstrate that the arts and appliances of barbarous nations are much more effective for human maintenance than a superficial examination of them would lead us to suppose.

A comparison of the principal regions of North America, north of Mexico, will reveal material differences as to the abundance of spontaneous means of subsistence. East of the Mississippi the most valuable portion was that which bordered upon the great lakes. These inland seas produced fish in abundance. The aborigines were able to take them in the bays that indented their shores, in the streams flowing into them, and in the rivers by which they were connected in a continuous chain. Although the shore line of these lakes measures thousands of miles, there were particular districts which concentrated the advantages of each. Of these, the rapids at the outlet of Lake Superior, held by the Ojibwas,[1] the straits of Mackinaw, held at a later day by

---

[1] The Crane tribe of the Ojibwas have the following legend of their origin: "The Great Spirit created two cranes, a male and a female, in the upper world, and, having let them through an opening in the sky, directed them to seek a habitation for themselves upon the earth. They were told, when

the Otawas,[1] the Georgian bay, held by the Hurons, may be cited as examples. The south shore of Lake Ontario, and particularly the inland lake region of central New York, occupied by the Iroquois, possessed excellent fisheries. But little inferior to these were the river districts of New England, in which fish from the ocean were found at particular seasons in great abundance, superadded to which were the shell-fish of the coast. From Hudson river southward to the James, the country, for similar reasons, was favorable for Indian occupation. It required, however, south of the great lakes, the additional resources of game and of a limited agriculture to sustain the numbers found in possession of these several areas at the time of their discovery. The gulf region was inferior to those already named in the means of subsistence it afforded. It was poorly supplied with fish, except upon the coast, and with game; but these disadvantages were compensated by a genial climate, and by the greater productiveness of the garden beds, upon which the inhabitants chiefly relied. There is a wide district of country upon both sides of the Ohio river, occupying half the space between the great lakes and the gulf, which formed the poorest part of the area east of the Mississippi. It was not destitute of game, but poor in fisheries, and therefore uninhabitable without cultivation of the soil. The absence of lakes throughout this area, and the turbid character of the waters of the Mississippi, which excluded ocean-fish, furnish a sufficient reason why this entire region was

---

they had found a place which suited them, to fold their wings close to their bodies as they alighted upon the chosen spot, when they should be immediately transformed into a man and woman. The pair flew down to the earth and spent a long time in visiting different parts of the continent. They went over the prairies, and tasted the meat of the buffalo, which they found to be good, but they also came to the conclusion that it would not last. They passed over the great forests and tasted the flesh of the elk, the deer, the beaver, and of many other animals, all of which they found to be excellent; but they feared the supply of food from these sources would also fail. After making the circuit of the great lakes, and tasting the various kinds of fish with which their waters were supplied they came at last to the rapids at the outlet of Lake Superior, where they found fish in great abundance making their way through its noisy waters. They discovered that they could be taken with ease, and that the supply was inexhaustible. 'Here,' they said to each other, 'is food forever; here we will make our homes.' Near the site of Fort Brady, upon a little knoll near the foot of the rapids of the St. Mary, which is still pointed out, the cranes alighted, folding their wings as directed. The Great Spirit immediately changed them into a man and woman, who became the first parents, and the progenitors of the Crane tribe of the Ojibwas." This legend was communicated to the writer by WÄ-bé-ge-sin (White Hawk) an Ojibwa of the Crane tribe.

[1] O-tÄ'-was: *ä* as in father, *a* as in ale.

a solitude at the period of European discovery. It also tends to show that the mound-builders, who occupied this area — chiefly north of the Ohio — were Village Indians (probably from New Mexico); otherwise they would not have selected this region in preference to others.[1] Along the east side of the Mississippi, above the Ohio, and upon its tributaries, were settlements of Algonkin nations; but the occupation of this region by them

---

[1] The earthworks of the so-called mound-builders seem to remain an insoluble problem in American ethnology. The authors of *The Ancient Monuments of the Mississippi Valley* remark in their preface (p. xxxiv), that "the ancient enclosures and groups of works personally examined and surveyed are upwards of one hundred..... About two hundred mounds of all forms and sizes, and occupying every variety of position, have also been excavated." Out of ninety-five earthworks (which probably mark the sites of Indian villages) figured and described in this memoir, forty-seven are of the same type, and may be assigned unhesitatingly to the mound-builders; fourteen are emblematical earthworks, mostly in Wisconsin, and may probably be assigned to them also; but the remaining thirty-four are doubtful. They may or may not belong to the class of Village Indians who constructed the works in the Scioto valley. If to these are added the fifty or sixty emblematical earthworks in Wisconsin figured and described by Mr. Lapham, there may be one hundred and forty such works, large and small, genuine and doubtful, indicating the sites of Indian pueblos, of which something more than one hundred may have been in actual occupation at the same time. The earthworks proper must be regarded as the sites of so many pueblo villages, constructed and occupied by the mound-builders. The question then recurs, for what purpose did they raise these embankments, at an expenditure of so much labor? If a sensible practical use for these embankments can be found it will be more satisfactory to adopt the suggestion than be subject to the mischief in ethnology which comes from handing such remains over to the category of mysteries. "A large, perhaps the larger portion of these works," observe the same authors, "are regular in outline, the square and the circle predominating..... The regular works are almost invariably erected on level river terraces,..... The square and the circle often occur in combination, frequently communicating with each other" (*Ibid.*, p. 6). " Most of the circular works are small, varying from two hundred and fifty to three hundred feet in diameter, while others are a mile or more in circuit" (*Ibid.*, p. 8). The walls of these embankments are for the most part slight, varying from three to six, eight, ten, and twelve feet in height, with a base of proportionate width, as appears from numerous cross-sections furnished by the authors. But the circular embankments are the lowest.

I am tempted to submit, for what it is worth, a conjectural explanation of the uses made of these embankments, on the reasonable assumption that the mound-builders were Village Indians from New Mexico, the nearest point from which such emigrants could have come into this area; who, as such, would have been apt to choose this region, so favorable for an agricultural subsistence, though so poor in fish and game. As Village Indians they would understand cultivation, the use of adobe brick, and the art of constructing communal houses, closed in the first story on the ground for defensive reasons, and entered through the flat roof by means of ladders, with which they ascended also. If, for example, a band of Village Indians, with such habits, emigrated from dry New Mexico to the Scioto valley in Southwestern Ohio, they would find it impossible to construct houses of adobe brick able to resist the frosts and rains of that climate. They would then be compelled to use stone, which they did not; or to build their houses of poles and bark upon the level ground, and thus change their habits; or *to raise embankments of earth as a substitute for the first story*, and construct their houses of poles and bark upon this foundation. It is not improbable that these embankments were constructed for this purpose, and were lined on their tops with long pueblo houses of poles and bark, the best they were able to build. This conjecture has a basis of probability, and will bear further examination. If we examine the Scioto valley, the earthworks of which are the best specimens of the class, we find within an extent of twelve miles the remains of seven large pueblo villages, four upon the east, and three upon the west side of the river. The remains of each

was comparatively modern, and their dependence more upon fish and game. The open prairies were also solitudes.

Bancroft estimates the number of Indians east of the Mississippi and south of the chain of lakes, at the beginning of the seventeenth century, at one hundred and eighty thousand.[1] This is as large a number as our information will justify.[2] There is not the slightest reason for supposing that they ever exceeded that number.

In the central prairie area, west of the Mississippi, there is

---

of the seven consist principally of an embankment of earth, several feet high, and correspondingly broad at the base, enclosing a square or slightly irregular area, each of the four walls or embankments being about a thousand feet long, with an opening or gateway in the middle of each, and usually at each of the four angles of the square. Attached, or quite near, to five of the seven are large circular enclosures, each formed by a similar but lower embankment of earth, and enclosing a space somewhat larger than the square enclosure. The height of the walls of four of the square enclosures are given respectively at four, six, ten, and twelve feet, with bases from thirty to fifty feet; and three of the circular embankments are five and six feet high respectively. The embankments around the squares were probably the sites of their houses, since as the highest they were best adapted to the purpose. When in use they were of course higher than at present, and probably with flat tops, and sides steeply graded. In houses thus erected upon elevated embankments, some of the features of security enjoyed in a house of the New Mexican model would be realized. Indians accustomed to such houses, and to spending their time upon terraced rooftops, would be apt to resort to such embankments, if unable to construct houses of stone after finding adobe brick unsuitable, rather than to live upon the level ground. A number of these enclosures are ten hundred and eighty feet square, which gives an aggregate length of embankment of four thousand three hundred and twenty feet, without deducting the openings, each of the four embankments being divided at the centre. With each of the eight surmounted by a house about five hundred feet long and of the width of one apartment, accommodations would be furnished for a band of twelve hundred Indians, about the average number in a large pueblo. The aggregate length of the apartments in the pueblo of Chetho Kette, on the Rio de Chaco, in New Mexico, including the several stories, is four thousand seven hundred feet, about equal in accommodations with one of those on the Scioto, constructed as supposed.

With respect to the embankments enclosing circular areas, the smaller ones might have been used in the same way, and even the larger, but for two objections; first, their want of sufficient height, and second, that if so used they would furnish accommodations for from two to four thousand additional persons, making, by the addition, too large a number for an Indian village. Other uses, such as that of a cemetery, or village common, might be suggested. In some of them mounds are found raised over the remains of deceased chiefs.

If the conjecture with respect to the higher embankments enclosing squares is well founded, charcoal and ashes, the remains of fire-pits, should still be found at intervals along their summits, unless the banks have been greatly reduced by the frosts and rains of centuries.

[1] "We shall approach and perhaps exceed a just estimate of their numbers two hundred years ago, if to the various tribes of the Algonquin race we allow about ninety thousand; of the Eastern Sioux, less than three thousand; of the Iroquois, including their southern kindred, about seventeen thousand; of the Catawbas, three thousand; of the Cherokees, twelve thousand; of the Mobilian confederacies and tribes, that is, of the Chickasas, Choctas, and Muskhogees, fifty thousand; of the Uchees, one thousand; of the Natchez, four thousand: In all, it may be, not far from one hundred and eighty thousand souls." — *History of the United States*, III, 253.

[2] Consult, further, Greenhalgh's estimate, 1677, *Col. Hist. N. Y.*, III, 250; Sir William Johnson's estimate, 1763, *Ibid.*, VII, 582, and French estimate, 1736, *Ibid.*, IX, 1052.

but one district which calls for special notice. It is the country upon the head-waters of the Mississippi, which was occupied by the Sioux, or Dakotas, at the period of European colonization. For Indian occupation it is not inferior to the best of those previously described. Being a combination of forest with prairie, and within the range of the elk and the buffalo, it was an excellent game country; but its chief advantages were the lakes with which Northern Minnesota is literally crowded, which were well stocked with fish.[1] The Dakotas were without agriculture, and depended upon fish, game, and wild rice (*Zizania aquatica*, Linn.). They ranged eastward to Lake Superior, and westward to the Missouri. Their numbers when first discovered we have no means of knowing accurately. They were one of the great stocks of the Northern Indians, and stood next to the Iroquois in character and strength. The French estimate of 1736 gave them about twelve thousand.[2] They now number upwards of thirty thousand.

The Lower Missouri, from the mouth of the Platte river, was a poor country for Indian occupation. Several small nations dwelt upon its banks, and continued to maintain a bare subsistence. Above the Platte the forest is confined to the bottom lands within the bluffs, except in places near the mountains, and is interrupted for long distances even within this narrow valley. This river, from its turbid character, is also poorly supplied with fish. Buffalo abounded upon the entire course of the Missouri. They existed in millions upon the central prairies, but without the horse to give chase the Indian hunter was powerless, except by accident of position.

Canada and the Hudson-bay territory were, in the main, countries unfavorable to the sustenance of Indians. Fish and rabbits were the principal food of their aboriginal inhabitants.

---

[1] These lakes, which are from one-fourth of a mile to ten and twenty miles in length, are connected, many of them, by continuous outlets, and are still well supplied with fish. It is a lacustrine region in the full sense of the term, about one-twentieth of the surface being covered with lakes. I counted within an extent of sixty-five miles sixty-one lakes, in which number were included such only as contained clear water and were from an eighth of a mile to ten miles in length. They were within a belt not exceeding ten miles in width upon the route traveled, which was as far as the country could be seen, from the rolling character of the surface. These lakes were usually wooded upon the north and east sides, and bordered with prairie on the south and west, thus showing the prevailing direction of the winds.

[2] *Colon. Hist. New York*, ix, 1052.

The thick wood region lying around Hudson's bay, and embraced within a circuit of three hundred miles from its shores, was cold, rugged, and swampy. Nearly half of this district is under water; and yet it was thinly peopled from Lake Winnipeg to the confines of the Eskimos on the coast of Labrador. There were no centres of population within this area. North of the prairie area, or of Peace river, there is a gradual descent of a thousand miles to the Northern ocean. Its rivers and lakes are well supplied with fish, and its dwarfed forest with some kinds of game. A short hot summer visits both the Mackenzie and Yukon river districts, but for the remainder of the year it is intensely cold. Rigor of climate, however, is not an absolute barrier to Indian occupation, although unfavorable to an increase of numbers. This region has always sustained a considerable Indian population, which, within the last two centuries, through the peaceful relations preserved among them by the Hudson-Bay company and by the trade in furs, has largely increased.

In 1857 Sir George Simpson estimated the entire Indian population of British America, east of the Rocky mountains, at sixty-seven thousand souls, including the Eskimos and excluding the half-bloods at Red-river settlement. Of this number he remarks: " Twenty-five thousand live principally upon buffalo meat, and thirty thousand live principally upon fish and rabbits."[1] West of the mountains, in a territory less than one-eighth of this in extent, he estimates the number of inhabitants at eighty thousand, and the reason for this great difference will presently appear. The significance of this disproportion is increased by the fact that the development of the larger part of the population upon

---

[1] Report from the Select Committee on the Hudson-Bay Company to Parliament in 1857, p. 96.
In the Appendix to this report, at page 376, is the following estimate, made by Simpson, of the number of Indians in the Hudson-bay territory:—

Thick Wood Indians, east side of the Rocky mountains.	35,000
The Plain tribes, Blackfeet, etc.	25,000
The Esquimaux	4,000
Indians settled in Canada	3,000
Indians in British Oregon and on the northwest coast	80,000
	147,000
Whites and Half-breeds in Hudson-bay territory	11,000
Total	158,000

the prairies east of the mountains was subsequent to their possession of the horse.

The general character of the country east of the Rocky mountains and north of New Mexico has now been sufficiently set forth to indicate the sections where a considerable population was developed, and the basis upon which it was sustained.

West of the mountains there is one particular district which rises in importance above all others upon the continent. On the northwest coast there is a region of ample extent, having Puget's sound as its centre on the Pacific, and the valleys of the Columbia and Frazer's rivers within its circumference, which combined so singularly all the advantages of the mountain, the forest, the prairie, and the sea coast as to give it a superiority over every other region either of North or South America. Within a radius of five hundred miles from the head of this sound — from the Umpqua river on the south to Queen Charlotte's sound on the north, and from the sea coast to the western slopes of the Rocky mountains — this country, embracing the greater part of the drainage of the two rivers before named, was singularly well supplied at the time of its discovery with the requisites for the subsistence of Indian tribes. A mild and genial climate was added to its other advantages. In the amount and variety of the means of subsistence spontaneously furnished, it had no parallel in any part of the earth. It deserves a somewhat minute examination from the relation in which, by reason of this fact, it stood to the remainder of the continent.

A combination of forest and prairie rendered it an excellent game country, although it was not entered by the buffalo. Elk, bear, deer, mountain sheep, the rabbit, and the beaver were abundant, and as they found refuge in the fastnesses of the mountains or on the open prairies their extermination was impossible. With water and land fowls of different species the region was well supplied, together with wild fruits and berries of various kinds. In the kamash (kă'-mash) root, from which they prepared a species of bread, and which was found in inexhaustible supplies upon the prairies, they possessed a resource of no small importance, particularly in seasons of scarcity.[1] Other bread roots were also found in this area, such as the cayuse and biscuit, and likewise a species of edible black moss,[2] each of which entered more or less into the subsistence of the aborigines. In these several respects this region was not greatly superior to some of those previously named. The signal advantages which it possessed were its inexhaustible salmon and shell fisheries. From these sources, and particularly from the first, arose that superabundance of food which tended to render this area the nursery of the Indian family. Along the inlets, bays, and islands of Puget's sound, which has a shore line of fifteen hundred miles, and in the connecting waters of the gulf of Georgia, oysters and clams are found in extensive beds, and at low tide are gathered with facility. The neighboring Indians not only subsisted upon

[1] The kamash is a white bulbous root resembling the onion. It has a blue flower, and ripens in June, in which month it is gathered. In Oregon and Washington it is found in abundance, literally covering, when in flower, some of the prairies. The kamash is first baked, then formed into cakes and dried in the sun and air, after which it will keep for a year. It is boiled with meat and also eaten alone. For the purpose of baking they make a cavity in the ground large enough to hold ten and even twenty bushels of the kamash, and line it with pebble stones. After it is filled to the level of the surface with kamash roots, a covering of pebble stones is placed over the mass, then a second covering of grass, upon which a hearth is formed of clay. Upon this hearth a fire is made, and continued for about seventy hours, the time required for baking. If the fire eats through the hearth, which is shown by a rise of steam from the kamash, the place is again covered with mortar. When the kamash is taken out it is black, soft, and very sweet to the taste. It is then made into cakes and dried, after which it is ready for use. The above particulars were communicated to the writer by Father De Smet, S. J., the distinguished Oregon missionary. Governor Stephen thus refers to this root: "The kamash root forms an important article of food when other supplies fail" (*Pres. Mess. and Docs.* 1854-55, pt. 1, p. 423); and George Gibbs, Esq., remarks: "The Skagits have a natural resource in their camash, which grows abundantly on the prairies of Whitby's Island..... The camash, it is worth mentioning, improves very much by cultivation, and it is said to attain the size of a hen's egg in land that has been ploughed" (*Explorations for a Railroad Route*, etc., I, 4, 33).

[2] This moss grows abundantly as a parasite on the pine trees of Oregon and Washington, some of which will yield several bushels. It is gathered and washed, after which it is formed into balls, and baked in ovens in the same manner as the kamash, the baking requiring about forty-eight hours. It comes out in a fluid state, and is much like liquorice to the taste. After drying it in the sun they cut it into cakes and put it aside for use. They also mix it with the kamash after both are cooked, and let them harden together. When they are hardened separately they are pounded together and made into a kind of cheese. The kamash is highly nutritious; the moss only moderately so. The biscuit root yields a white flour when pulverized, and is eaten dry. Besides these they have a black edible root called the tobacco root, and the inner bark of a species of pine, which is sweet in flavor and used as food. There is a small oak, both in the Rocky and Cascade mountains, which yields plentifully an acorn of which they make a palatable and nutritious soup. The acorns are gathered in bags holding about eighty pounds, and buried in the sand. After a sufficient time they are taken up, the shells are removed, and the kernels dried and pounded into flour. From this flour the soup is made.

them at certain seasons, but dried them on strings for exchange with inland inhabitants and for winter use.[1] It was the salmon fisheries, however, that gave to this region its preëminence. The salmon were not confined to the bays upon the coast, but they entered all the rivers of the country, and penetrated the recesses of the mountains as far as the tributary streams were sufficient in volume to admit their passage. Besides the annual run of the Chinook salmon, some species of this fish were found in the Columbia at all seasons of the year. The testimony of all observers is the same with respect to their marvelous abundance, their large size, and their excellent quality. Dr. Suklcy, a surgeon in the United States army, thus remaks: "They come up annually in great numbers on their way to the head-waters of the Columbia. The Indians, as before stated, all collect in the neighborhood of these and other falls, where they riot in feasting on their captured prey. They kill hundreds and thousands of these fish by spearing. The myriads of salmon that ascend the rivers of the Pacific coast are almost incredible. In many places the waters appear alive with them, and the shores are thickly lined with the dead and dying fish...... The Columbia river salmon weigh from six to forty pounds. The Indians along the river collect during the summer the fish which they want for winter use; these are split open and the bones removed, after which they are scarified in various directions, and then hung up for a short time in the smoke of a fire. They are then hung on poles or the branches of trees, where they are freely exposed to the wind. In a month they become perfectly dry, and are then housed in small storehouses.... Salmon thus dried form the

---

[1] The Indians of Queen Charlotte's island, as late as the year 1800, were accustomed to go down by sea to Vancouver's island and spend the winter there to benefit by these shell-fisheries. They went in red-wood canoes, each large enough to carry fifty persons, and safe for miles out at sea. Mr. Gibbs remarks that "the tribes living upon the eastern shore possess also territory upon the islands, and their usual custom is to resort to them at the end of the salmon season, that is, about the middle of November. It is there that they find the greatest supply of shell-fish, which form a large part of their winter stock, and which they dry both for their own use and for sale to those of the interior" (*Explorations, etc.*, I, 432). Speaking of the Chinooks, at the mouth of the Cowlitz, the same writer remarks: "It was really the principal seat of the Chinooks proper, who resorted to the Columbia mostly for their spring salmon, while they dug their clams and procured their winter supplies on the bay. It formed, in fact, a perfect Indian paradise in its adaptation to canoe travel and the abundance of scale and shell fish which it furnished" (*Ibid*, I, 427). *Vide* also p. 408, for an account of the mussel-shell beds on the Yakima.

principal food of the natives during the winter."[1] He elsewhere observes: "The salmon of these waters, unlike those of other parts of the world, do not take the hook, and strange as it seems, they are said never to stop searching after the source of the stream they are in. Their march is always ahead until they spawn and die; they never return to the sea. This seems to be the general opinion of the people with whom I have conversed." Mr. Gibbs, before mentioned, in speaking of the salmon-fisheries of the Yakima river, one of the tributaries of the Columbia, says: "Besides the fisheries at the Dalles, the Yakimas have others on their river, up which the salmon run without interruption far into the mountains. On the main fork in particular they penetrate to Lake Kitchelus, at the very foot of the dividing ridge. In addition to the different kinds of salmon proper, they have also the salmon-trout, two varieties of the speckled trout — the red and black spotted, both of them growing to a large size — and some other species of fresh-water fish. The salmon they take in wears and cast-nets. The wears are constructed, with considerable skill, upon horizontal spars and supported by tripods of strong poles erected at short distances apart, two of the legs pointing up stream and one supporting them below. There are several of these wears on the main river, fifty or sixty yards in length. The cast-net is managed by two men in a canoe, one of whom extends it with a pole and the other manages the rope."[2] Elsewhere the same writer remarks: "The fishery at the Kettle falls is one of the most important on the river; and the arrangements of the Indians, in the shape of drying-scaffolds and storehouses, are on a corresponding scale. They take the fish by suspending immense baskets upon poles beneath the [water as] traps, into which the salmon spring."[3]

Father De Smet described to the writer this method of basket-

---

[1] *Explorations for a Railroad Route, etc., to the Pacific*, I, 299.

[2] *Ibid.*, p. 407. At the Sault Ste. Marie, the Ojibwas use a scoop-net to take white-fish in the rapids. Two men push out into the stream in a birch-bark canoe, one at the stern to manage the boat with a pole and force it up the rapid, while the other, standing at the bow, takes the fish by plunging the net to the bottom and bagging them as they attempt to run up the rapids. The pole to which the net is attached is about ten feet long. This method is highly successful.

[3] *Explorations for a Railroad Route, etc., to the Pacific*, I, 413.

fishing, which he had frequently witnessed at these falls. The basket is made of willow, from fifteen to twenty feet long, five or six wide, and about four feet deep, with a high back upon one side, which is designed to rise above the surface of the water. A stick of timber is firmly anchored in the rocks below the falls, extending out over the stream twenty or thirty feet. To this the basket is suspended, and so far submerged as to leave the back just above the water up stream, while the opposite side is several inches below the surface of the water, and down stream. The ascending salmon rise up the side of the basket and spring into it, where they are held, their passage up being arrested by the high back; and as they never turn their heads down the current they are retained securely. After the basket in this manner is well filled, a man descends into it and hands out the fish. Two hundred salmon, weighing from six to forty pounds each, have been caught in this way in a few hours. They are also speared in great numbers. It was a common occurrence, he remarked, to take three thousand salmon in a day, since there was no limit to their numbers, and a whole band of Indians were engaged in the work. The fish were divided equally among the women each day, the number of females in each family forming the basis of distribution. He further observed that he once spent thirty days at these falls, in the fishing season, with the Kootenays, and received for his share of the fish taken a sufficient quantity, when dried, to load thirty pack mules.[1] These falls are fifteen feet high, but they present no barrier to the passage of the salmon up the river. He had often seen them leap these falls in great numbers; in doing which they keep near the surface of the descending water, and shoot themselves up at one dart, and then continue their course. It is simply swimming up at a faster rate than the water falls. In these attempts they often fail, and are thrown back into the stream. They ascend to the head waters of the Columbia and its tributaries, filling the small streams, where, worn out and exhausted, they perish in myriads.

---

[1] The natives also prepare fish pemmican from the salmon. After it is dried they pulverize it and mix it with fish oil, and then form it into cakes. It will not, however, keep as long in this form as when dried.

They are not found in Clarke's river, however, above the great falls.

Lewis and Clarke, the first explorers of the Columbia, make frequent reference to the salmon fisheries, the methods by which the fish were taken, and their unlimited numbers. "The multitudes of this fish," one of them remarks, "are almost inconceivable. The water is so clear that they can readily be seen at fifteen or twenty feet, but at this season [October, 1805] they float in such quantities down the stream, and are drifted ashore, that the Indians have only to collect, split, and dry them on scaffolds. . . . . . The Indians assured me by signs that they often used dried fish as fuel for the common occasions of cooking."[1] Farther on they write: "At the distance [of] two miles below [on the Columbia] are five new huts, the inhabitants of which are all engaged in drying fish, and some of them in their canoes killing fish with gigs; opposite to this establishment is a small island in a bend towards the right, on which there were such quantities of fish that we counted twenty stacks of dried and pounded salmon."[2] These stacks are subsequently explained as follows: "When it [the fish] is sufficiently dried it is pounded fine between two stones till it is pulverized, and is then placed in a basket about two feet long [deep] and one in diameter, neatly made of grass and rushes, and lined with the skin of a salmon, stretched and dried for the purpose. Here they are pressed down as hard as possible, and the top covered with skins of fish, which are secured by cords through the holes of the basket. The baskets are then placed in some dry situation, the corded part upwards, seven being usually placed as close as they can be put together, and five on the top of them. The whole are then wrapped in mats, made fast by cords, over which mats are again thrown. Twelve of these baskets, each of which contains from ninety to one hundred pounds, form a stack."[3] Twenty such stacks would contain about twenty-four thousand pounds of dried fish.[4]

---

[1] *Travels, etc., to the Pacific Ocean*, London ed., quarto, 1814, p.353.   [2] *Ibid.*, p. 363.
[3] *Travels, etc., to the Pacific Ocean*, p. 365.
[4] Irving, in his *Bonneville* (p. 385), gives an account of the salmon fisheries of Snake river, one of

The Columbia-river Indians changed their residences at the different seasons of the year, much in the same manner as the aborigines east of the Mississippi at the period when they were first visited by Europeans. The Iroquois, for example, after planting their garden beds in the spring, most of them, left their villages for their different fishing encampments, to return again in midsummer when the corn was in the green ear. In the autumn, and again in the winter, parties went out upon the autumn and winter hunts, to return before winter and spring. Lewis and Clarke describe the routine of the Columbia river Indians at the period of their visit, by saying that "the inhabitants of the Columbia plains, after having passed the winter near the mountains, come down as soon as the snow has left the valleys, and are occupied in collecting and drying roots till about the month of May. Then they crowd the river, and, fixing themselves on its north side to avoid the incursions of the Snake Indians, continue fishing until about the first of September, when the salmon are no longer fit for use. They then bury their fish and return to the plains, where they remain gathering quamash till the snow obliges them to desist. They then come back to the Columbia, and, taking their store of fish, retire to the foot of the mountains and along the creeks which supply timber for their houses, and pass the winter in hunting deer and

---

the tributaries of the Columbia, as follows: "They take these fish in great quantities and without the least difficulty, simply taking them out of the water with their hands, as they flounder and struggle in the numerous long shoals of the principal streams. At the time the traveler passed over these prairies, some of the narrow deep streams by which they were traversed were completely choked with salmon, which they took in great numbers. The wolves and bears frequent these streams at this season to avail themselves of these great fisheries." And again on page 396: "It was on the 20th of October when they found themselves once more on this noted stream. The Shoshonees, whom they had met with in such scanty numbers on their journey down the river, now absolutely thronged its banks, to profit by the abundance of salmon and to lay up a stock of winter provisions. Scaffoldings were everywhere erected, and immense quantities of fish drying upon them. In some places the shores were completely covered with a stratum of dead salmon, exhausted in ascending the river, or destroyed at the falls — the fetid odor of which tainted the air."

In the rivers of Maine the same thing is occasionally witnessed, where wagon loads of fish are sometimes found dead upon the banks, and carried away for manure. This is said to be occasioned by stampedes or panics among the fish themselves, when moving in large numbers up stream and encountering some obstruction like shoal water — the momentum of those below crowding those above into a mass, and forcing them finally upon the land, where they remain to perish. In like manner the beds of dead salmon found upon the tributaries of the Columbia are probably to be explained.

elk, which, with the aid of their fish, enables them to subsist till in the spring they resume the circle of their employments."[1]

Another prominent characteristic of this region is the mildness of the climate as compared with that upon the same parallels on the Atlantic coast. It is important, since it rendered less clothing and less subsistence necessary, and thus favored an increase of numbers. The mean temperature for spring ranges from 45° to 50°; for summer, from 60° to 65°; for autumn, from 50° to 52°; and for winter, from 35° to 40°; giving a mean temperature for the year ranging from 50° to $52\frac{1}{2}$°. The annual precipitation varied from thirty to sixty inches in different parts of the area.[2]

The superior advantages which abundance and variety of food and fineness of climate gave to this region over every other part of North or South America cannot fail to arrest attention. Its superiority for Indian occupation is created in the main by the concurrence of a good climate with the possession of the most bountiful and widely distributed fisheries to be found in any part of the earth. These two elements, superadded to other advantages not surpassed if they are equalled elsewhere, must have exercised a potent influence upon population. From the superabundance of the means of subsistence, which belongs to this region above every other already described, or remaining to be noticed, the inference arises that this area would develop a surplus of population from age to age; and that it would become permanently the point of departure of migrations to different parts of the continent. The facts are sufficient to raise a presumption that the valley of the Columbia was the region from which both North and South America were peopled in the first instance, and afterwards resupplied with inhabitants.

A larger population would be expected in this area than in any other of equal extent, with the exception of districts where agriculture was the basis of subsistence; and the population was, in fact, denser, but the excess was not large. The reason must be sought in the nature of the institutions of the Indians, which

---

[1] *Travels, etc., to the Pacific Ocean*, p. 444.
[2] Blodgett's *Climatology of the United States; Isothermal and Hyetal Charts*.

precluded the formation of a state. They were found subdivided into a large number of petty nations, speaking dialects of several different stock languages, which are more numerous in this area than in any other of equal extent in North America, thus affording decisive evidence of the great antiquity of its occupation. It also shows that no single nation had been able to consolidate these several nations into one in this, any more than in other parts of the continent. The constant tendency was to disintegration, subdivision, and displacement. This tendency is inherent in the institutions of barbarous ages, and continues in force until the institutions of pastoral or advanced agricultural life supplant them. Confederacies of nations serve in some measure to counteract these results; but none existed, of which a knowledge is preserved, in the valley of the Columbia.

The first estimate of the number of the Indians in that region was made by Lewis and Clarke, in 1805. It included all the nations upon the Columbia and its tributaries of which he obtained knowledge, those upon Puget's sound, and those in the southern part of British Columbia. They were estimated in the aggregate at eighty thousand souls, which was probably an unexaggerated estimate. In 1857, the Indian population in British America, west of the Rocky mountains, was estimated, as has been stated, at eighty thousand. This included the Louchoux or Kutchin (Kŭ-tchin),[1] of the Yukon and Peel rivers,[2] and some small bands scattered along the narrow belt of land between the Russian possessions and the Rocky mountains, north of the fifty-fourth parallel of latitude. The bulk of these Indians were south of this line, and within the area described. Vancouver's and Queen Charlotte's islands and the valley of Frazer's river were well adapted to Indian occupation, and undoubtedly, in 1805, sustained a very considerable Indian population. For that part of the area not covered by the estimate of Lewis and Clarke, about fifty thousand may be added, which would give a much larger aggregate number than was found in any other region of equal extent north of Mexico.

[1] ŭ as *oo* in *food*.

[2] Mr. Murray, before mentioned, who established the first trading-post on the Yukon, informed the writer, in 1861, that this nation numbered from three to four thousand.

California, which embraces a large area, possessed only ordinary advantages for the support of an Indian population. In 1802, the Spanish missionaries estimated the number of Indians at thirty-two thousand and a fraction over; and in 1852 the secretary of state of California estimated them at about the same number.[1]

The Roving and partially Village Indians have now been sufficiently considered with respect to their centres of population, their means of subsistence, and their numbers. It remains to notice briefly the strictly Village Indians, who inhabited the comparatively small area from New Mexico to the isthmus of Panama. Portions of this area were occupied by Roving Indians, other portions by partially Village Indians, and still other portions were either solitudes or neutral grounds separating hostile nations. The largest development of numbers was in and around the valley of Mexico, and in Yucatan and Guatemala. A dense and unsubdued forest overspread the greater part of Central America, and Mexico was, in the main, a forest country. Since the Village Indians depended upon agricultural subsistence, and occupied a section of the continent poorly supplied with fish and game, inquiry should be directed to the nature and extent of their agriculture. If the degree of its productiveness could be ascertained, it might afford means of ascertaining their probable numbers, and whether it secured to them any positive advantages over the barbarous nations in a contest for the mastery of the continent. Before considering the subject of Indian agriculture, the geographical location of the several nations of Village Indians should be noticed.

Of New Mexico they were the chief possessors, occupying the valley of the Rio Grande and its tributaries, and the valleys of the eastern and southern tributaries of the Colorado. They were found, in 1540, living in great communal houses constructed of stone or of adobe brick, and several stories high. They dwelt not in single houses with one family in each, nor in many houses grouped together, but in one great house constructed upon a definite model, containing two hundred apartments, more or less,

---

[1] *President's Message and Documents*, 1855-56, pt. I, p. 575, and note.

and large enough for an entire band or nation. In rare cases several such houses were grouped together, as at Zuñi; but usually they were situated a mile or more apart, in the same valley, the different bands being leagued together for mutual defence where they spoke the same dialect, or dialects of the same stock language. Castañeda, who accompanied the expedition of Coronado to New Mexico, in 1540–1542, estimated the population of the fourteen villages of Cibola and Tucayan at four thousand men (probably warriors) and that of the numerous villages on and near the Rio Grande and its tributaries at sixteen thousand souls — which would give an aggregate of about fifty thousand Village Indians.[1]

From New Mexico southward for about eight hundred miles the country was unfavorable to Indian occupation. As it was thinly peopled, probably its inhabitants never came into prominent notice. But thence southward to the isthmus the country was more favorable to a population depending upon agriculture for sustenance. With a tropical climate, relieved by table-lands, the disadvantage of the absence of fisheries and of the larger forest-animals was more than counterbalanced by increased agricultural production, and by wild fruits and useful plants. These advantages were again lessened by geographical location and contracted areas. The drift of population seems to have been down the mountain chains to the valley of Mexico, and thence toward the isthmus, the only means of exit from the northern half of the continent. Any nation attempting to hold the table lands of Mexico, forming as they do a natural gateway to the distant south, must have been able to repel and turn back this flow of migrating bands, or have been swept away by the current. Moreover, barbarous nations are strongly attracted to the seats of even partial civilization for purposes of rapine and plunder: witness the continuous assaults of the Apaches and Navajos, within the last hundred years, upon the Village Indians of New Mexico, and the ruined and abandoned pueblos within that area. History furnishes some evidence tending to show that no nation, previous to the Aztec, had been able to hold per-

---
[1] *Coll. Ternaux-Compans*, vol. IX.

manently the table-land of Mexico, or to develop a population upon the basis of agriculture, able to maintain itself there, much less to extend its power and influence northward. The Toltecs, of whose previous occupation, advancement in civilization, and retirement from the valley we have some information, doubtless repeated the experience of nation after nation which had preceded them. At the time of the Spanish conquest the Aztecs had been dominant in the valley about two hundred years, and coming, like their predecessors, from the north, they had neither extended their conquests, nor planted a colony north of the borders of the valley. On the contrary, they were confronted by hostile and independent nations on the west, northwest, northeast, and east sides; that is, upon all sides except the southwest, south, and southeast, in which latter directions they had extended their authority over the more feeble portion of the southern Village Indians.

With respect to the numbers and the social and civil condition of the Village Indians of Mexico and Central America at the time of the conquest, our information is very far from satisfactory. From the outset the phenomena of their civilization appear to have been to the invaders an enigma of marvelous interest; but we have lost the principal facts necessary for its elucidation, in gaining volumes of romance.

At that period the areas above named were occupied by forty petty nations — more or less — speaking dialects of several different stock languages, living chiefly in villages, and depending upon agriculture for a subsistence. Their villages were constructed in eligible situations upon the margins of lakes, the banks of rivers and streams, and sometimes in positions of natural strength. Since their agriculture was confined to garden beds around and near their villages, the greater portion of these countries was a wilderness without inhabitants, except as it was traversed by hunting parties or roving bands. Each nation, or confederacy of nations, was under its own chiefs, and governed in accordance with those usages and customs which were the common inheritance of the Indian race. The evidence that any considerable number of these nations were consolidated into a state is not satisfactory. In other words, it cannot be affirmed that any number of these nations speaking different stock languages had become absorbed into one national organization, with common laws, and one executive government to which they all acknowledged allegiance and from which they received protection. The Aztec confederacy, the dominant Indian power of the period, had subdued the nations south of the valley, in a westerly and southerly direction to the Pacific, southeasterly to Guatemala, Yucatan, and the gulf of Mexico, and along the western shores of the gulf near Vera Cruz; and they are said to have been the terror of surrounding nations, from their confederate organization, their numbers, and their sanguinary character. The nations which they had conquered were subjected to tribute, and held in the nominal connection which its payment implies; but the Aztecs and their confederates did not spread over the territories of these nations, nor attempt to impose upon them either their language, their customs, or their direct civil administration. At least there is no satisfactory evidence that they did. Traces are found among these nations of the three stages of political organization common among the northern Indians: first, the tribe, composed of persons of the same immediate descent; second, the nation, consisting of several tribes intermingled by marriage and speaking the same dialect; and lastly, the confederacy of nations speaking dialects of the same stock language. Most of them appear to have been in the second stage, organized into nations; but a portion of them had reached the third, of which the Aztec, the Tlascalan, and perhaps the Cholulan and Michuacan confederacies are examples. With respect to the tribal organization, the evidence is fragmentary. Among the Aztecs the descent of the office of chief from brother to brother, or from uncle to nephew, can be explained only by the hypothesis of a division into tribes, with descent limited to the female line, as among the Iroquois.[1]

The Aztec confederacy embraced the Aztecs, Tezcucans, and Tlacopans,[2] who spoke either the same, or dialects of the same

---

[1] *League of the Iroquois*, p. 87.

[2] There is some uncertainty concerning the correct name of the third nation. Tlacopan, on the west side of the lake, was the name of the pueblo of the Tepanecans, one of the seven nations who "came from the far countries which lie toward the north, ... to people the land of Mexico" (Joseph Acosta, *Nat. and Mor. Hist. East and West Indies*, Lond. ed. 1604, Grimstone's Trans. p. 500). The latter would seem to be the correct name of this nation.

language, and occupied, in conjunction with other villagers of kindred descent, the valley of Mexico. It is not improbable that the Chalcans, and other villagers who maintained a distinctive name, were independent members of the confederacy. The valley is oval in form, being longest from north to south, and is about one hundred and twenty miles in circuit. A large portion of it is covered with lakes. It is surrounded by a series of hills, one rising above the other, with depressions between, encompassing the valley with a mountain barrier. Within it the nations just named resided at the time of the Spanish conquest, in about thirty pueblo villages, more or less. There is no evidence that any considerable portion of the confederates resided outside of the valley and the adjacent hill-slopes; but, on the contrary, there is satisfactory evidence that the remainder of modern Mexico was then occupied by nations who spoke stock languages different from the Aztec, and most of whom were independent of the Aztec power. This fact has a material bearing upon the probable numbers of the people thus confederated. Any estimate here must be purely conjectural. There are no materials from which an approximation to accuracy can be made. There is no doubt that a much larger population was found in particular districts of Mexico and Central America than in any other equal area in North America, and that the valley of Mexico contained a larger number of people than any other district of equal extent. But there is no ground for reckoning this population by millions;[1] a much smaller number would have exhausted the resources of the country as developed by Indian agriculture. In the

---

[1] It is a common statement, running through most of the histories of the conquest, that the pueblo of Mexico contained *sixty thousand houses*. Zuazo, who visited Mexico, in 1521, cited by Prescott (*Conquest of Mexico*, II, 112, note), wrote *sixty thousand inhabitants*; the Anonymous Conqueror, "sixty thousand fires;" but Gomara and Martyr wrote *sixty thousand houses*, and the last has since been steadily repeated by Clavigero (*Hist. of Mexico*, Phila. ed. 1817, II, 360); by Herrera (*Hist. of America*, Lond. ed. 1725, II, 360); and by Prescott (*Conquest*, etc., II, 112). Solis says *sixty thousand families* (*Hist. Conquest of Mexico*, Lond. ed. 1738, I, 399). Torquemada, cited by Clavigero (*Ibid.*, II, 360, note) increases the number to *one hundred and twenty thousand houses*. There cannot be a reasonable doubt that the houses of the Aztecs were most of them great communal edifices like those in New Mexico, some of them large enough to accommodate a thousand or more people. This magnifies the exaggeration to an impossibility. If these later writers had any real knowledge of the subject, it must be supposed that they meant apartments, instead of houses, treating each great house as a block of houses, and estimating the number of rooms. Zuazo's estimate is probably the nearest to the truth.

valley of Mexico, excluding the lakes, and including a liberal belt of surrounding hills, there may be fifteen hundred square miles of land. If we allow one hundred and seventy inhabitants to the square mile, which is double the average number to the square mile in the state of New York, it would give to the nations of the valley two hundred and fifty-five thousand souls. It is difficult to see how so large an estimate can be sustained.

With respect to the nations and languages of Mexico, modern research has advanced but little beyond the sketch of Clavigero, except in relation to the grammatical structure of some of these languages. It will be sufficient to follow his authority for the names and locations of the principal remaining nations. He enumerates fourteen stock languages in Mexico and Yucatan.[1]

The most prominent Indian nations cotemporary with the Aztecs were the Chichemecs, who occupied the country on the northwest border of the valley, and ranged westward well towards the Pacific. They were non-agricultural and independent of the Aztec confederacy.[2] South of them were the Otomies, who for the most part were non-agricultural and independent. A portion of them near the valley appear to have been subdued by the Aztecs. These nations spoke different languages. South of the Otomies and immediately west of the valley of Mexico were the Michuacans, who occupied a large area extending towards the Pacific. They spoke the Tarasca language, and were independent of the Aztecs. Southwest of the valley, and bordering upon it, were the tributary Matlatzincas, an inconsiderable people, who spoke a language of the same name, and occupied, with a portion of the Otomies, the valley of Talocan. On the northeast of the valley, and about eighty miles distant, were the Meztitlans, who spoke a dialect of the Aztec, but were independent. East of the latter, and ranging to the gulf of Mexico, in the region around Tampico, were the Huastecas, who spoke the Huastec language, and were inde-

---

[1] *History of Mexico*, III, 371.

[2] The ancient and first inhabitants of New Spain were men very barbarous and savage, which lived only by hunting; for this reason they were called Chichemecas. They neither sow nor till the ground (Acosta, *Nat. and Mor. Hist.*, etc., p. 497). Although Acosta makes this a general name for the Roving Indians in Mexico, there was a distinct nation of this name in the region referred to.

pendent. South of them, and ranging along the gulf as far as Vera Cruz, were the Totonacs, who spoke the language of the same name, and acknowledged the supremacy of the Aztec confederacy. Between them and the valley of Mexico, but confined to an area of moderate dimensions, were the sturdy Tlascalans, also independent. Southwest of them were the Cholulans, supposed to have been a subdivision of the Tlascalans. Whether the Tlascalan was an independent stock language is not ascertained. It is asserted that the Cholulans were subdued by the Aztecs shortly before the Spanish conquest; but Clavigero places them in the list of independent republics.[1] In the areas south of the several nations named, between the valley of Mexico and the Pacific, and extending eastward to Guatemala and Yucatan, were several other nations, of whom the names and locations are preserved, and but little besides. Among them were the Mixtecas and Zapotecas, who spoke the Mixtec and Zapotec languages; the Chinantecas, Mazatecas, Tlahuicas, Cohuicas, Popolocas, and several others scarcely needing enumeration — all supposed to have been tributary to the Aztec confederacy.[2] Whether these Village Indians were permanently subjugated, and acknowledged their dependence by paying periodical tribute, or whether their submission ended with the foray that enforced the tribute, we are not precisely informed.

The Village Indians of Yucatan and Guatemala were, probably, the highest of the class in North America, as well as the oldest in their civilization. They possessed some advantage in their sheltered position behind the gulf of Mexico, and off the great highway of migration to South America, toward which the movements of the northern Indians tended to drive the fragmentary and broken nations. The remains of their pueblos in ruins bear testimony to their higher development. Their agriculture must have been more efficient, to overcome the superior activity of the forces of nature in a tropical climate. "The

---

[1] *History of Mexico*, I, 6.

[2] Doña Marina, the interpreter of Cortes, was born in the province of Coatzacualco, on the gulf of Mexico, near the Tabasco river, and spoke a dialect of the Aztec language. "Doña Marina understood the language of Guacacualco and Mexico, which is one and the same" (Bernal Diaz, *True Hist. Conq. of Mexico*, London ed. 1803, I, 76).

kingdom of Yucatan," says Las Casas, bishop of Chiapa, who wrote in 1539 the relation from which we quote, " contained a prodigious number of people; the air of the country is very temperate and pleasant; it has great plenty of fruits, and all the necessaries of life; it exceeds Mexico itself in fertility. . . . . The inhabitants of it are more polite, more civilized, and better civilized in morals and in what belongs to the good order of societies, than the rest of the Indians. There is a remarkable prudence and justness of mind in them, which is not to be found in others."[1] And Herrera remarks to nearly the same effect: These people were then found living together very politely in towns, kept very clean, without any ill weeds growing about, but with fruit-trees orderly planted. Their temples were in the midst of their towns, and near to them the houses of their prime men and priests, those of the commonalty being farther off; and the common wells were in the squares or market places; and the reason of their being so close together was because of the wars which exposed them to the danger of being taken, sold, and sacrificed; but the wars of the Spaniards made them disperse."[2] From the references of Las Casas to the number and location of the pueblo villages in Yucatan and Guatemala, it is to be inferred that they were numerous, and, when constructed upon the banks of rivers, were so near together as to be in sight of each other, in some cases, for miles together. These tribes seem to have followed precisely the same method of building as the Village Indians of New Mexico.

Within a few years after the conquest of Mexico the pueblo villages of Yucatan, Guatemala, and Honduras were ravaged by military adventurers, and the people driven from their pueblos into the forests. The Spaniards destroyed in a few years a higher civilization than they substituted in its place. "The pretence," says Las Casas, "of subjecting the Indians to the government of Spain is only made to carry on the design of sub-

---

[1] *An Account of The first Voyages and Discoveries made by the Spaniards in America*, London ed. 1699, p. 59.

[2] *Herrera*, IV, 108.

jecting them to the dominion of private men, who make them all their slaves."[1]

The Maya language was spoken in Yucatan; the Quiche, Poconchi, and some other languages in Guatemala; and the Chontal in Nicaragua. Oviedo, who was in the last-named province in 1526, states that there were five languages spoken there, of which the one most extensively used was the same as the Aztec.[2]

It is not improbable that the nations of Mexico and Central America above enumerated were so described on the ground of a common language, and that some of them were subdivided into nations speaking dialects of the same stock language. The continuity of territorial possession is usually well preserved by nations of the same speech; but this did not arrest the inevitable tendency to disintegration inseparable from their institutions. The number of nations must be measured by dialects, and not by stock languages. It is further probable that each group of pueblos occupied by people speaking the same dialect was independent, except as several such groups were confederated for mutual protection. In strictly village life the tendency to disruption was even greater than in the non-stationary condition; and consequently the Village Indians, although more numerous in equal areas, were probably more disunited and less efficient and warlike than the barbarous nations.

Having now considered the most important districts of North America with reference to the means of subsistence which they respectively afforded, and compared the particular advantages of each with such statistics of actual population, except as to the Village Indians, as our limited information furnishes, inquiry should next be made into the nature and extent of Indian agriculture; and this for the purpose of ascertaining whether a sub-

---

[1] *Account of the first Voyages*, etc., p. 119. Elsewhere he quotes from the letter of the bishop of St. Martha to the king, as follows: "To redress the grievances of this province, it ought to be delivered from the tyranny of those who ravage it, and committed to the care of persons of integrity, who will treat the inhabitants with more kindness and humanity; for if it be left to the mercy of the governors, who commit all sorts of outrages with impunity, the province will be destroyed in a very short time" (p. 61). He also says, "Fourscore towns and villages at least were burned in the kingdom of Xalisco" (p. 51). The good bishop's numbers must be received with caution.

[2] *Trans. Am. Ethn. Soc.*, I, 7.

sistence derived from agriculture, or one procured by fishing and the chase, tended to the more rapid production of a surplus population to be sent forth as emigrants into other areas.

Indian agriculture was based upon one cereal, Indian corn, and upon three indigenous plants, the bean, the squash and tobacco. To these, cotton, a species of pepper, and of onion, were added in some areas. The Aztecs, and some of the nations south of them, had, without cultivation, several useful fruits and plants, such as cocoa — from which they prepared chocolate — the banana, and the maguey. The art of cultivating the ground doubtless sprang up as a happy accident, after the Indians had overspread North America and discovered these "gifts of the Great Spirit to the red man." Where it originated it is impossible to ascertain, though one may reasonably conjecture that it must have been in a tropical climate, in some moist, hot region, where corn is most prolific and was probably indigenous. Its introduction was a great event in the primitive history of the Indians. Without agriculture they could not have reached the second stage of their development, namely, that of permanent villagers. After the art of cultivating corn was acquired, agriculture would spread with the people; but it would not be restricted to the lines covered by their migrations. In many fortuitous ways it might be transferred from nation to nation by the opportunities of aboriginal life. The art spread, in the course of time, throughout Central America, Mexico, and the West India islands. Northward it was carried, it must be supposed, first into New Mexico, and thence to the Mississippi valley, whence it spread from the gulf of Mexico to the chain of lakes and as far east as the Kennebec river. The Hurons introduced it on the Georgian bay of Lake Huron, the Shiyans on the river of that name, a tributary of the Red river of the north, and the Minnitarees on the Upper Missouri. It was unknown in all other parts of North America, and confined to mere patches of land within the areas named.

Indian agriculture was rude, and of moderate productiveness. It was limited to garden beds upon alluvial soils, where the climate was moist, and to irrigated garden beds where it was dry. This kind of cultivation is the most productive in equal areas, and with irrigation is immensely productive; but there was a drawback in the smallness of the areas that could be cultivated. The thought of subduing the forest never entered the Indian mind. To clear it was impossible without metallic implements, and field agriculture equally impossible without the horse or ox and the plough, neither of which were known to the American aborigines. They cultivated therefore only small patches of alluvial land upon the margins of rivers and lakes, and such shreds of prairie as they were able to dig over, and such bottom lands, in the dry regions, as they were able to irrigate by means of canals. But little is known of their implements for horticulture (for it was horticulture, rather than agriculture, which they practiced). The Northern Indians probably used the common stone chisel, set in a handle like a pick, as a pointed instrument to break the soil; but even this is partly conjectural. A stick or a bone was the usual implement. In Mexico and Central America implements of native copper were used to some extent. Clavigero remarks that, "to hoe and dig the ground they [the Aztecs] made use of the *coatl*, which is an instrument made of copper, with a wooden handle, but different from a spade or mattock. They made use of an axe to cut trees, which was also made of copper, and was of the same form as those of modern times, except that we put the handle in the eye of the axe, whereas they put the axe into an eye of the handle." And he naively concludes: "They had several other instruments of agriculture; but the negligence of ancient writers on this subject has not left it in our power to attempt their description."[1] Herrera, speaking of the Village Indians of Honduras, observes that they have "also Indian wheat, and kidney beans, which they sow thrice a year; and they were wont to grub up great woods with hatchets made of flint, which all could not get before they had the use of iron. They turned up the earth with long staves that had two hooks or branches coming from them, one above and another below, to press hard with the arm and foot, as also sharp shovels; being wont to sow little, as they were very slothful and often in want, eating several

---

[1] *Conquest of Mexico*, II. 177.

sorts of roots."[1] Bernal Diaz remarks that "copper axes and working tools" were offered for sale in the markets of Mexico, but gives no particulars of them.[2] The implements that they used were doubtless of the simplest and rudest kind. After their garden beds were once formed, the work of planting and cultivating them would be moderate from year to year; but the reduction of the ground in the first instance was the permanent obstacle to the use of large areas. Amongst the partially Village Indians labor was despised by the males; the cultivation, consequently, fell upon the overtaxed females. Nevertheless this class of Indians, east of the Mississippi, raised crops of corn, not large enough to save them at all times from famine, yet sufficient to sustain them in considerable numbers. In New Mexico and southward the labor of cultivation appears to have been shared more equally between the sexes, which serves to explain the greater productiveness of the horticulture of that region.

/Irrigation was the favorite method of cultivation with the Village Indians. It was extensively practiced in Mexico, and appears to have been the exclusive method in New Mexico./ A brief explanation of the ancient method in the latter territory, where it is still practiced, will assist materially to an understanding of Indian agriculture. The sites of their pueblos were usually in narrow valleys, watered by streams often of inconsiderable size. The pueblo was located upon high ground within the valley, but the garden beds were upon the first river terrace. An acequia, or canal, commencing sometimes a mile or more above the village, was excavated deep enough to draw off a portion of the water of the river and conduct it back of the garden beds to be irrigated, and not unfrequently one or two miles below the pueblo, where it was discharged into the river. The acequia, starting from the river, was led back to the outer margin of the valley as soon as the descent would permit, and then carried past the pueblo at such an elevation that the bottom of the canal would be higher than the garden beds, which were laid out between the canal and the river. These canals were usually

---

[1] *History of America*, IV, 133.
[2] *History of the Conquest of Mexico*, I, 106.

about ten feet wide at the bottom, with sloping banks, and the flowing water within them about a foot and a half deep. If the soil was loose, and the water not abundant, the bottom was often paved with cobble stones, or, in some cases, with flat tiles of clay.[1] Lots were laid off with a frontage upon the main canal, and separated from each other by dividing ridges. Each family, or group of families of related persons, had their own lot which was private property. These lots measured on the canal, varied from fifty to two hundred feet in width, and extended from the canal to the river, or as far as the proprietor chose to cultivate. Each lot was subdivided into garden beds about twenty feet square, surrounded by embankments about a foot high; so that a lot sixty feet front on the canal and two hundred feet deep would contain thirty such beds. After the ground was prepared, and before the seeds were planted, a sluice was cut from the main canal to the first lot, and the several garden beds overflowed with water to the depth of about eight inches; openings being made through the low embankments separating the several garden beds, until the water was conducted over the entire lot. In thus irrigating it was necessary to dam the main canal, below the side cut, in order to turn the flow of water into the garden. This process was repeated from day to day, until all the garden lots of the pueblo had been submerged, and by the absorption of the water brought into a proper condition for the seeds. The same process of irrigation was repeated when the growing corn was about eight inches high; and usually a third time at a later stage of its growth, the number of times depending upon the amount of rain which might fall during the growing season. Very large crops of corn, beans, and squashes were thus raised upon small areas; but it will be seen that it involved such an amount of labor to prepare and grade the ground as to restrict the area cultivated to

---

[1] There are miles of acequias now in use in New Mexico, and the remains of miles of abandoned acequias near the pueblos in ruins. Captain Johnson, U. S. A., thus speaks of a district on the Gila fifteen miles long: "The ground in view was about fifteen miles, all of which, it would seem, had been irrigated by the waters of the Gila. I also found the remains of an acequia, which followed the range of houses for miles. It had been very large."—*Reconnoissance in New Mexico*, Journal Captain A. R. Johnson, Ex. Doc. No. 41, 30th Congress, 1847–48, p. 598.

a small one for each pueblo.[1] This simple but ingenious method of cultivation is the highest evidence that can be adduced of the progress made by the Village Indians in civilization.

Another method of irrigation appears to have been practiced, and upon a very extended scale, by the Aztecs and their confederates in the valley of Mexico. It is a difficult and hazardous subject to touch. Few nations as small have elicited such masses of historical writing; and none have had their public affairs decorated with such wealth of imagination; yet, when it comes to a practical question as elementary as the means whereby they lived, these histories afford very little direct information. It appears that they cultivated in garden beds, and upon a large scale, corn, beans, and pepper; that they raised cotton and tobacco; and that they had cocoa, the banana, and the maguey, the latter of which was utilized in many different ways. Provisions, such as they were, seem to have been abundant. But the support of the excessive population credited to this valley, upon the products named, in the absence of a field agriculture, would have required horticultural cultivation upon a much more extended scale than there is reason to suppose could ever have existed. The necessity of resorting to conjecture to explain the cultivation of this valley is the best evidence of the imperfect state of our knowledge. The one about to be offered must be taken for what it is worth.

In a previous article in this *Review*,[2] the writer observed that "Mexico appears to have been surrounded by shallow artificial ponds, which answered as an exterior defence. It may be conjectured that the water was held there by means of dikes and causeways, and that the supply of water was obtained by damming Lakes Xochimilco and Chalco. These lakes at present

---

[1] A mistaken idea prevails in regard to the great advantages of artificial irrigation over that of natural rains. It is true that when the cultivator can depend upon an ample supply of water at all seasons in the irrigating canals, he possesses an advantage over him who relies exclusively on nature. But the misfortune is that when water is most needed the supply is the scantiest. In February and March there is always enough [in New Mexico] for the first irrigation. In April and May the quantity is much diminished; and if the rise expected to take place in the middle of May fails, there is not enough to irrigate properly all the fields prepared for it; the consequence is a partial failure of the crops."— Bartlett's *Personal Narrative*, I, 187.

[2] April, 1860, p. 492, note.

are a little less than five feet higher than the plaza of Mexico, which, in turn, is about six feet higher than the present level of Lake Tezcuco. By means of dams and dikes, with both of which the Aztecs were familiar, this result might have been attained." These suggestions need further development. In the absence of any evidence that the climate of Mexico has changed since the Spanish conquest, it must be assumed that the level of Lake Tezcuco was the same then as now; less the amount of water discharged into it by the small lakes to the northward of Mexico, the outlets of which were turned out of the valley by the tunnel of Huehuetoca, constructed in the beginning of the seventeenth century. The level of the lake would vary with the relative amounts of precipitation and evaporation. Lake Tezcuco, which is now three miles east of Mexico, is thirteen miles long and nine broad. Lake Chalco is now nine miles south of Tezcuco; and Lake Xochimilco, at its west end, is five and half miles south of Mexico. These last lakes are connected by an outlet, and together are fifteen miles long,[1] and discharge into Lake Tezcuco, through an outlet seven miles long, running along the borders of the present city of Mexico. At the time of the Spanish invasion, in 1519, there is no doubt that the waters of the three lakes were united by a narrow neck, and covered more than twice their present areas, and that the pueblo of Mexico was entirely surrounded by water. " The city of Mexico was then situated," says Clavigero, " as we have already said, upon a small island in Lake Tezcuco. . . . . For the convenience of passing to the mainland, there were three great causeways of earth and stone raised in the lake. That of Iztapalapan, towards the south, upwards of seven miles; that of Tlacopan, towards the west, about two miles; and that of Tepejacac, toward the north, of three miles in length; and all three so broad, that ten men on horseback could pass abreast."[2] And Herrera to the same effect: " Mexico, Tenochtitlan, is every way encompassed with fresh water, though thick, and, being in the lake, has only three avenues along the causeways. One of them

---

[1] *Map of the Valley of Mexico*, by Lieut. Hardcastle, U. S. A.; General Scott's *Expedition to Mexico*, 1847; *President's Message and Documents*, 1847–48, p. 256.

[2] *History of Mexico*, II, 859.

comes from the west, about half a league in length, another from the north, a league long. On the east there is no causeway, but only canoes to come at it. The other causeway is on the south, two leagues in length, along which Cortes and his men entered. It is to be observed that, as the lake of Mexico stands, it seems to be but one, yet there are two, and of very different nature; for the water of one of them is brackish, bitter, naught, and neither breeds nor will bear any sort of fish, and the water of the other is fresh, and has fishes, though small. The salt ebbs and flows, more or less, according as the wind blows on it. The fresh is higher, and so runs into the salt, and not the reverse, as some have thought, through six or seven large gaps that are in the causeway that divides them, over which there are large wooden bridges. The salt lake in some places is five leagues over, and eight or ten in length, the compass of it being about fifteen. The fresh water is about the same compass."[1] The problem then is to explain the former presence of a lake where none now exists, with no change of climate in the interval; the lake having two sections, one of them brackish, and the other fresh. Since the lake of brackish water still remains, and has no outlet, it explains itself; but the fresh-water lake around Mexico has disappeared. Lakes Xochimilco and Chalco are also much reduced in size.

The Aztecs as cultivators were familiar with the uses of water, both for irrigation and as a solvent to assist in the reduction of land. They were also familiar with dams and canals, and constructed dikes miles in length. The marsh lands around the pueblo then, as around the city now, were not available for cultivation. A series of dams upon the outlet of the fresh-water lakes, from their mouth to Lake Tezcuco, would be the first expedient, followed by lateral dikes for the formation of ponds over the lowlands around the pueblo. These ponds would serve to irrigate the patches of higher and better land. This plan or method of irrigation, followed up for years, would finally produce the result of covering the entire region around the pueblo with water, serving as a defence also, and necessitating the construction of the great causeways as they were

[1] *History of America*, II, 363.

afterwards found. Earth and mud were thrown up on the margins of the ponds and formed into gardens, and every patch rising above the water or which could be raised by artificial means was put under cultivation. Even floats were constructed upon an extensive scale, covered with earth and mud and planted as garden beds. They were rather a necessity of their method of cultivation, as Clavigero states, than the result of luxury and taste.[1] Some of the pleasure gardens attracted the attention of the conquerors from their great size and orderly arrangement, among which are those of Istapalapan and Huaxtepec. Of the first, Clavigero observes: "It was laid out in four squares and planted with every variety of trees, the sight and scent of which gave infinite pleasure to the senses; through these squares a number of roads and paths led, some formed by fruit-bearing trees, and others by espaliers of flowering shrubs and aromatic herbs. Several canals from the lake watered it." And of the latter: "The garden of Huaxtepec was still more extensive and celebrated than the last. It was six miles in circumference, and watered by a beautiful river which crossed it."[2] There were fields of maize and pepper around Cholula, near Chalco, and other towns as well as near all the pueblos in the valley. Most of them appear by the accounts to have been cultivated by irrigation. "For the refreshment of their fields," says the same author, "they made use of the water of rivers and small torrents which came from the mountains, raising dams to collect them and forming canals to conduct them."[3] There is no doubt that land was also cultivated without irrigation, but with a greater

---

[1] "Necessity and industry together taught them to form movable fields and gardens, which floated on the waters of the lake. The method which they pursued to make those, and which they still practice is extremely simple. They plait and twist willows and roots of marsh plants together, which are light, but capable of supporting the earth of the garden firmly united. Upon this foundation they lay the light bushes which float on the lake, and, over all, the mud and dirt which they draw up from the bottom of the lake. Their regular figure is quadrangular; their length and breadth varies; but as far as we can judge, they are about eight perches long, not more than three in breadth, and have less than a foot of elevation above the surface of the water. They were the first fields the Mexicans owned after the foundation of Mexico; there they first cultivated the maize, great pepper, and other plants necessary for their support. In progress of time, as those fields grew numerous from the industry of those people, there were among them gardens of flowers and odoriferous plants." — *History of Mexico*, II, 175.

[2] *History of Mexico*, II, 180.

[3] *Ibid*, II, 177.

expenditure of labor in its reduction. The topographical map of Lieutenant Hardcastle shows low grounds around Mexico in the precise areas covered by the ancient ponds. It is probable that the great square of the Aztec pueblo was lower than the present level of the plaza of Mexico; and if about two feet above the level of the ponds, there would be about two feet difference between the level of the latter and of Lake Tezcuco, which was then probably several inches higher than at present. A series of low dikes between the pueblo and Lake Tezcuco would produce this result with apparently one lake, yet in reality two, as described by Herrera, the fresh water lake being higher and flowing insensibly into the lower.[1] In a short time after the conquest the lake around Mexico had entirely disappeared. Bernal Diaz, who was writing his work in 1558, remarks : "That which was a lake is now a tract of fields of Indian corn, and so entirely altered that the natives themselves could hardly know it."[2] If this conjecture with respect to the formation of a great artificial pond or ponds around the pueblo of Mexico, by means of dams and dikes to hold the waters discharged by Lakes Xochimilco and Chalco and by the mountain streams, is accepted as probably true, it tends very much to raise our estimate of the intelligence and industry of the nations of the valley, as well as to bring distinctly before the mind the formidable obstacles which, in their condition, impeded their progress in civilization. The evidence which it also affords as to the great amount of labor connected with the reduction and cultivation of land by their methods, places a limit to the possible population of these areas.

Whether, at the time of the discovery of this continent, a subsistence derived from the chase, or one resting upon agriculture, was more favorable to an increase of the numbers and development of the power of the American aborigines, and whether the preponderating influence in peopling North America belonged to the Roving and partially Village Indians, or to

---

[1] "Around the city there were many dikes and reservoirs for collecting water when it was necessary, and within it so many canals that there was hardly a district that could not be approached by boats." — *History of Mexico,* II, 231.

[2] *Conquest of Mexico,* I, 188.

the Village Indians proper, cannot be determined from the facts thus far presented. It will be necessary to consider the actual migrations, and to find the source whence the emigrants came, to procure the remaining facts necessary to settle these questions. For the present it may be remarked, that the first effect of substituting agriculture in the place of a subsistence obtained from fisheries and the chase, was to break up the roving propensity by localizing the people in villages. This was a substantial advance. It is found to be nearly universally true of both divisions of the American aborigines, that nations speaking dialects of the same stock language maintained a territorial continuity with each other. This may have sprung, in part, from the influence of the bonds of kinship of language in securing mutual protection. It often resulted in confederacies. But the areas occupied by kindred nations of Village Indians were much smaller than those held by an equal number of nations of the other class. Moreover, from the direct personal nature of Indian government, each pueblo tended towards a state of independence of every other, while village life increased rather than moderated the tendency to political subdivision. This was a hindrance to progress. The inability of the Indians to rise out of the condition in which they were found was the result of the arrested growth of the idea of government. In the first place, they could not prevent the divergence of language into dialects, consequent upon geographical separation and diminished intercourse; secondly, when confederacies were formed, they were established generally too late to include all the nations of the same immediate descent; and thirdly, they were unable, with their means of subsistence, to develop population of the same descent in sufficient numbers within the folds of one confederacy to establish a formidable power. Their form of government was not adapted to overstep the barrier of diversity of language and include nations alien in speech, except as tributary, dependent, and humiliated. The idea of government is a growth through successive periods of development. It has its stages of development in barbarous society, and its after stages in civilized society, which are continuations the one of the other, and all stand together in a logical series. Its successive forms are founded upon the growth of man's experience in society. The American aborigines, as elsewhere remarked, had developed the first three stages, which belong to the period of barbarism: first, that of chief and followers, as represented by the tribe; second, that of a council of chiefs over a number of tribes, as represented by the nation; and third, that of a great council of chiefs over several nations, represented by the confederacy. Out of this came a tendency to advance a head-chief from among the members of the council, as the executive agent of its will. For the sufficient reason that the council remained supreme,[1] it was rather a tendency towards, than the establishment of, an executive, a necessity of their form of government rather than a lodgement of irresponsible power in a single person. In judging of the degree of their progress, the permanent existence of a council which held the powers of government must be kept in view. For another significant reason Indian chiefs did not govern according to their sovereign pleasure: because the power of deposition, as well as of election, was held by the respective tribes. The idea of a state is essentially modern in man's history. In its perfect development it is a government of equal and impartial laws enacted by the people themselves, through representatives of their own selection. In such a state the law rules, and not the executive, not the legislature, not the magistrate. The American aborigines were very many stages below this idea of a state.

From these various considerations it may be seen why it was that the Village Indians did not rise to a supremacy over the continent by reducing the Roving Indians to contracted areas, occupying their best positions, and holding them powerless for aggression. The Aztecs were unable to carry their power a hundred miles beyond the valley of Mexico, either north, west, or east. In warfare they possessed no advantages over the barbarous nations. On the contrary, there are reasons for believing that the latter were in general superior to the Village Indians in hardihood and courage, and in warlike inclinations.

---

[1] Acosta, after defining four grades of Aztec chiefs, observes that "all these four dignities were of the geat council, without whose advice the king might not do anything of importance."—*Nat. and Mor. Hist. East and West Indies*, p. 485.

Between the years 1600 and 1700 A.D., the entire area from the Atlantic to the Mississippi, and from Hudson's bay to the gulf of Mexico, had been sufficiently explored by traders, missionaries, and colonists, to render both the English and the French familiar with the location and condition of the several Indian nations within these limits. Some knowledge of the Dakotas and of the Missouri nations had also been obtained. But it was not until the eighteenth century that the same degree of information was acquired of the nations in the interior of the continent and upon the Pacific coast. Our systematic knowledge of the American aborigines belongs to the present century.

Having previously considered the means of subsistence of the aborigines, both natural and agricultural; the centres of Indian population; and the natural highways of migration suggested by the topographical features of North America; it remains to investigate their migrations for the purpose of finding, if possible, the initial point or centre from which, in successive streams, these nations spread abroad. The additional evidence and the conclusions must be sought in their systems of consanguinity, languages, mutual relations, and traditions, and in such actual migrations as are known to have occurred.

The aboriginal languages, north of Mexico, have been sufficiently studied in their vocables and in their grammatical structure to enable us to resolve them into a number of stock languages, which are found to be all constructed upon the same plan, and to remain in the same stage of development. But investigation has not been carried far enough to unite them in a family of languages upon strict linguistic principles. Philologists, therefore, have not claimed for these nations the position of a linguistic family of mankind, like the Aryan and Semitic families. It is very material to the further progress of American ethnology that the unity of origin of the American aborigines should be established, if evidence sufficient to demonstrate the fact can be discovered. Inasmuch as their languages are now spoken in a hundred and forty dialects, more or less, it is not probable that these will ever be investigated with sufficient minuteness, in their grammatical structure, to elicit from this source the proofs it might afford. If more than one original speech exists, that fact, however, may yet be ascertained by an analysis of a limited number of these languages.

Another class of facts, however, which may yield the evidence desired is to be found in their systems of consanguinity and affinity.[1] In this connection it will be sufficient to present such general results of a comparison of these systems as have a bearing upon Indian migrations. The Indian nations, from the Atlantic to the Rocky mountains, and from the Arctic sea to the gulf of Mexico, with the exception of the Eskimo, have the same system. It is elaborate and complicated in its general form and its details; and, whilst deviations from uniformity occur in the systems of different stocks, the radical features are, in the main, constant. This identity in the essential characteristics of a system so remarkable tends to show that it must have been transmitted with the blood to each stock from a common original source. It affords the strongest evidence yet obtained of the unity of origin of the Indian nations within the region we have defined. These several stocks, therefore, may be united into a family of mankind upon the basis of their joint possession of the same system of relationship. The same system has also been found, with more or less distinctness, amongst the nations in the valley of the Columbia, and in the Hudson's-bay territory, and also among the Village Indians of New Mexico and Central and South America. Treating the stocks first named as of one blood, under the name of the Ganowanian family,[2] such nations of the American aborigines as may be hereafter found to possess this system in its essential characteristics may be admitted, upon the basis of this common institution, into the same connection. Occasional references to this system of relationship will be made in the course of this article.

The migrations of the North American Indian nations are now to be considered, both those which have occurred within

---

[1] This subject, with the evidence, has been fully treated in a memoir now in course of publication by the Smithsonian Institution.

[2] *Gá-no-wá'-ni-an*. This proposed name for the American Indian family is in the Seneca-Iroquois language, from *gá-no*, an arrow, and *wá-á'-no* a bow — family of the Bow and Arrow. (*á*, as *a* in *father*; *a*, as *a* in *at*; *a*, as *a* in *ale*.)

the historical period, or a knowledge of which has been preserved by tradition, and those which, from the various sources of information previously indicated, it may be inferred have taken place. The classification of several stocks into sub-groups is founded upon a comparison of dialects.

I. *Algonkin Migrations.*

A much larger area was occupied by the Algonkin stock than by any other of the Ganowanian family. North of the chain of the great lakes the nations of this lineage were spread from the eastern slopes of the Rocky mountains to the coast of Labrador. South of these lakes, and between the Mississippi and the country of the Iroquois, they were found in possession as far south as the area between the Tennessee and the Mississippi. Along the Atlantic seaboard they were distributed from the St. Lawrence to the northern confines of South Carolina, occupying the whole of New Brunswick, New England, and Virginia, and portions of the intermediate states. They were thinly scattered throughout this immense region; but they held it free from the intrusion of other stocks, with the exception of the Winnebagoes in Wisconsin, and the Iroquois and their congeners in New York and the territories adjacent to New York on the north, south, and west. They were subdivided into a large number of petty nations, all speaking dialects of a common language, but living without unity of organization, or political relations, and without any knowledge of the order of their separation from each other. A comparison of their dialects resolves them into several groups, and tends to show that each member of each group was a subdivision of an original nation, or that they were descended from a common parent nation.

1. *Atlantic Nations.*[1]—No movement was in progress among

Localities.

[1]. Sheshatapoosh } On the northern shores of the gulf of St. Lawrence.
2. Scoffies ....
3. Micmacs ....Western shores and rivers of this gulf, and in Nova Scotia.
4. Etchimons ......River St. John, and between it and the Penobscot.
5. Abenakis ....The Kennebec, and ranging to the Saco.
6. Massachusetts. }
7. Narragansetts. } These nations extended from the vicinity of the Saco to the Hudson river.
8. Mohegans .... }
9. Montaks... ....Long Island.

the Atlantic Algonkins at the epoch of their discovery. They were stationary within certain geographical limits. From the relation of the Eastern Algonkin dialects to the western no certain inference can be drawn as to which was original, and which derived; but from the greater amount of divergence among the western dialects, it is a reasonable inference that the western part of the Algonkin area was first and longest occupied. There is also traditionary evidence of a western origin of the Eastern Algonkins. The Mohegans, who inhabited the country between the Connecticut and Hudson rivers, had a well-defined tradition, which was shared by some other New England nations, that they came originally from the northwest; but they were without any definite knowledge of the country from which they came. The Delawares communicated to Heckewelder a similar tradition of their western origin. Such evidence, standing alone, possesses but little weight, but, taken in connection with corroborating facts, it is not without significance. It is plainly to be inferred that the Iroquois area was originally Algonkin, and that the irruption of the Iroquois into this area explains the spread of the Algonkin nations southward along the Atlantic coast.

2. *Great Lake Nations.* — The Ojibwas, Otawas, and Potawattomies were derived immediately from each other, or from a common stem.[1] This fact is still shown by the close relationship of their dialects. In point of development the Ojibwa language stands at the head of the Algonkin tongues, unless the Shawnee or the Cree may dispute this preëminence. The country of these nations extended from the Otawa river to and along the north shore of Lake Huron, through the peninsula between Lakes Michigan and Superior, and thence into Northern Wisconsin. In the central area, at the outlet of Lake Superior,

---

10. Delawares,....
11. Minsi ... .} Between the Hudson and Susquehanna rivers.
12. Nanticokes... ..Eastern shore of Chesapeake bay.
13. Powhattans... .. Virginia.
14. Pampticoos .....North Carolina.

The affiliation of the four nations first named is closest with the Kenistenaux, or Crees, of whom the first two were probably detached bands.

[1] The Missisagas were chiefly of the Eagle tribe of the Ojibwas. Their range was north of the Georgian bay of Lake Huron.

were the Ojibwas, from which point they ranged west to Ontonagon along its south shore, and upon its northeast shore to the country of the Crees. Shortly before the discovery of the country the Otawas had retired westward from the Otawa river district to the Manitoulin islands and to the straits of Mackinaw, where they were first known to the French; and from this region they were then spreading southward over Lower Michigan, to the vicinity of Detroit. The third nation, the Pottawattamies, after occupying several localities in Upper Michigan and Wisconsin,[1] were then drawing southward, to the south end of Lake Michigan, near Chicago, and east of that district. At the time of their discovery the Ojibwas, who held the great fishing place at the Sault Ste. Marie, were advancing westward upon the "disputed ground" which separated their territory from that of the Dakotas. The original boundary between these nations was the Montreal river and the Porcupine mountains, a few miles west of Ontonagon; but the Ojibwas were then occupying the south shore of Lake Superior, as far west as Chegoimegon, near La Pointe. Father Allouez, however, met the Dakotas in 1665, at the head of the lake."[2] At the time of their discovery, these nations were receding westward.[3] An explanation is found in the rising power of the Iroquois at that period under their confederate organization. They had forced the Otawas westward from their original seat on the river of that name, and had attacked the Ojibwas on the south shore of Lake Superior.

A still more extended region was occupied by the Kenistenaux, or Crees. They ranged from the north shore of Lake Superior

---

[1] In the Memoir of M. Du Chesnau on the Western Indians, written in 1681, they are mentioned in territorial connection with the Sawks and Winnebagoes, which would place them between Green bay and the Mississippi. This was probably their country in 1640, when the Jesuit missionaries first reached Lake Superior (Vide *Colonial History of New York*, IX, 161).

[2] Bancroft's *History of the United States*, III, 151. "There too, at the very extremity of the lake, the missionary met the wild, impassive warriors of the Sioux, who dwelt at the west of Lake Superior."

[3] After the separation of the three nations, a confederacy was formed among them, which they called *Na-nod'-ba-ne- zid'*, the Three Council-fires. In this confederacy the Ojibwas were styled Elder Brother, th: Otawas, Next Older Brother, and the Pottawattamies, Younger Brother. It was organized for common defence against the Iroquois, and was of modern date. Sir William Johnson, in his enumeration of Indian nations, made in 1736, speaks of the Otawa confederacy, but includes under it other nations (*Doc. History N. Y.*, I, 26).

to Hudson's bay, and from Lake Winnipeg on the west to the neighborhood of the Saguenay, east of Quebec. The Montagnars, who have been represented as holding the eastern part of this area, and of whom as a distinct people but little is known, were probably of Cree descent. With respect to the Cree language, which is now spoken in three slightly different dialects, it finds its nearest affinity in the Ojibwa, with the exception of the two Eastern Algonkin dialects, first named in a note on a previous page. The principal facts here ascertained are the establishment of the great lake nations around Lake Superior when first discovered, the closeness of their dialectical connection, and the southern movement then progressing in the case of two of these nations. There is a tradition still preserved among the Ojibwas that they came originally from the northwest. It is highly probable that the shores of Lake Superior were the central seats of the Algonkin stock, from its earliest appearance on the eastern side of the continent, and that emigrants went forth from this secondary centre of population to occupy the valley of the St Lawrence and the Atlantic coasts, and also the eastern banks of the Mississippi and its smaller tributaries.

3. *Mississippi Nations.*— This group of nations occupied the east side of the Mississippi, from the country of the Ojibwas southward to the Ohio, and south of this river between the Tennessee and the Mississippi. They ranged eastward to Lake Michigan and to the state of Indiana. By a comparison of dialects they are resolved into five sub-groups, as follows: (1.) The Miamis; (2.) The Kaskaskias, Peorias, Weas, and Piankeshaws, who appear to have been known collectively, at one time, as the Illinois; (3.) The Sawks and Foxes; (4.) The Menominees; (5.) The Shawnees. To these the Shiyans (Cheyennes) and Arapahoes, now of Colorado territory, should be added, as a sixth and displaced member of the group.

The first two groups, consisting of five nations, who occupied the southern and eastern portion of the area just described, lying north of the Ohio, are so nearly allied in dialect as to show that they are subdivisions of one original nation; the last four nations speaking substantially the same dialect, while that of the first is distinct from the others. These dialects again resemble the Ojibwa and Otawa so closely as to render it probable, if not certain, that the nations above named were derived from the two last named by subdivision or descent. The southern movement of the Otawas and Pottawattamies, before mentioned, seems to have been made upon the lines of migration of their kindred who had preceded them. It also tends to confirm the position elsewhere taken, that the great region of fisheries upon the south shores of Lake Superior and the north shores of Lakes Michigan and Huron had been secondary initial points of emigration of the Algonkin nations to the south and east.

In the central parts of Wisconsin the Sawks and Foxes were found by the first explorers, and south of them the Kikapoos. Their dialects still resemble each other, but they show such an amount of divergence from those of the great lake nations as to preclude the supposition of a direct descent from them. They were, undoubtedly, an early offshoot from the Algonkin stem. This last remark is equally true of the Menominees, who, when first known, occupied the wild-rice regions upon the Menominee river in Northern Wisconsin, and the upper peninsula of Michigan.

Lastly, the Shawnees were the southernmost nation, in territorial position, of the Central Algonkins. They held originally, and before the period of colonization, the western part of Kentucky, between the Mississippi and Tennessee rivers.[1] Their dialect shows a great divergence from all the dialects of the Mississippi nations. If they came originally from the great lake region, or, which seems more probable, from the head-waters of the Mississippi, their language indicates a separation from the parent stem at an early period. The name by which they call themselves, *Sä-wän'-wä-kee'* (in Otawa, *O-shä'-wä-noke'*, whence Shawnee), signifying southerners, implies a previous location farther north. It seems probable that they took this name in a boastful sense, to indicate that they were the southernmost of the Algonkin nations.

---

[1] They removed eastward, first to North Carolina, as is supposed, and afterwards to Pennsylvania. They were a party to William Penn's treaty, in 1682.—Harvey's *History of the Shawnees*, p. 22.

There are strong reasons for classing the Shiyans and Arapahoes with the Mississippi nations, notwithstanding their territorial displacement.. The original seat of the former nation was upon the Cheyenne river, a tributary of the Red river of the north, from which they were expelled by the Dakotas. In 1804 they were found by Lewis and Clarke west of the Missouri. Their nearest congeners, the Arapahoes, were high up on the Missouri when first discovered. The dialects of these nations, which are closely allied, show an excessive amount of divergence from those of the great lake nations, but their nearest affinity is with the Shawnee, Kikapoo, and Menominee. This fact renders it extremely probable that the original seat of all these nations, except the first, second, and third sub-groups, was upon the head-waters of the Mississippi, the area occupied by the Dakotas at the time of their discovery; and that the Dakotas not only were intruders into territory previously Algonkin, but in their progress to the eastern side of the continent dispossessed this stock of the first and most important seat occupied by them.

Whether or not the great lake nations emigrated from the south is a question hardly worth considering. It must be assumed that they were originally non-agricultural; because if they had ever been agriculturists, it would be difficult to explain the migration of the present northern nations from districts where agriculture was known into the northern wilderness, where it is impossible. The mound-builders had practiced agriculture north of the Ohio before the advent of the Algonkin stock, and it is not probable that the art of cultivation was afterwards lost in this area. On the other hand, the territorial and dialectical connections of the Mississippi nations, except the first, second, and third sub-groups, tend to refer the immediate original stock from which they were derived, not merely to a northern position, but directly to the attractive and desirable area for Indian occupation upon the head-waters of the Mississippi. This is the only region in the western part of the Algonkin area, except that around Lake Superior, which could have developed, without agriculture, the population necessary for the gradual formation of these nations. When forced out by increase of numbers, and finally by an alien people, they would naturally have sought the prairie area bordering the Mississippi, and a knowledge of agriculture would have become necessary to secure them a subsistence. Agriculture was practiced by all of these nations when discovered, except the Menominees and Arapahoes. The whole period of time covered by the occupation of the Algonkin stock, and by their dispersion over the areas in which they were found, is not a long one in comparison with that during which the Ganowanian family had possessed North America. This is shown by the present close connection between the Algonkin dialects, the divergences among which may have required a thousand years, more or less, for their production. It is evident that this stock was recent upon the eastern side of the continent. From these and other considerations a portion of the Mississippi nations may reasonably be referred to the Lake Superior region, and the remainder to the head-waters of the Mississippi, as the centres from which they issued. A further subdivision occurred, in some cases, in their newly acquired territories.[1]

4. *Rocky Mountain Nations.*— Upon the eastern slopes of the Rocky mountains, and eastward upon the open prairies, ranging from the Missouri to the Saskatchewan, dwell the Blackfeet, a powerful nation of horsemen, who hold undisputed sway over that section of the continent. Since the time of European colonization, a portion of the Crees, receding westward, have possessed themselves of the lower half of the district on the Saskatchewan river, where they now confront the Blackfeet; thus completing the continuity of territorial possession from the Rocky mountains to the Atlantic coast. The Blackfoot, spoken in three closely connected dialects, belongs to the Algonkin speech, but it exhibits a large amount of divergence from all the other dialects of this stock, as well as the presence of a large number of vocables from foreign or indigenous sources. Nothing is known of the early history of the Blackfeet or their previous location. Im-

---

[1] *O-je-bic*, the root of the name Ojibwa, signifies *root, trunk*, or *stem people*, whence *O-jib-wa* an Ojibwa; *O-jib-wa-ka* and *O-jib-wage* (plural), Ojibwas. The etymology of this term, however, carries with it no special significance, as it was a common practice amongst Indian nations to call themselves *original*, and often *autochthones*.

mediately south of them, at the present time, are the Ahahnelins (*Gros-ventres* of the prairie), who also speak an Algonkin dialect. This completes the summary of the nations of Algonkin lineage.

From the foregoing brief statement of the locations of the several Algonkin nations, and of the relations of their dialects to each other when they severally became known, two important facts are made apparent: first, that the Algonkin stock still inhabit the slopes of the Rocky mountains, over against the valley of the Columbia, thus pointing to that valley as the initial point from which they emigrated to the great lake region, and thence to the Atlantic coasts; and secondly, that they were climatically a northern people. With respect to the first statement, it is sufficient, for the purposes of this discussion, to show that the Algonkins were found in uninterrupted possession of a continuous area from points within a hundred miles of the head-waters of the Columbia to the Atlantic seaboard. If sufficient reason be found, in the superabundance of natural subsistence in the Columbia valley, for holding that remarkable area to be the land from which they originally spread, the entire course of their migrations will stand revealed. It may be observed, with respect to the second fact, that the main body of the Algonkin stock was found around Lake Superior and along the St. Lawrence, from which their diffusion to the south was nearly balanced by that towards the north. The only feature in itself peculiar, in the area occupied by them, was its elongation southward along the Atlantic seacoast, which, as before remarked, seems to find a full explanation in the intrusion of the Iroquois within their original limits.

II. *Dakotan Migrations.*

Some evidence, both with respect to the separate migrations of the Dakotan nations, and the general direction of their advance as one of the great stocks of the Ganowanian family, may be derived from the relations of the dialects, and the geographical positions, of the numerous nations of this lineage. The bulk of these nations were strictly River Indians, which gave a peculiar character to their occupation of the area possessed by them. Since the rivers traversing the central prairies had a narrow border of forest, while all beyond was open prairie unsuitable for Indian occupation, the nations of this stock spread over great distances north and south, along the banks of rivers, without any corresponding lateral expansion. Besides, as this area, with the exception of one district, was comparatively a poor one, it created a tendency among the more vigorous and warlike bands, like the Iroquois — who were probably an early offshoot of the Dakotan stem — to seek new habitations in distant and disconnected regions.

1. *Dakotas.* — The Dakotas proper held a broad as well as compact area. When first discovered, they were established upon the head waters of the Mississippi, in the present state of Minnesota, whence they ranged eastward to Lake Superior and westward to the Missouri. A portion of them were permanently established upon the latter river. They are now subdivided into twelve great bands, or embryo nations, and occupy the plains between the Missouri and the Rocky mountains — forced westward, as other nations have been, by the progress of the whites. Down to the time of their discovery they had remained in such intimate intercourse with one another that their language had developed but two dialects — the Isauntie, on the Mississippi, and the Teeton, on the Missouri; with a third, the Yankton, in the incipient stages of formation out of the first. The three forms, however, vary so slightly as to be mutually intelligible with entire facility. From this fact it may be inferred that the Dakotas were comparatively recent in this area, while the superior advantages of this district for Indian subsistence are demonstrated by their unusual numbers. When Carver visited the Dakotas in 1756, they were divided into eleven bands.[1] They acknowledged seven nations or divisions, as stated by Riggs,[2] of which the seventh, the Teetons, was subdivided into eight bands. They are now organized into twelve nations, known as Isaunties, Yanktons, Yanktonais, Sissetons, Ogalallas, Brulés, Uncpapas, Blackfoot Dakotas, Ohenonpas, Minikanyes, Sansarcs, and Itazipcos. Isaunties is a generic term used by the Western Dakotas,

[1] Carver's *Travels*, Phila. ed. 1796, p. 37.
[2] Riggs's *Dakota Lexicon* (Smithsonian Contributions, IV.), Intro., p. xv.

to designate their kindred on the Mississippi; and Teetons, another, employed by the latter to describe the former. It will be seen that the distinction is dialectical. *Dakota* in the Isauntie dialect, *Lacota* in the Teeton, which signifies *leagued* or *allied*, is the name by which they call themselves. They also speak of their confederacy as the Seven Council-fires, from their seven political divisions. The Dakotas proper, who are more numerous than all of their recognized congeners united, are of immediate common descent.

2. *Asiniboines.* — This nation was one of the constituent bands of the Dakotas, and became detached and independent shortly before the period of European discovery. They moved northward, and became established upon Rainy lake, and ranged thence westward to the Red river of the north, and northward to the vicinity of Lake Winnipeg. At the present time they dwell west of the last named river, and range westward to the Missouri, and northward well towards the Saskatchewan.[1] Since the separation the Dakotas have regarded them as enemies. After a geographical separation of more than two hundred years, their dialects are mutually intelligible, with entire facility.

3. *Missouri Nations.*— The nearest congeners of the Dakotas were the eight nations of the Lower Missouri, who inhabited both banks of this river, and the banks of some of its tributaries, from the mouth of the Punka river on the north, to the mouth of the Missouri, and thence southward upon the west side of the Mississippi, to the Arkansas. Their dialects are distinct from each other, but may be resolved into three groups : 1st, That of the Punkas and Omahas, the northernmost nations, whose dialects, although greatly divergent, are more nearly allied to each other than either is to any of those remaining. These nations are probably subdivisions of one original band. South of them, upon the Missouri, and ranging over Iowa, were the Iowas, Otoes, and Missouris, whose dialects likewise are more nearly related to each other than to those remaining. These nations also were probably subdivisions of one original nation.

---

[1] In 1862, I met a band of this nation on the Upper Missouri, below the mouth of the Yellowstone river. They are a hardy stock, but inferior to the Dakotas in character and personal appearance.

INDIAN MIGRATIONS. 221

South of these were the Kaws, Osages, and Quappas, who were in like manner subdivisions of one nation, as is shown by the relation of their dialects. The Osages have a tradition that they once occupied the east bank of the Mississippi, south of the Ohio, in what afterwards became the Shawnee area; and that while there the Quappas separated from them, and emigrated to the mouth of the Arkansas,[1] where they were found by De Soto, in 1540.[2] All of the Missourian nations have changed their seats, from time to time, within their modern areas. The Kaws, when first known to explorers (under the names of Okames and Kansas), resided upon the Kansas river; but they were formerly established, as one of their chiefs informed the writer in 1859, upon the west bank of the Mississippi, a few miles above the mouth of the Missouri. Their village, at this point, was called *Ne-bla-zhe-tä'-mä*, which signifies the blue river, and this was their name for the Mississippi; whilst they called the Missouri *Ne-sho'-ja*, the muddy river. These eight nations, as before stated, were probably derived from three original nations by subdivision, and the three again from one; but the degree of the divergence of their dialects from each other, and from the Dakota, indicates a long period of separate national existence.

4. *Winnebagoes.* — In intimate connection with the Missouri nations, dialectically, must be placed the Winnebagoes. They were first known as Puants, and ranged from Lake Winnebago to Green bay in Wisconsin. They were an early offshoot from the Dakotan stock, which advanced eastward into the forest area; and their progress seems to have been arrested by Lake Michigan, and very likely by the nations in possession of the narrow peninsula between Lakes Michigan and Superior. This was the natural route of migration to the St. Lawrence valley from the Missouri and Mississippi regions.

When an original stock subdivides, and the process is repeated from century to century, it becomes impossible to ascertain which was the parent nation. They are, in effect, the common

---
[1] Report of William Clarke and Lewis Cass to the Secretary of War, in 1825. Schoolcraft's *History, Condition, and Prospects of the Indian Tribes*, III, 594.
[2] Bancroft's *History of the United States*, I, 54; Schoolcraft's, III, 594.

descendants of this original stock, which exists only in its branches. That branch only from which a particular nation is immediately derived stands to the latter in the relation of a parent. While this would be true, as to each band emigrating from the territorial and political connection of the mother nation, the constitution of Indian society tended to subdivision as the people spread abroad over larger areas. It is evident, from the relations of the dialects of the nations we are considering, that the Missouri nations were not derived from the Dakotas. Neither can the latter, nor the Winnebagoes, be derived from either of the former; but each is a branch of a common stem back of them all in point of time. There was a definite order of separation, but it is not now ascertainable. The Winnebagoes affirm that the Missouri nations were descended from them.

5. *Upper Missouri Nations.* —North of all the nations we have named on the Missouri were the Mandans, who speak a dialect of the Dakotan stock language, and also the Minnitarees, and Crows (*Ab-sar'-o-kas*), whose dialects have so large an infusion of Dakotan vocables that they are believed to be an offshoot of this stock, or rather of common descent with them. The Mandan dialect appears to be more advanced than any other of the Dakotan stock, unless the Dakota proper is the superior. Any person familiar with the articulation of Indian languages can form a very correct opinion of their development when heard from the lips of native speakers in council. The Mandan, as used by the chiefs in formal addresses, is a clear sonorous language, with quantity and accent strongly defined; but it is disfigured with scraping and gutural sounds. It could not have attained its degree of advancement without a long and prosperous national career. This dialect is in closer affiliation with those of the Lower Missouri nations than with the Dakota proper; at the same time, judging from a comparison of vocables, it resembles the latter more closely than the latter does the Missouri dialects, thus giving to the Mandans an intermediate position. The Minnitarees and Crows, who are subdivisions of an original nation, seem to form a connecting link between the Dakota and Missouri nations on the one hand, and the gulf nations, namely,

the Creeks, Choctas, Seminoles, etc., on the other. In their dialects they must be classed with the former, but in their system of consanguinity with the latter. There is a concurrence, in one striking feature, of their respective systems of relationship, which is found in their systems alone, and which seems to require a connection by blood for its explanation. It has elsewhere been stated as probable that the Minnitarees carried agriculture to the Upper Missouri and taught it to the Mandans and Arickarees, and that they were emigrants from the south. The remembrance of this migration seems still to be preserved in their national name *E-năt'-zä*, signifying the people who came from afar.

It thus appears that the nations of Dakotan lineage held a territory, when first discovered, substantially continuous through thirteen parallels of latitude, that is, from the Arkansas river to Rainy lake; and, in the upper part of the area, of several hundred miles in width. There is no direct evidence, either from tradition or other sources, as to the country from which they came. Their subdivision into the existing nations occurred, presumptively, after they became possessed of this area, or else they must have followed each other at short intervals from a common original seat; in either case, after the Dakotan stock language had become distinct. So much may be inferred from the present relation of its dialects, of which fifteen have been enumerated, and also from the continuity of their territorial possessions. The initial point from which they migrated into this area was necessarily remote; for they held an isolated position in the midst of the central prairies, and in precisely that portion of North America which would be occupied last in point of time by non-agricultural nations.

On the assumption that the Ganowanian family originated outside of the American continent and reached it in prehistoric ages, there are no facts of positive weight pointing to a European or African source. There were no people on either of these continents of the same or even similar type, from whom they could have been derived; consequently there is no occasion to include, as supposable, an hypothesis of their spread westward from the Atlantic coast. On the contrary, there are weighty, even conclusive indications that they commenced their dispersion over North America from the northwest coast. Their migrations, retraced to the valley of the Columbia, seem next to point back to the Asiatic continent, with which there are two possible routes of connection, and which still contains within its borders nations of a type strikingly similar to theirs.[1]

With respect to the Dakotan stock, the original home of their ancestors must, of necessity, be referred to the western side of the continent. There were but three routes through the prairie area available; first, by the Saskatchewan, from the eastern slopes of the Rocky mountains to Lake Winnipeg, and thence south by the Red river of the north to the head of the Mississippi, a distance of fifteen hundred miles; second, by the Platte river, from the same mountains to the Missouri — a distance of about eight hundred miles, nearly all the way through open prairies; and third, by the Arkansas river to the Mississippi, about the same distance, and through a similar region. A migration by the Saskatchewan or by the Arkansas is far less probable than by the Platte. If by the first, it would seem necessary to derive the Missouri nations from the Dakotas; if by the second the reverse; and both of these suppositions present linguistic difficulties. But if they reached the Missouri by way of the Platte, and spread thence northward and southward along the former river, and eastward to the sources of the Mississippi, into the several areas in which they were found, their movements would seem to have been more in accordance with their present relations. This supposed route is rendered probable by other facts. The Dakotan stock were, climatically, a northern people, and, with the exception of the Quappas, and, to a limited extent, of the Osages and Iowas, also non-agricultural. Had they reached the Mississippi as low down as the Arkansas, they would have come in contact with the gulf nations, who were agricultural in their habits when first discovered by De Soto in 1540; and would themselves have become agricultural, as the Quappas did at a later period,

---

[1] I have recently seen a photograph of a Mongolian woman whose face and features resembled those of Seneca-Iroquois females so closely that one might be taken for the other if they stood side by side.

from their geographical position. That the latter nation was a recent arrival upon the Arkansas in 1540 is shown by the Osage tradition before referred to. If the Dakotas had been acquainted with the art of cultivating the ground, and afterwards migrated to their northern location, they would probably not have abandoned the advantages to be derived from it. There is another class of facts bearing upon this question. At the time Marquette descended the Mississippi, in 1673, a portion of the Mississippi Algonkins resided on its west side, near the mouth of the Des Moines river in Iowa, whence they were afterwards expelled. The Kithigami, an Algonkin people, are located on Marquette's map upon the west side of this river, from which they afterwards retired.[1] Whether this occupation was an encroachment upon areas previously Dakotan, or indicates that this region was then a part of the Algonkin domain, cannot be determined with certainty. It seems most probable that the latter was the case, and that the Dakotan stock wrested this area, as well as their principal seat in Minnesota, from the Algonkins. When the Dakotas were discovered, in 1665, they were attempting to gain a foothold in the forest area on the south shore of Lake Superior; and the Winnebagoes, as elsewhere stated, had penetrated the Algonkin area as far eastward as Lake Michigan, and were then surrounded by Algonkin nations.

There is still another significant fact, in the name of the Shiyans, and of the river upon which they dwelt. They were formerly established in Dakota territory on the great bend of the Cheyenne river, a tributary of the Red river of the north, from which they were expelled by the Dakotas. Their name was bestowed on them by the latter, who called them *Shi-yä*, people of an unintelligible tongue. They also called the river *Shi-yä wo-zu-pe*, the last word signifying *plantation* or *garden*. Since the Shiyans are of Algonkin lineage, if the Dakotas had emigrated from the north or east, the Shiyan language would not have been new to them, and much less so strange as to have elicited such a name; and if from the south, planting or garden

---

[1] Bancroft's *History of the United States*, III, 160.

beds would not have been such a novelty as to have found expression in this way. On the contrary, from well-known Indian idiosyncrasies in bestowing names, had the Dakotas, advancing eastward from Nebraska toward the Mississippi, heard for the first time the Algonkin speech from the Shiyans, and on their river witnessed for the first time the cultivation of the earth, these names, or something equivalent — it might have been predicted — would be applied to them.

It seems therefore extremely probable that the Dakotan stock commenced the occupation of their modern area at some point on the Missouri as high up as the mouth of the Platte, from which they advanced northward, southward, and eastward, and subdivided into independent nations, as they increased in numbers and dwelt apart from each other. With this conclusion established, a prior migration from the eastern slopes of the Rocky mountains, by way of the Platte river and the Black hills of Nebraska, becomes a necessary inference, although the safe transit of a band of Indians by this or any route through the prairies must have been a happy accident. The next preceding movement connects them with the valley of the Columbia. This general conclusion will be materially strengthened by the facts bearing upon the migrations of the remaining stocks.

6. *Hodenosaunian Nations.*— This group consists of the five Iroquois nations (Senecas, Cayugas, Onondagas, Oneidas, and Mohawks), the Hurons, or Wyandotes, Eries, Neutral nation, Susquehannocks, Nottowas, and Tuscaroras.

The earlier home of the Iroquois, before they occupied New York, was upon the north bank of the St. Lawrence, in the vicinity of Montreal.[1] Their last migration, of which they have a clear tradition, was from that district into the lake region of Central New York, where they had been established for at least a century and a half when first discovered, in 1608. The Hurons remained in Canada, and were found on the Georgian bay of Lake Huron, around Lake Simcoe, and ranging southward toward Lake Erie. The Wyandotes, now of Kansas, are the remains of

---

[1] *League of the Iroquois*, p. 5.

the ancient Hurons. Upon both banks of the Niagara river, and ranging westward along the northeast shore of Lake Erie, was the Neutral nation, probably a subdivision of the Hurons. On the southeast shore of Lake Erie were the Gakwas, or Eries, supposed to have been a subdivision of the Senecas. Both the Neutral nation and the Eries were defeated and expelled by the Iroquois about 1650–1655, and are now extinct. The Susquehannocks lived on the banks of the lower Susquehanna, in Pennsylvania, and the Nottowas on the river of the same name in Virginia. These nations are also extinct. Upon the Neuse river, in North Carolina, were the Tuscaroras, who, upon their expulsion, in 1712, moved northward to the country of the Iroquois, and were admitted as a sixth nation into the Iroquois confederacy. Of the dialects of these nations the Tuscarora was the most divergent, but they were all closely affiliated.

It will be noticed that these nations are classed as a sixth branch of the Dakotan stock. There are strong reasons for assigning to them this position. Notwithstanding the general conclusion that the Hodenosaunian speech is a distinct stock language, a comparison of its several dialects with those of the Dakotan nations shows that if the words do not reach the point of clear identification, they have, nevertheless, a strong family likeness so plainly marked as to arrest attention, whilst corresponding words from Algonkin dialects are in striking contrast. Their respective systems of relationship are more nearly identical in minute details than those which belong to independent stocks. Among the Wyandotes there is a tradition that the Dakotas were derived from them, which is equivalent to a tradition of common descent.[1] They still recognize each other as *brothers*, which is a recognition of blood relationship when applied by one Indian nation to another.[2] There is some evidence to the same effect in the com-

---

[1] This tradition was communicated to the writer in 1859, at the Wyandote reservation in Kansas, by Matthew Walker, an educated half-blood Wyandote, who had lived among the Dakotas. He accepted the tradition as true. The war-dance of the Iroquois was obtained by them of the Dakotas, and is still called the Dakota dance. *Wā-sd-sa-o-no* is their name for the Dakotas, and *Wā-sd-sa*, for the war-dance.

[2] An investigation of the terms by which Indian nations address each other would lead to valuable historical results. They generally use these terms in such a way as not only to imply blood relationship, but also relative equality, inferiority, or superiority in age as nations. Thus the Dakotas

mon name applied by the Algonkin nations to the Iroquois and to the Dakotas. It gains importance from the fact that the Algonkin and Dakotan nations have confronted each other during the centuries of their occupation of conterminous areas, and have been mutual witnesses of each other's subdivision and changes of location. The Great Lake nations call the Iroquois *Nä-do-wage'*, which signifies *marauders*. It has a primary meaning equivalent to enemy, but it was applied to the Iroquois, as a specific national name, by the Algonkin nations. It was also their name for the Hurons, although the latter, while residing upon Lake Huron, were in alliance with the Ojibwas and Otawas, and made common cause with them against the Iroquois. It is still applied to the Wyandotes. Moreover the name Nottowas, given to a small nation of the same lineage, in Virginia, who called themselves *Che-ro-ha'-kä*, confirms the view that this term was a generic one among the Algonkins for this particular stock. In the next place, the French first learned of the existence and name of the Dakotas proper through the Otawas and Ojibwas, and from French sources came the name Nadoüessi, or Naudouescioux, whence probably the name Sioux, by which the Dakotas were first known. To the early English explorers the same name was given, and written Naudowissies. It is evident that the Ojibwa *Nä'-do-wä* was the root of both terms.[1] Whilst the strength of the argument in favor of a direct blood relationship between the Iroquois and Dakotas, from the application of this term to both, is weakened by its etymological signification, it is not overthrown.

---

and Wyandotes call each other *brothers* thereby admitting equality as well as kin. The Missouri nations call the Winnebagoes *uncles*, by which they recognize a common descent, and admit that the Winnebagoes are an older branch of the same stem. The Great Lake nations call the Shawnees *uncles*, thus acknowledging their superior rank as well as greater age. It seems to imply that the former separated from the main stock, possibly in Minnesota, when they took up their residence at the foot of Lake Superior. Most of the Algonkin nations call the Delawares *grandfathers*, thus recognizing their greater age as a nation, and implying descent from them as the mother nation. On the contrary, the Iroquois called the Delawares *nephews*, although belonging to a different linguistic stock. It was used in this case to express inferiority and the fact of their subjugation. The Mohawks, Onondagas, and the Senecas called each other *brothers*, and called Oneidas, Cayugas, and Tuscaroras *sons;* while the last three called each other *brothers*, and called the first three *fathers*.

[1] Now, there is a slight difference made in the two terms. In Ojibwa, *nä-dink* signifies the act of getting; *nä-yä do-wa*, one who comes stealthily and takes; whence *Nä-do-wa*, an Iroquois — a marauder; *Nä-ko-wage* (plural), Iroquois; *Nä-do-wa-see*, a Dakota; *Nä-do-wa-see-wug* (plural), Dakotas.

The force of the term is not exhausted by the fact that these nations, as aliens in speech, were, for that reason, both enemies of the Algonkin stock. These great branches of the Ganowanian family had long confronted each other, and it seems a reasonable supposition that a name applied originally to the Dakotan stock would be continued to each of its subdivisions as they occurred, thus preserving a knowledge of their blood connection.

From what quarter the Hodenosaunian nations entered the Algonkin areas, there is neither positive knowledge nor tradition. It seems at least probable that they were an advanced band or offshoot of the Dakotan stem, who worked their way through the narrow peninsula separating Lakes Michigan and Superior, and thence to the valley of the St. Lawrence, where their traditional history commences. It seems also not unlikely that the Winnebagoes were following on the same general line, and striving to enter the forest area, when their further progress eastward was arrested by the superior power of the nations which held this peninsula. Both migrations antedate, probably, the occupation of Minnesota by the Dakotas. The aborigines progressed slowly in these movements, living upon the territory they inhabited, and, if this was poor and unfavorable, constantly striving for the possession of a better area. Centuries might elapse before a Missouri nation, moving eastward, would have become established on the east side of the Mississippi, which formed a great natural barrier; and still other centuries, with many changes of location, before the same nation would reach the valley of the St. Lawrence. The valley of the Ohio, and particularly the region between that river and Lake Erie, so poorly supplied with fish, seems to have been avoided by the Roving Indians. Not until after European colonization had commenced did the Iroquois extend their occupation over this area, as far west as Indiana, although agricultural in their habits. Migrations eastward over the territory between the Ohio and Lake Erie were therefore extremely improbable.

III. *Migrations of the Gulf Nations.*

Philologists have recognized five stock languages among the nations inhabiting the regions, east of the Mississippi, between the Ohio and Neuse rivers — which may serve for the northern boundary — and the gulf of Mexico. These are the Catawba, the Natches, the Uche, the Creek, and the Cherokee.

Of the Catawba, there is but one vocabulary published, and that a scanty one. Of the existence of anything beyond this the writer is not aware. The conclusion that it is a distinct stock is, therefore, a negative one. A comparison of this vocabulary — which is found in the Mithridates, and also in Gallatin's collection — with those of the Dakotan dialects discloses strong similarities, rising in some words to the point of identity. It is not improbable that it will ultimately be found to be a dialect of that stock language.

Neither the Uche nor the Natches language has been investigated sufficiently to demonstrate its independent position. The Uches, and the remains of the Natches who survived their overthrow by the French, became afterwards, and are now, constituent members of the Creek confederacy. This fact alone tends to prove a remote connection by blood with the Creeks, although it is not conclusive.

The dialects of the Creek language are the Muscoke, or Creek proper, the Seminole, the Alabama, the Chocta, and the Chickasa. The last two are subdivisions of one nation, and the Seminoles are an offshoot from the Creeks, of no ancient date.

The Cherokee, which is spoken in two dialects, and has been thoroughly investigated, has some affinity with the Creek, and also with the Iroquois, but it still holds the position of an independent stock language. Concerning the migrations of these nations, and of the small bands west of the Mississippi, along the northern shores of the gulf, no knowledge is preserved. It is only by ascertaining their connection with nations whose migrations are traceable, that this knowledge can be recovered. We can only say that such of them as possess, in reality, independent languages, are presumptively the earliest occupiers of the country east of the Mississippi.

IV. *Migrations of the Prairie Nations.*

The Pawnees and Arickarees speak closely allied dialects, and are subdivisions of an original nation. When first known, the former nation occupied in four divisions the upper waters of the Kansas, and ranged from there to the Platte river. They were numerous and powerful for an Indian nation. After their separation, the Arickarees emigrated to the Upper Missouri, near the Mandans, where they became agricultural, and stationary in villages. Neither they nor the Pawnees ever lived east of the Missouri.

The only known congeners of the Pawnees and Arickarees are the Huecos, Witchitas, Keechies, and Towaches of the Canadian river, and of the Red river of Arkansas. They speak dialects of the same stock language. All these nations have been Prairie Indians since they were first known to the whites, and they have been able to occupy the prairies — subsisting upon the buffalo — through the possession of horses. This branch of the Ganowanian family is thus referred by its known past history to the Rocky mountain chain, near the head-waters of the Arkansas river, along which, in all probability, they traversed the prairies into their modern areas. The line of their migration, which was undoubtedly subsequent both to the Algonkin and Dakotan, points to the valley of the Columbia as its starting-point.

V. *Shoshonee Migrations.*

The nations speaking dialects of the Shoshonee stock-language are the Shoshonees, or Snake Indians, in subdivisions, who now inhabit Lewis's fork of the Columbia river, and range southward to the Humboldt river, and eastward to the Wind-river mountains; the Utes in several subdivisions, who inhabit the territory of Utah, from the region of Great-salt lake south-ward to New Mexico, and the west side of the Colorado as far south as Arizona; the Comanches of Texas; and the Cawios, Netelas, and other small bands in the peninsula of Lower California. In this stock of the Ganowanian family, the Shoshonees and Comanches are the most conspicuous in number, influence, and character. The former, since their discovery, have held the same area substantially, although a portion of them, according to a tradition of the Crow Indians, occupied, several centuries ago, the head waters of the Yellow-stone river, from which the Crows displaced them.

The Comanches, called at different times Paducas and Hictans, have been known from an early period. It is within a century, however, that they have come into prominence. Mountaineers originally, they became Prairie Indians through possession of the horse, and have far outstripped all of their congeners in number and intelligence. At the time of Coronado's expedition to New Mexico, in 1540, if they were met with at all by those adventurers, which is not certain, they were a feeble and inconsiderable nation. When first known to Americans they ranged northward to the Arkansas, and beyond into Kansas, and southward through the western part of Texas, well towards the gulf of Mexico.

In some respects the Shoshonee migration is more significant than that of any other stock of the Ganowanian family. Its course is still manifest, as well as the precise region in which it took its rise. The greater part of the area overspread is still held by nations of the Shoshonee speech. It extends from the principal branch of the Columbia southward, to the Colorado, where it divides into two streams: one, turning southeasterly, and migrating apparently by way of the Arkansas, reached Texas; while the other, keeping west of the Colorado, flowed southwesterly, until its most advanced bands penetrated Lower California — the two extremes being a thousand miles apart from east to west. There is no doubt whatever that the initial point of this migration was in the valley of the Columbia, where a greater abundance of the means of subsistence than was to be found in other areas favored a rapid increase of numbers; this surplus population being constantly forced outward by subdivisions resulting from the nature of their institutions. This statement will serve to illustrate the manner in which Indian migrations probably proceeded. The people, flowing out from a permanent centre of population, spread, slowly and step by step, over a continuous area which they strove to hold, and did retain until they were displaced by other emigrants. After portions of a particular stock had become separated by intervening and hostile nations, there was a strong tendency in the separated parts to reunite, by abandoning one of the areas and removing to the other. Thus their territorial positions were constantly shifting. A common language was the bond of peace and the means of confederation for mutual protection; whilst differences of language in nations confronting each other were the prolific source of interminable warfare. It is not unlikely that successive stocks had occupied the Dakotan and Algonkin areas before the appearance of the latter on the Missouri and the great lakes, and that many nations perished or were absorbed in the struggles of Indian nations with each other for the possession of particular areas. The Shoshonee migration was going on at the time of European discovery, and was consummated within the historical period by the development of the Shoshonee nation in the present territory of Idaho, and of the Comanche power in Western Texas. Their possessions were still substantially continuous and unbroken, and stretched back to the valley from which the stream had flowed. It was in the order of time the last stock language which, having become distinct in the valley of the Columbia, flowed out from that fruitful nursery of tongues, and took its place in the Ganowanian family of languages in distant parts of the continent — a language certainly the most opulent, in the number of its dialects, ever developed by any portion of the human family.

Four definite streams — the Algonkin, the Dakotan, the Pawnee, and the Shoshonee — have now been considered, all of which seem to proceed from the valley of the Columbia as their original source. In point of time the Algonkins apparently held the advance in the eastern movement, and were thus able to follow the isothermal line, by way of the Saskatchewan, to the great lake region, and thence to the valley of the St. Lawrence; while the Dakotas, striving to move in the same general direction, took a more southern route, by way of the Platte; and the Pawnees and Shoshonees, moving still later, followed a route still farther south. This, at least, seems to be the most probable solution of the order and course of these migrations.

VI. *Athapasco-Apache Migrations.*

The Athapascans, who inhabit the Hudson's-bay territory, and the Apaches and Navajoes of New Mexico, speak dialects of the same stock language. Their migrations present the remarkable spectacle of a stock dividing in some central area, one branch moving northward and becoming established in a nearly arctic climate, and the other moving southward into a semi-tropical region; and illustrate the truth that the habitat of man is co-extensive with the earth; his superior and flexible organization enabling him to become arctic or tropical in his habits, as circumstances may direct his migrations.

We are indebted to the late Professor W. W. Turner for the identification of the two great branches of this stock. The evidence, which is derived from a comparison of vocables, clearly establishes the fact.[1] The northern branch consists of the Cheppeyans, Hares, Dog-Ribs, Beavers, Red-Knives, Acheotennes, Kūchin (Koo-tchin'), Mountaineers, and some other bands, east of the Rocky mountains; and the Tacullies, Umkwas, and Hoopahs, west of those mountains; as well as several small nations in Alaska. The southern branch is formed by the Apaches in several subdivisions or embryo nations (Lipans, Miscaleros, Jicarillos, Coyoteros, and some other bands), who occupy an extensive district of country, from the ranges of the Comanches on the east nearly to the gulf of California on the west — including the northern parts of the Mexican states of Chihuahua and Sonora, and the parts of New Mexico not occupied by the Village Indians. In the northern part of the latter territory are the Navijoes and Pinols, who belong to the Apache stock.[1] The Apaches did not come into notice until after they obtained the horse, which has raised many Indian nations from obscurity. They were mentioned by Father Kino in 1694. At the time of Coronado's expedition, before referred to, they were probably in possession of some part of these regions as wild bands.[2]

In the migrations of this stock a fifth stream is recognized — earlier in point of time than the Shoshonee, and probably later

---

[1] *Explorations for a Railroad Route, etc., to the Pacific*, vol. III, Report on Indian tribes, page 84.

[2] Gregg's *Commerce of the Prairies*, I, 285.

[3] For a Spanish account of the Apaches in 1799, *vide* report of Don Jose Cortez (*Explorations for a Railroad Route*, III, 119). Cf., also, report of M. Steck (*President's Message and Documents*, 1859, I, 712); and report of E. A. Graves (*Ibid.*, 1854, 1855, I, 385).

than the Algonkin — which divided at some point between the two extremes in which they were found, and moved in opposite directions. The only intermediate region to which they can be referred as the place of their origin is the valley of the Columbia. It is a further and important confirmation of the superior claims of this valley, over the remainder of the continent, to be regarded as the nursery of the Ganowanian family.

VII.— *Migrations of the Village Indians.*

1. *The Village Indians of New Mexico and Arizona.*— Without a doubt, the valleys of New Mexico and Arizona have been the seats of the Village Indians from a very ancient date. This view is sustained by the number and position of the present pueblos, by the ruins of deserted pueblos surrounded with traces of cultivation, and by the number of stock languages still spoken in these limited areas. There are some reasons, derived from the number and extent of the pueblos in ruins in New Mexico and on the San Juan, and on its northern tributaries in the southern part of Utah, for supposing that Village Indian life in this region was in a state of decadence at the time of its discovery. It seems probable that the more northern Village Indians had been overpowered and forced southward by the roving nations. For upwards of three centuries the Pueblo Indians, as they are called, have been known to us, and have remained substantially in the same condition; but of their previous history and movements there exists no knowledge. No connection has as yet been discovered between their languages and those of the northern or southern Indians. Their village life probably commenced with the introduction of agriculture into this region. It is not necessary to assume that they migrated from the south and carried agriculture with them, in order to explain its presence in New Mexico, any more than it is, to infer that the Shiyans and Hurons emigrated from the gulf region into the Dakota territory and Canada, to explain their knowledge of agriculture. In many ways the art of cultivating the ground would spread from place to place by the mere accidents of aboriginal life, as well as through deliberate efforts made for its acquisition. It would be a fatal

error to adopt the track of agriculture as the line of original migration. Indian agriculture must have originated in a tropical climate, from the nature of the cereal upon which it rested, and long after both North and South America had become peopled with roving Indians. No supposition of the dispersion of the aborigines from a centre within the tropics is necessary. Whilst agricultural nations would be certain to carry cultivation wherever they migrated, the tendency of its practice was, to localize a people and arrest changes of dwelling, except within short distances. Agriculture was quite as likely to be propagated backward on the line of migration as forward.

The Village Indians of the lower Colorado, who speak the Pima and Yuma stock languages, are cultivators of the ground, but not house-builders either in adobe brick or stone. They still use the round-roofed wigwam, constructed of rude materials, but large enough for several families. From this fact it may be inferred, notwithstanding the evidence of their long-continued village habits, that their transformation from a non-agricultural to an agricultural life occurred within their present areas, and more recently than that of the other Village Indians of New Mexico. For their ancestors, it is not necessary to look beyond the Northern Roving Indians. It is not improbable that the more advanced class of Village Indians were equally slow in attaining their knowledge of architecture, and that centuries elapsed, after they became agricultural, before they learned or invented the art of constructing houses with adobe brick and stone. The evidence is decisive, of a very great antiquity of Village Indian life in New Mexico; but the probability is strong that the ancestors of all these nations were immigrants from the valley of the Columbia.

2. *The Village Indians of Mexico and Central America.* — In both of these areas the evidence of occupation from a very ancient date is equally decisive from architectural remains and from the number of stock languages. It is not probable that the number of these languages could be reduced below eight or ten, if the materials for comparison were ample. There are supposed to be eighteen. "We can safely affirm," says Clavigero, "that

there are no living or dead languages which can differ more among each other than the languages of the Mexicans, Otomies, Tarascas, Mayas, and Miztecas — five languages prevailing in different provinces of Mexico."[1] Such a result might have been expected from the number of inhabited localities and of independent nations. Moreover, the higher development of architecture and of stone sculptures in Chiapa and Yucatan affords evidence of a long period of village life in these areas — much longer than that of the Aztecs in the valley of Mexico, if we may judge from a comparison of corresponding works. It does not follow, however, that the whole of their experience in village life was acquired within the areas in which they were found.

It is a singular as well as instructive fact that the principal historical nations of Mexico found in possession of the country at the time of the Spanish invasion had resided there but a few hundred years. Their respective migrations were so recent in point of time, that the knowledge of the event, and of the direction from which they came, had not fallen out of remembrance. The particulars, with some degree of minuteness, were preserved by tradition. It becomes then a question of importance how far historical credit can be given to traditions, which are necessarily verbal, and liable to alteration in their transmission. The question is one worthy of a brief discussion.

Indian nations usually have a definite tradition of their last migration, particularly when it resulted in a prosperous establishment in a new home. It would require several centuries to efface all remembrance of such an experience among a people of ordinary intelligence. An oral tradition of a great migration, embodying an event so influential upon the subsequent life of a nation, would preserve the principal facts with great tenacity. In the absence of improbable circumstances, its essential statements must be accepted as historical evidence. These Indian traditions usually contain internal evidence of probability; and

---

[1] *History of Mexico*, III, 100. He names (*Ibid.*, page 371), the following languages, fourteen in number, of which a grammar, a dictionary, or both had been prepared, viz: Mexican, Otomie, Tarascan, Zapotecan, Miztecan, Maya, Totonacan, Popolucan, Matlazincan, Huaxtecan, Mixe, Cakciquel, Taraumaran, and Tepehuanan.

when they speak of no extravagant periods of time or unreasonable occurrences, their credibility may be admitted, on the ground of the extreme improbability that the remembrance of such events should have been lost. These suggestions apply to the historical traditions of the principal Mexican nations, to be stated hereafter, which have an important bearing upon the general conclusions to which the main discussion in this article tends. Whatever support the written or pictorial records of the Aztecs may add is left out of view. After the lapse of a few centuries, it is not uncommon for a claim to autochthony to spring up, and dispute possession with the tradition of a previous migration from a distant land. Thus the Iroquois have a well-defined tradition that they came from the north bank of the St. Lawrence near Montreal into Central New York, by way of the Oswego river, coasting the lake in canoes; and this tradition is confirmed by sufficient independent evidence. They also have a tradition that they sprang out of the ground, the Onondagas near Oswego, and the Senecas near Canandaigua. The traditions of the principal Mexican nations concerning their migration from the north are more specific than that of the Iroquois. They contain such internal evidence of probability that it is difficult to perceive upon what just ground of criticism their authority can be denied.

The Aztecs had a full and circumstantial tradition, not only of their own migration from the north, but also of the migration of several other kindred nations. It is given by Acosta, whose work was first published at Seville in 1589.[1] He visited Mexico prior to that date,[2] and consequently was in the country early enough to reach original sources of information. Substantially the same tradition is given by Herrera and Clavigero. Acosta remarks: "These second peoples, Navatalcas [the first inhabitants he calls Chichemecas], came from other far countries which lie towards the north, where now they have discovered a kingdom which they call New Mexico. There are two provinces in this country — the one called Aztlan, which is to say, a place of

---

[1] *Natural and Moral History of the East and West Indies*, Lond. ed. 1604, Grimstone's Trans., pp. 497—504.

[2] Acosta states in his work (p. 502) that he was in Mexico in 1585.

herons; the other Teaculhuacan, which signifies a land of such whose grandfathers were divine. .... The Navatalcas paint their beginning and first territory in the figure of a cave, and say they came forth of seven caves to come and people the land of Mexico." He fixes the time of the migration of the first of the seven nations at 720 A. D. — which of course must be considered as an approximate date only — and the length of time consumed in the movement at eighty years. In like manner the migration of the Aztecs, the last of the seven nations, was commenced in 1022 A. D., according to the same authority. Acosta states the names of these nations and the order of their arrival in Mexico as follows: 1. Suchimilcos, nation of the seeds of flowers. They settled upon Lake Xochimilco. 2. Chalcas, people of mouths. They came long after the former, and settled near them. 3. Tepanecans, people of the bridge. They settled on the west side of the lake of Mexico. Their chief town, Azcapuzalco, signifies the ants' nest. They were numerous. 4. Culhuas, a crooked people. These were the Tezcucans, who came some time after, and settled upon the east side of the lake. 5. Tlatluicans, men of the sierra, or mountain. This nation, finding the country around Lake Tezcuco occupied, passed southward, to the other side of the mountain. 6. Tlascaltecans, men of bread. They settled Tlascala. 7. Aztecs, or Mexicans. "Three hundred and two years afterwards [1022] those of the seventh cave or line arrived, which is the Mexican nation; the which, like unto the rest, left Aztlan and Teaculhuacan a polite, cultivated, and warlike nation."

Clavigero gives substantially the same tradition. "But of all the nations," he remarks, "which peopled the region of Anahuac, the most renowned and the most signalized in the history of Mexico were those vulgarly called Nahuatlacas. This name ..... was principally given to those seven nations, or rather those seven tribes of the same nation, who arrived in that country after the Chichemecas, and peopled the little islands, banks, and boundaries of the Mexican lakes. These tribes were the Sochimilcas, the Chalchese, the Tepanecas, the Colhuas, the Tlahuicas, the Tlascalans, and the Mexicans. The origin of all these tribes was the province of Aztlan, from whence came the Mexicans, or from some other contiguous to it, and peopled with the same nation. All historians represent them as originally of one and the same country; all of them spoke the same language."[1] Elsewhere he observes: "The Chichemecas, like the Toltecs, who preceded them, and other nations, which came after them, were originally from the north countries, as we may call the north of America, like the north of Europe, the seminary of the human race."[2]

Besides this general tradition, there is another of the Aztec migration exclusively, giving a circumstantial account of the motive in which it originated, the various localities in which the emigrants were established for a time on the way, and the incidents connected with their arrival in the valley, and with the foundation of the pueblo of Mexico. They left Aztlan, according to Clavigero, in 1160, arrived at Tulla, north of the valley, in 1196, at Chapultepec in 1245, at Acoloco in 1262, were enslaved by the Cholulans in 1314, freed themselves in 1325, and that year founded Mexico.[3]

The first and general tradition was evidently derived immediately from original sources. Omitting the attempt at a fixed chronology, which is necesarily conjectural even in regard to the century, and also the previous cave-life, which may embody a more ancient tradition, we may accept as credible the principal fact of a migration of these nations from the north, in the order stated, and within a period not remote. It is probable that this tradition, which may possibly have been derived from Aztec re-

---

[1] *Hist. of Mexico* (Phila. ed. 1817), Cullen's Trans., I, 141. Herrera adopts this tradition, and remarks upon their northern origin as follows: "They came from remote parts northward, where New Mexico was afterwards found" (*History of America*, Lond. ed. 1725, Stevens's Trans., III, 188, 189).

[2] *Ibid*, II, 119. Prescott (*Hist. Conq. of Mexico*, III, 397), thus refers to the several traditions: "They are admitted to agree in representing the populous north as the prolific hive of the American races. . . . . From this quarter the Toltecs, the Chichemecs, and the kindred races of the Nahuatlacs came successively up the great plateau of the Andes, spreading over the hills and valleys down to the gulf of Mexico." Again (*Ibid*., I, 15): "The Mexicans, with whom our history is principally concerned, came also, as has been seen, from the remote regions of the north, the populous hive of nations in the new world, as it has been in the old."

[3] *History of Mexico*, I, 150.

cords, rests upon the authority of Acosta alone, in which case its repetition by other authors does not increase its weight. Whether Acosta obtained it directly from aboriginal sources or at secondhand, it is probable in itself, and both in style and matter bears genuine marks of the Indian mind. The names given to these several nations are in strict accordance with the Indian method of national designation, and find their analogues in the names of northern Indian nations at the present time.[1] It is also intrinsically probable that these nations migrated at intervals of time, one following the other, and that years were consumed while these several movements were progressing. Since they must have passed through regions partially inhabited, and were striving to enter a highly desirable area already occupied by other nations, their migrations were necessarily military migrations, in which they contended with hostile nations for the mastery of each area. A successful migration, followed by a prosperous establishment in a desirable home, would involve years of effort and several changes of location. The special and more elaborate tradition of the Aztec migration which rests upon the authority of Clavigero corroborates the first. It is not necessary to adopt the minute circumstances or the chronology. The Aztecs, before their arrival in Mexico, could scarcely have possessed an accurate method of recording time; but the principal events which occurred between the time when they are supposed to have left Aztlan (A.D. 1160) and the Spanish conquest (1520), embracing a period of three hundred and sixty years, would be kept in remembrance. Within this period also the lapse of time between particular events would be known with reasonable nearness. It is another confirmatory fact that no extravagant antiquity is claimed for the foundation of the pueblo of Mexico. The Aztec records fixed the period at about 1325, but one hundred and ninety-six years prior to the Spanish conquest. To have increased their numbers and their influence from a small and feeble band, such

---

[1] Thus, Senecas, *Nun-da-wá-o-no*, great hill people; Onondagas, *O-nun-dá-ga-o-no*, people on the hills; Iowas, *Pa-ho-cha*, dusty noses; Missouris, *Ne-oo-cha-tá*, at the mouth of the stream; *Mi-ni-kan-ye*, those who plant by the water; and *O-ga-lal-lá*, raising camp — the last two being Dakotan nations.

as they doubtless were when they founded Mexico, to their prosperous condition at the latter date, must have required all the time assigned. It would seem also to create the further necessity of moderating materially the current estimates of their advancement and numbers. These several traditions could scarcely have been fictions of Spanish writers. They are so intrinsically probable in their main recitals, that they may fairly claim to be regarded as historical evidence.[1]

But little is known of the migrations of the Village Indians of Yucatan and Central America, and this little rests upon tradition. The Chiapanese had a similar tradition of a northern origin. "They say," observes Clavigero, "that the first peoples came from the quarter of the north, and when they arrived at Soconusco they separated, some going to inhabit the country of Nicaragua, and others remaining in Chiapan." It has elsewhere been stated that Oviedo, in 1526, found a people in Nicaragua who spoke an Aztec dialect which would refer them also to an original home in the north.

With these traditions of a northern origin, which seem to have been current in several nations in Mexico and Central America, and with what is still a matter of obvious inference from the

---

[1] The Honorable John R. Bartlett, whose conclusions as an investigator are entitled to great respect, questions these traditions as evidence that the Aztecs were immigrants from the north. He observes: "I am unable to learn from what source the prevailing idea has arisen, of the migration of the Aztecs, or ancient Mexicans, from the north into the valley of Mexico, and the three halts they made in their journey thither. This is another idea which has been so widely promulgated that it has settled down into an acknowledged fact, although I confess I have seen no satisfactory evidence of its truth. . . . . . The traditions which gave rise to this notion are extremely vague, and were not seriously entertained until Torquemada, Botnrini, and Clavigero gave them currency; but they must now give way to the more reliable results from linguistic comparisons. No analogy has yet been traced between the language of the old Mexicans and that of any tribe at the north in the district from which they are supposed to have come; nor in any of the relics, ornaments, or works of art do we observe a resemblance between them."— *Personal Narrative*, II, 283.

That a particular Indian language has passed beyond identification with any other in its vocables, and become an independent stock language, is not decisive evidence against a migration of the people speaking it from any place in which we have reason to suppose it once dwelt. It may be mentioned, however, that some words have been detected in the Koluschian of Sitka, and in some other far northern language, which are believed to be identical with the corresponding words in the Aztec speech. Latham (Notes to *Prichard's Eastern Origin of the Celtic Nations*, p. 21), refers to this fact in the following language: "The Aztec or Mexican words found in this language were indicated in the Mithridates. Since the publication, however, of that work, they have been shown to exist in other American languages — some inland, some southern, some interjacent to the Kolosh and Mexican areas, e. g. in California and elsewhere."

geographical features of North America, and the relation of the valley of the Columbia to all its other areas, it is difficult to arrive at any other conclusion than that the ancestors of all these nations were emigrants from that remarkable valley.

3. *The Mound Builders.*— The inquiry, thus far, has been restricted to the Indian nations in actual possession of the country at the period of European discovery. It is not to be supposed, however, that the nations found in particular areas were the first occupants. In very many cases the contrary is known to be true. Under the inexorable law which perpetually worked the subdivision of the Indian tribes as they spread abroad, there was a constant tendency towards an obliteration of many of these fragmentary nations, through collisions with one another. Large numbers of these nations, both in North and South America, undoubtedly perished in the course of centuries, not necessarily by the process of extermination, but rather from inability to maintain successfully the struggle for independence. They disappeared under the blow of some calamity, their fragments becoming incorporated with other nations. The several stocks belonging to the Ganowanian family, who were found in possession of the land, are to be regarded as the descendants and representatives of an original stock, which flowed out in successive streams from some original centre. The remoteness in the past of their first establishment must be estimated by the time required to create the present diversity of speech, both in dialects and stock languages.

Among those nations who are without recognized descendants are the mound-builders who lived east of the Mississippi. It is evident that they were agricultural and Village Indians, from their artificial embankments, their implements and utensils, and from their selection of the areas most poorly provided with fish and game. From the absence of all traditionary knowledge of their existence, amongst the nations found in possession of their territories, it is also to be inferred that the period of their occupation was ancient. Their disappearance was probably gradual, and completed before the advent of the present stocks, or simultaneously with their arrival. The small number of sites of ancient villages, and the scanty population assignable to Indian villages even of the largest class, particularly in cold climates, are good reasons for supposing they were never very numerous. It is a reasonable conjecture, as elsewhere stated, that they were Village Indians from New Mexico. In fact, there is no other region from which they could have been derived; unless it be assumed that, originally Roving Indians, they had become, after their establishment east of the Mississippi, Village Indians of the highest type — of which there is not the slightest probability. It seems more likely that their retirement from the country was voluntary, than that they were expelled by an influx of roving nations. If their overthrow had been the result of a protracted warfare, all remembrance of so remarkable an event would scarcely have been lost among the nations by whom they were displaced. A warm climate was to some extent necessary for the successful maintenance of the highest form of Village Indian life. In the struggle for existence in the colder climates, Indian arts and ingenuity have been taxed quite as severely to provide clothing as food. It is, therefore, not improbable that the attempt to transfer the type of village life of New Mexico to the Ohio valley proved a failure; and that after great efforts, continued for more centuries than one, it was finally abandoned, and they gradually withdrew, first into the gulf states, and lastly from the country altogether.

No reference has been made to the Eskimo, for the reason that their system of consanguinity and affinity disconnects them from the Ganowanian family. The Eskimo were originally emigrants from Asia, if the fact that a portion of this stock still exists upon the Asiatic side of the strait of Behring can be considered sufficient evidence. On the assumption that the Ganowanian family came out of Asia, their migration was necessarily very much earlier than that of the Eskimo. This is sufficiently demonstrated by the number of stock languages and dialects now existing in the former family, which, on the supposition of an Asiatic origin, would have required for their formation immensely long periods of time after their arrival on this continent. On the contrary, the dialects of the Eskimo, from the gulf of Anadyr in Asia, through

Arctic America and Greenland, still belong to the same stock language, which precludes the supposition of any great antiquity of the Eskimo on the American continent.

This concludes the suggestions the writer intended to make with respect to particular migrations. The discussion has been made sufficiently comprehensive to include the body of the American aborigines found in possession at the period of European discovery. If the views herein presented as to these stocks are sound, those which have disappeared, and those which remain unnoticed, must have followed the same routes. Some general considerations will conclude these articles.

With respect to the influence of agricultural subsistence in tending to create separate centres of population, either in South or North America, able collectively to offset the superior advantages in point of natural means of subsistence possessed by the valley of the Columbia, some further discussion may be necessary, lest a doubt should remain upon this material question. An outgrowth of civilization in a particular area, founded upon a subsistence obtained by agriculture, might, if carried far enough, have neutralized the previously superior advantages of the valley of the Columbia, and thus have created a more fruitful centre of population, able to send forth larger streams to overpower those issuing from that area. But there is not a fact to show that the Village Indians of Central America or Mexico ever spread northward, or competed with the Northern Indians for the possession of any part of the continent north of the immediate valley of Mexico; while several reasons may be assigned against the supposition of a movement in that direction. In the first place, the principal historical nations found in Mexico were themselves emigrants from the north. Secondly, climatic considerations, in the absence of overcrowded territories, would tend to repress migrations from a warm to a colder region. Thirdly, their type of village life was not adapted to cold climates. Although possessed of cotton, and the art of spinning and weaving it into light fabrics, this was incapable of affording them a warm apparel. The Village Indians of New Mexico, although well advanced in Indian arts, wore buffalo-robes and other robes of skins, like the Roving Indians. Friar Marcos de Niza, in his relation, speaking of the Cibolans in 1540, remarks: "Their apparel is of cotton and ox-hides, and this is their most commendable and honorable apparel."[1] They possessed no manufactured fabric capable of becoming a substitute for skins in the winter season. Fourthly, their institutions were unfavorable to the formation of a state capable of embracing and governing the descendants of an original stock as it increased in numbers and spread over larger areas. It was impossible to comprehend great numbers of the same lineage and language under one Indian government, and thus create a large homogeneous population; and it is extremely doubtful whether there ever were at one time, in any part of North America, one hundred thousand Indians who spoke the same dialect. This, if true, is so remarkable as well as important a fact, that the disproval of it would be a valuable contribution to the history of the American aborigines. These were organized into small bands or nations, the people of which spoke the same dialect. In many instances two or more such nations speaking dialects of the same stock language were united into a confederacy. The government of each was an oligarchy of chiefs in council, and the system failed to arrest the tendency to repeated subdivision, followed by territorial separation, independence, and the gradual formation of new dialects. As a necessary consequence of this multiplicity of nations and dialects, without any comprehensive governmental organization, perpetual warfare was superadded to the other hardships of their condition which tended to prevent their increase. The Aztec confederacy was the highest and most successful effort of the North American Indian nations to establish an Indian power. Yet it created neither an empire nor a state, in any proper sense of those terms. It subdued and placed under tribute a number of feeble petty nations, chiefly south of the valley; but it failed to consolidate them into one people, even for governmental purposes. On the contrary, it is plain that the confederacy was unable to wield the power of these tributary nations for common

---

[1] Hakluyt's *Collection of Voyages*, London, England, 1600, III, 872.

national objects.[1] A government founded upon territory, resting upon the body of the people, and administered by law, is the growth of ages. The American aborigines were thousands of years behind the modern idea of a state in their development. The table-lands of Mexico have no history prior to the Aztec occupation, except the dim account of their Toltec predecessors, and the unimportant history of their contemporaries. No people were ever able to hold these table-lands and valleys long enough to found a state; to rise by force of numbers out of the tribal, national and confederate organizations into a true political life, with a government of fixed and equal laws in the place of the arbitrary will of chiefs and the equally fluctuating determinations of councils. The time had not arrived, in the successive stages of progressive experience, for the American Indian to arrive at the forms of civilization. Fifthly, agriculture transformed them from Roving into Village Indians, which tended to localize them, as has been elsewhere stated; but this, although the numbers speaking the same dialect were thereby considerably increased, restricted them to much smaller areas than those occupied by nations of Roving Indians. Lastly, the productiveness of their agriculture was very limited, from the small extent of land cultivated, imperfect implements, and the amount of labor involved.

It does not appear, therefore, that there was any centre of population, either in Mexico or elsewhere, which became, on the basis of agricultural subsistence, a competitor with the fish-producing country of the Columbia in populating the continent. On the contrary, we are compelled to look to the last named region for that constant surplus of numbers, which would furnish successive streams of emigants, through indefinite periods of time, until an equilibrium of population was reached throughout the continent. Since physical causes were superior to human arts and institutions in influencing the movements of the aborigines, these causes remained unaffected, except to a limited extent, by the indigenous civilization which sprang up in particular areas.

---

[1] But one of these nations responded to the call for aid against the Spaniards; and this tardy force was dispersed before it reached the scene of action.

It is surprising how small an excess of natural advantages will invest a single district of country with permanent control over an entire continent in the primitive periods of man's existence; and with how great difficulty that superiority is neutralized and overcome. The reason is found in the uniformity of the operation of physical causes. We have seen that the Shoshonee migration was in progress at the time of European colonization; and that, at the last moment of the exclusive possession of North America by its aboriginal inhabitants, the valley of the Columbia was sending out another stock language and an independent people, to take their place in the midst of the languages and nations that had preceded them from the same land. Likewise the ultimate fact is reached, that a fish subsistence created the surplus of numbers which first spread abroad from this initial point to people North America, and from time to time supplied the successive bands of emigrants which replenished the continent with inhabitants.

It remains to apply the facts and conclusions, thus reached in relation to the North American Indians, to the aborigines of South America, for the purpose of ascertaining whether they are sufficient to sustain a similar hypothesis with regard to the peopling of the southern from the northern continent.

We are now prepared to recognize the existence of a constant tendency of the aboriginal population to flow southward from the valley of the Columbia, down the mountain chains toward the isthmus of Panama. A movement northward would be less probable, from climatic reasons, and eastward still less, from the barrier of the central plains. Mexico and Central America presumptively were first reached and occupied. Each successive stream of population would press upon its predecessors, tending to force the first emigrants southward through the isthmus into South America, where the Andes, a continuation substantially of the Rocky mountain chain, would direct the movement toward Patagonia. It is also probable, as has been elsewhere suggested, that both divisions of the continent were overspread with Roving Indians before the discovery of corn and the art of cultivating it. Neither can it be supposed that the remote ancestors of the

American aborigines were as far advanced in the arts of life as the Roving Indians were when first discovered; for there are many stages of progress in the ages of barbarism, as well as in the age of civilization. Whatever may be the experience of particular nations or stocks, the human family forever progresses. Century after century might have elapsed before the thought of utilizing corn and the bean dawned upon the Indian mind. The art of cultivating the earth, upon the limited scale on which they practiced it, created a new epoch in the Indian family. It not only favored, but necessitated village life, imperfectly attained before, which in turn tended to a rapid development of Indian arts. The condition and antecedents of the Mexican and Central American nations, at the period of the Spanish conquest, render it probable that the struggle between the Roving and Village Indians for the possession of these regions had been continuous from age to age, the former expelling the latter and becoming themselves Village Indians, to be afterwards forced southward by succeeding immigrants. The attractive character of the table-lands and valleys of Mexico, and their position on the narrowing highway to the gate of Panama, made it extremely difficult to hold these lands against advancing bands, except by superior numbers, or a higher knowledge of the art of war. In the latter respect it is well known that the Village Indians had made no advance beyond the Roving Indians, except in the art of constructing great communal edifices of the nature of fortresses, which the Aztecs had carried a step farther by surrounding their pueblo with water defences. The bow and arrow and the war-club were the principal weapons of all alike, and the most destructive of which they had any knowledge.

The first people in the valley of Mexico, of whom any knowledge has been preserved, were the Toltecs. They are supposed to have made considerable progress in civilization; but this did not enable them to hold the valley any more successfully than their predecessors, whoever they may have been. They evidently yielded to the influence of some calamity, and silently departed, none knew whither. After the discovery by Oviedo, in 1526, of a people in Nicaragua who spoke a dialect of the

Aztec language, this was supposed to be the remains of that nation;[1] and whether it was so or not, the finding of an Aztec stock in this extreme southern position seems to confirm the general conclusion, that the drift of population, particularly of fragments of nations, was southward. The facts collectively seem to sustain the inference that nation after nation, through century after century, had tried the experiment of holding these table lands and valleys against the Roving Indians constantly flowing down upon them, and that, one after the other, they had been borne on toward the south, and many of them, doubtless, swept through the isthmus into South America. Last, the Aztecs and their confederates tried the experiment, with the probable additional advantage of reaching the valley as agricultural and Village Indians. Sufficient time, however, had not elapsed to demonstrate their ability to hold an area lying across the natural highway of the continent southward. It should be observed that, within the short period of two hundred years before the Spanish conquest, the Aztec confederacy had risen from very small beginnings.[2] At the time of the Spanish invasion they were still confronted upon the east, north, and west by independent and hostile nations, whose power they had not been able to break. It may be a question whether the confederacy would have been able to maintain its position permanently, if it had been left to the natural course of events, free from European interference. Its position, surrounded by water defences substantially impregnable to Indian warfare, was the strongest

---

[1] *Trans. Am. Ethn. Soc.*, I, 8.

[2] Immediately prior to the founding of the pueblo of Mexico (1325) they were living at Acoloco, which consisted, says Clavigero, "of a number of small islands in the southern extremity of the lake. .... There, for the space of fifty-two years, they led the most miserable life; they subsisted on fish and all sorts of insects, and the roots of the marshes, and covered themselves with the leaves of the amoxtli, which grows plentifully in that lake. .... Their habitations were wretched huts, made of the reeds and rushes which the lake produced. It would be totally incredible that for so many years they were able to keep in existence in a place so disadvantageous, where they were so stinted in the necessaries of life, were it not verified by their historians and by succeeding events."—(*Hist. Conq. Mexico*, I, 156.)

The Aztecs were the first occupiers of the site of Mexico. But other nations of the same descent, who entered the valley before them, were in possession of the margins of the lakes, and would hardly have overlooked the great natural strength of this site, had it then been surrounded by Lake Tezcuco. Their neglect of it confirms the suggestion, elsewhere made, that the pueblo of Mexico was surrounded by artificial ponds made by the Aztecs.

guaranty of successful resistance, and the accumulation of independent bands on its northern frontier was the source of its greatest danger. With the possession of this fertile valley, and with the advantages of climate and of agricultural productions, it might have been expected that some native stock would have been able to develop a nation within this area, sufficiently numerous and powerful to influence materially the peopling of both divisions of the continent. But the Aztecs would probably have failed of such a destiny, as all previous confederacies, if such existed, had failed, and for reasons inherent in their institutions.

It cannot have escaped attention that the general course of Indian migrations upon the North-American continent, under the influence of physical causes, would tend to an early peopling of South America. If the general views which have been now presented with reference to the initial point and general direction of these migrations are considered established, they are sufficient to create a strong presumption that South America received its first inhabitants from the north; and this presumption would require strong evidence to rebut it. Whether the discovery of corn and the introduction of agriculture occurred north or south of the isthmus of Panama, it is at least plain that it spread at a remote period over Central America and Mexico; and from that time forward the effect of the general course of Indian migrations was to expel agricultural and Village Indians from North into South America. This process, long continued, would tend to give to South America a superior class of inhabitants, and, possibly, an older and higher civilization. The northern continent, in which barbarous nations preponderated, was thus impoverished to some extent by losing a portion of its most advanced and cultivated inhabitants for the benefit of the southern. The geographical features of America, and the relative distribution of the natural means of subsistence, are such as to render it extremely probable that a primitive family planted in the valley of the Columbia, and migrating from this area under the exclusive influence of physical causes, would have reached Patagonia, as I have elsewhere suggested, sooner than they would Florida. It may therefore be claimed, with a strong degree of probability, that the ancestors of the South American Indians originated in this valley.

In this and a preceding article, an attempt has been made to embody the principal facts bearing upon the migrations of the North American Indians, in order to form an hypothesis for explaining the initial point of those migrations and their general courses. It was found that these migrations were controlled almost exclusively by physical causes; and that their natural highways were indicated by the direction of the mountain chains, and the courses of the great rivers; while a free communication between the western and eastern sides of North America was interrupted by the formidable barrier of the central prairie area. In the second place, a comparison of the several districts of North America, with reference to the natural means of subsistence afforded by them, revealed great differences, and showed that the valley of the Columbia surpassed all other regions of America in the abundance and variety of food it furnished, to which was added the advantage of a mild and genial climate. There, and there alone, was found a region capable of furnishing a surplus population developed from the stable, unvarying supply of *fish subsistence*, and thrown off at such intervals of time as would explain the relations of the several stocks to each other, and to the land of their common origin. In the third place, certain facts were presented tending to show that Indian agriculture was never carried far enough to counterbalance the advantages of the abundant fish subsistence of the Columbia river. It was further shown that the Village Indians were unable to develop, upon agricultural subsistence, numbers sufficient to overflow the areas of the Roving nations and accomplish their displacement; and that, on the contrary, the latter nations from time to time penetrated the agricultural districts and became themselves Village Indians, thus contributing to their numbers; and finally, that the Roving and partially Village Indians seem, from first to last, to have taken the leading part in peopling the areas of North America. The migrations of particular stocks were then considered, and the relations of the subdivisions of each were indicated. Comparisons were also made of the relative amounts of subsistence afforded by nature in different parts of the continent, in order to find the secondary centres from which population spread. After these had been pointed out, we next endeavored, through the general relations of these stocks to each other, and from their languages, traditions, and known migrations, to find the initial point where these several streams took their rise. These investigations and comparisons seemed to establish, with a reasonable degree of certainty, the following conclusions: first, that the distribution of the aborigines over North America began on the Pacific side of the continent: second, that the several stock languages east of the Rocky mountains and north of New Mexico had become distinct before these stocks migrated eastward; third, that the nations of Mexico and Central America were emigrants from the north; and last, that the initial point of all these migrations was in the valley of the Columbia. In this valley a land is discovered so amply endowed by nature with the means of subsistence, and standing in such geographical relations to the remainder of North America, as to explain and harmonize the phenomena under consideration. All the conditions of an adequate and satisfactory hypothesis for the explanation of the migrations of the American Indians seem to have been fulfilled. Since subsistence on the bounties of nature necessarily precedes agriculture in the order of time, any hypothesis looking to any other nursery of population will fail for the want of the indispensable condition of a superabundant supply, by nature, of the means of subsistence. It is entirely immaterial at what place on the shores of the Pacific, between the Arctic sea and Mexico, the Indian family made its first appearance. If, in fact, it came from beyond the sea, it would gravitate irresistibly to the valley of the Columbia. That valley and the adjacent sea-coasts contained the paradise of the red man in the age of stone, when fish was his main sustenance, and game and bread-roots accessories for the promotion of his physical development. It will be impossible to explain the peopling of North America from any other centre. Had the Indian family been first planted in South America, and their descendants in course of time reached this valley, it would, from and after that event, have reversed the course of Indian migrations and become the source from which both divisions of the continent would have received inhabitants. No other area in either could compete with it in advantages for the support and increase of population. Ample time must have elapsed since the first occupation of this valley to efface beyond recovery all traces of a migration from South America, if such ever occurred.

With respect to the anterior question, whether the Indian family reached North or South America first, on the assumption that it had an Asiatic origin, we are left to a choice of probabilities. It is plain, however, that physical considerations and the types of man in northeastern Asia point to this section of Asia as the source, and to the Aleutian islands as the probable avenue, of this antecedent migration. This is no new hypothesis. A belief in his Asiatic origin was one of the first conclusions which followed the discovery of the Indian and a knowledge of his physical characteristics. Subsequent investigations have strengthened the grounds upon which this belief was based.

It will furnish a not appropriate conclusion to these articles to restate briefly the facts and reasons which support the inference of a derivation of the Indian family from northeastern Asia.

In the first place the number of distinct types of mankind in Asia, contrasted with the single type, aside from the Eskimo, existing in America, shows conclusively that the Asiatic continent has been occupied by man much the longer of the two. The striking affinities in physical characteristics between the Mongolian and Tungusian stocks of Asia and the Indian stocks of America, and the near approach of other Asiatic stocks to both, seem to compel us to assume an Asiatic origin for the American Indian, unless the independent creation of man in America be assumed. Secondly, there are two existing avenues between the two continents; one of which, across the straits of Behring, has been actually proved to be practicable, by the Eskimo migration; and the other, by the Aleutian islands, is rendered a probable route by the fact that most of these islands are now inhabited by a people of common descent, who have spread from island to island. Whether the Eskimo had been forced northward in Asia by the pressure of circumstances is immaterial, since it was necessary that they should be hyperborean in their habits to render possible their transit across the icy strait, which is about fifty miles wide where it is narrowest.[1] But it was not necessary that the ancestors of the American aborigines should have become hyperboreans in Asia, to explain their migration to America. The Aleutian islands furnish a possible as well as much more probable route. It is not to be supposed that it was a deliberate migration in numbers which brought the Ganowanian family to America, if they came from Asia. The natural obstacles presented to a transit by the Aleutian islands lead to the inference that the migration must have been purely accidental, and limited, it is not unlikely, to a canoe load of men and women. It may have been repeated at several different times in different ages, under similar circumstances, but limited in each case to inconsiderable numbers. If such accidental emigrants chanced to be of different stocks, the later ones would make but a slight impression upon the first stock that reached America. These islands, the summits of a chain of submarine mountains, stretch continuously and substantially in sight of each other from the peninsula of Alaska to the cape of Kamtchatka, with the following principal interruptions: The Amoukhta pass, separating two groups of these islands, is about sixty miles across; from the island of Goreloi to the island of Semisopochnoi is the same distance; from the latter to Semitchi island is about fifty miles; from the island of Attou to Copper island — which is much the widest interval between any two islands of the chain — is two hundred and thirty miles; and from Behring's island, the last, and one of the largest, of the series, to Cape Kamtchatka on the Asiatic coast is one hundred miles.[1] A migration by way of these islands is not improbable, and there are two facts which create a presumption in favor of the occurrence of such a migration by the mere accidents of the sea before

---

[1] *Map of Alaska and the Aleutian Islands*, U. S. Coast Survey Office, attached to speech of Hon. Charles Sumner in the Senate of the United States on *The Cession of Russian America*, 1867.

the lapse of many ages after Asia was overspread with inhabitants. The first is the ocean stream of the Asiatic coast — the counterpart of the gulf stream of the North Atlantic — which, rising in the South Pacific and flowing northward, skirts the shores of the Japanese and Kurilian islands nearly to the Cape of Kamtchatka, where it is deflected to the eastward, and divides into two streams. One of these, following the coast, enters Behring's strait, but the other, the main stream, crosses the Pacific eastward along the south shores of the Aleutian islands to Alaska, where it turns down the American coast. It is not entirely lost until it reaches the shores of California. This ocean stream might easily bear off canoe-men, once thrown upon its current, from the Kurilian islands, and from the coasts of Asia, to the Aleutian islands. After Attou island, which is but four hundred and forty miles from the nearest point in Asia, was gained, the problem of reaching Alaska would be substantially solved. It would thus seem that an instrumentality was provided in this ocean stream, whereby the American continent might become accessible from Asia in the early ages of the human family. The second fact is the character and position of the Amoor, one of the great rivers of Asia, which stands in nearly the same relation to the northeastern section of that continent that the Columbia does to the northwestern portion of the American. This river, from its fisheries, although inferior to the Columbia, must have attracted inhabitants to its banks at a very early period in Asiatic history. Its occupation would, in due time, have led to boat navigation, to familiarity with the sea, to the exploration and occupation of the adjacent sea coasts and islands, and would thus have prepared the way for peopling the Aleutian islands in the manner stated. It is a striking fact that the Tungusian and Mongolian stocks, the nearest in type, of existing Asiatics, to the American aborigines, still hold the Amoor river, upon which they have lived from time immemorial.

In the third and last place, the systems of consanguinity and affinity of several Asiatic stocks agree with that of the American aborigines. Omitting all discussion of the results of a comparison of systems, it may be stated that the system of the

Seneca-Iroquois Indians of New York is identical, not only in radical characteristics, but also in the greater portion of its minute details, with that of the Tamil people of South India.[1] This identity in complicated and elaborate systems is hardly accidental. There are but four hypotheses conceivable for its explanation — first, by borrowing one from the other; second by accidental invention by different peoples in disconnected areas (the system being treated as arbitrary and artificial); third, by spontaneous growth or development, in similar conditions of society (the system being treated as natural); and fourth, by inheritance with the blood from a common original source. The first assumes territorial connection, and the consequent Asiatic origin of the Ganowanian family. The second is an impossible hypothesis. As the system embodies upwards of twenty arbitrary particulars, the improbability of their accidental concurrence in the Seneca-Iroquois and the Tamil, increasing with the addition of each particular from first to last, becomes finally an impossibility. The third hypothesis is substantial, and deserves consideration. It assumes that the system is natural in its origin, and in accordance with the nature of descents. It must therefore further assume that the ancestors of the Seneca-Iroquois, and of the Tamilian people of India, if created in independent zoological provinces, have not only passed through the same experiences, but also have developed through great reformatory movements the same sequence of customs and institutions, and have wrought out by organic growth the Ganowanian system in America and the Turanian system in Asia; the two remaining identical after having been severally transmitted with the blood through centuries of time. In view of these difficulties, it will probably be found, in the sequel, that the fourth hypothesis, that of transmission with the blood from common ancestors, is the most satisfactory.

---

[1] For a comparison of the Tamil and Seneca-Iroquois systems, see *Proceedings of American Academy of Arts and Sciences*, Vol. VII, p. 456.

A PERILOUS FOSSIL HUNT.[1]

By William C. Wyckoff.

The early days of the present century, when Cuvier first identified in the gypsum quarries of Paris the remains of mighty extinct quadrupeds, and the years shortly following when nations quarreled over similar discoveries, have often been called the golden age of palæontology. But ten times as many fossil bones have been recently brought to the museum of Yale college as Cuvier ever saw in his whole lifetime — the remains of animals as large, as varied, and as unlike the creatures of the present day as those which he so accurately described. There is reason for believing that the year 1874 marks the extreme point in this class of discoveries; certainly its collections will be hard to surpass in number and quality.

During the summer months Prof. O. C. Marsh, whose annual journeys in search of vertebrate fossils at the west have become well known, was deeply absorbed in planning and supervising the construction of the new museum of Yale college. But although unable himself to take part in explorations in the field, Prof. Marsh's life-work has not halted. The *bone business*, as his western friends call it, did not slacken with the hard times. Not less than twelve parties of men inured to the business were kept at work by Prof. Marsh at his own expense, and under his constant instructions were exploring various regions at the west for fossils and packing and sending forward the accumulations. Patient study of the remains thus collected was leading Prof. Marsh to certain conclusions, in respect to the characteristics of extinct vertebrates, that cannot yet be stated. Notwithstanding the accumulated arrivals, the information to be gleaned proved unsatisfactory in determining vexed questions. To insure accuracy, the careful comparison of great numbers of specimens is necessary.

---

[1] Reprinted from the *New York Tribune Extra*, No. 27, March, 1875.

A Perilous Fossil Hunt.

Last October news came to Prof. Marsh that a most promising deposit of fossils had been discovered in the Bad lands, south of the Black hills; the character and condition of these bones, as they lay imbedded in position, would throw additional light on the problem which he was then engaged in working out. It may here be mentioned also that there is no certainty that beds of fossils will remain permanently undisturbed, even where the region is only occupied by savages, for the Indians frequently carry a fossil tooth or bone as an amulet or charm — or as they phrase it, as *medicine*. The discovery of fossil remains in the locality just mentioned was originally made by an Indian, who brought into camp the molar tooth of an animal which Prof. Marsh has named the Brontotherium. The finder carried the tooth in his tobacco pouch; his notion about it was that it had belonged to "a big horse, struck by lightning."

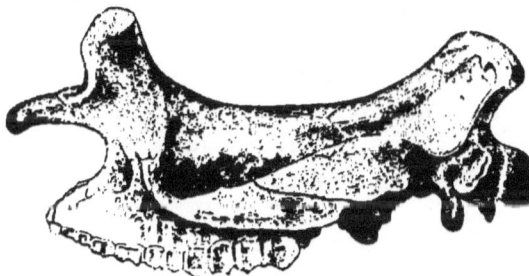

SKULL OF BRONTOTHERIUM — SIDE VIEW.

Gen. E. O. C. Ord, commanding the department of the Platte, and Col. T. H. Stanton, to whom Prof. Marsh was first indebted for information respecting the newly found fossil bed, fully appreciated the importance of the discovery, and promised him every assistance in utilizing it. The weather was already cold, the season rapidly advancing, and the Indians feverishly sensitive about the approach of white men to the Black hills. But great as were the perils, the attractions were greater; besides, the professor had not yet had his annual vacation, and everybody conversant with college traditions knows that a vacation is something to be taken like old-school medicine, at all hazards. That he anticipated special hardship and danger from Indians may be inferred from the fact that he took with him no party from New Haven, this expedition differing in that respect from all previous ones. He depended for assistance in the field on a number of frontiersmen who had been in his employ as collectors and guides in previous expeditions, and on whom he knew he could implicitly rely. Among these was Hank Clifford, who had been his chief guide in the Niobrara expedition of 1873, and whose knowledge of the country and of the Indians had been fully tested. Other less famous but promising aspirants for honors upon the bone fields were attached to the expedition.

Leaving the rail road at Cheyenne, Prof. Marsh reached Fort Laramie in the early part of November, and thence proceeded to the Red-Cloud agency, where he concentrated the men and materials of the expedition. The outfit on such occasions includes a great variety of articles: implements of war, of science, and of the kitchen, with abundant means for so packing the specimens obtained that they shall be not injured by the roughest kind of transportation. Gen. L. P. Bradley, Col. Stanton, Capt. Mix, and Lieut. Hay were of the party that went from Laramie to the Red-Cloud agency; the escort was M Company of the 2d Cavalry, Capt. John Mix in command; Major A. S. Burt and Lieut. W. L. Carpenter joined the expedition at the agency, and greatly contributed to its success. It was ascertained that the locality of the fossils was not within any of the reservations, and hence the Indians would have no evident right to obstruct the explorations. The XVIth section of the treaty of 1868 with the Sioux would make their permission necessary, if strictly interpreted: but this treaty has become in part a dead letter, being, for instance, not enforced south of White river, while by its provisions it extends to Platte river, which is further to the southward. Unfortunately the bone field lay north of the White river. Prof. Marsh was anxious to have a willing assent from the Indians; a fight with them was no part of his programme. Shortly after the arrival of the party at the agency, Red Cloud himself put in an appearance and was welcomed to dinner. He is still the tall, straight, intellectual-looking chieftain that he was when he visited our seaboard cities; temperate in his habits, and preserving his native dignity. It is certain, however, that he has lost no inconsiderable part of the influence over his tribe, especially among the young warriors, that he possessed when he was their leader in battle. As he cannot talk English, all conversation with him had to take place through the medium of an interpreter. The proposed expedition was only partially discussed at the dinner table, and Red Cloud's sentiments in respect to it were judged not to be unfriendly.

But there were many circumstances making the time unpropitious. The affair of the flagstaff was recent; it occurred before Prof. Marsh left Cheyenne, and occasioned there many misgivings as to his prospects; in fact there was for a while some alarm as to the possible fate of the agency. The occurrence was described at the time; it may here be briefly recapitulated. An attempt was made to raise a flagstaff and hoist the United States flag at the Red-Cloud agency, as is always done at military posts in the west. This aroused the animosity of Indians encamped in the vicinity; they cut down the flagstaff and made preparations to fire the large wooden structure occupied by the Indian agent. He sent to the post for aid. Lieut. Crawford was dispatched with about thirty men. The resolute bearing of this small force held the Indians for a while in check, and by energetic persuasion on the part of Red Cloud, Sitting Bull, and other chiefs, they were induced to relinquish their design. Great credit is due to Lieut. Crawford for his courageous attitude on this occasion, as the odds against him in case of battle were fearful.

The general danger was greatly increased at this time by the presence in the neighborhood of an extraordinary number of Indians, gathered to obtain their annuities. Their numbers did not probably fall short of 13,000. They were encamped within a radius of ten miles around the agency. There were about 9,000 of Red Cloud's band, the Ogallallas; the Cut-Off band under Little Wound, the Arapahoes under their chief Friday, of whom there are romantic stories told which there is not space for here. Besides these there were about 3,000 Northern Indians, of the wilder tribes, Minneconjous, Uncpapas, and Sansarcs, who boast that they have never eaten white man's bread; who fought Gen. Custer in the Yellowstone expedition. These Indians refused to be registered, having a superstition about being counted. The orders from Washington forbade the issue of annuities to any except those who were registered. Cheyennes were there, sulky because they had been ordered further south. The Arapahoes were fresh from their fight and losses in the battle on Powder river with Lieut. Bates. Outlaws, renegades and bad Indians, swelled the numbers that surrounded the agency, and made the neighborhood unquiet, not to say dangerous. An incident will illustrate the real temper of the class that claim to be good Indians. Within gunshot of the agency a teamster, whom Prof. Marsh had noticed a few minutes before busily engaged in cooking his supper, was indiscreet enough to leave his rifle a few steps away. A young Indian brave passed the professor on horseback, and seeing him well armed, gave him a respectful salutation. Not so with the teamster; the weakness of his position was apprehended by the brave at a glance. In less time than it takes to tell it, the Indian rode between the teamster and his rifle, and snatching up the latter, made off, pointing a pistol backward in defiance. The despoiled teamster ran up to the camp, and was very free in the use of "cuss-words;" but it was the general opinion that he might be considered fortunate in having, while he lost his gun, preserved his hair.

In short the whole vicinity was alive with Indians, their families, and their ponies; they had with them their entire possessions, and their lodges diversified the landscape in every direction. It was impossible to move even a few paces without encountering Indians, Indians everywhere. The agent at the post recommended that a guard should be selected from these warriors to accompany the expedition, and very soon assembled a council of leading chiefs to discuss the matter. As soon as they were brought together, it became evident that they mistrusted the intentions of the bone-hunters, as stated by the agent. Instead of waiting some moments, as they usually do after the object of a council has been stated, White Tail, one of the principal chiefs, sprang at once to his feet and harangued the audience, recounting previous grievances and declared that the proposed bone-seeking was merely a ruse to begin digging for gold and invading the Black hills region. His speech evidently conveyed the sentiments of the other chiefs; they listened intently, giving vent to applause and sympathy with guttural ejaculations of "How! How!" But a speech from Prof. Marsh, through the medium of an interpreter, promising that their just complaints should be heard at Washington, stating specifically the objects of the expedition, and holding out the prospect of pay for Indian services in bone-hunting, turned the scale at once. Consent was obtained for the expedition to proceed, but coupled with an agreement to take a selected guard of young warriors. The nominal object of this guard was to be a protection against Northern Indians who were encamped across the White river; the real intent was to keep watch on the proceedings of the bone-hunters. Sitting Bull, one of the most influential chieftains, was to select the guard, and himself to go at their head. Prof. Marsh was to let Sitting Bull know when he was ready to move forward.

The next day three or four inches of snow fell; this itself unfortunately delayed the expedition. Meanwhile the annuities were issued to the Indians, and this quite changed the aspect of affairs. Having got their annuities, the Indians were no longer on their good behavior; they could raid around for another year. There is at best always a great deal of dissatisfaction among them after the annuities are issued, but even those who had got all they hoped for exhibited a sauciness in marked contrast with their previous demeanor. In frontier phrase, "the Indians didn't care a cuss for Uncle Sam." The bone-hunting expedition was discussed in every lodge. They all arrived at one conclusion, that the pretense of seeking fossils was much "too thin." The chief of the bone-hunters was certainly in search of gold.

Quite unaware of the change of sentiment the expedition went on with its preparations, and on the second morning after the issue of annuities, broke camp and proceeded to the agency, expecting to get the Indian guard. The whole party, including the soldiers, were drawn up ready for the start. To reach the agency they had to pass between several villages composed of Indian lodges. The sight of the soldiers and the wagons excited the Indians. They gathered in great numbers about the agency. They were armed quite as well as our soldiers, with breech-loading rifles and revolvers of the most recent patterns.

Sitting Bull declared that the young men promised as a guard refused to go, being afraid of the Northern Indians. Red Cloud, when Prof. Marsh appealed to him, said that his young men believed the object of the search was gold, not bones, and the listening crowd approved his words. Pretty Crow, a chief of note, suddenly precipitated a crisis by shouting: "The white men are going into our country to find gold; we must stop them at once." A cry of warning was given. The women and children instantly started and ran out of harm's way. Guns were pointed at the party on every side, and a line of mounted Indians formed on their front and rear. In all directions runners were seen galloping off to the villages and calling together the warriors. The Indians outnumbered the expedition at least thirty to one. A single shot, or the order "Forward!" would have brought down their fire.

To push on under such circumstances would have been madness. The agent and the friendly chiefs pointed out to Prof. Marsh that the presence of the soldiers aggravated the excitement of the Indians. There was but one thing to do with safety; that was to withdraw. The entire expedition turned about and retreated to Camp Robinson, a distance of one and a half miles. It is not worth while here to repeat the jeers which this movement elicited from the Indians; they showered insults on the retreating party; the language of signs is never more efficient than for such a purpose, and it was freely used. Bad as were these insults, they were preferable to bullets. The rest of the day was spent in consultations. The advice of Mr. J. W. Dear and his assistance proved of great service to the party. On the following day beef was issued by the agent to the bands entitled to it. Meanwhile, as a result of many consultations, two conclusions were arrived at. 1. That something must be done to win the consent of the Indians. 2. That a feast given by Prof. Marsh and a few presents to leading chiefs were the most promising means of attaining consent. The professor was becoming very much disgusted with councils and talks, but decided to have another one.

On the day after the beef issue the feast was given. The

A Perilous Fossil Hunt.

order of precedence is as well established on these occasions as at a European court. Only the more eminent chiefs were admitted; the following were among them: Red Cloud, Red Dog, Old Man Afraid of his Horses, Spider (a brother of Red Cloud), Sword (son-in-law of Red Cloud), Sitting Bull, Pawnee Killer, Conquering Bear, Friday, American Horse, Torn Belly, Red Leaf, Rocky Bear, Little Wound, Three Bears, White Tail, Young Man Afraid of his Horses, Stabber, Hand, Pretty Crow, and some 30 others of less note. The feast was given in one of the largest lodges, and every detail of Indian etiquette was strictly observed. At its close, after Prof. Marsh had again stated the object and character of the expedition, a reluctant consent was again accorded, with the warning that the Minneconjous were likely to kill the professor if he crossed the White river. A band of scouts was promised under the leadership of Sword, whose influence is little less than that of his father-in-law, Red Cloud. It was again left with Prof. Marsh to name the hour for starting, all else being apparently provided for.

MAP OF THE REGION OF FOSSIL DISCOVERIES.

Fearing that a consent coupled with so much hesitation might prove unavailable, the professor resolved to test it, and sent word quietly, late in the night after the feast, to his interpreters and guides, to be ready the next morning. The dread of the Minneconjous and Uncpapas overcame the blandishments of the feast. Indian scoutes, guides, and interpreters all alike refused to go. Disappointed and not a little exasperated by these repeated delays, **Prof. Marsh** resolved upon the most extraordinary move of this expedition. He decided to give the Indians the slip. That night, shortly after midnight, he carried out this intention. Marching down between the Indian villages as silently as possible, the expedition sought the White river at the only spot where, for many miles, it is fordable. The Indian dogs barked furiously as the party defiled between the lodges, but fortunately their owners slept. If the expedition had been attacked at this time, their case would have been hopeless. It was a bitter night, and after crossing the river, as they ascended the highlands, the cold was so intense that those on horseback had to dismount and walk to keep from freezing.

The stolen march was soon discovered. By daylight scouts could be seen riding from village to village giving the alarm. Before the bone region was reached, Indian sentinels on horseback, posted on the high buttes, were watching the party. Both on account of the cold and the danger, the march was made with rapidity. On arriving at the locality, a position for the camp was chosen by Lieut. W. L. Carpenter, of great natural strength, flanked by ravines. But the field of research included a circuit of ten miles, mainly in a deep gorge. From the highest buttes in the vicinity, Harney's peak was visible. The party went to work immediately on their arrival on the grounds; in fact the weather was so intensely cold that work became a necessity. They could not sit on the ground to dig; moving about was necessary to keep from freezing. As fast as fossils were secured, they were heaped together, and piles of stones were placed to mark the localities of the bones, in the event of a snow-storm. For several days this bitter cold continued. The frugal meal rarely included water, ice-water ceasing to be a luxury. When a tumbler was filled, its contents rapidly froze solid, and before the table in the tent could be set, it was advisable to punch with a fork the ice that was forming in the glasses, and drink what remained fluid as quickly as possible. The bearded members of the party were festooned with icicles, like the Vikings of old, and had to break holes under their mustaches to put food in. During this exceptionally cold weather, there were four officers and many soldiers severely frost-bitten, but none of the bone-hunting party suffered injury, probably because they were so actively employed.

At length the cold moderated and there came a snow storm. The places marked by piles of rock were then the scene of renewed labors. Brooms made of bushes and grass were employed at these points to brush away the snow. Meanwhile, in spite of the cold, the Indians had kept their mounted sentinels on the neighboring hills, watching the operations of the party. One night some Indians attempted to surprise the camp; its guard, instead of shooting the approaching savages, awakened the members of the expedition. The Indians perceiving that the camp was alarmed, withdrew. This was far better than shooting would have been, since if an Indian had been shot, the act would have drawn down vengeance on the party. Occasionally in the daytime a few Sioux dropped in with proffers of friendship, probably to obtain a nearer look at the work of the expedition. When success was well nigh assured, and the labor of collecting was nearly completed, there were fears that a snow-storm which was threatened would check the work. A more serious cause for alarm was found in the representations of a party of Indians, headed by Spider and Sword, who came out to forewarn the expedition of its immediate dangers. They had ascertained that the Northern Indians had taken their wives and children to the Black hills, and were coming to make an attack on the camp. There was good reason to expect the attack that night. To throw the specimens into the wagons and rattle off with them unpacked was simply to break them to pieces. To pack them at night, burning lights in the tents, would be to invite an attack; the Indian asks no better mark for a shot at long range, than a lighted tent. Great as was the risk of remaining, Prof. Marsh, after due consultation with the officers in command of the escort, decided to stay long enough to pack properly. The expedition broke camp the next day, and not too soon; subsequent reports state that a large war party of Northern Indians scoured the Bad lands on the following day, in a vain search for the Bone-hunting chief and his band, then *en route* for New Haven.

On his return to the agency, Red Cloud was among the first to welcome Prof. Marsh. Some of the chiefs to show their good will, proposed to give a dog-feast in his honor, the tender canine being considered by them a special delicacy. The professor has eaten a variety of Indian viands and frontier dishes, ranging from mule meat to grasshopper short-cake, and would doubtless have partaken of fricaseed puppy, but for his haste to return. Moreover, his previous banquets had proved somewhat expensive, and it was understood that there should be a *quid pro quo* on his part, which might have made his second joint of bow-wow a costly dish. He sent his regrets and pleaded a previous engagement.

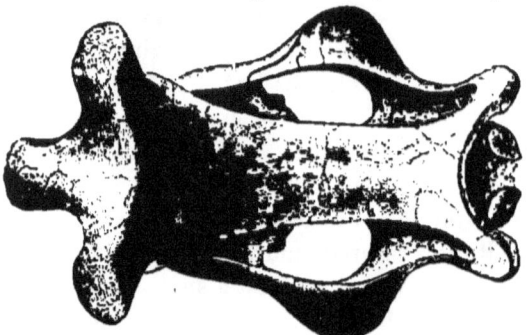

SKULL OF BRONTOTHERIUM—TOP VIEW.

Did the results obtained justify the expenditure, the time, the danger? Yes, amply. The bones obtained are those of tropical animals, of the miocene era. There are nearly two tons of these fossils; most of them are rare specimens, illustrative of entire families of quadrupeds, of which all that is known has been ascertained within a very few years; some of the bones are those of animals entirely new to science. The brontotherium is one of the larger quadrupeds whose remains are entombed in the bed of this miocene lake. It was as large as an elephant, and bore a general resemblance of form to that animal, but differed in many essential particulars. Its shorter limbs were like those of the rhinoceros; its nose was adorned with a pair of huge horns, placed crosswise. Its skull is a yard in length. It had no tusks, or long proboscis, such as the elephant possesses; but its nose was probably elongated and flexible, like the snout of a tapir. In fact its head and neck were so long that it had no need of an elephantine proboscis. These animals must have lived together in herds. Probably their remains were washed into the lake by a freshet, and thus were buried in the mud with which the lake was finally filled, which now has hardened into stone. Among other remains found are those of animals nearly allied to the rhinoceros, the camel, and the horse of to-day. It is not necessary to burden this page with their scientific names, which would convey no ideas of their form or characteristics to most readers. The stratum in which the fossils lay was of the lowest miocene, and could only have been reached by the upper miocene and the pliocene above that, having been washed away by a water-course in this cañon. Hence the locality of the fossils was narrow, and the expedition was able to get at and remove them entirely. A careful examination of the surrounding region showed that nowhere else had any watercourse cut deep enough to lay bare this stratum.

Aside from the novel points obtained concerning specific fossils, the expedition has made an important determination respecting the geology of the region. The fact was ascertained that the miocene lake was of more limited extent than has hitherto been asserted, although larger than any two great lakes of the northwest at the present day would be if combined in one. Its northern limit was the southern slope of the Black Hills; its western margin the Rocky mountains; its southern limit near the northern line of Kansas. Long after this lake was filled and dried, another tropical lake covered the same region, having the same boundaries at the north and west, but extending southward even to Texas. The sands and clay deposits of this more recent lake basin are of the pliocene age; they are of great thickness, in some places, not less than 1,500 feet. No inconsiderable part of the beds which Prof. Hayden has regarded as belonging to the miocene or lower lake formation proves to be of the pliocene or upper lake, the true miocene being visible in occasional depressions where the pliocene has been washed away. All or nearly all the high table lands from the White river to the Arkansas are formed of the deposits of the pliocene lake; it has proved rich in organic remains, especially in fossil horses; but all the animals found in it differ from those of the lake below as well as from those now living. Many obscure and some contested points in science will be determined by the material which Prof. Marsh's expedition of 1874 has gathered, and the Indians have already found compensation for their "medicine" ravished to adorn the shelves of Yale's new museum.

INDIAN AFFAIRS AROUND DETROIT IN 1706.[1]

TRANSLATED FROM A FRENCH Ms. BY COL. CHARLES WHITTLESEY.

[These transcripts, brought with other historical papers from Paris by Gen. Lewis Cass, are so negligently made, on poor paper and in a hurried chirography; that it is frequently difficult to read them. They give a vivid idea of Indian ferocity, duplicity and cruelty, depicted by one of their own number; from personal observation. It is not known that this remarkable speech; or the reply of Vaudreuil, have before this appeared in print.]

SPEECH OF MISKOUAKI, BROTHER OF JEAN LE BLANC, AN OTTAWA OF DETROIT, WHO CAME FROM MACKINAW TO THE MANOIR MENARD[2] TO MONSIEUR THE MARQUIS DE VAUDREUIL SEPTEMBER 26th, 1706.

My father, you will be surprised by the bad affairs that I am about to inform you of on the part of Pesant, and of Jean Le Blanc touching what has passed at Detroit. I desire you my father to open to me your door, as to one of your children, and listen to what I have to say.

When I left Mackinaw, my father, our old men did not expect me to come so far as this place, hoping you would be still at Montreal. The time is short for me to return. I desire you to be willing to listen to me.

Listen — The Ottawa nations who were at Detroit, the Kikiakous the Sinagoes and the nation DuSables have been killed, and such as have returned to Mackinaw, came in the greatest distress. It is the Miamis, my father, who have killed us.

The reason we were obliged to fight the Miamis is, that having gone to war against the Sioux, as we have said to Sieur Bourmont, we had been informed by a Potawatomie encamped near the fort of the Hurons, that the Miamis, who were at Detroit, had resolved to allow us to depart and march three days, after which they would attack our village, and eat our women and children. My father, we were unable to comprehend, and you yourself will be surprised, as well as we, when you know that Quarante Sous, who was employed by Le Sieur La Mothe to bring all the nations to Detroit, made use of this pretext, to give them wampum pri-

---

[1] Reprinted from Tract No. 8, *Western Reserve and Northern Ohio Historical Society* (Cleveland, O.), December, 1871. Revised by the translator for the *Indian Miscellany*.

[2] The Manoir Menard is presumed to be near Quebec.

vately, to engage them to destroy us. I have not come, my father, to lie to you, I have come to speak the truth. You will do after this what shall please you.

We have learned by a Pottowatomie named ———, who married a Miami, that the Miamis would eat our villagers. Upon this news, my father, the war chiefs of three nations of Ottawas with whom we had set out, held a council, and concluded that we should not deliberate upon an affair of this consequence without the consent of Pesant and of Jean Le Blanc, who are their principal chiefs, and who were sent for at once. Le Pesant and Jean Le Blanc, after having heard the news told us by the ———, concluded by stamping his foot, that since the Miamis had resolved to kill and boil us, it was necessary to forestall them.

When Pesant had said it was necessary to strike, we soon saw, and Jean Le Blanc first of us all, that he was going to do a wicked thing, but no person dared contradict him, on account of his influence and because we should then have made ourselves contemptible, in the eyes of the young men. My father, my brother and myself inquired what Pesant thought of striking, while our people were divided. Some were at war with the Hurons, some at Montreal, and what would the commandant at Detroit say if we struck at his gate.

We said thus to Pesant, but he would not listen. It is he, my father, who has caused all the misfortunes that have happened.

Jean Le Blanc, my father, would have come with me but being stripped of everything, and not daring to come as a malefactor he told me to come, and know your mind. He would have come, my father, but according to our custom during all the time we were at war, being at Detroit; he had given the Sieur Bourmont all that we had, thinking it more safe there, than in our fort, and in consequence of the misfortunes that have happened, since our departure to the war with the Sioux, it remains there, and all I can do is to offer you this wampum, on the part of my nation, which is all I have, and have taken this from my pouch.

According to our resolution, we resumed the way to our fort, and as we approached the fort of the Hurons, we found eight

Miami chiefs, who were going there to a feast. As we met them Pesant said, behold our enemies. These are the men which wish to kill us. Since there are the leaders, it is necessary to rid ourselves of them, and thereupon made a cry as a signal, encouraging us to let none of them escape. At the first cry no person moved. But Pesant having made a second, as we marched along on each side of the way, and as we were in the midst, we fired; and none of them saved themselves but Pamakona, who escaped to the French fort.

I dare tell you one thing, that I have never said before, and it is, that he is a strong friend of mine. I made a signal to him before the discharge to withdraw, and it is thus he was saved.

After those were killed, our young men rose to take such as might remain in the lodges, and as LePesant and Jean Le Blanc could not go as fast as the others, I was one of the first to reach there, but to prevent this some one forced me between the French and our people.

The Miamis being camped near their fort when I arrived I found the Miamis had withdrawn into the fort of the French, and one of our young men, a chief, had been killed, and that our youth in despair on account of his death, resolved to burn the fort. I threw myself in the midst of them, and many times snatched the burning arrows repeatedly imploring them with vehemence, not to do the French any injury, for they were not connected with the quarrel we had with the Miamis.

I heard during this time a voice crying there is a Black Robe (a priest) and I saw my brother sending the Pere Recolet into the fort, having not harmed him, and having desired him to say to Sieur Bourmont, that he should not fire upon us, nor give any ammunition to the Miamis, but put them out of the fort and leave us alone.

We had not known, my father, that a Pere Recolet and the French soldiers, had been killed, but the next day those who had fired upon them, not being (illegible) then I blamed my brother very much, that he had not detained the Recolet father and the soldiers; who replied that he thought they would be more safe there than in our fort, on account of the irritation among our young men, for the death of two chiefs that we had lost.

The next day, my father, my brother took a flag that you had given him, and insisted on speaking to Monsieur Bourmont, desiring him, our arms reversed all around, to give us missionaries, an opportunity to explain. He said he had no reply for us, but that the Sieur De La Foret, whom he had expected early in the spring, would soon arrive with five canoes when we could give our reasons. Seeing he did not wish to listen to us, we were obliged to return; and that night our young men determined to burn the fort. Our old men were embarrassed, and to prevent them passed three entire days in council.

After having been three days in council Jean Blanc rose and said to Pesant, "since it is you who has caused all this difficulty what do you say? what do you think? As for me I say we are dead, and that we have killed ourselves by striking the Miamis, at the French stockade. In turn the Miskouakies and the Sinagoes will say the same thing.

As soon as the Sieur De Tonty was gone, we were well agreed that affairs were becoming embroiled, of which there were sure signs in this last matter; since the Sieur De Bourmont being able to arrange everything did not wish to listen to us, referring us always to the arrival of the Sieur De La Foret.

However we had certain signs that he wished to fight (illegible) for he put swords at the end of his pike staves. We continued some time to have parleys with him, and went without fear to the fort of the Hurons, believing that they were our allies, but for fear of the Miamis we always went in canoes.

My father, the Hurons called the Ottawa Sinago, and said to him, "My brothers it is a long time that we have been brothers, and that together we have fought the Iroquois. When we speak to you we speak to all the nations, Outawase (Ottawas), Sacs, Sauteurs, Poutawatamies, Saukies, Chippeways and Mississaugies. Look at this string of beads, my brothers, I take it out for you to look at. It is a long time our old men have preserved it. Upon this string there is seen the figures of men. This string (or belt) signifies much. It is never shown unless we give life or death to those to whom we speak. I return it, and say to you on the part of the French, that he wishes you to meet him at the feast. It will not be in the lodges, for you might thus have apprehensions, but it will be near this spot, on the prairie, where the French flag will be planted, and there you will come to the feast."

On the morrow, the day of the feast we were to have, Jean Le Blanc having his garden near the place where the French flag was planted, was walking there and saw a number of the French bring wheat and throw it upon a sail cloth, spread out upon the prairie. The Huron women did the same, and brought the wheat and poured it upon the cloth. Then my brother thought the Hurons had spoken truly, and that we should have a good time, nevertheless being with Pesant they reflected, that the French had never been willing to speak to them.

It might be that under the name of this feast, the Hurons would betray them, and give the Miamis the opportunity of attacking them, while their women and children were gone to fetch the wheat. They resolved to send out scouts for discovery in the woods, and four young men departed, who returned and said, they saw many ways which led into the depths of the forest, and seemed to encircle those which led to the wheat. As some of our people had already departed we caused them to be recalled seeing clearly it was a bait which they had spread for us. We then knew it was a design of the French, of the Miamis, as also of the Hurons, as soon as we should leave our fort to go to the wheat which was intended for us; and when they thought as we were very hungry, we should enjoy ourselves very much, the greater part of the Miamis and the Hurons, who were in the thick woods, were to come to take the fort, and the other portion, composed of French, Hurons and Miamis, were concealed in the glades opposite the flag, and from thence would fall on us. As we had recalled all of our people, and no one went for the wheat, they were much deceived on their part, and the Miamis who were in the thick wood, thinking that we had gone out of our fort, or at least a great part of us, rushed forward with great shouts to take it. Our young men who were in the bastion, having discovered them afar off, we fought them all day with guns, and lost one of our men, who was killed by a woman.

In the evening the Miamis returned, without our being able to determine how many of their people were killed. In returning they met Katalibou and his brother, whom they killed and scalped.

The Miamis in attacking our fort took the precaution to form two companies, and one of them came along the water, where they threw away such of our canoes as they found, for the purpose of depriving us of the means of escape.

The next day, my father, we were convinced that the Hurons had joined the Miamis. They came together to attack us at our fort, and this day more of the Miamis were killed, than the day before. They returned again the next day. We attacked the Hurons, who undertook to overwhelm us with injuries. We had so little powder we dare not fire, though we had some. They took new life since Onontio had abandoned (manuscripts not legible here).

Cletart, the brother of Quarante Sous, said then that our young men, indignant at the injuries that the Hurons had done us, should make a sortie, and we fought against them and the Miamis, a long time out of the fort. The Hurons held their ground, but the Miamis fled, although there were four hundred of them.

On this day one of our people who had been at war with the Hurons at the (not legible), arrived at our fort, and said that all the others who had started with him and had returned, were bound in the French fort; that the Hurons had bound them, and that they had sent him to let us know of it; that two of our war allies of the Hurons were prisoners in their fort, and that the rest had been taken to the French fort, for what reason we did not know.

The next day the Hurons and Miamis came again and attacked our fort. They had apparently lost some person of consideration among them. They shot, before they left one, of their prisoners, who was one of our allies.

Some time after the Hurons (Wyandots) sent for the relatives of those who were confined in the French fort, saying that they well remembered what we had done to them, and that it was by way of reprisal that they had bound our people, but that they did not wish to kill them. We had but to come and cover them according to custom. We caused some to carry blankets thither, and they told us to come and cover them to-morrow (manuscripts defective), we observing a place at the gate of the French fort where the cannon was, and where they placed poles.

They ordered us to bring presents then, according to the favors they were granting us. Our people, believing them to act in good faith, returned, and each one exhausted their goods and carried them, even to the beads of our children.

Scarcely had we put on the poles (or pickets) ten pieces of porcelain beads, twenty kettles, two packs of beaver, and all that we had brought, when Quarante Sous gave his hand to Jean Blanc. At this moment Jean Blanc received a shot, and at the same time a discharge was made from the fort, upon us, who being there in good faith, were without arms, relying upon the sincerity of the French, and were obliged to fly. The Hurons and the Miamis having made a sortie, those of our people who remained in the fort came to the assistance of those who fled, and the remainder of the day was passed in fighting on both sides. We lost in this treachery, two men, killed at the discharge from the French fort, and five wounded. The last stroke which the Miamis have given us, my father, was done at our homes by their young men. There they killed a woman and took another prisoner, and as we sent after them to know what they would do with her, our people heard cries in the French fort where they were burning her.

The exhaustion of war and hunger, obliged our people to send (not legible) one of our chiefs to speak to the Ouyatanons. Heretofore the Ouyatanons (a tribe on the waters of the Wabash, a Miami tribe) had danced with him the calumet of peace. Our people employed this man to speak to the Miamis. He said, my father, the Ouyatanons had treated us as sons in dancing this calumet, and also "I am astonished that you remain so long to kill us at our palisades. Art thou not wrong in killing us, and dost not thou kill thyself also, hast thou no pity on thy young men."

An Ouyatanon replied " that it was not his tribe who had done that, but it was the Hurons and the French who wished to oblige them to remain until the Ottawas should perish in their fort by hunger," and the Ouyatanons ceased to speak. Having determined to return the slaves, we separated. Two of our people were given to the Ouyatanons, two were given to the nation of the Crane, Miamis, who are of the river St Josephs; one was burnt in the French fort, another shot, and the son of Aiontache a Mississauga saved from death by the commandant of a French fort. There was one of our men married to a woman of whom we have no news. The two others, Sieur De La Mothe has restored to the Mississaugas. Behold my father all which I know, and the old men have requested me to say to you, that on account of all the treachery that the Hurons have done them, it is with difficulty they can restrain their young men from going against him, so long as he remains at Detroit, from whence we have withdrawn only to be less exposed.

The two Ottowas, my father, who were given to the Ouyatanons saved themselves on the way and came to rejoin us. They say they were not misused by the Ouyatanons. They report that the Miamis have in killed and wounded fifty persons; and we have lost twenty-six, including those who were returned from the war, and those the Hurons bound through treachery.

My father, I speak in the name of all nations, Ottowas, Poutawotomies, Saukis, Outagamies, Kickapous, Quinepigs, Matamini, Sauters and Mississaugas, all the people of the country bordering upon the lakes, in short of all our allies, and of their indignation against the Hurons for the treachery they have done us. They desire you through me to allow us to fight him. I desire you, my father, to tell me your thoughts, so that I may report the same to our people, and that we may fully know each other's wishes.

REPLY OF MONSIEUR DE VAUDREUIL TO MISKOUAKI, BROTHER OF JEAN LE BLANC, AN OTTOWA CHIEF OF THOSE WHO WERE AT DETROIT, SEPTEMBER 28, 1706.

I have listened quietly Miskouaki to all you have said, and although I am already informed of what has passed at Detroit, could not fail to be greatly surprised by your recital. I do not reply, because it does not appear to me that you are sent by all

the nations, as you say: but only by your brother, Jean Le
Blanc, to preoccupy my mind; and for this purpose you left
Mackinaw, intending to remain here. It is only the arrival of
your brother that has given you a desire to return. However
that may be, I am not sorry to have seen you, and am glad to
hear what you have said, touching the conduct of your brother.

You wish to know my thoughts, Miskouaki, you desire me to
give them to you. Listen to me well, I am a good father, and
so long as my children listen to my voice, no evil will happen
to them. You have proofs of this in what happened at Detroit,
and if Le Pesant and Jean Le Blanc, had not undertaken anything
without knowing my wishes, you would not have attacked the
Miamis. You would not have killed of mine, and you would
not have been in the distress and misery where you are now.

We have been killed, Miskouaki, and until I see all the nations
whom I have always regarded as my children, come here, recognize their fault and ask pardon, I cannot forget that I have
lost at Detroit a missionary and a soldier, who are of value among
us.

This is what you can say to your brother and to all the nations,
when your arrive there. I have seen and examined the speech
you have delivered. As you have yourself said that the belt you
drew from your pouch, was not given you by your people when
you departed, I return it to you, and do not receive it, not because
I despise it as coming from you, but because I cannot reply to it,
since it does not come directly from them, and I am pleased to
return it to you as a thing that belongs to you, that you may use
it to accommodate the bad affairs which might happen.

In regard to what has passed at Detroit, I say to all your people that I stop the tomahawk, and prohibit them from going to
war, either with the Hurons or Miamis, or any one else, and
order them to remain strictly on the defensive, until I am better
informed. As to other matters, I expect news daily from
M. De La Mothe, and during the winter I shall examine all you
have said, and that which he shall advise, in order to be able to
regulate affairs.

If the recital you have made us is true, as a consequence of the present state of things, you cannot move aside very far in hunting this winter. Your people will be able to come here early in the spring, with the Frenchmen I leave above, to know my thoughts.

This is what they should have done this year, and not to have sent you alone, and without belts on the part of all the nations. It is not beads, Miskouaki, that I demand, neither presents where my children have disobeyed, and done such wrongs as you have. The blood of Frenchmen is not paid by beaver skins.

It is constant reliance in my goodness that I demand, a real repentance of faults they have committed, and entire resignation to my will. When your people shall be in this state of mind, I will accomodate everything as before; but for this it is necessary to come early in the coming spring, or at least a part of the chiefs. It is necessary that they lead here all the French, and that your young men assist them to bring down their furs.

It is necessary also that they remain quietly upon their mats, without going to war, either with the Hurons or the Miamis or others, that they remain entirely on the defensive, and even if they are attacked at home, to be content until the coming year to defend themselves, and to come here and make their complaints to me.

These, Miskouaki, are my thoughts and it is thus you can speak to all the nations on my part. I do not make you presents for your brothers nor the other chiefs, it not being natural to recompense children when in a state of disobedience like you. I take pity however on you on account of the trouble you have been at, and the confidence you have shown in me. I give you a blanket, a shirt, some trinkets, powder, lead and tobacco, to excite you to diligence on your return and in the expectation you will behave yourself in the upper country, and also that the father Marest will report to me, in such a manner that I shall have consideration for you, and it will be for you to conduct yourself, so as to receive evidences of my goodness, when you shall return here with the others.

THE ABORIGINAL INHABITANTS OF CONNECTICUT.[1]

By Luzerne Ray.

The Indians of North America, when they first became known to Europeans, were separated into subdivisions almost numberless. Every prominent feature in natural scenery; the river — the bay — the mountain — gave its name to the few natives that clustered round it. Without central government; with no systems of general law, and no very definite limits of territory; the separate fractions of the race presented, at first view, none of the external marks which lead at once to a wider classification. But a longer and more intimate acquaintance with the multitudinous tribes, has fully established the fact, that a few great classes or families embraced them all. In the inquiry before us, our attention will be fixed, for the most part, upon one of these families — upon that, namely, which, sometimes called the Chippeway, is best known, however, by its French name, Algonquin.[2]

The Algonquin tribes were once the most numerous, and so far as numbers can give strength, the most powerful in North America. Beginning at the gulf of St. Lawrence, their territory ran along the Atlantic coast as far south as southern Virginia; bounded in this quarter by the country of the Cherokees and Tuscaroras, it passed westward across the mountains, reaching the Mississippi at the mouth of the Ohio, and separated by the former river from the great family of Dahcotas, which inhabits its western bank; from this point advancing northward, it embraced the present states of Kentucky, Illinois, Indiana, and

---

[1] Reprinted from *The New Englander* (New Haven), for July, 1843.

[2] For the facts and statements contained in this article, we have depended mainly upon the following works: Trumbull's *History of Connecticut*, Bancroft's *History of the United States*, Hutchinson's *History of Massachusetts*, Mather's *Magnalia*, Adair's *North American Indians*, Gookin's *Historical Collections of the Indians in New England*, Wood's *New England Prospects*, Winslow's *Relation*, and Roger Williams's *Key to the Indian Languages*. We make this general acknowledgment, to avoid the tediousness of repeated reference; but in all cases where information has been derived from other sources than these, the proper credit will be given by the way.

Michigan; the territory of Wisconsin; the lakes Michigan and Superior; and penetrating the wild regions beyond them, found at last its northern limit in the high latitude of the Great-Slave lake. All the Indians of New England were branches of the Algonquin stock, a fact which rests its proof upon their general resemblance in form and feature; the similarity of their habits and manners, and more than all, the radical identity of the languages spoken by the various tribes.

Historians have been accustomed to reckon five principal Indian nations within the present boundaries of New England. This enumeration, however, is far from perfect, as it makes no mention of the tribes inhabiting Maine, and fails also to include a considerable number of the smaller and less important clans which were scattered, here and there, over the other New England states. These five nations or confederacies were as follows: the Pawtuckets, inhabiting the sea-coast of New Hampshire; the Massachusetts, surrounding the bay which still bears their name; the Pokanokets, a tribe made famous by the exploits of their renowned sachem, Philip, whose territories lay in the neighborhood of the Plymouth colony; the Narragansets, occupying a part of Rhode Island, and finally, the Pequods. These last were almost wholly within the limits of Connecticut, and they were destined to fill one brief but terrible chapter of the history of the state.

At the first settlement of the country, the tribe of Pequods was the most warlike and powerful that could any where be found east of the Hudson river. The pestilence which but a short time before had spread such desolation among the neighboring Indians; which reduced the Pokanokets to five hundred warriors; the Pawtuckets to two hundred and fifty, and left scarcely one hundred men among the once numerous Massachusetts;[1] this destroying scourge passed lightly over the country of the Pequods, and, certainly not for any virtues in them, spared this nation of ferocious savages. Not to this fact alone, however, did they owe their relative preëminence among the natives, for they were outnumbered by their immediate neighbors, the Narragansets, with whom they were continually at war. The Narra-

---

[1] *Historical Memoir of Plymouth*, by Baylies, **I**, 45.

gansets also surpassed them in civilization, if such a word can be properly applied to any portion of the Indian race. It was their bravery and ferocity in battle; their love of warfare and cruelty to their captives, which made the very name of Pequod a fearful sound in the ear of every native whom their power could reach.

The tradition is, that this tribe came down from the interior at some period not very remote, and conquering for themselves the fine country in the southeastern part of Connecticut, established their chief quarters in the territory now occupied by the towns of New London, Groton, and Stonington. When the English first visited the state, Sassacus, the chief sachem of the Pequods, held his royal residence in a large fortress on a commanding hill in Groton, from whence he was continually making hostile incursions into the surrounding country, and whither he was wont to retire, whenever he could not safely keep the field.

Directly north of the Pequods, and separated from them by uncertain boundaries, lay the country of the Mohegan tribe; the only one which from first to last, proved friendly to the whites. The dominion of this tribe extended to the northern limits of Connecticut, including by conquest, a portion of the Nipmuck territory, which, for this reason, was sometimes called the Mohegan conquered country. The numbers of the Mohegan tribe were originally small. There is reason indeed to believe that it was no more than a fractional portion of the Pequods, living in separation and rebellion. It is certain at least that Uncas, the sachem to whose talents as a warrior and ruler, the tribe owed its subsequent importance, was himself of Pequod origin, and that he married a Pequod wife.

Having thus ascertained the aboriginal inhabitants of the eastern section of the state, we pass next to the rich and beautiful valley of the Connecticut. Perhaps no other part of the United States, certainly none in New England, was so densely populated as this. The fine meadows which lay spread out on each side of the river, were easy of cultivation, and abundant in their harvests; the river itself was full of fish, and in the forests which skirted the valley, might be found great numbers of bears, wolves, deer, foxes, and such other wild animals as the Indian hunted for amusement, or sought for food.

The inhabitants of the Connecticut valley were known among the English by the general appellation of River Indians. There was, however, no bond of political connection between the various tribes included by this single name. Each was governed by its own chieftain, independent of all the rest, so far at least as any government was found necessary or possible. In the ancient town of Windsor alone, there were no less than ten distinct sovereignties. Perhaps no place in the United States, of equal territory, could count so many Indian inhabitants as Windsor. They were also numerous in Hartford and Wethersfield. In East Hartford, upon the river to which they have left their name, the Podunks could muster about two hundred warriors. In Middletown, dwelt the Mattabeset tribe, and in Chatham, on the opposite bank of the river, the Wongungs. Lyme was occupied by the Nehantics, and East Haddam, then called Machemoodus, by a tribe, whose reported intercourse with evil spirits, was formerly supposed to have some connection with the celebrated Moodus noises. The Indians on the river were generally well disposed toward the English, to whom they looked for protection from their terrible enemies, the Pequods on the one side, and the Mohawks on the other.

In many places west of the river they were likewise numerous. At Guilford there was one small tribe, and another in Branford and East Haven. New Haven was occupied by the Quinnipiacks. They were also scattered in considerable numbers along the shores of the sound, in the direction of New York, at Milford, Derby, Stratford, Norwalk, Stamford and Greenwich. Milford especially was full of them. Back in the interior of the state they had but few settlements; their dread of the Mohawks having driven them away from the whole western border. They were found, however, as far west as Woodbury, New Hartford, and Simsbury, and the pleasant banks of the Tunkis in Farmington, were inhabited by a warlike tribe whose numbers, according to President Stiles, were greater than those of any other in the neighborhood of the Connecticut.[1]

---

[1] Porter's *Historical Discourse*, p. 26.

Allusion has been more than once made to the Mohawks. Although surrounded by the territory of the Algonquins, this tribe belonged to another and a hostile race, speaking a different language, and possessing a different character — the Huron-Iroquois. The country of the Iroquois embraced large portions of Pennsylvania and Ohio, the greater part of New York, together with the whole peninsula of Upper Canada. Less numerous than the surrounding Algonquins, but far more bold and warlike, they made the terror of their name felt for more than a thousand miles beyond their boundaries. Accustomed to estimate the glory of the warrior only by the number of scalps which hung in his cabin, they were ever on the alert, far and near, to snatch from the heads of their enemies, these ghastly tokens of their prowess. Departing on their distant expeditions, not usually in large numbers, for they trusted more to cunning than to open force, they glided unseen through the closest paths in the forest, patiently enduring cold and hunger and fatigue, they wandered, sometimes over mountains apparently inaccessible, sometimes along the beds of rivers, that they might leave no trail behind them, until they found themselves in the immediate neighborhood of the enemy they sought. There they awaited, with patient expectation, the favorable moment for attack, and when it came, sudden and secret as the lightning, their blows were never seen before they fell. When their object was accomplished, they vanished once more into the forest, baffling all pursuit, and leaving no token of the foray, save the ruin which they had wrought.

It is not strange, therefore, that the warriors of this daring nation were held in the highest fear by the feebler natives of Connecticut. The latter had no confidence in themselves, howevermuch superior in numbers, when opposed to their more powerful neighbors; for the very name of Mohawk was enough to scatter their forces in a moment. All the tribes west of the river were found by the English with the usual marks of subjection upon them; paying an annual tribute, and groaning under the capricious cruelties which savage masters know so well how to inflict.

With regard to the total number of Indians in Connecticut at the settlement of the state, nothing now can be certainly known. Trumbull has reckoned them at twenty thousand, an estimate which is probably not very far from the truth. Bancroft, however, gives to the whole Algonquin race a population of only ninety thousand; so that allowing both estimates to be substantially correct, Connecticut must have been populated out of all proportion to the rest of the Algonquin territory. We know, indeed, that Vermont was wholly without aboriginal inhabitants; that large portions of Maine, New Hampshire, and Massachusetts, were in the same condition, and that from some cause unknown, the fruitful fields and flowing rivers of the west were in a great measure destitute of the abundant population which they are so well calculated to sustain. It is possible, therefore, that the opinions of both historians may be correct, although they make it necessary to suppose that the narrow limits of Connecticut embraced more than one-fifth of the whole population of the vast Algonquin country.

The origin of the American aborigines has been a favorite subject of speculation ever since the discovery of the continent. The history of populating the various theories which have been elaborated for the purpose of the country in a legitimate manner, would furnish the reader with an inexhaustible fund of amusement or of sorrow, according as he might be disposed to laugh at intellectual folly or to weep over it. But we have neither time nor inclination to enumerate all these theories — two or three of them may be taken at random to set forth their general character.

Some writers on this subject have supposed the aborigines of America to be descendants of the Canaannites, who were driven by Joshua out of the promised land.[1] Some profess to deduce their origin from the old Norwegians; excluding, however, Yucatan and the parts adjacent, which according to this theory were peopled by Ethiopic Christians, thrown upon the coast by storm or otherwise.[2] With not a few it has been a favorite speculation,

---

[1] "Gomara et Jean de Lery font descendre tous les Amériquains des Cananéens, chassé de la terre promise par Josué."—Charlevoix: *Dissertation sur l'origine des Amériquains.*

[2] Grotius; *De Origine Gentium Americanum.* In his opinion respecting Yucatan, Grotius follows Peter Martyr.

that the American Indians are the pure-blooded offspring of the lost tribes of Israel;[1] a theory which is likely to profit little by later discoveries of the same wandering race in other parts of the globe. Some have ventured to maintain that the separation which now exists between the eastern and western continents, is of comparatively recent origin; that the century is not very distant when South America was united with Africa, and North America with Asia and Europe.[2] Earthquakes of course, the ever ready helpers of a theorist in dilemma, were the causes of the disruption which has taken place. The honor of beginning the population of this continent has also been given by different writers to the Phenicians, the Carthaginians, the Germans, the Welch, the Icelanders, the Moors, the Scythians, the Chinese — indeed scarcely a nation exists in the eastern hemisphere, which some philosophic speculator has not made the undoubted original of the Indian tribes. To this superabundance of theory, Cotton Mather has added a singular notion of his own. His love of the supernatural would not suffer him to admit any agency in this matter less distinguished than that of the great enemy of mankind. It was he who first moved in the business of emigration, and his devilish object was to carry at least a portion of the human race to a land so distant that the gospel of peace and pardon would never reach them there.[3]

After this partial enumeration of the various methods of supplying America with inhabitants which the ingenuity of the learned has devised, it is no more than just to allow the Indians to speak for themselves upon the question. "They say that they have sprung up and grown in that very place like the trees of the wilderness."[4] Let no one smile at the simplicity of this solution, for even the brilliant and learned Voltaire has presented the same. These are his words; "The providence which placed

---

[1] Adair occupies a large part of his voluminous work in earnestly advocating this opinion.

[2] Abbé Clavigero: *History of Mexico*, III, 109.

[3] "Probably the devil decoyed those miserable savages hither, in hopes that the gospel of our Lord Jesus Christ would never come here to destroy or disturb his absolute empire over them." *Magnalia*, Book III.

[4] Roger Williams, in *Mass. Hist. Col.*, III, 205.

mankind in Norway, planted them also in America, and under the southern polar circle, even as it planted trees there and made the grass to grow."[1] This remarkable coincidence completes the circle of folly. Infidel science ends where ignorance began. Learned philosophism and savage superstition rest lovingly together upon the same broad basis.

From this wilderness of opinions it is not easy to emerge without a hearty acquiescence in the opening remark of Gookin, " concerning the original of the Indians in New England, there is nothing of certainty to be concluded." If any one chooses, however, to rest in the theory of Robertson[2] and Dwight,[3] he will probably find less to disturb him there than in almost any other position. This theory holds that the northeastern part of America was colonized from the north of Europe, and that the whole continent beside received its population from Asia by way of Behring's strait and the Aleutian archipelago. A glance at the map must convince any one that such an opinion is perfectly rational, for even the White bear, on his cake of ice, has a hundred times made longer voyages than the distance which separates the two worlds.[4]

Almost without exception the Indians were tall, straight and muscular. Their manner of life from the earliest period of youth was such as to insure a free and full development of the physical system; and born as they were of sturdy mothers, they inherited none of those bodily weaknesses which, self-caused or otherwise, so heavily curse the females of a later race. Nearly white when new-born, the young Indian turns more and more to the tawny hue as he advances in years, until the copper-color of his nation is finally fixed upon him. A broad, square face, with considerable elevation of feature; hair black and coarse, but never curling;

---

[1] La providence qui a mis des hommes dans le Norvége, en a planté aussi en Amérique et sous le cercle polaire meridional, comme elle y a planté des arbres et fait croître de l'herbe."— *Œuvres*, XVI, 10.

[2] *History of America*, Book IV.

[3] *Travels in New England*, Letter IX.

[4] Bradford's *American Antiquities* is the last, and perhaps the best work on the subject which I have here lightly touched.

eyes small, dark and keen; these complete his outward, personal description.

Among the moral characteristics of the Indian, his passive courage was perhaps the most remarkable. The endless state of warfare in which he delighted to live, together with the cruelties so generally practiced upon captives taken in battle, gave numberless occasions for the exercise of a fortitude which the stoic or the fatalist might have wondered to behold. When fastened to the stake, and yielding up his life by the keenest tortures, not a rebellious muscle testified to the agony of death. No sound escaped his lips; or if his voice was heard among the yells of his tormentors, it was neither the shriek of pain nor the cry for deliverance, but a song as defiant and triumphant as any that burst from the lips around him. To the extremities of heat and cold, he was in a great degree insensible. The longest journeys could scarcely be said to fatigue him. With a little cake made from the meal of parched corn for his food, and water from any stream for his only drink, he would travel day after day with but scanty resting, and arrive fresh and unwearied at his post. His patient endurance of fatigue and suffering was marked with one exception, however, which the faithful pen of Williams has not hesitated to record, although it presents a ludicrous contrast to the high heroism with which death was uniformly met. He says that the Indians could not endure the toothache with any kind of equanimity, but that they cried aloud for very pain, when this tormentor was upon them.

The Indian was also characterized by a remarkable sense of justice, as we may call it, manifested alike in the opposite directions of revenge and gratitude. The *lex talionis* was his only law. An injury was never forgiven until expiation had been made, and on the other hand, a benefit never forgotten until repaid in kind. He lived under the great law of nature; life for life and limb for limb; a law which was made by Divine authority the rule for the administration of justice by magistrates under the Mosaic system; which Pharisaic interpretation perverted into a Divine rule of private conduct; and which Christ forbids as a law of action between individuals, because God has said, "Vengeance is mine; I will repay." Let us not therefore condemn the Indian with too great severity, if in his utter ignorance of the Divine command, and without any competent tribunal of earthly justice to which he might appeal for redress, he so often obeyed the instinctive impulses of his nature, and made himself the judge and avenger of his own wrongs. Let us rather contemplate the more agreeable manifestations of this same principle of retribution, when instead of evil for evil, it aimed only at rendering good for good.

The elder Winthrop has left an anecdote on record which curiously illustrates the ingenuity of Indian gratitude. Massasoit, the sachem of the Pokanokets, was once restored from dangerous sickness to health by the medical skill of Edward Winslow, a leading man among the first settlers of the Plymouth colony. This friendly service he never forgot, but manifested to the whites in every possible manner, his grateful sense of the benefit which he had received from one of their number. On a certain occasion, Winslow, who had been absent for some time in Connecticut, returned through the country of his friend Massasoit, and stopped at his quarters to spend the night with him. Immediately after his arrival, the sachem secretly dispatched his swiftest runner to the colony, bidding him announce with the most truthful air which he could assume, the sudden death of his honored guest; even the very time and manner of it were minutely dictated. The next morning, refreshed by the hospitalities of the wigwam, Winslow pursued his homeward journey. On his arrival at Plymouth, he was not a little surprised to find the whole population lamenting his untimely departure, while they were certainly not less amazed to behold him once more in the flesh. When Massasoit next visited the colony, he was requested to explain the object of this singular falsehood. Without seeming to suspect the least impropriety in the course he had taken, the old sachem replied, that he was strongly desirous of making his white friends happy, and that he could think of nothing which would give them greater pleasure than to have their friend and counselor suddenly restored to their arms in the very midst of their mourning for his loss. The story stops at

20

this point, but we may reasonably conjecture that while the benevolent motive of the old chieftain was properly acknowledged, he was at the same time taught that truth is even more sacred than friendship.[1]

Hospitality was another characteristic of the Indians. The stranger was always welcome. If he came in the night, hungry and weary, men and women roused themselves from slumber, and cheerfully provided for his wants. The best wigwam, usually that of the sachem, was appointed for his habitation while he remained, and he was troubled with no questions concerning the object of his visit or the time of his departure.

Generosity was also a common virtue. They had little to give, it is true, but whatever they had was freely offered. Whenever one of them had been unusually successful in the chase or on the water, a part of his fish and flesh was always distributed among his neighbors. Of the sick their friendship was never forgetful. They filled his hut and crowded round it with offers of aid; not always judicious, indeed, but giving the most ample testimony to the generous warmth of their hearts. On the recovery of the invalid, it was a general custom with them to send him presents, as some compensation for the expenses attendant upon disease; a custom beautiful in itself, and rendered especially necessary by the improvidence of the Indian, for it was no part of his practical wisdom to make health labor for sickness, or youth for old age.

His aversion to labor was such, indeed, that nothing but the urgency of natural wants could rouse him to exertion; and when the immediate necessity was satisfied, no thought of the future prevented his return to idleness. He might suffer the severest pangs of famine in the long and dismal winters of the north; the winds might pierce his miserable dwelling, and cause even his hardened flesh to shrink from their icy touch, but the experience of these and similar evils could not persuade him to make any effectual provision against them. War and the chase alone excepted, the *dolce far niente* was the paradise of the Indian.

But war was his delight, and whenever his energies were roused

---

[1] Winthrop's *History of New England*, 1, 188.

by an impulse of this nature, he exhibited the most abundant resources of cunning, courage, patience and perseverance; of nearly all the qualities, indeed, which were best calculated to insure success. In the conduct of warfare, the Indian fought with little regard to military discipline or to the commands of his leader. He trusted to himself in a remarkable degree. Sometimes a single warrior, in search of glory or revenge, would leave his tribe hundreds of miles behind him, and penetrate alone the country of his enemy. The history of civilized nations can furnish no example of greater self-reliance than was exhibited in such enterprises as these.

Among the moral characteristics of the Indian, it only remains to notice his comparative indifference to sensual pleasures. In this one respect he presented a striking contrast to nearly every other savage, removed as far as he was from all the restraints of civilized and Christian life. Food of the most simple character was all that his appetite demanded; his thirst was always slaked and satisfied with a little water from the spring. If, as was sometimes the case, he was obliged to fast two or three days in succession, he submitted in patience to the necessity, never seeming to regard it as a hardship worthy of complaint. But it may be said that the Indian was indifferent to the pleasures of the palate, only because he was ignorant of the sources of gratification. He knew no food more inviting than his half-cooked fish and flesh; no drink more pleasant to the taste than water; and not being conscious of deficiency, he therefore sought for nothing better than that which he already possessed. It may be so. Let us, however, venture to extend the inquiry to another appetite, which, next to hunger and thirst, is the most imperious of all in its demands; to that upon which the continued existence of the race depends. Passing upon this ground, we find the same characteristic of comparative indifference; the Indian is still "the stoic of the woods." To him the female of his race was not, as in civilized society, a companion and friend; nor yet, as elsewhere, the mere object of voluptuous desire; but he seemed to look upon her as little other than a slave and beast of burden. His conduct exhibited none of those tender sentiments which, grounded on the difference of the sexes, soften and harmonize their intercourse, but he stood aloof in his cold superiority, waited on with trembling by his female drudges.

During the wars which he so frequently and fiercely waged against the whites, many of their wives and daughters were taken captive and carried into his own country. Although these prisoners were entirely at his disposal; although they were subject to insult and injury of every other kind; there is yet no instance recorded of the perpetration of that violence which female virtue reckons worse than death. How shall we account for this remarkable temperance? How can it be accounted for, except upon the ground that the Indian master, whether from natural temperament or manner of life,[1] or indeed from the joint influence of both these causes, was in a great measure insensible to the ordinary power of female beauty? No other explanation is free from insuperable difficulties. The lust of the savage is his law. Whatever desire urges and opportunity presents to his hand, he does; restrained even by the slightest barriers of external prohibition, and hearing the faintest whisper from the voice within. If then, at any time, he seems to respect the claims of virtue, his continence must be attributed, not so much to a kindred virtue in himself, as to the absence of every impulse toward its violation.

When the young Indian arrived at marriageable years, he began to look about him for a companion in life. Having found one that suited his fancy, he paid his addresses to her by the gift of such trinkets and treasures as he supposed would be most pleasing to her taste. If his presents were rejected, his suit was lost; if received, it was the token of his own acceptance, but marriage did not immediately follow. The young couple lived together for a time on trial. At the end of the probationary period, if they were pleased with each other, they were united in wedlock; if not, they separated, each to make another experiment in a different quarter. After marriage, the first object of the young husband was to provide a dwelling for his wife and

---

[1] "Sine Baccho et Cerere friget Venus."

himself. This was accomplished in the following manner. Having chosen a spot for his house, with especial reference to the convenient neighborhood of wood and water, he proceeded to form its roof and walls by bending down toward a common center, the tops of a circle of stout saplings, and closely interlacing their trunks with strips of bark. This done, it only remained to cut a hole in the top of the hut for the passage of the smoke; to make an opening on the side for the ingress and egress of its inhabitants; to cover the structure, within and without, with mats to keep it warm, and then the simple dwelling of the Indian was completed.

In the division of family duties, the whole drudgery of life was imposed upon the female. While the husband was engaged in hunting or fishing, the wife was compelled to cultivate the field; to supply the wigwam with food and water; to carry home the game which her husband had taken — in short, whenever toilsome and inglorious work of any kind was to be done, she was the only laborer. There was but a single exception to this domestic law. The Indian *could* condescend to labor in the field for one purpose. His darling plant, tobacco, was thought worthy to receive his personal care. The manner of life to which the Indian female, even from a child, was bred, although in itself most ungenerous and oppressive, was attended with at least one salutary effect. It gave her a strength of bodily constitution scarcely inferior to that of her master. Her powers of endurance were astonishing. The curse of her sex was nearly lost upon her. "I have often known," says Williams, "in a quarter of an hour, a woman merry in the house, and delivered and merry again; and within two days abroad, and after four or five days at work." The number of wives was unlimited, yet polygamy, though not rare, was by no means universal among them. Divorces frequently took place, for little beside the inclination of the parties kept them together. Adultery was considered a heinous crime, although the sexual intercourse of the unmarried was under no restraint, either of law or public opinion. The children of the Indians were treated by their parents with great affection and indulgence, but parental kindness was seldom repaid or even remembered. The aged and helpless were frequently left to perish in neglect, without the slightest token of love or offer of aid from those to whom they had given birth. In the heart of the Indian, the current of affection, forsaking the parents, ran always forward toward the children: and this truth continuing from one generation to another, it came to pass that filial ingratitude was ever justly punished in the very manner of its own sin. The child who had neglected his parent, becoming a parent himself, was in turn neglected by the children whom he had begotton.

Of iron and steel the Indian had no knowledge. All the tools which he used were made of wood, shells, and stone. The hoe with which the Indian women cultivated the fields, was a clam-shell. Their axe was of stone, having a withe fastened round the neck of it for a handle. Their mortars, pestles, and chisels, were also of stone; and they had moreover stone knives, sharpened to so keen an edge that they could easily cut their hair with them. Two methods of hunting were in use among the natives. Sometimes they followed their game in companies of two or three hundred men, scouring the forests, and destroying multitudes of the sylvan inhabitants, with the same weapons which they used in war. Sometimes they filled the woods with traps of various fashions, and spent their time in passing from one trap to another, to secure whatever had been taken in them. In fishing, they employed nets made of hemp; lines terminating in a hook of bone; and in shallow water, arrows or sharpened sticks, in the use of which they were very skillful.

Their weapons of war were the bow and arrow, the spear, and the tomahawk. The string of the bow was made either of hemp or of the sinew of some wild animal. The arrow was commonly headed with a sharp stone, but sometimes with the horn of the deer, and the claw of the eagle. The spear was nothing more than a long pole, sharpened at the end, and hardened in the fire. The tomahawk, by no means the deadly weapon which the Indian has used since iron was given him, was merely a stick of two or three feet in length, headed with a knob or a stone. Such were the simple arms of the aborigines, and although with these they were able to carry on the warfare of ambushment and surprisal, which they loved so well, yet we cannot wonder that a few shots of European musketry so often drove hundreds of them from the open field.

The Indian was not without a circulating medium, to represent the value of the little property which he possessed. His coin was called *wompumpeag*, or more briefly, *wampum*, and was of two kinds, the white and black. The black was double in value to the white It was wrought from shells into the form of beads, to be strung as beads are, and reckoned by the fathom. A fathom of wampum was worth not far from five English shillings. This Indian money served a double purpose, being used for ornament as well as trade. Chains and bracelets were made of it, and worn upon the neck and wrists, while belts curiously wrought, encircled the body. Indeed nearly the whole dress of the more wealthy was covered by it, for the ostentation of riches is confined to no state of society, and to no period of the world. There was not any restriction upon the manufacture of this money, but whoever chose to make it, was at liberty to do so.

In what is called driving a bargain, the Connecticut Indian was scarcely inferior to the Connecticut white. An old historian says, "they will be at all markets, and try all places, and run twenty, thirty, yea, forty miles and more, and lodge in the woods, to save six pence." Their trade was principally in furs; but sometimes in corn, venison, and fish. It was never safe to allow them credit, for whoever did so, most commonly lost both his debt and his customer.

The political institutions of the Indians were of the very simplest character. A hereditary sachemdom was the only authority recognized among the tribes. In theory, the power of the sachem was absolute; but whenever a question of more than usual interest or difficulty arose, he always sought the advice, and was guided by the wisdom of his counselors. His actual influence with his subjects depended far more upon personal character, than upon birth or station. The sachem who was not the leader of his tribe, in fact as well as name, could not long command their respect or obedience. Females were not excluded from the regular line of succession, although the early history of New England presents but few examples of such government.

The dignity of the crown was sustained by the liberal contributions of the people. Offerings of corn and other productions of the soil were annually made to the sachem, who received also one-fourth of all venison taken in the chase. If his dominions included any portion of sea-coast, whatsoever was cast upon the shore, were it ship or whale, belonged to him.

The administration of justice was among the duties of the sachem, who united in his single person, the legislative, judicial, and executive functions. The Indian who had transgressed the laws of his tribe, not only received his sentence from the lips of his chief, but ordinarily, the punishment decreed, was inflicted by the hand of the judge himself. In every such instance, the criminal submitted in silence to the discipline of his master.

The sachem was assisted in council by a certain order of men called the *paniese*. He availed himself of their wisdom in time of quiet, and in war they formed his body-guard. Selected as the *paniese* were, from the most promising of the young men, trained to dare every danger, and endure all hardships, they constituted not only the defense of the sovereign, but, in a great measure, the strength of the whole tribe. They founded their claim to the respect of the people, not more upon their personal merits, than upon their pretended intercourse with the invisible world. They were wise enough to know that the great weakness of the savage is his superstition, and taking advantage of this weakness, they established their power in this world on a firmer basis, by deriving their authority from the powers of the world to come.

The mind of the Indian, degraded and dark as it might be, was nevertheless not without a few faint glimpses from the eternal world. Although among the lowest of mankind, he was still a man, and therefore not utterly destitute of those religious ideas which, by nature, belong to every human soul. He believed in a Supreme Being, and in a future state; he recognized a ruling Providence in the affairs of this world, and a retribution hereafter. These great principles of natural religion were as really, if not so beautifully, developed in the wilds of North America, as they ever had been in the porch and the academy of ancient Greece; for wherever the Almighty enkindles the immortal fire of a human soul, he never leaves it without implanting in its nature a witness of himself.

The religion of the Indian was polytheistic in the very highest degree; but like every other polytheist, he had his greater and his lesser deities. *Kiehtan* was his name for the good God, the creator of the world, and the bountiful bestower of every blessing. His home was in the southwestern heavens, and to his presence went the souls of the good, when death called them to leave the earth. He named his devil, *Hobbamock*. This bad spirit was the fountain of all evil; and fear, which among savages is always stronger than love, led the Indian to court his favor with prayers and offerings, and nearly every form of deprecatory worship. Beside these two principal deities, there was a multitude of local gods who were known by the general name of *Manitou*. With these subordinate spirits the whole world of the Indian was overflowing. The classical student is familiar with the beautiful superstition of that land where every wood has its dryad; every fountain its naiad — where the rainbow was the garment of one god, and the sun the golden chariot of another — where the Lares and Penates watched over the household hearth — where Jupiter thundered in the heavens, and Neptune rose from the sea. But the fancy of the Indian was even more than prodigal of its treasures than the poetry of brilliant Greece. He filled and crowded every object in nature with spiritual existence. The great points of the compass, east, west, north, south, had each its peculiar god. The sun, the moon, the sea, and the fire, were all the abodes of supernatural beings. Even the involuntary motions of the body were attributed to the power of resident spirits. It was a god who made the heart to beat; yet another god who filled the lungs with vital air. It was a god (Somnus by a different name), who sat upon the eyelids and pressed them down in slumber; still another god who lifted those lids, and let in the light of the morning. So also whenever any thing took place, the cause or manner of which they did not at once perceive, they were always accustomed to say, *Manitou*, it is a god. "At the apprehension of any excellency in man, woman, birds, beasts, fish, etc.," they still cried out, with a kind of reverential admiration, it is a god. When the English first came among them, and they beheld the ships which brought them over; the buildings which they erected; their manner of cultivating the fields; their arms and clothing; and above all, their books and letters, they exclaimed one to another, *Manitouwock*, they are gods. In all this we discover, carried out to its full extent, the universal tendency of the untaught mind to refer all appearances, unusual or difficult of explanation, to the immediate agency of supernatural beings. The grand idea of something above and beyond nature, pervades the whole region of humanity, whether developed in the pantheism of the philosopher, the polytheism of the savage, or the heaven-inspired faith of the Christian.

With a belief so constantly active in the existence and power of spiritual beings, the Indians were ever seeking to propitiate their favor, by prayers and sacrifices and solemn feasts; the customary methods to which nature seems to direct the unenlightened soul. *Kiehtan*, the good god, they approached chiefly with thanksgiving, for benefits received. When victory crowned their warfare, or plenty smiled upon their fields, or success attended their efforts in any direction, it was piously attributed to the friendly aid of this benevolent spirit, and they expressed their thanks to him in song and dance, and every utterance of grateful joy.

But their principal worship was paid to *Hobbamock*, whose disposition to do them injury they strove by every means to change. They were accustomed to ascribe all their sufferings to the mischievous agency of this spirit of evil. Disease, death, defeat in battle, famine, and pestilence; these and other calamities proceeded forth from him, and fear of his power compelled them to supplicate his mercy with all the earnestness of prayer. The Indian who had lost a child, called up his family at break of day, to join him in his lamentation, and with abundance of tears, exclaimed, "Oh! God! thou hast taken away my child! thou art angry with me. Oh! turn thine anger away from me, and spare the rest of my children."[1] A fearful dream they conceived to be

---

[1] Key, chap. xxi.

a threatening of evil from *Hobbamock*, and whenever their rest was so disturbed, they would rise at all times of the night and fall at once to supplication.

But not with prayers alone did the Indian seek the favor, and deprecate the wrath of his gods. Sacrifices were also common among them, and it has even been asserted that human life was occasionally taken for this purpose. The truth of this statement, however, is doubtful, and so long as entire certainty is wanting, we should hesitate to admit that the Indian was ever guilty of so horrible a crime. But whether or not they gave the fruit of the body for the sin of the soul, there is no question of their liberality in separating to religious purposes the most valued of their worldly possessions. Kettles, skins, hatchets, beads, and knives, all were cast by the priests into the sacred fire, and consumed to ashes; and while the conflagration was going on, they gathered around it, sometimes by hundreds, dancing and shouting, and making all kinds of discordant noises. In these religious exercises, they were led on by the priests, or as they named them, *powows*, who to sustain their official character, made their devotion so excessively earnest, that it often left them utterly exhausted with fatigue.

The Indian *powow* was a physician as well as a priest. In every case of sickness, he was sent for to the cabin of the sufferer, where his mere presence, or if that failed, his magical incantations, were thought sufficient to restore the invalid. The credulous historian of the Narragansets, who was frequently a witness of these superstitious rites, acknowledges that "by the help of the devil, they do most certainly work great cures," although "they administer nothing, but howl and roar and hollow over them."

The heaven of the Indian was in the house of *Kichtan*, far away in the southwest, where the spirits of the good who had left the earth, were gathered in a most happy society, enjoying in constant fullness those pleasures which, to the simple mind of the Indian, were enough to constitute a paradise. There they engaged in the occupations which delighted them most in the world they had left behind. War, followed always by victory — the chase, with a never-failing abundance of game — feasting and dancing — these brightened the hours as they rolled along, and filled up the measure of their heavenly happiness. But this heaven is open only to the good. The souls of thieves, liars, and murderers, go also to the house of *Kiehtan*, and ask for admission, but he replies that there is no place for them; he bids them depart, and so "they wander forever in restless want and penury."

It is worthy of remark, that the southwest was so generally distinguished by the aborigines as the peculiar quarter of their God and their heaven. This sentiment prevailed not only in Connecticut and New England, but throughout the United States. The reason of this common belief must occur to every one familiar with the climate of the country. The east wind is damp and chilly, bringing clouds and rain from the ocean; the north wind is piercingly cold; but the wind from "the sweet southwest," which unites the freshness of the west with the mildness of the south, was to the Indian, as well as to the Greek of old, the Zephyr, *the bringer of life*. Whenever his cheek was touched by the summer softness of the breezes which came from that quarter of the sky, it was not difficult for him to believe, with a literal confidence, that they were "airs from heaven."

When the Indian died, all his relations and friends went into mourning, to testify their sorrow for his loss. In the beginning of sickness, indeed, it was customary for the females of the family to blacken their faces with soot and charcoal, and to keep them in this condition day after day; but only when disease terminated in death, did the men disfigure themselves in the same singular manner. This visible token of grief was accompanied by cries and wailings of the most mournful character. Tears plentiful as rain coursed down the cheeks of the mourners, and mingling with the soot and charcoal which covered them, presented a spectacle of woe calculated to move far other feelings than those of sympathetic sorrow. When the body was brought to the place of burial, it was not immediately committed to the earth, but left at the side of the grave, until the friends of the dead had united once more in vociferous and long-continued lamentation. At such times, not only the women and children suffered their tears to flow freely, but even the "stoutest captains" wept in company. This duty done, the corpse was laid in the ground, wrapped in skins and mats, and covered by the same ornaments which had graced it when a living body. Whatever treasures belonged to the deceased, were also laid by his side, together with all the utensils and implements which he had been accustomed to use — as if his soul would need them in the world to which it had gone. Sometimes the body was covered with a fine red powder, of a strong scent, but not offensive, which was evidently used as " a kind of embalment."[1] The wigwam in which he had died, was considered thenceforth uninhabitable, and always burned down or otherwise destroyed. The mat upon which the dead had lain, was spread over his grave, and his coat of skins hung up on a neighboring tree, where it was suffered to remain until it dropped to pieces. The continuance of mourning depended very much upon the dignity of the deceased; in some cases it lasted but a short time; in others a year was not thought too long to bear about the emblems of sorrow. After the funeral ceremonies had been performed, the relatives of the dead were visited by all their acquaintances, who came to express sympathy, and offer consolation. The Indian was never guilty of neglecting this important office of friendship.

A singular custom prevailed among them in regard to pronouncing the names of the dead. Whoever did so was subjected to a fine, and if the offense was repeated, death was not regarded as a punishment too severe. In 1655, the Sachem Philip crossed from the main land to the island of Nantucket, for the single purpose of taking the life of John Gibbs : an Indian whose only crime was that he had spoken the name of a deceased relative of Philip. Gibbs had notice of his coming and concealed himself; the English interfered, but all arguments, together with all the money which they could collect for the ransom of the offender, were scarcely able to calm the anger of Philip, and lead him to lay aside his murderous designs.[2]

The inquiry in which we have thus engaged is not without a mournful interest, when we remember how like a dream when

---
[1] *Chronicles of the Pilgrims*, p. 142.
[2] Macy's account of Nantucket, in *Mass. Hist. Coll.*, III, 159.

one awaketh, the old lords of the land have passed away. The pestilence which destroyed thousands of the eastern tribes just before the landing of the pilgrims of the Plymouth colony, was more rapid in its work of death, but not more sure than the surge of emigration which, but a few years later, began to roll in upon the valley of the Connecticut. Whether by sickness, by sword, or by the mere neighborhood of a stronger and wiser race, the destiny of the Indian drove him into one path, and that path led only to destruction.

But while it is impossible to regard the disappearance of whole tribes and nations without a feeling near akin to sadness, yet when we estimate aright, in all its bearings and results, the wonderful change in which their ruin was involved, who shall say that there is any room for sorrow? It is a questionable philanthropy that weeps at such a revolution. Behold the contrast. Barbarism has given place to civilization. Heathenism has yielded to Christianity. The depths of the forest, which for ages had been sacred to darkness, are now laid open to the light of the sun. The resources of the soil, which the Indian wanted industry and skill to develop, are no longer hidden beneath the surface, but on every side we behold, in all abundance and variety, the harvest of his indefatigable successor. Physical comfort, knowledge, peace, liberty, and religion — all that is accounted excellent and desirable in the world — have become the common inheritance of the people, even upon the same soil where, two centuries, ago, they were totally unknown. The whimsical Rousseau might profess to regard the savage state as the most perfect condition of humanity, yet surely, no sound mind, or benevolent heart, can remember with any thing but joy the change which two hundred years have wrought in New England.

THE INDIAN RESERVATIONS OF CALIFORNIA.[1]

By J. Ross Browne.

When the state of California was admitted into the Union, the number of Indians within its borders was estimated at one hundred thousand. Of these, some five or six thousand, residing in the vicinity of the missions, were partially civilized, and subsisted chiefly by begging and stealing. A few of the better class contrived to avoid starvation by casual labor in the vineyards and on the farms of the settlers. They were very poor and very corrupt, given to gambling, drinking, and other vices prevailing among white men, and to which Indians have a natural inclination. As the country became more settled, it was considered profitable, owing to the high rate of compensation for white labor, to encourage these Christian tribes to adopt habits of industry, and they were employed very generally throughout the state. In the vine-growing districts they were usually paid in native brandy every Saturday night, put in jail next morning for getting drunk, and bailed out on Monday to work out the fine imposed upon them by the local authorities. This system still prevails in Los Angeles, where I have often seen a dozen of these miserable wretches carried to jail roaring drunk of a Sunday morning. The inhabitants of Los Angeles are a moral and intelligent people, and many of them disapprove of the custom on principle, and hope it will be abolished as soon as the Indians are all killed off. Practically, it is not a bad way of bettering their condition; for some of them die every week from the effects of debauchery, or kill one another in the nocturnal brawls which prevail in the outskirts of the pueblo.

The settlers in the northern portions of the state had a still more effectual method of encouraging the Indians to adopt habits of civilization. In general, they engaged them at a fixed rate of wages to cultivate the ground, and during the season of labor

[1] Reprinted from *Harper's Magazine* (New York), for August, 1861.

fed them on beans and gave them a blanket or a shirt each; after which, when the harvest was secured, the account was considered squared, and the Indians were driven off to forage in the woods for themselves and families during the winter. Starvation usually wound up a considerable number of the old and decrepit ones every season; and of those that failed to perish from hunger or exposure, some were killed on the general principle that they must have subsisted by stealing cattle, for it was well known that cattle ranged in the vicinity; while others were not unfrequently slaughtered by their employers for helping themselves to the refuse portions of the crop which had been left in the ground. It may be said that these were exceptions to the general rule; but if ever an Indian was fully and honestly paid for his labor by a white settler, it was not my luck to hear of it. Certainly, it could not have been of frequent occurrence.

The wild Indians inhabiting the coast range, the valleys of the Sacramento and San Joaquin, and the western slope of the Sierra Nevada, became troublesome at a very early period after the discovery of the gold mines. It was found convenient to take possession of their country without recompense, rob them of their wives and children, kill them in every cowardly and barbarous manner that could be devised, and when that was impracticable, drive them as far as possible out of the way. Such treatment was not consistent with their rude ideas of justice. At best they were an ignorant race of Diggers, wholly unacquainted with our enlightened institutions. They could not understand why they should be murdered, robbed, and hunted down in this way, without any other pretense or provocation than the color of their skin and the habits of life to which they had always been accustomed. In the traditionary researches of their most learned sages they had never heard of the snakes in Ireland that were exterminated for the public benefit by the great and good St. Patrick. They were utterly ignorant of the sublime doctrine of General Welfare. The idea, strange as it may appear, never occurred to them that they were suffering for the great cause of civilization, which, in the natural course of things, must exterminate Indians. Actuated by the base motives of resentment, a few of them occasionally rallied, preferring rather to die than submit to these imaginary wrongs. White men were killed from time to time; cattle were driven off; horses were stolen, and various other iniquitous offenses were committed.

The federal government, as is usual in cases where the lives of valuable voters are at stake, was forced to interfere. Troops were sent out to aid the settlers in slaughtering the Indians. By means of mounted howitzers, muskets, Minie rifles, dragoon pistols, and sabres, a good many were cut to pieces. But, on the whole, the general policy of the government was pacific. It was not designed to kill any more Indians than might be necessary to secure the adhesion of the honest yeomanry of the state, and thus furnish an example of the practical working of our political system to the savages of the forest, by which it was hoped they might profit. Congress took the matter in hand at an early day, and appropriated large sums of money for the purchase of cattle and agricultural implements. From the wording of the law, it would appear that these useful articles were designed for the relief and maintenance of the Indians. Commissioners were appointed at handsome salaries to treat with them, and sub-agents employed to superintend the distribution of the purchases. In virtue of this munificent policy, treaties were made in which the various tribes were promised a great many valuable presents, which of course they never got. There was no reason to suppose they ever should; it being a fixed principle with strong powers never to ratify treaties made by their own agents with weaker ones, when there is money to pay and nothing to be had in return.

The cattle were purchased, however, to the number of many thousands. Here arose another difficulty. The honest miners must have something to eat, and what could they have more nourishing than fat cattle? Good beef has been a favorite article of subsistence with men of bone and muscle ever since the days of the ancient Romans. So the cattle, or the greater part of them, were driven up to the mines, and sold at satisfactory rates — probably for the benefit of the Indians, though I never could understand in what way their necessities were relieved by this speculation, unless it might be that the parties interested turned over to them the funds received for the cattle. It is very certain they continued to starve and commit depredations in the most ungrateful manner for some time after; and, indeed, to such a pitch of audacity did they carry their rebellious spirit against the constituted authorities, that many of the chiefs protested if the white people would only let them alone, and give them the least possible chance to make a living, they would esteem it a much greater favor than any relief they had experienced from the munificent donations of congress.

But government was not to be defeated in its benevolent intentions. Voluminous reports were made to congress, showing that a general reservation system, on the plan so successfully pursued by the Spanish missionaries, would best accomplish the object. It was known that the missions of California had been built chiefly by Indian labor; that during their existence the priests had fully demonstrated the capacity of this race for the acquisition of civilized habits; that extensive vineyards and large tracts of land had been cultivated solely by Indian labor, under their instruction; and that by this humane system of teaching many hostile tribes had been subdued, and enabled not only to support themselves but to render the missions highly profitable establishments.

No aid was given by government beyond the grants of land necessary for missionary purposes; yet they soon grew wealthy, owned immense herds of cattle, supplied agricultural products to the rancheros, and carried on a considerable trade in hides and tallow with the United States. If the Spanish priests could do this without arms or assistance, in the midst of a savage country, at a period when the Indians were more numerous and more powerful than they are now, surely it could be done in a comparatively civilized country by intelligent Americans, with all the lights of experience and the coöperation of a beneficent government.

At least congress thought so; and in 1853 laws were passed for the establishment of a reservation system in California, and large appropriations were made to carry it into effect. Tracts of land of twenty-five thousand acres were ordered to be set apart for the use of the Indians; officers were appointed to supervise the affairs of the service; clothing, cattle, seeds, and agricultural implements were purchased; and a general invitation was extended to the various tribes to come in and learn how to work like white men. The first reservation was established at the Tejon, a beautiful and fertile valley in the southern part of the state. Head-quarters for the employés, and large granaries for the crops, were erected. The Indians were feasted on cattle, and every thing promised favorably. True, it cost a great deal to get started, about $250,000; but a considerable crop was raised, and there was every reason to hope that the experiment would prove successful. In the course of time other reservations were established, one in the foot-hills of the Sacramento valley, at a place called Nome Lackee; one at the mouth of the Noyo river, south of Cape Mendocino; and one on the Klamath, below Crescent City; besides which, there were Indian farms, or adjuncts, of these reservations at the Fresno, Nome Cult or Round valley, the Mattole valley, near Cape Mendocino, and other points where it was deemed advisable to give aid and instruction to the Indians. The cost of these establishments was such as to justify the most sanguine anticipations of their success.

In order that the appropriations might be devoted to their legitimate purpose, and the greatest possible amount of instruction furnished at the least expense, the executive department adopted the policy of selecting officers experienced in the arts of public speaking, and thoroughly acquainted with the prevailing systems of primary elections. A similar policy had been found to operate beneficially in the case of collectors of customs, and there was no reason why it should not in other branches of the public service. Gentlemen skilled in the tactics of state legislatures, and capable of influencing those refractory bodies by the exercise of moral suasion, could be relied upon to deal with the Indians, who are not so far advanced in the arts of civilization, and whose necessities, in a pecuniary point of view, are not usually so urgent. Besides, it was known that the Digger tribes were exceedingly ignorant of our political institutions; and required more instruction, perhaps, in this branch of knowledge than in any other. The most intelligent of the chiefs actually had no more idea of the respective merits of the great candidates for senatorial honors in California than if those distinguished gentlemen had never been born. As to primary meetings and caucuses, the poor Diggers, in their simplicity, were just as apt to mistake them for some favorite game of thimble-rig or pitch-penny as for the practical exercise of the great system of free suffrage. They could not make out why men should drink so much whisky and swear so hard unless they were gambling; and if any further proof was necessary, it was plain to see that the game was one of hazard, because the players were constantly whispering to each other and passing money from hand to hand, and from pocket to pocket. The only difference they could see between the different parties was that some had more money than others, but they had no idea where it came from. To enlighten them on all these points was, doubtless, the object of the great appointing powers in selecting good political speakers to preside over them. After buildig their houses, it was presumed that there would be plenty of stumps left in the woods from which they could be taught to make speeches on the great questions of the day; and where a gratifying scene might be witnessed, at no remote period, of big and little Diggers holding forth from every stump in support of the presiding administration. For men who possessed an extraordinary capacity for drinking ardent spirits; who could number among their select friends the most notorious vagrants and gamblers in the state; who spent their days in idleness and their nights in brawling grog-shops — whose habits, in short, were in every way disreputable — the authorities in Washington entertained a very profound antipathy. I know this to be the case, because the most stringent regulations were established prohibiting persons in the service from getting drunk, and official orders written warning them that they would be promptly removed in case of any misconduct. Circular letters were also issued, and posted up at the different reservations, forbidding the employés to adopt the wives of the Indians, which it was supposed they might attempt to do from too zealous a disposition to cultivate friendly relations with both sexes. In support

The Indian Reservations of California. 309

of this policy, the California delegation made it a point never to indorse any person for office in the service who was not considered peculiarly deserving of patronage. They knew exactly the kind of men that were wanted, because they lived in the state and had read about the Indians in the newspapers. Some of them had even visited a few of the wigwams. Having the public welfare at heart — a fact that can not be doubted, since they repeatedly asserted it in their speeches — they saw where the great difficulty lay, and did all in their power to aid the executive. They indorsed the very best friends they had — gentlemen who had contributed to their election, and fought for them through thick and thin. The capacity of such persons for conducting the affairs of a reservation could not be doubted. If they had cultivated an extensive acquaintance among pot-house voters, of course they must understand the cultivation of potatoes and onions; if they could control half a dozen members of the legislature in a senatorial contest, why not be able to control Indians, who were not near so difficult to manage? if they could swallow obnoxious measures of the administration, were they not qualified to teach savages how to swallow government provisions? if they were honest enough to avow, in the face of corrupt and hostile factions, that they stood by the constitution, and always meant to stand by the same broad platform, were they not honest enough to disburse public funds?

In one respect, I think the policy of the government was unfortunate — that is, in the disfavor with which persons of intemperate and disreputable habits were regarded. Men of this kind — and they are not difficult to find in California — could do a great deal toward meliorating the moral condition of the Indians by drinking up all the whisky that might be smuggled on the reservations, and behaving so disreputably in general that no Indian, however degraded in his propensities, could fail to become ashamed of such low vices.

In accordance with the views of the department, it was deemed to be consistent with decency that these untutored savages should be clothed in a more becoming costume than Nature had bestowed upon them. Most of them were as ignorant of covering as they were of the Lecompton constitution. With the exception of a few who had worked for the settlers, they made their first appearance on the reservations very much as they appeared when they first saw daylight. It was a great object to make them sensible of the advantages of civilization by covering their backs while cultivating their brains. Blankets, shirts, and pantaloons, therefore, were purchased for them in large quantities. It is presumed that when the department read the vouchers for these articles and for the potatoes, beans, and cattle that were so plentifully sprinkled through the accounts, it imagined that it was "clothing the naked and feeding the hungry!"

The blankets, to be sure, were very thin, and cost a great deal of money in proportion to their value; but, then, peculiar advantages were to be derived from the transparency of the fabric. In some respects the worst material might be considered the most economical. By holding his blanket to the light an Indian could enjoy the contemplation of both sides of it at the same time; and it would only require a little instruction in architecture to enable him to use it occasionally as a window to his wigwam. Every blanket being marked by a number of blotches, he could carry his window on his back whenever he went out on a foraging expedition, so as to know the number of his residence when he returned, as the citizens of Schilda carried their doors when they went away from home, in order that they should not forget where they lived. Nor was it the least important consideration, that when he gambled it away, or sold it for whisky, he would not be subject to any inconvenience from a change of temperature. The shirts and pantaloons were in general equally transparent, and possessed this additional advantage, that they very soon cracked open in the seams, and thereby enabled the squaws to learn how to sew.

As many of the poor wretches were afflicted with diseases incident to their mode of life, and likely to contract others from the white employés of the reservations, physicians were appointed to give them medicine. Of course Indians required a peculiar mode of treatment. They spoke a barbarous jargon, and it was not possible that any thing but barbarous compounds could operate on their bowels. Of what use would it be to waste good medicines on stomachs that were incapable of comprehending their use? Accordingly, any deficiency in the quality was made up by the quantity and variety. Old drug stores were cleared of their rubbish, and vast quantities of croton oil, saltpetre, alum, paint, scent-bottles, mustard, vinegar, and other valuable laxatives, diaphoretics, and condiments were supplied for their use. The result was, that, aided by the peculiar system of diet adopted, the physicians were enabled very soon to show a considerable roll of patients. In cases where the blood was ascertained to be scorbutic, the patients were allowed to go out in the valleys, and subsist for a few months on clover or grass, which was regarded as a sovereign remedy. I was assured at one reservation that fresh spring grass had a more beneficial effect on them than the medicines, as it generally purged them. The department was fully advised of these facts in elaborate reports made by its special emissaries, and congratulated itself upon the satisfactory progress of the system. The elections were going all right — the country was safe. Feeding Indians on grass was advancing them at least one step toward a knowledge of the sacred scriptures. It was following the time-honored precedent of Nebuchadnezzar, the king of Babylon, who was driven from men and did eat grass as oxen, and was wet with the dews of heaven till his hairs were grown like eagles' feathers, and his nails like birds' claws. An ounce of croton oil would go a great way in lubricating the intestines of an entire tribe of Indians; and if the paint could not be strictly classed with any of the medicines known in the official dispensary, it might at least be used for purposes of clothing during the summer months. Red or green pantaloons painted on the legs of the Indians, and striped blue shirts artistically marked out on their bodies, would be at once cool, economical, and picturesque. If these things cost a great deal of money, as appeared by the vouchers, it was a consolation to know that, money being the root of all evil, no injurious effects could grow out of such a root after it had been once thoroughly eradicated.

The Indians were also taught the advantages to be derived from the cultivation of the earth. Large supplies of potatoes were purchased in San Francisco, at about double what they were worth in the vicinity of the reservations. There were only twenty-five thousand acres of public land available at each place for the growth of potatoes or any other esculent for which the hungry natives might have a preference; but it was much easier to purchase potatoes than to make farmers out of the white men employed to teach them how to cultivate the earth. Sixteen or seventeen men on each reservation had about as much as they could do to attend to their own private claims, and keep the natives from eating their private crops. It was not the policy of government to reward its friends for their "adhesion to the constitution" by requiring them to perform any practical labor at seventy-five or a hundred dollars a month, which was scarcely double the current wages of the day. Good men could obtain employment any where by working for their wages; but it required the best kind of administration men to earn extraordinary compensations by an extraordinary amount of idleness. Not that they were all absolutely worthless. On the contrary, some spent their time in hunting, others in riding about the country, and a considerable number in laying out and supervising private claims, aided by Indian labor and government provisions.

The official reports transmitted to congress from time to time gave flattering accounts of the progress of the system. The extent and variety of the crops were fabulously grand. Immense numbers of Indians were fed and clothed — on paper. Like little children who cry for medicines, it would appear that the whole red race were so charmed with the new schools of industry that they were weeping to be removed there and set to work. Indeed many of them had already learned to work "like white men;" they were bending to it cheerfully, and could handle the plow and the sickle very skillfully, casting away their bows and arrows and adopting the more effective instruments of agriculture. No mention was made of the fact that these working Indians had acquired their knowledge from the settlers, and that if they worked after the fashion of the white men on the reservations, it was rarely any of them were obliged to go to the hospital in consequence of injuries resulting to the spinal column. The

THE INDIAN RESERVATIONS OF CALIFORNIA. 313

favorite prediction of the officers in charge was, that in a very short time these institutions would be self-sustaining — that is to say, that neither they nor the Indians would want any more money after a while.

It may seem strange that the appropriations demanded of congress did not decrease in a ratio commensurate with these flattering reports. The self-sustaining period had not yet come. On the contrary, as the Indians were advancing into the higher branches of education — music, dancing, and the fine arts, moral philosophy and ethics, political economy, etc.— it required more money to teach them. The number had been considerably diminished by death and desertion; but then their appetites had improved, and they were getting a great deal smarter. Besides, politics were becoming sadly entangled in the state, and many agents had to be employed in the principal cities to protect the women and children from any sudden invasion of the natives, while the patriotic male citizens were at the polls depositing their votes.

The department, no doubt, esteemed all this to be a close approximation to the Spanish mission system, and in some respects it was. The priests sought the conversion of heathens, who believed neither in the Divinity nor the Holy Ghost; the department the conversion of infidels, who had no faith in the measures of the administration. If there was any material difference, it was in the Head of the church and the missionaries appointed to carry its views into effect.

But the most extraordinary feature in the history of this service in California was the interpretation given by the Federal authorities in Washington to the Independent Treasury Act of 1846. That stringent provision, prohibiting any public officer from using for private purposes, loaning, or depositing in any bank or banking institution any public funds committed to his charge; transmitting for settlement any voucher for a greater amount than that actually paid; or appropriating such funds to any other purpose than that prescribed by law, was so amended in the construction of the department as to mean, " except in cases where such officer has rendered peculiar services to the party and possesses strong influences in congress." When any infraction of the law was reported, it was subjected to the test of this amended reading; and if the conditions were found satisfactory, the matter was disposed of in a pigeon-hole. An adroit system of accountability was established by which no property return, abstract of issues, account current, or voucher, was understood to mean what it expressed upon its face, so that no accounting officer possessing a clew to the policy adopted could be deceived by the figures. Thus it was perfectly well understood that five hundred or a thousand head of cattle did not necessarily mean real cattle with horns, legs, and tails, actually born in the usual course of nature, purchased for money, and delivered on the reservations; but prospective cattle, that might come into existence and be wanted at some future period. For all the good the Indians got of them, it might as well be five hundred or a thousand head of voters, for they no more fed upon beef, as a general thing, than they did upon human flesh.

Neither was it beyond the capacity of the department to comprehend that traveling expenses, on special Indian service, might just as well mean a trip to the convention at Sacramento; that guides and assistants were a very indefinite class of gentlemen of a roving turn of mind; that expenses incurred in visiting wild tribes and settling difficulties among them did not necessarily involve the exclusion of difficulties among the party factions in the legislature. In short, the original purpose of language was so perverted in the official correspondence that it had no more to do with the expression of facts than many of the employés had to do with the Indians. The reports and regulations of the department actually bordered on the poetical. It was enough to bring tears into the eyes of any feeling man to read the affecting dissertations that were transmitted to congress on the woes of the red men, and the labors of the public functionaries to meliorate their unhappy condition. Faith, hope, and charity abounded in them. "See what we are doing for these poor children of the forest!" was the burden of the song, in a strain worthy the most pathetic flights of Mr. Pecksniff; "see how faithful we are to our trusts, and how judiciously we expend the appropriations!

Yet they die off in spite of us — wither away as the leaves of the trees in autumn! Let us hope, nevertheless, that the beneficent intentions of congress may yet be realized. We are the guardians of these unfortunate and defenseless beings; they are our wards; it is our duty to take care of them; we can afford to be liberal, and spend a little more money on them. Through the judicious efforts of our public functionaries, and the moral influences spread around them, there is reason to believe they will yet embrace civilization and Christianity, and become useful members of society." In accordance with these views the regulations issued by the department, were of the most stringent character — encouraging economy, industry, and fidelity; holding all agents and employés to a strict accountability; with here and there some instructive maxim of morality — all of which, upon being translated, meant that politicians are very smart fellows, and it was not possible for them to humbug one another. "Do your duty to the Indians as far as you can conveniently, and without too great a sacrifice of money; but stand by our friends, and save the party by all means and at all hazards. *Verbum sap!*" was the practical construction.

When public clamor called attention to these supposed abuses, and it became necessary to make some effective demonstration of honesty, a special agent was directed to examine into the affairs of the service and report the result. It was particularly enjoined upon him to investigate every complaint affecting the integrity of public officers, collect and transmit the proofs of malfeasance with his own views in the premises, so that every abuse might be uprooted and cast out of the service. Decency in official conduct must be respected and the public eye regarded! Peremptory measures would be taken to suppress all frauds upon the treasury. It was the sincere desire of the administration to preserve purity and integrity in the public service.

From mail to mail, during a period of three years, the agent made his reports; piling up proof upon proof, and covering acres of valuable paper with protests and remonstrances against the policy pursued; racking his brains to do his duty faithfully; subjecting himself to newspaper abuse for neglecting it, because no beneficial result was perceptible, and making enemies as a matter of course. Reader, if ever you aspire to official honors, let the fate of that unfortunate agent be a warning to you. He did exactly what he was instructed to do, which was exactly what he was not wanted to do. In order to save time and expense, as well as further loss of money in the various branches of public service upon which he had reported, other agents were sent out to ascertain if he had told the truth ; and when they were forced to admit that he had, there was a good deal of trouble in the wigwam of the great chief. Not only did poor Yorick incur the hostility of powerful senatorial influences, but by persevering in his error, and insisting that he had told the truth, the whole truth, and nothing but the truth, he eventually lost the respect and confidence of the "powers that be," together with his official head. I knew him well. He was a fellow of infinite jest. There was something so exquisitely comic in the idea of taking official instructions literally, and carrying them into effect, that he could not resist it. The humor of the thing kept him in a constant chuckle of internal satisfaction ; but it was the most serious jest he ever perpetrated, for it cost him, besides the trouble of carrying it out, the loss of a very comfortable per diem.

The results of the policy pursued were precisely such as might have been expected. A very large amount of money was annually expended in feeding white men and starving Indians. Such of the latter as were physically able took advantage of the tickets-of-leave granted them so freely, and left. Very few ever remained at these benevolent institutions when there was a possibility of getting anything to eat in the woods. Every year numbers of them perished from neglect and disease, and some from absolute starvation. When it was represented in the official reports that two or three thousand enjoyed the benefit of aid from government within the limits of each district — conveying the idea that they were fed and clothed at public expense — it must have meant that the territory of California originally cost the United States fifteen millions of dollars, and that the nuts and berries upon which the Indians subsisted, and the fig-leaves in which they were supposed to be clothed, were embraced within the cessions made by Mexico. At all events, it invariably happened, when a visitor appeared on the reservations, that the Indians were "out in the mountains gathering nuts and berries." This was the case in spring, summer, autumn, and winter. They certainly possessed a remarkable predilection for staying out a long time. Very few of them, indeed, have yet come back. The only difference between the existing state of things and that which existed prior to the inauguration of the system is, that there were then some thousands of Indians living within the limits of the districts set apart for reservation purposes, whereas there are now only some hundreds. In the brief period of six years they have been very nearly destroyed by the generosity of government. What neglect, starvation, and disease have not done, has been achieved by the coöperation of the white settlers in the great work of extermination.

No pretext has been wanted; no opportunity lost, whenever it has been deemed necessary to get them out of the way. At Nome Cult valley, during the winter of 1858–'59, more than a hundred and fifty peaceable Indians, including women and children, were cruelly slaughtered by the whites who had settled there under official authority, and most of whom derived their support either from actual or indirect connection with the reservation. Many of them had been in public employ, and now enjoyed the rewards of their meritorious services. True, a notice was posted up on the trees that the valley was public land reserved for Indian purposes, and not open to settlement; but nobody, either in or out of the service, paid any attention to that, as a matter of course. When the Indians were informed that it was their home, and were invited there on the pretext that they would be protected, it was very well understood that as soon as government had spent money enough there to build up a settlement sufficiently strong to maintain itself, they would enjoy very slender chances of protection. It was alleged that they had driven off and eaten private cattle. There were some three or four hundred head of public cattle on the property returns, all supposed to be ranging in the same vicinity; but the private cattle must have been a great deal better, owing to some superior capacity for eating grass. Upon an investigation of this charge, made by the officers of the army, it was found to be entirely destitute of truth; a few cattle had been lost, or probably killed by white men, and this was the whole basis of the massacre. Armed parties went into the rancherias in open day, when no evil was apprehended, and shot the Indians down — weak, harmless, and defenseless as they were — without distinction of age or sex; shot down women with sucking babes at their breasts; killed or crippled the naked children that were running about; and, after they had achieved this brave exploit, appealed to the state government for aid! Oh, shame, shame! where is thy blush, that white men should do this with impunity in a civilized country, under the very eyes of an enlightened government! They did it, and they did more! For days, weeks, and months they ranged the hills of Nome Cult, killing every Indian that was too weak to escape; and, what is worse, they did it under a state commission, which in all charity I must believe was issued upon false representations. A more cruel series of outrages than those perpetrated upon the poor Indians of Nome Cult never disgraced a community of white men. The state said the settlers must be protected, and it protected them — protected them from women and children, for the men are too imbecile and too abject to fight. The general government folded its arms and said, "What can we do? We can not chastise the citizens of a state. Are we not feeding and clothing the savages, and teaching them to be moral, and is not that as much as the civilized world can ask of us?"

At King's river, where there was a public farm maintained at considerable expense, the Indians were collected in a body of two or three hundred, and the white settlers, who complained that government would not do any thing for them, drove them over to the agency at the Fresno. After an expenditure of some thirty thousand dollars a year for six years, that farm had scarcely produced six blades of grass, and was entirely unable to support over a few dozen Indians who had always lived there, and who generally foraged for their own subsistence. The new-comers, therefore, stood a poor chance till the agent purchased from the white settlers, on public account, the acorns which they (the Indians) had gathered and laid up for winter use at King's river.

Notwithstanding the acorns they were very soon starved out at the Fresno, and wandered away to find a subsistence wherever they could. Many of them perished of hunger on the plains of the San Joaquin. The rest are presumed to be in the mountains gathering berries.

At the Mattole station, near Cape Mendocino, a number of Indians were murdered on the public farm within a few hundred yards of the head-quarters. The settlers in the valley alleged that government would not support them, or take any care of them; and as settlers were not paid for doing it, they must kill them to get rid of them.

At Humboldt bay, and in the vicinity, a series of Indian massacres by white men continued for over two years. The citizens held public meetings, and protested against the action of the general government in leaving these Indians to prowl upon them for a support. It was alleged that the reservations cost two hundred and fifty thousand dollars a year, and yet nothing was done to relieve the people of this burden. Petitions were finally sent to the state authorities, asking for the removal of the Indians from that vicinity; and the state sent out its militia, killed a good many, and captured a good many others, who were finally carried down to the Mendocino reservation. They liked that place so well that they left it very soon, and went back to their old places of resort, preferring a chance of life to the certainty of starvation. During the winter of last year a number of them were gathered at Humboldt. The whites thought it was a favorable opportunity to get rid of them altogether. So they went in a body to the Indian camp, during the night when the poor wretches were asleep, shot all the men, women, and children they could at the first onslaught, and cut the throats of the remainder. Very few escaped. Next morning sixty bodies lay weltering in their blood — the old and the young, male and female — with every wound gaping a tale of horror to the civilized world. Children climbed upon their mothers' breasts, and sought nourishment from the fountains that death had drained: girls and boys lay here and there with their throats cut from ear to ear; men and women, clinging to each other in their terror, were found perforated with bullets or cut to pieces with knives — all were cruelly murdered! Let any who doubt this read the newspapers of San Francisco of that date. It will be found there in its most bloody and tragic details. Let them read of the Pitt river massacre, and of all the massacres that for the past three years have darkened the records of the state.

I will do the white people who were engaged in these massacres the justice to say that they were not so much to blame as the general government. They had at least given due warning of their intention. For years they had burdened the mails with complaints of the inefficiency of the agents; they had protested in the newspapers, in public meetings, in every conceivable way, and on every possible occasion, against the impolicy of permitting these Indians to roam about the settlements, picking up a subsistence in whatever way they could, when there was a fund of $250,000 a year appropriated by congress for their removal to and support on the reservations. What were these establishments for? Why did they not take charge of the Indians? Where were the agents? What was done with the money? It was repeatedly represented that unless something was done the Indians would soon all be killed. They could no longer make a subsistence in their old haunts. The progress of settlement had driven them from place to place till there was no longer a spot on earth they could call their own. Their next move could only be into the Pacific ocean. If ever an unfortunate people needed a few acres of ground to stand upon, and the poor privilege of making a living for themselves, it was these hapless Diggers. As often as they tried the reservations sad experience taught them that these were institutions for the benefit of white men, not Indians. It was wonderful how the employés had prospered on their salaries. They owned fine ranches in the vicinity; in fact, the reservations themselves were pretty much covered with the claims of persons in the service, who thought they would make nice farms for white men. The principal work done was to attend to sheep and cattle speculations, and make shepherds out of the few Indians that were left.

What did it signify that thirty thousand dollars a year had been expended at the Tejon? thirty thousand at the Fresno? fifty thousand at Nome Lackee? ten thousand at Nome Cult? forty-eight thousand at Mendocino? sixteen thousand at the Klamath? and some fifty or sixty thousand for miscellaneous purposes? that all this had resulted in the reduction of a hundred thousand Indians to about thirty thousand? Meritorious services had been rewarded, and a premium in favor of public integrity issued to an admiring world.

I am satisfied, from an acquaintance of eleven years with the Indians of California, that had the least care been taken of them these disgraceful massacres would never have occurred. A more inoffensive and harmless race of beings does not exist on the face of the earth. But wherever they attempted to procure a subsistence they were hunted down; driven from the reservations by the instinct of self-preservation; shot down by the settlers upon the most frivolous pretexts; and abandoned to their fate by the only power that could have afforded them protection.

This was the result, in plain terms, of the inefficient and discreditable manner in which public affairs were administered by the federal authorities in Washington. It was the natural consequence of a corrupt political system, which, for the credit of humanity, it is to be hoped will be abandoned in future so far as the Indians are concerned. They have no voice in public affairs. So long as they are permitted to exist, party discipline is a matter of very little moment to them. All they ask is the privilege of breathing the air that God gave to us all, and living in peace wherever it may be convenient to remove them. Their history in California is a melancholy record of neglect and cruelty; and the part taken by public men high in position in wresting from them the very means of subsistence, is one of which any other than professional politicians would be ashamed. For the executive department there is no excuse. There lay the power and the remedy; but a paltry and servile spirit, an abject submission to every shifting influence, an utter absence of that high moral tone which is the characteristic trait of genuine statesmen and patriots, have been the distinguishing features of this branch of our government for some time past. Disgusted with their own handiwork; involved in debt throughout the state, after wasting all the money appropriated by congress; the accounts in an inextricable state of confusion; the creditors of the government clamoring to be paid; the "honest yeomanry" turning against the party in power; political affairs entangled beyond remedy; it was admitted to be a very bad business — not at all such as to meet the approval of the administration. The appropriation was cut down to fifty thousand dollars. That would do damage enough. Two hundred and fifty thousand a year, for six or seven years, had inflicted sufficient injury upon the poor Indians. Now it was time to let them alone on fifty thousand, or turn them over to the state. So the end of it is, that the reservations are practically abandoned — the remainder of the Indians are being exterminated every day, and the Spanish mission system has signally failed.

THE DOG SACRIFICE OF THE SENECAS.[1]

BY SAMUEL CROWELL.

On the second day of February, 1830, I witnessed an interesting, and to me, a novel religious ceremony of the Seneca tribe of Indians, then occupying that portion of territory now comprising a part of the counties of Seneca, and Sandusky, Ohio, familiarly known to the inhabitants of this region, as the Seneca reservation.

The fact that this nation had recently ceded their reservation to the United States, and were now about to commemorate, for the last time in this country, their annual festival, previous to their emigration to the Rocky mountains, contributed not a little, to add to it an unusual degree of interest.

To those acquainted with the characteristic traits of the red men, it is unnecessary to remark, that there is a reservedness attached to them — peculiarly their own; but, especially when about to celebrate this festival, they seem, so far at least as the pale-faces are concerned, to shroud their designs in impenetrable secrecy. And the festival of which I now speak, might have been, as many others of a similar character were, observed by themselves with due solemnity, and without the knowledge or interference of their white neighbors, but that the general poverty and reckless improvidence of the Senecas were proverbial. And those were the causes which awakened the suspicions of the inquisitive white man.

In order, therefore, that the approaching festival should not lack in any thing necessary to make it imposing, and impress a permanent recollection of it, on the mind of their rising race — no effort was spared, and no fatigue regarded, that would tend to promote this object. Thus for some time previous to the period of which I am now speaking, by the unerring aim of the Seneca rifle, the antlers, with the body of many a tall and stately

[1] Reprinted from the Cincinnati (O.) *Miscellany* for February, 1845.

buck, fell prostrate; and in crowds the Indian now came into Lower Sandusky with their venison, and their skins; and the squaws, with their painted baskets and beaded moccasins, not as heretofore, to barter for necessaries, but chiefly for ornaments!

To the penetrating mind of the merchant, they thus betrayed their object; to wit: that they were preparing to, in the vulgar parlance of the day, "burn their dogs."

Inquiry was now on the alert to ascertain the precise period; and to the often repeated interrogatory put by the boys of our village, "Indian, when will you burn your dogs?" — an evasive reply would be given; sometimes saying, "may be" (a very common expression with them), "two days," — "may be, three days," — "may be, one week." Their object being to baffle the inquirer; so that the further off the intended period was, they would give the shortest time — and *vice versa*.

The principal head-men, or chiefs of the Senecas, were Good Hunter, Hard Hickory, and Tall Chief; there were also some sub or half chiefs; among those of the latter rank, Benjamin F. Warner, a white or half-breed, had considerable influence. In this, as in other nations, civilized as well as savage, though there may be several men of apparent equal rank, yet there usually is one, who either by artificial, or universally acknowledged talent, directs in a great measure, the destinies of the nation; and such among the Senecas, was Hard Hickory.

To a mind of no ordinary grade, he added, from his intercourse with the whites, a polish of manner, seldom seen in an Indian. The French language he spoke fluently, and the English, intelligibly. Scrupulously adhering to the costume of his people, and retaining many of their habits, this chief was much endeared to them; while on the other hand, his urbanity, and for an Indian, he possessed, as already observed, a large share of the *suaviter in modo* — his intelligence, his ardent attachment to the whites — and above all, his strict integrity in business transactions, obtained for him, and deservedly, the respect and confidence of all with whom he traded. Such was the trust the merchants of Lower Sandusky reposed in this chief, that when an indigent Indian came to ask for goods on credit, if **Hard**

Hickory would say he would see the sum paid, no more was required. Thus his word passed current with, and current for, the whole nation. And as in the mind of man there is something intuitive, better known than defined, by which instinctively, as it were, we find in the bosom of another a response to our own feelings; so in the present case, this noble Indian soon discovered in the late Obed Dickinson, a merchant of Lower Sandusky, a generous, confiding and elevated mind, whose honorable vibrations beat in unison with his own.

To Mr. Dickinson, therefore, he made known the time when they would celebrate their festival, and cordially invited him to attend as a guest, and if so disposed, he might bring a friend with him. Correctly supposing that I never had an opportunity of witnessing this religious rite, Mr. D. kindly requested me to accompany him to their council-house, on Green creek, in that part of Sandusky county included in the present township of Green Creek. On giving me the invitation, Mr. D. remarked, that by taking a present in our hand, we would, probably, be made the more welcome. In accordance, therefore, with this suggestion, we took with us a quantity of loaf sugar and tobacco.

It was sometime in the afternoon of Feb. 1st when we arrived, and immediately thereafter, we were ushered into the council house with demonstrations of public joy and marked respect. As soon as seated, we gave our presents to Hard Hickory, who, rising, held one of them up, and pointing to Mr. Dickinson addressed the Indians in an audible voice, in their own tongue; then holding up the other, he pointed to me, repeating to them what he had before said — this done, he turned to us, and said: "You stay here long as you want, nobody hurt you." Confiding in the assurances of this chief, I hung up my valise, in which were some important papers, for I was then on my way further east, attending to my official duties as sheriff of Sandusky county, and felt perfectly at home.

To the inhabitants of this section of Ohio, a minute description of the council house would be deemed unnecessary. Suffice it to say, that its dimensions were, perhaps, sixty by twenty-five feet; a place in the centre for the fire, and corresponding therewith, an aperture was left in the roof for the smoke to ascend. Contiguous to the fire place were two upright posts, four or five feet apart; between these posts, a board, twelve or fifteen inches broad, was firmly fastened; and over this board the skin of a deer was stretched very tight. On a seat near this board, sat a blind Indian with a gourd in his hand, in which were beans or corn — with this he beat time for the dancers. Such was the musician, and such the music.

The dancing had commenced previous to our arrival; and was continued with little intermission for several successive days and nights. An effort by me to describe their manner of dancing would be fruitless. I have witnessed dancing assemblies in the populous cities of the East, among the refined classes of society — but having seen nothing like this, I must, therefore, pronounce it *sui generis*. I was strongly solicited by some of the chiefs to unite with them in the dance: I, however, declined the intended honor — but gave to one of them my cane, as a *proxy*, with which he seemed much delighted. Several of their white neighbors, both male and female, entered the ring.

There was on this occasion a splendid display of ornament. Those who have seen the members of a certain society, in their most prosperous days, march in procession, in honor of their patron saint, decorated with the badges and insignia of their order, may have some conception of the dress and ornamental decorations of those head-men, while engaged in the dance. I will select *Unum e Pluribus*, their *Doctor*, as he was called, who wore very long hair, and from the nape of his neck, to the termination of his cue, there was a continuous line of *pieces of silver* — the upper one being larger than a dollar, and the lower one less than a half dime.

Some of the more inferior Indians were "stuck o'er with baubles, and hung round with strings." Many of them wore small bells tied round their ancles; and those who could not afford bells, had deer hoofs in place thereof; these made a jingling sound as they put down their feet in the dance. The *squaws* also exhibited themselves to the best advantage. Several of them were splendidly attired and decorated. Their dresses were chiefly of silk, of various colors, and some of them were of good old fashioned queen's gray. These dresses were not cut, as our fair belles would say, *a la mode* — but they were cut and made after their own fashion: that is; not so long as to conceal the scarlet hose covering of their ancles, their small feet, or their moccasins, which were so ingeniously beaded, and manufactured by their own *olive* hands. Nor must I omit saying, that the sobriety and correct demeanor of the Indians, and the modest deportment of the squaws, merited the highest commendation.

At the commencement of each dance, or, to borrow our own phraseology, each set dance, a chief first arose, and began to sing the words, " *Ya-ico-hah!*" with a slow, sonorous, and strong syllabic emphasis, keeping time with his feet, and advancing round the house; directly, another arose, and then in regular succession, one after the other, rising, and singing the same word, and falling in the rear, until all the men had joined in the dance; next the squaws at a respectable distance in the rear, in the same manner, by seniority, arose, and united in the dance and the song. Now the step was quicker and the pronunciation more rapid, all singing and all dancing, while *Jim*, the blind musician, struck harder and faster with his gourd, on the undressed deer-skin; thus they continued the same dance for more than one hour, without cessation!

The Indian boys, who did not participate in the dance, amused themselves the meanwhile discharging heavy loaded muskets through the aperture in the roof the reverberations of which were almost deafening. Taken altogether, to the eye and ear of the stranger, it seemed like *frantic* festivity. Tall Chief, who was confined to his bed by indisposition, felt it so much his duty to join in the dance with his people, that he actually left his bed, notwithstanding it was mid winter, came to the council house, and took part in the dance as long as he was able to stand.

About the "noon of night," Hard Hickory invited Mr. D. and myself to accept a bed at his residence; to this proposition we readily assented. Here we were not only hospitably provided for, but entertained in a style which I little anticipated. Even among many of our white inhabitants, at this early day, a *curtained* bed was a luxury not often enjoyed — such was the bed we occupied.

Shortly after our arrival at the house of this chief, Mr. D. retired; not so with our friendly host and myself — while sitting near a clean, brick hearth, before a cheerful fire, Hard Hickory unbosomed himself to me unreservedly. Mr. D. was asleep and the chief and I were the only persons then awake in the house.

Hard Hickory told me, among other things, that it was owing chiefly to him, that this feast was now celebrated; that it was in part to appease the anger of the *Good Spirit*, in consequence of a dream he lately had; and as an explanation he gave me the following narration :

"He dreamed he was fleeing from an enemy, it was, he supposed, something supernatural; perhaps, an evil spirit; that, after it had pursued him a long time, and for a great distance, and every effort to escape from it seemed impossible as it was just at his heels, and he almost exhausted; at this perilous juncture, he saw a large water, towards which he made with all his remaining strength, and at the very instant when he expected each bound to be his last, he beheld, to his joy, a canoe near the shore; this appeared as his last hope; breathless and faint, he threw himself into it, and, of its own accord, quick as an arrow from the bow, it shot from the shore leaving his pursuer on the beach !"

While relating this circumstance to me, which he did with earnestness, trepidation and alarm, strongly expressed in his countenance, he took from his bosom something neatly and very carefully enclosed in several distinct folds of buckskin. This he began to unroll, laying each piece by itself, and on opening the last, there was enclosed therein, a canoe in miniature! On handing it to me to look at, he remarked, that no other person save himself and me, had ever seen it, and that, as a memento, he would wear it, as "long as he lived." It was a piece of light wood, resembling cork, about six inches long, and, as intended, so it was, a perfect model of a canoe.

This chief, being now in a communicative mood, I took the liberty to inquire of him "when they intended to burn their dogs?" for I began to fear I should miss the express object which I came to witness. After giving me to understand that "the red men did not care about the pale faces being present at, nor, if they chose, joining in the dance, but burning their dogs was another thing — this was offering sacrifice to, and worshiping the Great Spirit; and while engaged in their devotions they objected to the presence and interference of the whites; yet, as I had never been present, and coming as the friend of Mr. Dickinson, who was a good man, he would tell me they would burn their dogs soon to-morrow morning." The night being now far advanced, he pointed to the bed and told me to sleep there; but that he must go to the council house, to the dance, for his people would not like it, if he would stay away, and wishing me good night, he withdrew.

Anxiety to witness the burnt offering almost deprived me of sleep. Mr. D. and I, therefore, rose early and proceeded directly to the council house, and though we supposed we were early, the Indians were already in advance of us. The first object which arrested our attention, was a pair of the canine species, one of each gender suspended on a *cross!* one on either side thereof. These animals had been recently *strangled — not a bone was broken* nor could a distorted hair be seen? They were of a beautiful cream color, except a few dark spots on one, naturally, while the same spots had been put on the other, artificially, by the devotees. The Indians are very partial in the selection of dogs entirely white, for this occasion; and for which they will give almost any price.

Now for part of the decorations to which I have already alluded, and a description of one will suffice for both, for they were *par similes.* A scarlet ribbon was tastefully tied just above the nose; and near the eyes another; next round the neck was a white ribbon, to which was attached something bulbous, concealed in another white ribbon; this was placed directly under the right ear, and I suppose it was intended as an amulet or charm. Then ribbons were bound round the forelegs, at the knees, and near the feet — these were red and white alternately. Round the body was a profuse decoration — then the hind legs were decorated as the fore ones. Thus were the victims prepared and thus ornamented for the burnt offering.

While minutely making this examination, I was almost unconscious of the collection of a large number of the Indians who were there assembled to offer their sacrifices.

Adjacent to the cross, was a large fire built on a few logs; and though the snow was several inches deep, they had prepared a sufficient quantity of combustible material, removed the snow from the logs, and placed thereon their fire. I have often regretted that I did not see them light this pile. My own opinion is, they did not use the fire from their council house; because I think they would have considered that as common, and as this was intended to be a holy service, they, no doubt, for this purpose struck fire from a flint, this being deemed sacred.

It was a clear, beautiful morning, and just as the first rays of the sun were seen in the tops of the towering forest, and its reflections from the snowy surface, the Indians simultaneously formed a semicircle enclosing the cross, each flank resting on the aforesaid pile of logs. Good Hunter who officiated as high priest, now appeared, and approached the cross; arrayed in his pontifical robes, he looked quite respectable. The Indians being all assembled — I say Indians (for there was not a squaw present during all this ceremony — I saw two or three pass outside of the semi-circle, but they moved as if desirous of being unobserved), at a private signal given by Good Hunter, two young chiefs sprang up the cross, and each taking off one of the victims, brought it down, and presented it on his arms to Good Hunter, who, receiving it with great reverence, in like manner advanced to the fire, and with a very grave and solemn air, laid it thereon — and this he did with the other — but to which, whether male or female, he gave the preference, I did not learn. This done, he retired to the cross.

In a devout manner, he now commenced an oration. The tone of his voice was audible and somewhat chanting. At every pause in his discourse, he took from a white cloth he held in his left hand, a portion of dried, odoriferous herbs, which he threw on the fire; this was intended as incense. In the meanwhile his auditory, their eyes on the ground, with grave aspect, and in solemn silence, stood motionless, listening attentively, to every word he uttered. Thus he proceeded until the victims were entirely consumed, and the incense exhausted, when he concluded his service; their oblation now made, and the wrath of the Great Spirit, as they believed, appeased, they again assembled in the council house, for the purpose of performing a part in their festival, different from any I yet had witnessed. Each Indian as he entered, seated himself on the floor, thus forming a large circle; when one of the old chiefs rose, and with that native dignity which some Indians possess in a great degree, recounted his exploits as a warrior; told in how many fights he had been the victor; the number of scalps he had taken from his enemies; and what, at the head of his braves, he yet intended to do at the Rocky mountains; accompanying his narration with energy, warmth, and strong gesticulations; when he ended, he received the unanimous applause of the assembled tribe.

This meed of praise was awarded to the chief by three times three articulations, which were properly neither nasal, oral, nor gutural, but rather abdominal. Indeed I am as unable to describe this kind of utterance, as I am, the step in the dance. I have seen some whites attempt to imitate the step, and heard them affect the groan or grunt, but it was a mere aping thereof. Thus many others in the circle, old and young, rose in order, and *proforma*, delivered themselves of a speech. Among those was Good Hunter; but he

"Had laid his robes away,
His mitre and his vest."

His remarks were not filled with such bombast as some others; but brief, modest, and appropriate; in fine, they were such as became a priest of one of the lost ten tribes of Israel!

After all had spoken who wished to speak, the floor was cleared, and the dance renewed, in which Indian and squaw united, with their wonted hilarity and zeal.

Just as this dance ended, an Indian boy ran to me, and with fear strongly depicted in his countenance, caught me by the arm, and drew me to the door, pointing with his other hand towards something he wished me to observe. I looked in that direction, and saw the appearance of an Indian running at full speed to the council house; in an instant he was in the house, and literally in the fire, which he took in his hands, and threw coals of fire and hot ashes in various directions, through the house, and apparently all over himself! At his entrance, the young Indians, much alarmed, had all fled to the further end of the house, where they remained crowded, in great dread of this personification of the evil spirit! After diverting himself with the fire a few moments, at the expense of the young ones, to their no small joy he disappeared. This was an Indian disguised with an hideous false face, having horns on his head, and his hands and feet protected from the effects of the fire. And though not a professed fire king, he certainly performed his part to admiration.

During the continuance of this festival, the hospitality of the Senecas was unbounded. In the council house, and at the residence of Tall Chief, were a number of large fat bucks, and fat hogs hanging up, and neatly dressed. Bread also, of both corn and wheat in great abundance. Large kettles of soup ready prepared, in which maple sugar, profusely added, made a prominent ingredient, thus forming a very agreeable saccharine coalescence, and what contributed still more to heighten the zest — it was all *impune* (scot free). All were invited, and all were made welcome; indeed a refusal to partake of their bounty, was deemed disrespectful, if not unfriendly.

In the afternoon I left them enjoying themselves to the fullest extent: and so far as I could perceive, their pleasure was without alloy. They were eating and drinking (on this occasion, no ardent spirits were permitted), dancing and rejoicing — caring not, and, probably, thinking not of to-morrow.

*THE SPANISH MISSION COLONY ON THE RAPPA-
HANNOCK; THE FIRST EUROPEAN SETTLEMENT
IN VIRGINIA.*[1]

[Read before the New York Historical Society, October 1, 1872.]

BY JOHN GILMARY SHEA.

There is an episode in Virginia history, that will, I think, be new to many of my hearers — a most strange, romantic and tragic prelude to its annals, as we generally find them written: the history of the first house reared by white men on the soil of the Old Dominion.

This was the attempt of Spain to plant a missionary colony near the shores of the Chesapeake, which her navigators named St. Mary's bay, and visited years before Sir Walter Raleigh projected his settlement at Roanoke island.

When or from whom St. Mary's bay got its name, our most zealous antiquarians have failed to discover. The name is not on the curious copper globe made by Ulpius in 1540, which once belonged to Pope Marcellus II, and now adorns our library, but it is mentioned by Oviedo even earlier, and is found on Cabot's map of 1544.

Spanish vessels came and went. Cape St. Mary and Cape St. John lured them into the broad expanse, studded with so many islands charming to the sight, whether crowned with groves of stately trees or verdant with wild vines and bushes, that they called it the archipelago. While from the mountains seen afar came down a series of noble rivers, watering a land of forests so dense that grass was a rarity.

Doubtless to their eyes, as to those of the English who soon after visited the bay, it seemed "a country that might have the prerogative over the most pleasant places known. Heaven and earth it seemed never agreed better to frame a place for man's habitation."

---

[1] Reprinted from the original manuscript.

One day a Spanish vessel standing out to sea through the capes, bore on its deck a tall, well formed brave, the brother of a native chieftain, whom some Dominican fathers had persuaded to accompany them to Mexico.

The viceroy of that rich province, Don Luis de Velasco, just, upright and disinterested, who so lived that men could boast, that with all his opportunities for acquiring wealth, he died as he had lived poor and in debt — took kindly notice of the Virginian. He had him instructed in the truths of Christianity, and when with all the pomp of his time he was solemnly baptized in the Cathedral of Mexico, the viceroy became his sponsor and the chieftain from the shores of the Chesapeake was thenceforth known by the name of his patron, Don Luis de Velasco.

The time came for something more than mere flying visits to the bay. Don Pedro Melendez had scarcely accomplished his bloody task of stamping out French colonization in Florida, before he began his preparations for occupying St. Mary's bay. Through it he hoped to reach China. This in our present state of knowledge seems absurd and ridiculous, and we always laugh at Captain John Smith's voyage up the Chickahominy to seek a route to Cathay. But Hudson was seeking it in our harbor, as Gomez had already sought it, and to this day Lachine in Canada, which is simply French for China, records the attempt of the adventurous La Salle to reach the middle kingdom.

By the letters of the brave but cruel old seaman Melendez, we can see him in his moments of leisure during the winter of 1665, poring over the best maps of his time, some of which, like the copper globe in the library below, show the Pacific running far into our northern continent so as nearly to reach the Atlantic coast about Carolina. By him sits the calm, stoical Luis de Velasco, now a man of fifty, and also a missionary who has just come from China by the usual overland route of that time across Mexico, for Panama with its deadly fevers seems to have been avoided. Father Urdaneta is full of stories of the Pacific and points out where the charts should lay down the straits of Anian that separated America from Asia. Don Luis gave his descriptions of his native land which Melendez combined with the data on the maps, and the ideas of his Chinese missionary.

His letters from St. Augustine and Havana at this time show the result which he attained on these investigations. The rivers flowing into St. Mary's bay were to be ascended 80 leagues, then the mountain range was to be crossed. There two arms of the sea were found, one by which canoes go to Newfoundland, bearing their rich cargoes of furs to the French traders, the other leading to China.

With our knowledge of the country and of the history of northern exploration, we can readily comprehend what Melendez so evidently misunderstood.

The Salt river or narrow part of the bay receiving the waters of the Susquehanna, led up into the country of the Five Nations and by the Oswego to the lands of tribes who had already begun to carry down flotilla loads of furs to Brest, a French trading post of the time on the Labrador side at the mouth of the St. Lawrence, frequented in Cartier's time and later, but long since forsaken and forgotten. Of this fur trade Melendez, a native of northern Spain, had doubtless heard from the Basques who visited the great bank of Newfoundland. That even then an Indian trail well known in the land led from Upper Canada to the Chesapeake we can see by the fact that only forty years later than the period we treat of, the adventurous Champlain after founding Quebec pushed boldly on to the shores of Lake Huron — the Freshwater sea — and thence dispatched one of his fearless Frenchmen, Stephen Brulé, with a few Hurons, to the Carantouanais, a tribe on the Susquehanna, who were kindred and allies of the Hurons. And Brulé, not without danger indeed, succeeded in reaching them, and returned to report to Champlain. As intercourse was thus kept up between Lake Huron and the lower Susquehanna it is not surprising that the fur trade, which came down from the lakes to the French, was known in Virginia in the days of Melendez.

The Potomac, apparently the Espiritu Santo of the Spaniards, if ascended to the mountains led to the Monongahela and so to the Mississippi, bringing them to the land of gold and of civilized men.

Misled, however, by his idea as to the arms of the sea, Melendez in 1566 dispatched a vessel, bearing thirty soldiers and two Dominican fathers, to begin a station in Axacan, near the Chesapeake, escorted and guided by Don Luis de Velasco; but these missionaries, corrupted by an easy life in Peru, had no taste for a laborious mission, or perhaps learned the real state of facts. At all events the whole party took alarm and forced the captain to sail off for Spain.

Four years later Melendez himself trod the soil of the Spanish peninsula, full of his projects and bent on carrying them out. Jesuit missions had now sprung up in Florida, and though one of the fathers had already dyed the earth with his heart's blood, others pressed on. These were to Melendez's mind, the men to plant the standard of Christianity and the banner of Spain on the shores of the Chesapeake. So the adelantado arranged his plan with that saintly scion of unsaintly race, Francis Borgia. Don Luis de Velasco was still in Spain, a grave, intelligent man, thoroughly conversant with Spanish affairs, to all appearance a sincere and correct Christian and friend of the Spaniards. With every mark of joy he offered to return to Axacan, and do all in his power to further the labors of any missionaries sent over to instruct his brother's tribe. Ere long he was again on the Atlantic, a staunch Spanish ship bearing him from San Lucar with the Jesuit father Quiros and some associates. In November, 1570, this vessel anchored before the Spanish fort Santa Elena, on what still bears the name Saint Helena sound, South Carolina.

There Father Segura, the vice provincial or superior of the Jesuits, arranged the plan of the projected mission. So great a field, it was believed, lay open to the labors of his order, that he resolved to go in person, with Father Quiros, accompanied by five young members of the society, and four Indian boys as catechists and aids for temporal service. With the influence and support of Don Luis, they would require no Spanish guards, and as soldiers were sometimes a detriment to a mission, it was determined by the missionaries to trust themselves entirely alone in the hands of the Indians.

Don Luis made every promise as to the security of the persons of the missionaries confided to his honor. "They shall lack nothing," he declared, "I will be ever at hand to aid them."

On the fifth of August, 1570, this little mission colony sailed from Saint Helena sound, and must have crept very slowly along the coast and up the Chesapeake, for it was not till the tenth of September that they reached Axacan, the country of Don Luis and the scene of their intended mission and settlement.

Where precisely Axacan was no map or document has yet been found to show. We are therefore left to conjecture. It was evidently either on the Susquehanna or the Potomac, the two great rivers at the head of the bay mentioned in Spanish accounts and by which the object of their exploration, as conceived by Melendez, was to be attained.

That it could not have been on the Susquehanna is evident from the fact that that river was held by tribes of Huron race living in palisaded towns, while the tribe of Don Luis were according to all accounts manifestly a division of the nomadic Algonquins.

Axacan was then in all probability on the Potomac, the Espiritu Santo of the Spanish navigators. The vessel that bore the missionaries and two other vessels, subsequently ascended this river for a considerable distance to a point where they landed and proceeded over land six miles to another river leading to the country of Don Luis, and by which they might have sailed up directly to it, but had apparently passed as a less navigable stream. On the Potomac there is to this day a spot called Occoquan, which is near enough to the Spanish Axacan to raise a suspicion of their identity, and not far below, the Potomac and Rappahannock approach so closely as to lead us to suppose that the hamlets of Don Luis were on the Rappahannock.

The land which met the eyes of the Spanish missionaries was not one to raise fond hopes or sustain delusions. Of all that the descriptions of Don Luis had prepared them to find, there was absolutely nothing. Just come from the vicinity of Florida with its rich luxuriant vegetation, with fruits of spontaneous growth, and maize abundant, they beheld a land scourged by a six years' sterility, with the starving remnants of decimated and thrice decimated tribes. These wretched beings looked upon Don Luis as if sent back by heaven, and seeing him whom they had so long mourned as dead, treated with honor, they received the Spaniards with every demonstration of good will, though so destitute, that they could offer no fruit or maize.

With the winter fast approaching, it seemed almost madness for Father Segura and his companions to attempt to establish themselves in this unpromising land, but the previous failure of the Dominican fathers, and the deep interest taken by Melendez in the success of the attempt, doubtless decided the point in the mind of the missionaries.

The pilot of the vessel which brought them being short of provisions gave them little time for reflection. He reached there on the 10th of September, and hastily landing the missionaries and all that belonged to them, he was ready to sail on the following day. Segura had barely time to write to the king and to add a few lines to the letters which Quiros wrote to Melendez urging speedy relief.

Among the interesting documents discovered and copied by our late associate Buckingham Smith during his life-long investigations in Spain were these autograph letters written from Axacan to Melendez by Fathers Segura and Quiros, and sent back by the vessel which had brought them from St. Helena sound; and he traced a facsimile of the signatures of these daring heralds of the cross, the first to offer up any Christian worship on the soil of Virginia.

In this letter Father Quiros writes: "It is certain that these Indians of Don Luis, have shown their good will in such manner as they could. Don Luis seemed to them to have risen from the dead and come to them from heaven, and as most of all those who have remained here are his relatives, they have been consoled much in his company and have taken courage and hope that God will favor them. They say that they wish to be like Don Luis and ask us to remain in this land with them. The cacique, Don Luis's brother, had a child three years old very sick, some seven or eight leagues from here, and as it seemed to him on the point of death, he prayed us to go and baptize it. The vice provincial accordingly decided to send one of us by night to baptize it, as it was very near death.

"In view then of the good will manifested by these people, although on the other hand as already stated, they are so famine stricken and all expected to die of hunger and cold this winter, as many have done in previous winters, for the deep snows that fall on this land prevent their seeking the roots on which they are accustomed to live — in view however of the great hope we entertain of the conversion of this people, and the service of our Lord, and of his majesty and of reaching the mountain range and China, etc., it seemed proper to the father that we should venture to remain here, although with so little ship's stores and provisions, because we ate on the way two of the four barrels of biscuit and the little flour they gave us for the voyage."

After announcing this heroic decision, in which we cannot fail to admire their zeal and courage, if we doubt their prudence, they asked speedy relief. "It is very necessary that you should endeavor if possible to supply us with all dispatch, and if it is impossible to do so in winter, at least it is necessary that in March or at the furthest early in April, a good supply be sent, so as to furnish all these people with seed corn." He concludes, "From the great want of provisions felt by all in the ship, it has been necessary that arriving here as we did yesterday, they go off to-day leaving us here in this depopulated land, with the discomforts already described, and hence there has been no opportunity for further information or greater detail."

It was arranged by them that about the time the ship should return, Indians would be on the lookout at the mouth of the river on which Don Luis's tribe lived, the Rappahanock as I infer; where they would build signal fires to attract attention, and deliver to a boat sent from the ship a letter from the missionaries.

The little band beheld the vessel hoist her sail and glide down the Potomac. They doubtless lingered, watching what seemed the last tie between them and civilized man, then guided by Don Luis, they started on the six miles' portage to the Rappahannock, the Indians bearing some of their scanty, but precious supplies, the missionaries themselves carrying their chapel service, books and other necessaries. On reaching the river they were to ascend it about six miles in the wretched canoes of the natives, for in their misery they had scarcely a single one fit for any use.

The Indians of Virginia did not dwell in palisaded towns, like those on the Susquehanna, and their kindred the Hurons and the Iroquois. They seem to have lived only in scattered bands, each forming a little hamlet of from five to twenty cabins, each lodge in the midst of a rude garden, for they cultivated very little ground, depending almost entirely on the spontaneous productions of their forests and swamps.

The accounts of the subsequent proceedings of this strange colony are derived from a boy, and are somewhat obscure, for unfortunately we have not the formal examination, which must have been forwarded to Spain.

These statements seem to make the journey to the hamlets of Don Luis's tribe, a long and weary one through wood and desert and morass, loaded with their baggage, living on roots, and not the short journey that Father Quiros anticipated.

The hamlet first reached was a wretched one of naked and starving savages. Here amid the tent-like lodges of the Indians, made of poles bound together at the top and covered with mats or bark, Segura and his companions erected a rude house, a log cabin doubtless, the first white habitation in that part of America. One end was devoted to their chapel, the other was their dwelling.

Here, doubtless to the wonder of the natives, the service of the Roman church was solemnly performed.

Of the party Segura was the soul. He was a native of Toledo, who had become a Jesuit in 1566, and led by his zeal to seek a foreign mission, he had renounced the comforts of Europe and the positions of dignity offered him there, to come in 1568 to Florida. He had thus acquired two years' experience of the Indian character and manners and doubtless some insight into the languages spoken at Calos and Santa Elena. In his new mission we can see him attempting, under the guidance of Don Luis, to acquire the language of the Algonquin flock among whom he was now to labor.

As the missionaries had foreseen that they must winter there and might not receive supplies before March or April Segura doubtless began like his Indian neighbors to lay up a winter store from the woods and meadows around the clearing where his chapel stood. Acorns, walnuts, chestnuts and chinquapins were regularly gathered by the natives as well as persimmons and a root like a potato growing in the moist lands.

In those narrow tongues of land between the Virginian rivers larger game must have been very scarce, the hunting ground being off by the mountains. But the mission party had no means of hunting and though the rivers teemed with fish, we find no indication of their being supplied with any means of deriving food from that source.

For a time Don Luis remained with them, but as so generally happens in all attempts to elevate the redmen, old habits returned, he became Indian with the Indians rather than Spanish with the Spaniards. Ere long he abandoned the missionaries entirely and went off to another place, distant from it a journey of a day and a half.

The missionaries were not yet sufficiently versed in the language of the natives to dispense with his aid as teacher and interpreter, and his influence was constantly needed. Hence they felt his desertion keenly. Several times they sent one of the young men to urge his return, but he refused and the winter wore away with great suffering and hardship, not unmingled with gloomy forebodings.

As February approached and there seemed only a short interval left before the return of the vessel from Santa Elena which was their only hope of escape from the difficulties which surrounded them, Segura resolved to make a last effort to move Don Luis. He sent Father Quiros with two brothers, De Solis and Mendez, to the hamlet where he resided, to make a last appeal. He made many excuses for his absence and continued to beguile them by promises of which they saw too clearly the insincerity. They departed heavy hearted, but they had scarcely passed beyond the last cabin of the hamlet when a shower of arrows came whirring upon them. Quiros and his companions fell pierced in countless places by the flinty arrow heads. Their quivering bodies were at once stripped and subjected to all the indignities and mutilations that savage fancy dictated.

Father Segura and the remainder of his party had spent the interval in prayer. Anxiety deepened as no sign of Father Quiros appeared. On the fourth day, yells and cries announced the approach of a large party, and in a few moments Don Luis appeared arrayed in the cassock of Father Quiros, attended by his brother and a war party armed with clubs and bows, and dressed in all the finery of war.

The closing scene had come. Don Luis sternly demanded from those whom he had promised to protect and aid, all that could serve for a defence, their knives, the axes used for chopping wood. But Segura and his companions had no thought of resistance. They surrendered these things without a word of remonstrance. Then they knelt down before their rude altar to await the death they had expected. Don Luis gave the signal. His braves rushed upon the mission party and slaughtered all but one, a boy named Alphonsus who was protected by a brother of Don Luis and escaped.

The account states that Don Luis buried beneath their chapel house the bodies of his victims, Father John Baptist Segura, Brothers Gabriel Gomez, Peter de Linares, Sancho Levallos and Christopher Redondo, with their Indian attendants.

The authorities at the Spanish post, Santa Elena, seem to have shown great indifference as to the fate of this mission band. Under the pretext that no pilot could be found to run along the coast from South Carolina to the Chesapeake, they let the whole autumn and winter pass. In the spring Brother Vincent Gonzales succeeded in obtaining a vessel and sailed with some Spaniards to the relief of his associates. They ran up the Potomac and anchored at the spot where Segura had landed. At a distance they beheld men in the garb of the missionaries, but the Indians failed to lure them ashore by the device. Some of the natives even came out saying: "See the fathers who came to us: we have treated them well. Land and see them and we will treat you likewise." On the contrary suspecting treachery from the fact that the pretended fathers did not approach as the real ones would have done, the Spaniards seized two of the Indians and sailed back.

Melendez returning from Spain heard their report and at once sailed to the Chesapeake, to chastise the murderers. Taking a stout though light craft, he soon ran up the Potomac to the spot already twice visited. There a Spanish force fully armed and headed by this determined man, landed. Melendez unfurled the standard of Spain on Virginian soil, and marching inland soon captured several Indians. They confessed the murder of the mission party, laying all the blame on Don Luis.

Melendez announced that he would not harm the innocent, but ordered them to deliver up Don Luis. That Indian and his brother, the chief of Axacan, fled to the mountains. The brother, who had saved the life of little Alphonsus, brought him to Melendez, who received him with great pleasure. This boy gave an account of all that happened since they landed, and I need hardly say that it is the basis of all the accounts we have. He pointed out those concerned in the massacre and Melendez hung eight of them at his yard arm.

After this summary piece of justice, the founder of Saint Augustine with his mail-clad force embarked, and the Spanish flag floated for the last time over the land of Axacan.

So ends the history of the first settlement of white men on the soil of Virginia. The walls of the Capitol at Washington, might well be adorned with a painting of a scene that occurred almost in sight of its dome — the founder of Saint Augustine, the butcher of Ribault, the chosen commander of the Invincible Armada, as he stood surrounded by his grim warriors, planting the standard of Spain on the banks of the Potomac.

Raphe Hamor, author of one of the earliest Virginia tracts, says that Powhatan's tribe were driven by the Spaniards from the West Indies, a loose expression, that will mean any part of Spanish America. Powhatan's confederacy were Algonquins and could scarcely have come from the south. If driven from their original abode by the Spaniards, they may be the very tribe to which Don Luis belonged and which fled from the Potomac and Rappahannock to the shores of the York and James. If so Don Luis de Velasco honorably received at Mexico and Madrid, was a kinsman of Pocahontas treated as a princess in England.

ALASKAN MUMMIES.[1]

By W. H. Dall.

For nearly a hundred years it has been known, through the quaint accounts of the early voyagers, that certain tribes of southern Alaska preserved the bodies of their dead. Up to a very recent period, however, no examples of this practice had reached any ethnological museum, or fallen under the observation of any scientific observer. When the territory was purchased, had it continued as accessible as during 1868, it might have reasonably been expected to attract many investigators in natural history and ethnology, whose chief difficulty would have been an *embarras de richesse*. But private interest and public indifference united to seal it up from inspection. Naturalists generally are less easily muzzled than poorly paid political appointees, and hence the obstacles thrown in the way of exploration have been so great that we can hardly wonder that so few have been able to enter this rich and interesting field.

During the last four or five years, the investigations of M. Alphonse Pinart, and of the writer, have spread among the residents of the territory some knowledge of the value attached to the ethnological material which surrounds them, and to this fact we owe the collection and preservation of much that is of interest. Among other things which have come to hand in this manner are the only specimens of Alaska mummies extant.

The practice of preserving the bodies of the dead was in vogue among the inhabitants of the Aleutian islands and the Kadiak archipelago at the time of their discovery, and probably had been the custom among them for centuries. We find nothing of it on the mainland. It is curious to trace the customs of the wild tribes in this respect in connection with their external surroundings. In the Chukchee peninsula on the Asiatic side of Behring strait, there is no soil in many places. The substratum

---
[1] Reprinted from *The American Naturalist* (Salem, Mass.), for August, 1875.

of granitoid rock is broken by the frost into hundreds of angular fragments, which are covered with a thin coating of various mosses, which may be stripped off in great pieces like a blanket. There are no trees and but little driftwood. Burial is impracticable, cremation impossible, and the natives expose their dead on some hillside to the tender mercies of bears, dogs and foxes.

In the Yukon valley at a short distance below the surface the soil is permanently frozen, and excavation without iron tools extremely difficult. But timber abounds, and the bodies of the dead, doubled up to economize space, are placed in wooden coffins which are secured without nails and elevated above the surface of the earth on four posts. To scare away wild beasts poles are frequently erected around the coffin, bearing long strips of fur or cloth which are agitated by the wind.

The poor and friendless may be simply covered with a pile of logs, secured by heavy stones; but in general the method is as above. Various modifications are found in various localities; the coffin on the lower Yukon is sometimes filled in with clay, packed hard; and the Nowikakhat Indians sometimes place their dead erect, surrounded by hewn timbers secured like the staves of a cask.

On the islands the soil is unfrozen and there are no obstacles to digging. But wood is only found on the shores, drifted by the ocean currents, and usually not in large quantities. However there are no wild animals to disturb the remains; the beetling cliffs which are found on every hand, shattered by frequent earthquakes, afford in the talus of broken rock at their bases, abundant and convenient rock-shelters. Here the natural depositories exist, of which the natives have availed themselves. On all these customs, originally prompted by the bare necessities of the case, the slow development of sentiment and feeling (which undoubtedly does take place in savage people, though we may not be able to trace its growth) has grafted animistic ideas, and semi-religious rites and ceremonies. Thus, the original utilitarianism is more or less completely masked or concealed. It is a singular fact that no people have ever adopted the plan of committing their dead to the sea.

Without attempting, at present, to trace the growth of the custom, I will briefly describe the method adopted by the Kaniag and Alëut branches of the Eskimo stock, in preserving the dead. The details are partly given in the older voyages; and have been confirmed and supplemented by an examination of a large number of the mummies, and the traditions of the present natives.

The body was prepared by making an opening in the pelvic region and removing all the internal organs. The cavity was then filled with dry grass and the body placed in running water. This in a short time removed most of the fatty portions, leaving only the skin and muscular tissues. The knees were then brought up to the chin, and the whole body secured as compactly as possible by cords. The bones of the arms were sometimes broken to facilitate the process of compression. In this posture the remains were dried. This required a good deal of attention, the exuding moisture being carefully wiped off from time to time. When thoroughly dried the cords were removed and the body usually wrapped in a shirt, made of the skins of aquatic birds with the feathers on, and variously trimmed and ornamented with exceedingly fine embroidery. Over this were wrapped pieces of matting made of *Elymus* fibre, carefully prepared. This matting varies from quite coarse to exceedingly fine, the best rivalling the most delicate work of the natives of Fayal. It is, indeed, quite impossible to conceive of finer work done in the material used.

The matting was frequently ornamented with checks and stripes of colored fibre, with small designs at the intersections of the stripes, and with the rosy breast-feathers of the *Leucosticte* sewed into it. Over this sometimes a water proof material, made from the split intestines of the sea lion sewed together, was placed. The inner wrappings vary in number and kind but they are all referrible to one or the other of the above kinds. Outside of these were usually the skins of the sea otter or other fur animals, and the whole was secured in a case of scalskins, coarse matting or similar material secured firmly by cords and so arranged as to be capable of suspension.

The case was sometimes cradle shaped, especially when the

body was that of an infant. On these occasions it was often of wood, ornamented as highly as their resources would allow, painted with red, blue or green native pigments, carved, adorned with pendants of carved wood and suspended by braided cords of whale sinew from two wooden hoops, like the arches used in the game of croquet.

The innermost wrapping of infants was usually of the finest fur, and from the invariable condition of the contained remains it is probable that the bodies were encased without undergoing the process previously described. The practice of suspension was undoubtedly due to a desire to avoid the dampness induced by contact with the soil. The bodies of infants thus prepared were often retained in the house, by the fond mother, for a long time. Afterwards they were sometimes suspended in the open air: but adults were, as far as I have been able to find out, invariably consigned to caves or rock-shelters.

Among the localities which have been visited personally by the writer, are caves in Unga, one of the Shumagin islands, and others on the islands of Amaknak and Atka, further west. In all of these the remains of mummies existed; but the effect of falling rock from above, and great age, had in all the caves, except that of Unga, destroyed the more perishable portions of the remains, and in the latter place only fragments remained.

Many stories, however, came to hand in relation to a cave on the "islands of the Four mountains" west of Unalashka, where a large number of perfectly preserved specimens were said to exist, in relation to which the following legend was current among the natives.

Many years ago[1] there lived on the island of Kagámil (one of the Four mountains) a celebrated chief named Kat-hay-a-kut-chak, small of stature but much feared and respected by the adjacent natives for his courage and success in hunting. He had a son whom he fondly loved, and who was about fifteen years old. For this son he made a bidarka (or skin-boat) highly ornamented and of small size. When it was finished, the boy entreated his

---

[1] The date is fixed as being the fall before the spring in which the first Russians made their appearance at these islands, about 1760.

father for permission to try it, and after much coaxing was permitted to do so, on condition that he did not go far from the shore. After seeing the boat safely launched the father sat on the hillside watching its progress. The boy became interested in the pursuit of a diving bird at which he threw his dart and which receding from the shore carried the boy away in pursuit, forgetful of his promise. His father shouted to him but the boy was too far away to hear, and presently it becoming dusk, he could no longer see him and the chief returned to his dwelling. The boy did not become conscious of the distance he had paddled until out of sight of his own island, and in the darkness he made for the nearest shore.

In those days an Alëut marrying into another family was accustomed to leave his wife with her people, at least for a certain time; and a native of another island who had married a daughter of the chief was on his way to visit his wife when he saw a little canoe in front of him and recognized his little brother-in-law. The boy did not, however, recognize the native, and supposing himself pursued paddled away as fast as he could. The brother-in-law tried to frighten him by throwing darts at his canoe, and threw one so carelessly that it hit the boy's paddle and his canoe overturned. The brother-in-law made all speed to catch up with him and attempted to right the boat; but he could not do it, the boy, as is the custom, being tied into the aperture in the top; until, when he did succeed, he found that the boy was dead. His grief may be imagined, and at first he thought of abandoning the canoe where it was, but on reflection he took it to the landing at Kagámil and securing it in the kelp, that it might not float away, he returned to his own island without having seen his wife. In the morning the chief's servants brought it in, and to his great sorrow Kat-hay-a-kut-chak recognized his beloved son.

He caused the body to be prepared for burial, and when the preparation was complete he sent for all the people of the Four Mountain islands to unite in the ceremonies of depositing the body in the place where the Alëuts were used to put their dead. The people collected, and together with the chief and his family formed in procession, with songs of lamentation, beating the native tambourines on the way to the burying place. It was autumn and some snow was on the ground which the warm sun had partially melted. On the road lay a large flat stone. The sister of the boy, who was great with child, having her eyes covered, did not see the stone, slipped, and fell, injuring herself severely, and bringing on premature delivery, which caused her death with that of the infant, on the spot. Now the poor old chief had three to bury instead of one. So he ordered the procession to return to the village, bearing the dead with them.

He then had a cave near his house, which had been used as a place for storage, cleaned out, and after due preparation, the bodies were deposited in this cave, and with them many sea-otter skins, implements, weapons, and all the personal effects of the dead. He then distributed presents and food to the people, saying that he intended to make of this cave, a mausoleum for his family; and when he himself should die it was his desire to be placed there, with his children. He then told them to eat and drink as much as they desired, but as for himself he should fast and weep for his children. His wishes were carried out, and he was placed in the cave after his death, and since that time the Four Mountain islands have been abandoned as a place of residence by the natives and only occupied by casual parties of hunters.

The writer attempted in 1873 to reach this locality, but bad weather prevented anchoring; as the shores are mostly precipitous, and there are no harbors. In the summer of 1874, however, the captain of a trading vessel sent there to take off a party of hunters, was guided by some of them to the cave, and succeeded in removing all the perfect mummies and such implements and other ethnological material as could be found. Through the liberality of the Alaska Com. Co., these remains have been received by the National Museum and a careful and detailed account of them has been prepared.

Most of the mummies were wrapped up in skins or matting as previously described, but a few were encased in frames covered with sealskin or fine matting, and still retaining the sinew grummets by which they were suspended. These cases were five-sided, the two lateral ends subtriangular; the back, bottom and sloping top, rectangular, like a buggy top turned upside down. With them were found some wooden dishes, a few small ivory carvings and toys, a number of other implements, but no weapons except a few lance or dart heads of stone. Two or three women's work bags with their accumulated scraps of embroidery, sinew, tools and raw materials were among the collection.

While space will not suffice here to describe this material in detail, it may be mentioned that it contained thirteen complete mummies, from infants to adults, two of which were retained in California; and two detached skulls. None of the material showed any signs of civilized influences, all was of indigenous production, either native to the islands, or derived from internative traffic or drift wood. The latter comprised a few pieces of pine resin and bark, birch bark, and fragments of reindeer skin from Alaska peninsula.

It will thus be seen that this is one of the most important additions to our knowledge of the prehistoric condition of these people. So far as the specimens differed from those in use in more modern times they resembled more nearly the implements in use among the Eskimo of the mainland. The remains are all those of true aboriginal Aleuts.

The Kaniagmut Eskimo, inhabiting the peninsula of Alaska, the Kadiak archipelago and the islands south of the peninsula, added, to the practice of mummifying the dead, the custom of preparing the remains in some cases in natural attitudes, dressing them in elaborately ornamented clothing sometimes with wooden armor, and carved masks. They were represented, women as serving or nursing children; hunters in the chase, seated in canoes and transfixing wooden effigies of the animals they were wont to pursue; old men beat the tambourine, their recognized employment at all the native festivals. During the mystic dances, formerly practiced before a stuffed image, the dancers wore a wooden mask which had no eye-holes, but was so arranged that they could only see the ground at their feet. At a certain moment they thought that a spirit, whom it was death or disaster to look upon, descended into the idol. Hence the protection of the mask. A similar idea led them to protect the dead man, gone to the haunts of spirits, from the sight of the supernatural visitor. After their dances were over the temporary idol was destroyed. We found many relics of this practice in the Unga caves.

In Kadiak still another custom was in vogue. Those natives who hunted the whale formed a peculiar caste by themselves. Although highly respected for their prowess and the important contributions they made to the food of the community, they were considered during the hunting season as unclean. The profession descended in families and the bodies of successful hunters were preserved with religious care by their successors. These mummies were hidden away in caves only known to the possessors. A certain luck was supposed to attend the possession of bodies of successful hunters. Hence one whaler, if he could, would steal the mummies belonging to another, and secrete them in his own cave, in order to obtain success in his profession.

While M. Pinart was in Kadiak, he heard of the existence of one of these mummies but was unable to discover the locality. Afterwards Mr. Sheeran, the U. S. deputy collector of the port of Kadiak, through a peculiar superstition of the Christianized (?) natives, was able to discover and secure it. It appears that though nominally all members of the Greek church they still have great faith in the superstitions of their ancestors, and while the whaleman's supersition has passed away, the natives still regarded the mummy as possessing the power of averting the ill nature of evil spirits, and consequently were accustomed to take to it the first berries and oil of the season. This, they asserted, the mummy ate, as the dishes were always empty when they returned for them. Thus annually, they furnished the foxes and spermophiles with a feast. By watching, when the spring offering was made, the locality was detected. The mummy was secured by Mr. Sheeran and placed in an outbuilding near his house. During the season the natives came to him and remonstrated at his not feeding the dead man sufficiently; for he had been seen by a native watchman one foggy night, prowling about the town, presumably in search of food.

This mummy was only covered with a tattered gut-shirt or kamlayka, was in a squatting posture, and held in his hand a stoneheaded lance, on the point of which was transfixed a rude figure cut out of sealskin, supposed by the natives to represent the evil spirits which he held in check. It was that of a middle aged man with hair and tissues in good preservation.

DYEING, SPINNING AND WEAVING, BY THE CAMANCHES, NAVAJOES, AND OTHER INDIANS OF NEW MEXICO.[1]

By J. Henry Peters.

Thomas Ewbank, Esq.,

Dear Sir: Fully appreciating the heartiness and zeal, with which you direct your researches into the various branches of inquiry and learning connected with your important bureau, I with great pleasure, but with diffidence, accede to your request, and give you such information with regard to the manufactures of wool and cotton, as I have acquired in my rambles among our western Indians; and more especially, among the Camanches, Navajoes, and Apaches of western Texas and southern New Mexico. I have not been further west than Paso del Norte, in Texas, nor further north than Sonora, in New Mexico, and the surrounding county.

It is known to every observing traveler in those parts of our country — now no longer remote — that the brilliancy and durability of the various shades of primitive colors, and the few semi-colors that those Indians dye their wool in, are probably not equalled by the learned and scientific chemists of Europe, and our own country — an important fact, that seems not to have excited the curiosity of our otherwise enquiring countrymen. Should I be able, through your instrumentality, to bring to the public notice, such facts as will lead to enquiry and investigation, I should consider myself as having contributed somewhat to our national advancement in one branch of the arts at least, and that one of the most important.

The Camanche, Navajoe, and Apache Indians, present the curious spectacle of marauding bands of well mounted men; seemingly always committing predatory incursions upon their civilized neighbors, the Texans and Mexicans, apparently con-

---

[1] Reprinted from the *Report of the U. S. Commission of Patents*, for 1850, part 1.

stantly on the alert for evil, and yet, possessing great skill in the more peaceful and benevolent habits of the herdsman and shepherd.

The depredations of the immense number of sheep, almost daily chronicled in our gazettes, are not made to appease hunger only; but to add to the already immense flocks that overspread, as I have been told by them, the region of country lying west of the Sierra Madre, and east of California.

In the spring and summer of 1843, in company with an old friend — one of the Creeks who had emigrated west of the Mississippi, soon after the treaty with them in 1832 — I traveled westward. My guide and companion had acquired a good knowledge of the language and habits of the Camanches, Navajoes and Apaches, and had probably not altogether abstained from joining them occasionally in their irruptions upon the settlements of their timid neighbors of Chihuahua and Sonoro. I found him "as one having authority," and of course, very useful, both in the protection he afforded me, and the information he enabled me to acquire.

Among the first objects of interest to me, next to the matchless feats of horsemanship they perform, and which have so often been written of — was the number and variety of articles wrought by them, both useful and ornamental, and which might well vie with the skill of more civilized artizans. Among these were the beautiful fabrics composed of wool, and a kind of grass cloth, and some few of cotton. The object, however, of greatest interest to me, was the art of imparting to wool, etc., the beautiful colors I had often before admired, and to this I gave most attention. Like other Indians, I found them unwilling to impart knowledge voluntarily, and I had in my previous and long intercourse with the western tribes, early learned not to make inquiries that might excite their special attention to my designs. Our Indians are not disposed to impart to their white brethren, unless their citizens, any thing that might be useful out of their own country, in which particular, they are not unlike the Chinese, so that with the exceptions of their modes of dyeing and spinning, I will not now attempt to give you any certain account. The information

I derived, and minutes made at the time, will now only enable me to give you the modus operandi of extracting their dyes, without being able to give you the names of the ingredients. The specimens I had been enabled to collect have become dried up, and many have been lost by crumbling, and I was not enabled to procure seeds or other means of reproducing the plant, and am not sufficiently a botanist to give you a technical description of them. I can give you the facts only, but these are of sufficient importance to awaken curiosity, and lead to the investigations of secrets by those more intimately connected with the subject treated of, and I think of sufficient importance to have that enquiry efficiently made under governmental auspices.

The colors most admired by the Camanches and Navajoes are crimson, blue, purple and green; consequently these colors are the most common among them in all their shades; and though in their weavings they blend these with brown, yellow and other colors, with singular judgment and taste, yet it is the brilliancy of those that you most admire.

All their primitive colors are the products of the prairie and mountain flowers, and their semi-colors are composed of these and the inner bark and roots of but few other plants combined in such proportions as the hue intended to be produced. They have no mineral dyes that I am aware of. Many of these flowers are small, indeed most of them; and the plants of low size, and begin to bloom in February, March and April, and continue till summer. During the blooming, the flowers are gathered early in the morning, with the dew upon them, and dried of the dew under a shade. The leaves are carefully picked off, the stems and such as have their petals covered with pollen of another color —*e. g.*— such as are purple or scarlet with petals of yellow or white pollen, are carefully separated from it. Particular flowers only are selected; all flowers of purple color are not used to dye purple, and so of every other color, but such only as are known to make an indelible dye.

When the desired quantity of leaves are collected they are carefully and cleanly bruised and into them a small quantity of ley (I shall hereafter describe it) is put, but only enough to make a thick paste — which has the property of loosening the dye from the fabrics, and facilitating its extraction. A small bag shaped like a money purse, and but little larger, made of new dog skin, deer or wolf skin, tanned by the Indians in a manner peculiar to them, is used to compress the juice from the pulp. This bag, a foot or eighteen inches long and three or four inches wide, is half filled with the pulp. Two small handles of wood are stuck through the ends of the bag, about the length of a corkscrew handle, and used to grasp a firm hold, and as levers by which the bag is twisted until the juice is extracted through the pores of the skin, which are very open.

Whether extracted or not for immediate use, the dye is carefully bottled, in glass if it can be procured, or in small bladders, if glass is not to be had. I say small bladders, because if put away in large quantities, the dye sometimes spoils, they say, and produces dingy colors. When put away for future use the light is carefully excluded by overwrapping with skins, or any thing else, and generally buried in the ground under a shelter in which fire is not used, so as to exclude heat. The dyes, however, are generally used soon as extracted, as during the winter the women prepare their best wool, and have it ready in the spring and summer for the process of dying.

The pulp after compression is put into a small quantity of the same ley above spoken of, and permitted to remain several hours to extract any remaining dye that might be in it, and undergo the same squeezing process until no dye remains.

The ley is made with care of the ashes after burning, of the green wood of a shrub very similar to the *Auralia Spinosa,* if it be not the same of a stunted growth. So careful are they of procuring this ash unadulterated, that they have dry parcels of it laid by with which to ignite the green wood, that the ashes may not be commingled with those of other woods. The ley is usually made in a large gourd, well cleaned and dried, with the butt end cut off, and a small hole bored through the point of the neck to drip from. The gourd is three quarters filled with the ashes considerably compressed in it, and by a bale or handle suspended from a bar containing several of them. Each is then filled with rain or pure river water: the point is stopped, and the water allowed to remain on the ashes for a day and night, and then permitted to drip into the vessel placed to catch the ley.

This ley is a little colored, and is clarified by the same process of filtration through clean white sand, or sand that has been used for the same purpose before — when clarified, the ley is used as before stated, and especially to set the colors, which seems to be the principal use of it. It has no caustic quality after filtration, but an astringency peculiar to itself — rather a pungent than burning quality. It is sometimes used to dilute the darker dyes and produce lighter shades.

The wool to be dyed is washed in warm water until perfectly cleansed of the natural oil — using the root of a plant very abundant in Texas and southern New Mexico, as well as most of the southern states, of a very saponaceous quality, and known as the soap plant. In all their best fabrics — blankets, belts, leggings, etc., made of wool, their finest fleeces are used, and it is not unknown to many of our army officers and others, that the Navajoes give great attention to their management of sheep, and often produce fleeces almost or quite equal to the merino in fineness and softness of texture, by their skilful crosses and selections made after long and minute observations and care. A Camanche and Navajoe are as much delighted with the possession of a superior ram and ewe as of a fine horse, to the breeding of which they also give much attention. Von Thaer would not be more so with the possession of his finest buck. All their wool is dyed before spinning, and this is done by submerging it in the dye and letting it remain ten or fifteen days, the dye-pot being left covered: but during this soaking the wool is turned over once every day. Sometimes the lighter shades are imparted to the wool by soaking a shorter time — they say this produces a clearer tint. If not dark enough, the same process is repeated with fresh dye. I have been told by my guide, that the Camanches fumigate the wool after dying, over a smoke of the above described wood, to deepen the color, but I never saw it done.

Their green color is produced from the leaves of several plants, the juice of which is expressed in the same manner as from the flowers, and used in the same manner.

DYEING, SPINNING AND WEAVING BY THE CAMANCHES. 357

Their brown color is made from the inner bark, roots and nuts of the walnut and of other trees, much in the same manner as our farmer's wives now dye their wool for home-made jeans.

After the dyeing is finished, the wool is dried in the shade, and when well dried, exposed to the sun for a few hours; the dyeing is then complete, and the wool ready for spinning, except sometimes, perhaps, not always, they oil the wool slightly, and diffuse the dampness through it by rubbing and rolling it in the hands. I do not know the precise object of this, but they say it works better. This does not impair the color, for washing restores them to their first brightness. It seems to be the peculiar quality of the *set* that gives the lasting brilliancy of the color. I have seen the Camanche blankets, after being used for months, and abused by being put under the saddle, saturated with sweat, rained upon, slept in upon the naked earth, and when carefully washed, present the colors again, as bright as newly dyed silk.

The spinning is what you would call twisting the thread; this is done altogether by the fingers, and somewhat similar to the ancient distaff, though reversing the order of operation. The distaff was used to wrap the raw material upon, and the spool or quill was used not only to wind the thread upon, but as the spindle to twist it. The Camanches reverse this order, and use the raw material for the spindle, and the spool only to wind the thread upon. They use no distaff.

A CAMANCHE SPINNING.

In spinning, a small portion of wool only is used at a time — a mess, say, of a quarter pound weight, and shaped like an egg, say four or five inches long, and two or three in diameter, is wrapped around with a string sufficiently tight to keep it together, but loose enough at the point to permit the wool to be drawn out for spinning the thread — a small stone, of an ounce or so in weight, is tied on the middle of a stick of about six inches in length (see *d*), and inserted in the lower part of the bunch. This is to add weight to it without increasing the size, and is used as dead weight, to increase and continue the velocity when twirled round by the fingers.

The spinning is begun by first twisting a thread of five or six inches in length, which is wound around a stick of ten or so inches long, and half an inch in diameter, which is held in the left hand, and serves for the spool to wind the thread upon. After the thread is commenced, the spinning proper begins, and is then continued, by constantly keeping the bunch of wool swiftly rotating horizontally, by twirling it with the thumb and middle fingers; at the moment the twirl is given, a slight jerk downwards is made, to draw out the wool, and a simultaneous slight yielding of the left hand, to prevent the thread separating from the mass until the twist is given it, and when sufficiently spun, is wound upon the spool. They usually spin three or four or six inches at a time — and wind up every time. The thread is usually twisted hard, and always doubled before weaving. I have seen thread spun altogether by the fingers, and the spinning and weaving is by no means confined to the women; men are often engaged in it, and exhibit much taste and skill in devising the patterns, as well as blending the colors. After small parcels of the wool are well loosened by picking and straightening with the fingers, it is tied loosely together with a string, to prevent the bunch falling apart; or it is often put in a small bag, of four or six inches in diameter, and drawn together at the mouth, leaving portions of the wool protruding from it in a point, to facilitate its being drawn out to form the thread. A weight of an ounce or two — usually a flat stone, is tied in the middle of a stick of six inches in length, and half an inch in diameter, and is enclosed within the wool, or the bag, near the bottom of it, and acts as a dead weight to facilitate the momentum when turning round. The ends of the stick project from the mass of wool like two handles, and are used to twirl it with the fingers.

The thread is usually about the fineness of our good Osnaburg, and spun sufficiently hard to twist readily when doubled, and

DYEING, SPINNING AND WEAVING BY THE CAMANCHES. 359

makes the doubled thread not very hard. After the spinning is finished, and previous to weaving, the thread is measured, by *hanking* it over two pins a certain distance apart. This is only to ascertain the length of the thread required, and is then formed into a ball.

NAVAJOES SPINNING.

The Navajoes have another and a more artistic manner of spinning, for which it has been thought they were indebted to white instructors, but which they indignantly deny. Two boards, of two or three feet in length, and three to six inches in width, as may be procured, are pinned on opposite sides of the crotch of a tree of convenient height, or of two posts set in the ground near each other, or two trees growing near together. Two holes are bored in the boards, one opposite the other, and about one and a half inches in diameter. A limb of any kind of tree with a branch diverging at right angles, is procured. The larger limb is cut off about eighteen inches each way from the branch, so as to be about three feet long. The branch is trimmed off to fit the holes, and constitutes the spindle. The limb is used as the handle, and as a fly to continue the momentum. The whole apparatus is unique, simple and efficient, and I would say an original one. (See section S, where $a, a,$ is the spindle, $b, b,$ the boards, and $c,$ a pin to keep the spindle in its place.)

The spinning is commenced like the first process, by twisting with the fingers a short thread, then fastening it to the point of the spindle. The spinner has already prepared, by picking with her fingers, a quantity of wool which she has in her basket or bag, tied around her waist, or in a bundle like the one described in the previous process. A person twirls around the handle or fly (see d), and the spinner keeps moving backwards, as the thread is formed. The process is much the same as that by which our rope makers spin hemp by hand. A thread of six or eight feet in length, is spun before being wound up.

The Indian never spins until he or she has a specific work to perform. The size, plan, configuration, and every other requisite, is first determined. The quantity of thread required for any piece of work, is from long habit, pretty accurately known. I think I have said already, that all their weaving is done with a double and twisted thread. They waste no thread. They usually spin a small quantity and weave, and then spin again, and so on, until the work is completed. The process is the same for cotton, wool, grass, etc.

Weaving is the most elaborate of their arts, and they make beautiful work. Their blankets, or I should call them shawls, are often rich, strong and showy. Some have a resemblance to the Persian shawl. They frequently sell in Mexico for three hundred dollars, and I have seen them sell in New Orleans for two hundred dollars. I have one in my possession, taken by Gen. Houston at the battle of San Jacinto, which cost three hundred dollars. They are usually impervious to water, very heavy, and are rather plaited together than woven. The time occupied in making one of these, is from four to six, and sometimes eight months.

A FORTNIGHT AMONG THE CHIPPEWAS OF LAKE SUPERIOR.[1]

By Prof. I. I. Ducatel.

One of the conditions, in the purchase from the Chippewa Indians of the vast tract of land lying in Wisconsin territory, and partly in the state of Michigan to the south of Lake Superior, is the payment to them of a stipulated annuity, consisting of articles of clothing, blankets, kettles, guns, and ammunition, together with a certain amount in specie. To receive this annuity, they are notified by the Indian agents to assemble at the most convenient places for the transportation of the goods within some specified period. This year (1835), those inhabiting the southern coast of Lake Superior from the Ance up, those to the east of the Mississippi, and on the head waters of that river, as far as Leech lake, were required to assemble on the 10th of August at Lapointe, the principal trading post of the American Fur Company. It appears that the whole number of these Indians entered upon the rent roll of that year was 5030, of whom, however, not one-half of the number came forward, the remainder being represented by proxy. The amount to be distributed was twenty-eight thousand dollars in clothing, and twenty-two thousand dollars in cash, with a further allowance of five thousand dollars for provisions dealt out to them during their stay at the post and the balance of which they are permitted to take along with them. Among those admitted to this distribution are, not only the roving Indians, but likewise the settled half breeds; these being supposed to have inherited a share in the sovereignty of the soil.

The annual recurrence of this payment (*L'bahmahtin*, as the Indians call it), brings together a great many families; for not only do the men come, but they bring along with them the women and children and dogs. They build up their wigwams along the shores of the beautiful bay of Lapointe, locating themselves ac-

---

[1] Reprinted from *The United States Catholic Magazine* (Baltimore), for January and February, 1846.

cording to bands, but without any reference to conveniency of arrangement—the result seemingly of an unpremeditated impulse. Their lodges, that are dome-shaped, made of bent saplings and covered with birch bark, are carelessly put up and unsightly, and, being in scattered groups, without any line of bearing, as a geologist would say, they produce no picturesque effect by themselves, but require other adventitious circumstances to relieve the sameness of their appearance. On the present occasion there are not more than two thousand Indians assembled, and their personal appearance is far from being prepossessing — but very few good looking men and still fewer well looking women. The children alone are attractive by their healthful look, their playfulness, and their noise. The half-naked men are wrapped up in dirty blankets, with their faces horridly besmeared with paint; the women are decently covered, but unwashed and uncombed; their children pretty much in the same bodily condition, except that some have a little clothing on, whilst others have none at all.

The animation of an Indian camp consists in a motley set of half-clad human beings of the male sex, squatted upon the ground, sullenly smoking their pipes, or seated in circular groups playing cards, or their favorite and more animated *mukkesinnahdahdewug* (which will be presently described); women and little girls moving about the fires, cooking and fetching water, and a parcel of idle boys kicking at each other, wrestling and screaming at the top of their voices, or teasing a whole gang of half-starved dogs that bark and growl.

The old women scarcely ever leave the lodges; young women or maidens are never seen intermixed with the men, or participating in their amusements. They move at a distance from them; the mothers with their babes, swaddled, in a bod which is carried on the back, or simply supported, in the same way, by a blanket worn as a shawl. The young women are cheerful in their looks, and modest in their deportment. They have a more cleanly appearance than the squaws, are more talkative among themselves, and the better sort ornament their arms and ankles with bands of bead work, and wear decent ear rings with bead necklaces. They seldom disfigure themselves with paint. This folly is principally confined to the men, who seem, indeed, much fonder also of trinkets than the women. A warrior will be seen with a dozen of eagle's feathers banded round his head, his face painted red, blue, and black, with a red circle around one eye and a blue one around the other, a great slit in his ear, from which depends a profusion of tinselled ornaments and the like hung round his neck, a gaudily embroidered belt of bead work, with leggins of the same material, and thus attired, he struts about like a peacock. One of this class offered five dollars for a turkey cock; on being asked what he wanted to do with it, it was solely to possess its tail feathers to ornament his head. Strange are their notions of improvement in this conchoidal appendage to the human head. They will stick long plated arrows into them, even as our own fair countrywomen stick similar darts through their hair. They fix knives and forks into these auricular slits, and some have been seen with a comb thus preposterously located. The young female *barbarian* does not venture upon these extravagances; but, like a *Christian* daughter, is satisfied with a simple ear ring. Useless as it may be, this supererogatory fixture conveys no meretricious intention on the part of the Indian girl; for it is worn alike by the woman and the maid; but upon what notion of good taste do our civilized daughters imitate this savage custom? As our young women don't take snuff, why not hang rings to their noses, likewise? Surely a fine engraving of Queen Victoria would set off her royal majesty's head much better without the bodkins.

But to return to the payment. It is accomplished in this way. The agent having adjusted the rent-roll, which he does upon the returns of the chiefs of the several bands — each of whom is the bearer of a bundle of small sticks that represent the number of members belonging to his clan, and, strange to say, this is the only way they can be made to enumerate themselves — the goods are then allotted and distributed by bands.

This adjustment of the rent-roll is not, however, unattended with difficulties; the agent being the auditor of all claims and bars against the regular division of the property. Some of the claims against the payment in full to a band are peculiar to the

Indian social condition. Thus, if a manslaughter has been committed to the damage of a family of any one band, by an individual of another, the injured party demands indemnity from the aggressor out of his portion of the annuity, if he be able to give it; if not, he asks it from the whole band to which he belongs. In the same way any accidental or mischievous damage done by one band to another, or by the Indians to our own people, is sure to be met with a claim for indemnities, requiring not only judgment, but firmness on the part of the agent to allow or reject. To carry on this sort of litigation, there are numerous conferences and "talks," that afford not the least interesting occasions for studying the Indian character.

At one of these talks, *Biziki*, or Buffalo, spoke pretty much to this effect upon the subject of Indian aggressions. After offering his salutations, and those of his band who were seated round the hall, first to their great father at Washington, and then to the Indian agent, he said " that his people had been accused of committing aggressions upon the whites — he thought it probable that some of the thoughtless young men might have done so, and if he knew who they were he would certainly point out to them how much against their interest it is to do such things. He had made some inquiries about the alleged aggressions, and he thought that when they came to be examined into they would be found of a very trifling nature, and more intended as a retaliation for much greater aggressions on the part of the white men. He said that his people were satisfied with the assistance and the advice which the great father had caused to be given to them, and that they were thankful to him for his presents. He had advised his people himself, as the agent had last year asked him to do, to turn their attention, more than they had previously done, to the cultivation of their soil, to the planting of corn and of potatoes; but that the wide woods were still full of game, and the deep waters full of fish, and that it was difficult to prevail upon the young men to abandon these resources, to go about turning up the ground. They preferred to leave that to the care of the women, who seemed to be better fitted for such drudgery. He would, however, continue to advise them gradually to break themselves into this new system, if it were only to keep them from the temptation, when they were pinched by want, to trespass upon the potato patches of the white men. Yet he was of opinion that if the agent looked carefully into the matter, he would find that the aggressions came most frequently from the whites upon the Indians."

He now signified that he had spoken all he had to say. And, advancing to the agent, gave him his hand, and in succession to all those seated round the agent's table.

On another occasion, *Singoup*, or Balsam Tree, spoke in some such a strain as this. After making the usual salutation, he said that he probably would be considered as having spoken like a child. "The truth is," he said, "I am now a child — the time was when I was a man, and then I spoke like a man; but now I speak like a child, because my young men treat me as if I was a child. When I was a British Indian I was treated by the British agents like a man — they spoke well of me, which my young men heard, and they gave me presents, which my young men saw, and that caused them to respect me; but now that I am an American Indian, I am not noticed by the great father, and my young men think that I am not in favor, and, therefore, they treat me like a child. I used to give them good advice, which they heeded; but now they don't listen to what I say. It is not my fault. If they become dissatisfied, great mischief may arise out of it — they may again draw the knife — and there may be a great deal of bloodshed. It was not so when I was a British Indian; but now I am a child, and must expect to be treated like a child."

To which the Indian agent replied very appropriately, "that there was nothing more true than that he had spoken like a child; but it was not true that he had not been as well spoken of or treated as the other chiefs. Whenever it was known that he had given good advice to his people, he had been lauded for it, and received presents. As to his taunting him (the agent) with what he was when a British Indian, it was a matter of perfect indifference — the great father at Washington had ample power to keep all children under obedience, and would do so; that he would reward where reward was due, and punish where punishment was merited. He talked of bloodshed; he (the agent) could tell them, and he was glad to have an opportunity of saying so.in the presence of the young men here assembled, that if they dared to respond to such sentiments as those expressed by the chief, they would sorely repent of it. Yes, Singoup," said the agent, "you have indeed spoken like a child. At one time I thought you were a good man; I fear now that I was mistaken, though I still hope that your speech was prompted by some momentary ebulition of passion, that your better sense will cause you to repent of. If you wish to speak again, speak like a man, not like a whining child, or a woman." Singoup, who had been during this severe reprimand composedly smoking his pipe, then rose once more and blandly said " that what he had said amounted to nothing at all. He only wished to see what effect it would have upon his young men." He then advanced and shook hands, not a little to the amusement, though surprise of all, at this ingenuous way of getting out of a scrape.

There are two occasions when the Indian character shows itself strongly: at their dances and when they are gambling. During the period of the payment the performance of the pipe-dance, together with the war-dance, is a very frequent exhibition with them; and as they resort to it for the express purpose of levying a contribution upon the merchants and traders of Lapointe, it has been more significantly called the " begging-dance." Accordingly they make great preparations for its coming off with effect — such as annointing their limbs, painting their bodies in the most fantastical manner, and, barely saving decency, appear almost naked. After promenading the village, they assemble before the agency house, and other places where they expect to be treated, and commence their performances. The pipe-dance is usually a *pas seul*, danced by the most expert *balerini* of the troup in turns, and consists in grotesque and violent distortions of the body, indicative more of suppleness than of strength, but having no pretensions whatever to grace. It precedes the war-dance, in which the whole *corps de ballet* unite in equally violent contortions of limbs, and *quasi* martial exercises of marching and countermarching, interspersed with the firing off of pistols, brandishing of knives, going through the sham action of slaying and scalping an enemy, and making animated harangues. Both dances are accompanied by a monotonous beating upon a kettle, or a tight skin, and the jingling of bells, that are played by the elders of the band, who seem to delight in the sport, and contribute to it by an incessant chant. *Nemeewin* is their generic name for a dance; *opwagun-nemeewin* is the pipe-dance, and *medaweewin* the grand medicine dance. The boys sometimes fall into the dance; but the women never; and only a few, ensconced behind the fences, are even spectators of it. The dance being over, the party is usually at the factory treated with some crackers and cheese; and a pail of sweetened water into which has been poured a bottle or two of essence of peppermint, is brought out to which they help themselves at discretion. They are very fond of this sort of mint julep, which they call *mahkahwahgomik*.

The Indians are inveterate gamblers. They have combined a game of cards (*ahtahdewenog*) which is said by those who play it to be full of interest and ingenuity. But their favorite game is the *mukesinnahdahdewog*, or moccasin game. It is played with four bullets (one of which is jagged) and four moccasins. The four bullets are to be hid, one under each moccasin, by the first player, whose *deal* is decided by throwing up a knife and letting it fall on the blanket, the direction of the blade indicating the person who is to hide first. The four bullets are held in the right hand, and the left hand is kept moving from one moccasin to the other; whilst the player, with a peculiar manner calculated to divert the attention of the one with whom he is playing, and with an incessant chant accompanied by a swinging motion of the head and trunk, passes his bullet hand under the moccasins depositing a bullet under each. The other is to guess where the jagged bullet is, but not at the first trial; for if he strike upon it the first time, he loses four sticks — there being twenty altogether, that are used as counters; if the second time he make a similar guess, then he loses three sticks; but if he guess the situation of the jagged bullet the third time, then he *gains* four sticks; finally should the bullet remain under the fourth moccasin, the guesser loses four sticks. The game continues until the twenty sticks have passed from one hand to the other. At this game, of which they are very fond, they stake every thing about them and sometimes come away literally stripped. The groups that are thus collected present the most characteristic of Indian habits. There will be twenty sitting down and as many standing round, intent upon the progress of the game, which is carried on in silence, except on the part of the hider.

Another game of chance, and perhaps the only other after cards, and the one just described, is the *pahgehsehwog*, or pan-play, which consists in guessing at any thing, or number of things, enclosed between two pans. The men also amuse themselves at foot races for a wager, and shooting with the bow and arrow, which is termed *pahpahmetehgwahdah*. The boys have a few games of their own: one consists in pitching pins into a hole as our boys pitch marbles; this is called *ahtahdedah-nesaguahbedeun*. They also play at ball by throwing it out and catching it with a stick, the end of which is curled up and makes the opening a pocket of net work; this is their *pahgahto-wahnak*. But their favorite amusement seems to be a game at marbles, which must have been taught to them by the French Catholic missionaries;[1] for it is the same that is played at all the Catholic schools and colleges of our country, was at one time exclusively played at these institutions, though now known every where. It is what our boys call, if the recollection serves well, "knuckling." The Indian boys call it *ninijoweh-ehdehdah*. They play also at "hop-scop," and they have their *shosehman*, or snow stick, about the length of a common walking cane cut out in the shape of a sledge, which they cause to slide over the snow or ice. He who sends it farthest, upon a bet wins. The only plays observed among the girls, is the *pahpahjekahwewog*, a sort of substitute for our "graces," which simply consists in catching with two sticks a twine loaded at each end with a ball; and another, to which they give the name of *paskahwewog*, is a sort of "cup-and-ball," in which a pin is used instead of the ball, and is caught, by a similar arrangement to our game, on its point.

---

[1] Cards were introduced among them by the British and American traders.

The Indian boys (*kwewezens*) are very fond of wrestling, a gymnastic which they term *kahguahjewah-nahawin*. They never box; their usual mode of fighting being to kick at each other — *tunggishkoo-dahdawin*; they practice this exercise also for amusement. The men (*enenewug*) never fight except with bloody intentions. The women (*equawug*) and girls (*equesens*) do frequently, with all the destructive manipulations of the sex in every clime. A very remarkable trait of character in the Indians is, that they never quarrel, nor address insulting epithets to each other. If one wishes to speak ill of another, he will do so in his presence, but addresses himself to a third person; the insulted party either listens to it in silence, goes away, takes no notice of it, or resents it by a manslaughter.

The Chippewas appear not to be musical. The Ottowas who assemble at the Sault and at Mackinaw are much more so, as on the occasions of their payment they buy fifes, flutes, and fiddles, which they use *tant bien que mal;* but a Chippewa's notion of music is concentrated in his *tawahegun*, or drum, and the jewsharp *madwawechegance*. They have songs, but they could not be prevailed upon to sing them.

It may be said of the Indians that, either by temperament and some peculiarity of physical structure, or from a moral propensity, they are essentially a sluggish race — exhibiting none of that restlessness of the white man which is ever in quest of something beyond the complete gratification of the wants of the body. Hunger rather interrupts than overcomes their habit of bodily indolence; but it is a peculiarity of the Indian character to remain as long as possible in a state of quiescence. Hence they are essentially too improvident. The only provisions that are made for the long and dreary winter of their climate consist in planting and gathering a few potatoes and a v ry little corn; the only summer gifts that are hoarded are the wild rice and whortleberries, dried and put by, not as a delicacy, but for nourishment. The maple sugar is more an object of traffic than a provision. They rely, in fact, mainly upon game and fish. Some of the least improvident prepare a little smoked deer's meat, or other game, and render the tallow or lard of the slain animals, which they put in holes called *câches*. In these caches they also bury fish for great emergencies.

The only industrial arts practiced by the Indians are canoe building, making of nets and mats, and the manufacture of a variety of useful and ornamental articles with the birch bark. The birch, indeed, seems to have been made expressly for the Indian. With its bark he makes his canoe, named by him *gemaun;* the frame work of which is of yellow cedar, bound together with the fibrous roots of the spruce pine, and this is covered over with birch bark, rolled into sheets of various sizes that are sewed together with cords or threads of the spruce root; finally, the seams are covered over with gum, made of the exudation of the spruce boiled down to a proper consistency, to which is added powdered charcoal from the pine, to give color to the mastic. The birch bark is made into troughs (*pisketahnahgun*) in which the maple sugar (*sinzibuckwud*) is gathered in March and April, by merely cutting a gash in the tree from downwards up, and putting into it a chip of wood to direct the sap into the trough. With the birch bark is also manufactured the sugar basket (*mukknk*), and a variety of other baskets and boxes for useful purposes. There are some families that possess as household utensils from one to two thousand birch troughs, used to collect the saccharine juice of the maple. The *wegewan* is built of birch bark, and out of this bark the Indian makes himself a scroll (*totem*) upon which, in hieroglyphics of his own invention, he inscribes his coat of arms, a bird, a bear, a beaver, an owl, a fish, or animal of any kind, and marks down the number of members, old and young, belonging to his family. The bark is also used in preference to any other substance for kindling fires; it burns with a bright flame that adapts it for use as a torch-light in taking fish by night. The Indian seems to be aware of the peculiar adaption of this tree to his wants; for, if he has anything of value to preserve, he wraps it up carefully in its bark. The wood, too, is useful in its juice as a beverage; its young shoots collect a number of rabbits, and wild pigeons are particularly fond of its blossoms.

In the ornamental articles of Indian manufacture that serve as portions of their dress, such as the ties or garters for leggins, the belts, sashes, pouches, etc., that are made of colored beads, a prevailing idea of the cross is observed, probably imitated from the vestment of the Catholic priests who first settled among them, from whom also they have acquired many usages not riginally theirs. The moccasins worn by the females are frequently very neatly lined with blue cloth, and tastefully ornamented with bead work. Those of the men are decorated on the fore part of the foot, like the worked cloth slipper of the civilized gentleman. The most desirable article of female dress appears to be a shawl of superfine blue cloth, which is more frequently borne upon the head than the shoulders. Whether it be that the women have not so readily the means of procuring them, they do not wear as many ornaments as the men; but they are pleased to deck their children with them.

A very remarkable trait in the character of the Indian mother is her excessive fondness for her children, who are indulged in every way, are never chastised, and whose loss is bewailed with great demonstrations of sorrow. The men play with the young children, but take no notice of the growing up boys, who are suffered to do just as they please, and are very mischievous. When the men are too much annoyed by them, they knuckle them on the head, but have never recourse to flagellation. In this latter respect they have certainly an advantage over the white man, who has not yet discarded from his system of discipline the ferule and the whip. The Indian is also fond of his dogs; whenever a canoe is met coasting the shores of the lake, the sire is at the helm, the squaw and grown up boys or girls are paddling, the helpless children and a pack of dogs are the steerage passengers. The dogs have their litter in the wigwam; but if one is accidentally killed, or if necessity compels his slaughter, he is boiled into soup, and feasted upon as a great delicacy. The Indian pets them, as the white man does the lamb, and feeds them to gratify his appetite.

The Indians are certainly not what the French would call *gourmets*, but rather *gourmands;* in other words whenever the food is provided for them, they are great eaters, and not dainty at that. Their culinary art is even more circumscribed than their handicraft, since it extends no further than boiling their meat, fish and vegetables in one promiscuous *chowder*, with not even salt as a condiment. This disrelish for salt, or perhaps it might be better stated, this indifference to the use of it, is equally remarkable amongst the half breeds, and even with the Canadian *voyageurs* of Lake Superior, who seem to be quite satisfied with what is contained of it in the packed pork, of which they are so fond as to have richly merited the cognomen of "*mangeurs de lard.*"

At the distribution of the rations, during their sojourn at the post where the annuity is paid off to them, other traits of manners are observable, not at all of a disparaging character, as they evince a spirit of concession, and a sense of justice, which, on the contrary, are highly creditable to them. The rations are dealt from the store house of the American Fur Company, upon a requisition given by the Indian agent to the chief of each band, who sends the women and children to receive them — the drudgery of domestic affairs always devolving upon the women. It is amusing to see them trudging along under their load of provisions that are very liberally distributed, the little naked papooses, with their stomachs inordinately distended by a previous feeding, and carrying nearly their own weight of provender. The women have a full share of the burden, though, if a barrel of flour form a portion of the allotment, the chieftain, or his male subdelegate, faithful to his disrelish of manual exercises, kicks it to its destination. Arrived at their camping ground, the women and young members of the clan seat themselves in a circle two or three deep, and the chief proceeds in the distribution according to families, the whole procedure being conducted with much order, apparent mutual satisfaction, and without noise.

The only disturbances noticed during the encampment at Lapointe, took place once on the occasion of a trader beating his squaw, and then the excitement seemed to be principally amongst the travelers, who indignantly protested against this summary mode of punishing a refractory wife. The Indians took no part in the excitement, because it was understood that the discipline had been recommended by the woman's own parents. The poor thing was perfectly submissive under rather an unnecessarily severe castigation. The Indians themselves never beat their wives. On a second occasion, during a thunder storm of great violence which raged through the night, the whole camp suddenly became dreadfully distressed, the men expressing their alarm by yells, the women and children by moanings and loud sobs, as if they had already realized some dreadful calamity. At every vivid flash of lightning, as if to efface its trace, they would fire off volleys of musquetry, and each rolling peal of thunder was accompanied by shouts and whoops, calculated if not to drown, at least to divert the attention from the raging of the elements. There was some danger in this strife; for the unprotected store house contained a large number of powder kegs, whose explosion would have made sad havoc in the camp.

But a much more melancholy occurrence took place on the last night of the payment. It is a very judicious custom with the Indian agents to withhold the specie payment of the annuity until the final day, so as to prevent as much as possible any impositions to be practiced by the white traders upon the Indians, or to guard against any allurements by the unprincipled conduct of some of these mercenary venders, in the way especially of the sale of liquor. The cupidity of a few, however, will defy all laws, and notwithstanding the penalty of confiscation of their entire stock in trade, they contrive to introduce ardent spirits amongst the Indians, which is dealt out somewhat in this style. A whisky vender, standing upon a raised platform behind his groggery, lures them on, one by one, to a taste of his "vinegar," knowing full well that the unfortunate savage, when he has once tasted of it, can no longer control his thus excited insatiable appetite for more. The vender is of course willing to "accommodate" him for the trifling sum of fifty cents a gulp, and in the same accommodating spirit, repeats it until his victim from a savage has become a brute. One of the traders of notorious villainy had succeeded in introducing the poison into the camp, the consequences of which were exceedingly distressing if not alarming. Some of the men became infuriated, destroying their own lodges, to the great terror of their families, whilst others, completely unnerved, lay down to whine and drivel. The first care of the women, on such occasions, is to conceal the knives and other dangerous weapons, and they show the same solicitude that might be expected from a Christian wife.

Within what is called the Indian territory, the introduction of spirituous liquor is prohibited; but at places under the jurisdiction of the states, the federal government has not interfered, and can not; so that at Mackinaw, Green Bay, and the Sault, the excesses growing out of the use of ardent spirits are very great, and the women, and even the young people, are likewise maddened by it. The post, under such circumstances, becomes a true pandemonium. When in a state of intoxication, the women especially give vent to their sorrow in melancholy chantings and a profuse flow of tears; the burden of their songs being the death of their friends or other misfortunes. One who listens to these lamentations while darkness and distance interpose to conceal the too often disgusting objects who utter them, and to soften down and mellow the tone of high pitched voices, will often find something affecting in their honest and unpremeditated complaints. Before the whites introduced among them intoxicating drinks, it is probable that assembling together for feasts was their principal and most favorite source of excitement in times of peace, and comparative inactivity; for they are exceedingly fond of feasts, of which they have a great many, and at all of which they gather principally to eat and smoke. They seem to have a peculiar relish for the meat of dogs, which they simply boil without any salt. The soup is served up in a tin pan, from which each one, after taking a long sup, passes it to his next neighbor, and then falls to smoking. In no instance were they heard to enliven their conviviality by the help of a song.

Although the Indians, as before stated, are great eaters, yet they enjoin upon young and unmarried persons, of both sexes, rigorous and long continued fasts, that are begun at a very early age. "The parent," says Dr. James, in *Tanner's Narrative*, "in the morning, offers the child the usual breakfast in one hand and charcoals in the other: if the latter is accepted, the parent is gratified, and some commendations, or marks of favor, are bestowed on the child. To be able to continue long fasting confers an enviable distinction. They therefore inculcate upon their children the necessity of remaining long without food. Sometimes the children fast three, five, seven, and some, as is said, even ten days; in all of which time they take only a little water, and that at very distant intervals. During these fasts they pay very particular attention to their dreams, and from the character of these their parents, to whom they relate them, form an opinion of the future life of the child. Dreaming of things above, as birds, clouds, the sky, etc., is considered favorable; and when the child begins to relate any thing of this kind, the parent interrupts him, saying: 'It is well, my child say no more of it.' In these dreams, also, the children receive impressions which continue to influence their character through life. A man, an old and very distinguished warrior, who was some years ago at Red river, dreamed, when fasting in his childhood, that a bat came to him, and this little animal he chose for his medicine. To all the costly medicines for war or hunting, used by other Indians, he paid no attention. Throughout his life he wore the skin of a bat tied to the crown of his head, and in numerous war excursions he went into battle exulting in the confidence that the Sioux, who could not hit a bat on the wing, would never be able to hit him. He distinguished himself in many battles, and killed many of his enemies, but throughout his long life no bullet ever touched him, all of which he attributed to the protecting influence of his medicine, revealed to him, in answer to his fasting in boyhood. Of Net-no-kwa, his foster mother, the author of the foregoing narrative relates that at about twelve years of age she fasted ten successive days. In her dream a man came down and stood before her, and, after speaking of many things, he gave her two sticks, saying: 'I give you these to walk upon, and your hair I give it to be like snow.' In all her subsequent life this excellent woman retained the confident assurance that she should live to extreme old age, and often in times of the greatest distress from hunger, and of apparent danger from other causes, she cheered her family by the assurance that it was given to her to crawl on two sticks, and to have her head like the snow, and roused them to exertion by infusing some part of her own confident reliance upon the protection of a superior and invisible power."

Another occasion of excitement with the Indian is during the dying moments of one of the family, when, having satisfactorily proved the inefficacy of *gushkibitagun*, or medicine bag, they have recourse to the *biwinahkeek*, or medicine drum. The entrance to the lodge is then closed up with a black bear skin, and within its vitiated atmosphere a continuous drumming upon a tight skin is kept up, without intermission, for hours, accompanied by a monotonous chant, until the miserable sufferer is distracted first, and then literally asphyxiated. No sooner dead than he is buried; or rather is most usually laid out upon the surface of the ground and simply protected by a roof-shaped covering. Their *wake* over their dead takes place after this mode of burial, and consists in the lamentations of the women over the entombment for the rest of the day. This is what they are observed to do when thrown in the midst of a civilized settlement; but it is probable that when left to themselves their ceremonials, on such occasions, may be very different.

There is something impressive and affecting in their habit of preserving the *jebi*, or memorial of the dead, which like our weeds and crapes, finds a place in many a dwelling where little of mourning is visible. Yet, though the place which death had made vacant in their hearts, may have been filled, they seem never to forget the supply they consider due the wants of the departed. Whenever they eat or drink, a portion is carefully set apart for the *jebi*, and this observance continues for years, should they not, in the meantime, have an opportunity to send out this memorial with some war party; when, if it be thrown down on the field of battle, as they aim always to do, then their obligation to the departed ceases.

In sickness, the Indian is very desponding, and if relief be speedily administered to him, is equally grateful. He acknowledges services thus rendered to him, in manner and kind, to the utmost of his abilities. He seems to have fallen heir to all the diseases that afflict the human race, and is not known to have any one peculiar to his condition. In their own original and genuine custom, when the doctor — *muskekiwainni*, literally medicine man — is called in, it is usual to present him, as he enters the lodge of his patient, a kettle of the best food they are able to procure, and it is very generally the case that the medicine-man commences his treatment by assuring his patient that he is suffering from the malice of some enemy. He may possibly go still further, and not satisfied with telling his patient that he is under the influence of the incantations of some body, will name some person, either his own or his patient's enemy, as he may think most for his interest. In other words, the Indian medicine man is a rank impostor or quack.

After the distribution of the fresh blankets and new clothing, the Indian encampment assumes a gayer aspect. The women turn out in their newly acquired finery, displaying all the coquetry of their sex, in which the men are by no means deficient, except that with an inherent love, as it were, of paint, they daub their white blankets with red, blue and black earths, with grotesque representations of all sorts, which speedily brings them into the condition of dirty clothes, even before the time of departure for their forest homes.

Taking a final leave of the Chippewas a few reflections may be indulged, as respects the efforts to introduce our Christian civilization among them. It must be conceded, in the first place, that the Catholic missionaries have been most successful. And in reference to missionary labors, generally, among the Indians, it has been justly said that "they originate as well in a diffusive and amiable benevolence as a feeling of justice, and severe, though tardy compunction, which would seek, at this late day, to render to the starved and shivering remnant of the people who received us to their country in our day of small things, some recompense for the fair inheritance which we have wrested from their forefathers. The example of the Cherokees, and some others in the south, has been sufficient to prove that, under the influence of a mild climate and a fertile soil, these people can be taught habits of settled, if not persevering industry. From this condition of things we can already see how, among that people, habits of enterprise and industry are to spring up, and we look forward with confidence to a source of continued improvement. That all the other bands and tribes, under similar auspices and similar influences, would pursue a similar course, can not be doubted. Philologists and speculative theorists may divide and class as they please; to the patient and industrious observer, who has mingled intimately with this race in the low and fertile districts of the Mississippi, in the broad and smiling plains of Arkansas and the Red river, in the forests of the upper Mississippi, and among the pines and the mosses of the upper lakes, it will be evident that the aboriginal people of the United States territory are all of one family, not by physical constitution and habit only, but by the structure and temperaments of their minds; their modes of thinking and acting; and, indeed, in all physical and mental peculiarities which set them apart from the remainder of the human family as a peculiar people. Whatever course has, in one situation, proved in any measure effectual to reclaim them from their vague and idle habits, will certainly succeed in another situation, though perhaps more slowly, as they may be influenced by a less genial climate, or more barren soil."[1]

---

[1] *Tanner's Narrative.*

THE JANE McCREA TRAGEDY.[1]

By William L. Stone.

Probably no event, either in ancient or modern warfare, has received so many versions as the killing of Miss Jane McCrea during the Revolutionary war. It has been commemorated in story and in song, and narrated in grave histories, in as many different ways as there have been writers upon the subject. As an incident, merely, of the Revolution, accuracy in its relation is not, perhaps, of much moment. When measured, however, by its results, it at once assumes an importance which justifies such an investigation as shall bring out the truth in all its details. The slaying of Miss McCrea was, to the people of New York, what the battle of Lexington was to the New England colonies. In each case the effect was to consolidate the inhabitants more firmly against the invader. The blood of the unfortunate girl was not shed in vain. From every drop hundreds of armed yeomen arose; and, as has been justly said, her name was passed as a note of alarm along the banks of the Hudson, and, as a "rallying cry among the Green mountains of Vermont, brought down all their hardy sons." It thus contributed to Burgoyne's defeat, which became a precursor and principal cause of national independence.

The story, as told by Bancroft, Irving, and others, is that as Jane McCrea was on her way from Fort Edward to meet her lover at the British camp, under the protection of two Indians, a quarrel arose between the latter as to which should have the promised reward; when one of them, to terminate the dispute, "sunk," as Mr. Bancroft says, "his tomahawk into the skull" of their unfortunate charge.

The correct version, however, of the Jane McCrea tragedy, gathered from the statement made by Mrs. McNeal to General

---

[1] Reprinted from the *Galaxy* (New York), for January, 1867, with supplementary note, written by the author for the *Indian Miscellany*.

Burgoyne, on the 28th of July, 1777, in the *marquée* of her cousin, General Frazer, and corroborated by several people well acquainted with Jane McCrea, and by whom it was related to Judge Hay, of Saratoga Springs — a veracious and industrious historian — and taken down from their lips, is different from the version given by Mr. Bancroft.

On the morning of the 27th of July, 1777, Miss McCrea and Mrs. McNeal were at the latter's house in Fort Edward, preparing to set out for Fort Miller for greater security, as rumors had been rife of Indians in the vicinity. Their action was the result of a message sent to them early that morning by General Arnold, who had at the same time despatched to their assistance Lieutenant Palmer with some twenty men, with orders to place their furniture on board a *bateau* and row the family down to Fort Miller. Lieutenant Palmer having been informed by Mrs. McNeal that nearly all her effects had already been put on the *bateau*, remarked that he, with the soldiers, was going up the hill as far as an old block-house, for the purpose of reconnoitering, but would not be long absent. The lieutenant and his party, however, not returning, Mrs. McNeal and Jane McCrea concluded not to wait longer, but to ride on horseback to Colonel McCrea's ferry, leaving the further lading of the boat in charge of a black servant. When the horses, however, were brought up to the door, it was found that one side-saddle was missing, and a boy[1] was accordingly despatched to the house of a Mr. Gillis for the purpose of borrowing a side-saddle or pillion. While watching for the boy's return Mrs. McNeal heard a discharge of firearms,[2] and looking out of a window, saw one of Lieutenant Palmer's soldiers running along the military road toward the fort, pursued by several Indians. The fugitive, seeing Mrs. McNeal, waved his hat as a signal of danger, and passed on ; which the Indians perceiving, left off the pursuit and came toward the house.

---

[1] His name was Norman Morrison. It is not known with certainty what became of him, though tradition states that, being small and active, he escaped from the savages and reached his house in Hartford, Washington county, N. Y.

[2] So fatal was this discharge that out of Lieutenant Palmer's twenty men, only eight remained, Palmer himself being killed on the spot.

THE JANE MCCREA TRAGEDY.

Seeing their intention, Mrs. McNeal screamed, "Get down cellar for your lives!" On this, Jane McCrea and the black woman, Eve, with her infant, retreated safely to the cellar, but Mrs. McNeal was caught on the stairs by the Indians, and dragged back by the hair by a powerful savage, who was addressed by his companions as the "Wyandot Panther." A search in the cellar was then begun, and the result was the discovery only of Jane McCrea, who was brought up from her concealment,[1] the Wyandot exclaiming upon seeing her, "My squaw, me find um agin — me keep um fast now, foreber, ugh!" By this time the soldiers had arrived at the fort; the alarm drum was beaten, and a party of soldiers started in pursuit. Alarmed by the noise of the drum — which they, in common with Mrs. McNeal and Jenny, heard — the Indians, after a hurried consultation, hastily lifted the two women upon the horses which had been in waiting to carry them to Colonel McCrea's ferry, and started off upon the run. Mrs. McNeal, however, having been placed upon the horse on which there was no saddle, slipped off, and was thereupon carried in the arms of a savage. At this point Mrs. McNeal lost sight of her companion, who, to use the language of Mrs. McNeal, "was then ahead of me, and appeared to be firmly seated on the saddle, and held the rein while several Indians seemed to guard her — the Wyandot still ascending the hill and pulling along by bridle-bit the affrighted horse upon which poor Jenny rode." The Indians, however, when half way up the hill, were nearly overtaken by the soldiers, who, at this point, began firing by platoons. At every discharge the Indians would fall flat with Mrs. McNeal. By the time the top of the Fort Edward hill had been gained, not an Indian was harmed, and one of them remarked to Mrs. McNeal: "Wagh! um no kill — um shoot too much high for hit." During the firing, two or three of the bullets of the pursuing party hit Miss McCrea with fatal effect, who, falling from her horse, had her scalp *torn* off by her guide, the Wyandot

---

[1] Judge Hay was informed by Adam, after he became a man, that his mother, Eve, had often described to him how she continued to conceal him and herself in an ash-bin beneath a fire-place; he, luckily, not awaking to cry while the search was going on around them in the cellar. This was also confirmed by the late Mrs. Judge Cowen.

Panther, in revenge for the loss of the reward given by Burgoyne for any white prisoner — a reward considered equal to a barrel of rum.

Mrs. McNeal, however, was carried to Griffith's house and there kept by the Indians until the next day, when she was ransomed and taken to the British camp. "I never saw Jenny afterward," says Mrs. McNeal, " nor anything that appertained to her person until my arrival in the British camp, when an aide-de-camp showed me a fresh scalp-lock which I could not mistake, because the hair was unusually fine, luxuriant, lustrous, and dark as the wing of a raven. Till that evidence of her death was exhibited I hoped, almost against hope, that poor Jenny had been either rescued by our pursuers (in whose army her brother, Stephen McCrea, was a surgeon), or brought by our captors to some part of the British encampment." While at Griffith's house Mrs. McNeal endeavored to hire an Indian, named Captain Tommo, to go back and search for her companion, but neither he nor any of the Indians could be prevailed upon to venture even as far back as the brow of the Fort Edward hill to look down it for the *white squaw*, as they called Jenny.

The remains of Miss McCrea were gathered up by those who would have rescued her, and buried — together with those of Lieutenant Palmer — under the supervision of Colonel Morgan Lewis (then deputy quartermaster-general), on the bank of the creek, three miles south of Fort Edward, and two miles south of her brother's — John McCrea's — farm, which was across the Hudson, and directly opposite the principal encampment of General Schuyler.

The only statement which, while disproving Mr. Bancroft's relation, seems to conflict with the above account of the *manner* of her death, is the one made by Dr. John Bartlett, a surgeon in the American army. This occurs in his report to the director-general of the hospitals of the northern department, dated at Moses creek headquarters, at 10 o'clock of the night of July 27, 1777, and is as follows :

"I have this moment returned from Fort Edward, where a party of hell-hounds, in conjunction with their brethren, the British troops, fell upon an advanced guard, inhumanly butchered, scalped and stripped four of them, wounded two more, each in the thigh, and four more are missing.

"Poor Miss Jenny McCrea, and the woman with whom she lived, were taken by the savages, led up the hill to where there was a body of British troops, and there the poor girl was shot to death in cold blood, scalped and left on the ground; and the other woman not yet found.

"The alarm came to camp at two P.M. I was at dinner. I immediately sent off to collect all the regular surgeons, in order to take some one or two of them along with me to assist, but the devil of a bit of one was to be found. . . . There is neither amputating instrument, crooked needle nor tourniquet in all the camp. I have a handful of lint and two or three bandages, and that is all. What in the name of wonder I am to do in case of an attack, God only knows. Without assistance, without instruments, without everything."

This statement, however, was made, as is apparent on its face, hurriedly, and under great excitement. A thousand rumors were flying in the air; and there had been no time in which to sift out the kernels of truth from the chaff. But, in addition to this, the story of the surgeon is flatly contradicted by testimony both at the time of the occurrence and afterward. General Burgoyne's famous Bouquet order of the 21st of May, and his efforts, by appealing to their fears and love of gain, to prevent any species of cruelty on the part of his savage allies — facts well known to his officers and men — render it simply impossible to believe the statement of Surgeon Bartlett, that a "body of British troops" stood calmly by and witnessed the murder of a defenceless maiden — and a maiden, too, between whom and one of their comrades in arms there was known to be a betrothment. Leaving, however, probabilities, we have the entirely different and detailed account of Jenny's companion, Mrs. McNeal, "the woman with whom she lived," and who, as "the woman not yet found," was endeavoring — while the surgeon was penning his account — to prevail upon the savages to go back and search for Jenny's body, left behind in their hurried flight.

The whole matter, however, seems to be placed beyond all doubt, not only by the corroborative statement of the Wyandot Panther, when brought into the presence of Burgoyne — to the effect that it was not he, but the enemy, that had killed her — but by the statement of General Morgan Lewis, afterward governor of New York state. His account is thus given by Judge Hay in a letter to the writer:

"Several years after Mrs. Tearse had departed this, to her, eventful life, I conversed (in the hearing of Mr. David Banks, at his law-book store in New York), with Governor Lewis. Morgan Lewis then stated his distinct recollection that there were three gun-shot wounds upon Miss McCrea's corpse, which, on the day of her death, was, by direction of himself — and, in fact, under his own personal supervision — removed, together with a subaltern's remains, from a hill near Fort Edward to the Three Mile creek, where they were interred. The fact of the bullet wounds, of which I had not before heard, but which was consistent with Mrs. Tearse's statement, was to me 'confirmation strong as proof from Holy Writ' that Jane McCrea had not been killed exclusively by Indians, who could have done that deed either with a tomahawk or scalping-knife, and would not, therefore, be likely (pardon the phrase in this connection) to have wasted their ammunition. In that opinion Governor Lewis, an experienced jurist, if not general, familiar with rules of evidence, concurred."

This opinion of two eminent lawyers, as well as the statement of the Wyandot, receives, moreover, additional confirmation in the fact that when the remains of Jane McCrea, a few years since, were disinterred and removed to the old Fort Edward burial ground, and consigned to Mrs. McNeal's grave, Doctor William S. Norton, a respectable and very intelligent practitioner of physic and surgery, examined her skull, and found no marks whatever of a cut or a gash.[1] This fact, also, strongly confirms the opinion expressed at the time by General Frazer, at the *post mortem* camp investigation, that Jane McCrea was accidentally, or rather unintentionally, killed by American troops pursuing the Indians, and, as General Frazer said he had often witnessed, aiming too high, when the mark was on elevated ground, as had occurred at Bunker's (Breed's) Hill.

It thus appears, first, that Jane McCrea was accidentally killed

---

[1] Miss McCrea's remains have recently again been removed, for the third time, to a new Union Cemetery, situated about half way between Fort Edward and Sandy Hill. A large slab of white marble has been placed over the spot by Miss McCrea's niece, Mrs. Sarah H. Payne.

by the Americans; and, secondly, that the American loyalist (David Jones) did not send the Indians, much less the ferocious Wyandot, whom he abhorred and dreaded, on their errand.

Indeed, the falsity of this latter statement (which, by the way, General Burgoyne never believed) is also susceptible of proof. The well-established fact that Jones had sent Robert Ayers (father-in-law of Ransom Cook, Esq., now residing at Saratoga Springs), with a letter to Miss McCrea asking her to visit the British encampment and accompany its commander-in-chief, with his lady guests, on an excursion to Lake George, clearly shows how the charge against Jones had crept into a Whig accusation concerning supposed misconduct and meanness; and the dialogue (also well authenticated) between two of her captors, in relation to the comparative value of a living white squaw — estimated at a barrel of rum — and her scalp-lock, accounts, perhaps, for the story of the pretended proffered reward (a barrel of rum), alleged to have caused the quarrel among the Indians which resulted in the supposed catastrophy. All who had been acquainted with David Jones knew that he was incapable of such conduct, and so expressed themselves at the time.

The rumor, also, which is slightly confirmed in Burgoyne's letter to Gates, that Miss McCrea was on her way to an appointed marriage ceremony, originated in Jones's admission that he had intended, on the arrival of his betrothed at Skeensborough (Whitehall) to solicit her consent to their immediate nuptials — Chaplain Brudenell officiating. But Jones explicitly denied having intimated such desire in his letter to Miss McCrea or otherwise. "Such," he added, " was, without reference to my own sense of propriety, my dear Janet's sensibility, that the indelicacy of this supposed proposal would, even under our peculiar circumstances, have thwarted it." Indeed, this question was often a topic of conversation between General Frazer and Mrs. McNeal, who, with Miss Hunter (afterward Mrs. Tearse), accompanied him from Saratoga to Stillwater, and on his decease returned to Fort Edward after witnessing the surrender of the British general. Jones frankly admitted to his friends, that in consequence of the proximity of the savages to Fort Edward, he had engaged several chiefs who had been at the Bouquet encampment, to keep an eye upon the fiercer Ottawas, and especially upon the fierce Wyandot, and persuade them not to cross the Hudson; but if they could not be deterred from so doing by intimations of danger from rebel scouts, his employés were to watch over the safety of his mother's residence, and also that of Colonel McCrea. For all which, and in order the better to secure their fidelity, Jones promised a suitable but unspecified reward — meaning thereby such trinkets and weapons as were fitted for Indian traffic, and usually bestowed upon the savages, whether in peace or war.[1]

But partisanship was then extremely bitter, and eagerly seized the opportunity thus presented of magnifying a slight and false rumor into a veritable fact, which was used most successfully in stirring up the fires of hatred against loyalists in general, and the family of Jones in particular. The experiences of the last few years afford fresh illustrations of how little of partisan asseveration is reliable; and there is so much of the terrible in civil war which is indisputably true, that it is not difficult, nor does it require habitual credulity, to give currency to falsehood. One who a hundred years hence should write a history of the late rebellion, based upon the thousand rumors, newspaper correspondence, statements of radical and fierce politicians on one or another side, would run great risk of making serious misstatements. The more private documents are brought to light, the more clearly they reveal a similar, though even more intensified, state of feeling between the tories and the whigs during the era of the revolution. Great caution should therefore be observed when incorporating in history any accounts, as facts, which seem to have been the result of personal hatred or malice.[2]

---

[1] As showing how improbable exaggerations, originating in rumor, are perpetuated in print, reference is made to a book in the State Library at Albany, entitled, *Travels through America, in a series of letters, by an officer, Thomas Anbury*, 1783.

[2] NEW YORK, *Nov.* 1, 1876. — Before dismissing this subject, it may be well to state that the commonly received and romantic story, that Jones, the lover of Jane, never married, but died brokenhearted, is utterly destitute of truth. On the contrary, he married, and one of his grandsons, David Jones, as late as 1855, commenced four suits in the supreme court of New York state, for the recovery of the lands of his grandfather, confiscated by the state. He was unsuccessful, however; or failing to appear at the trial, judgement was rendered against him for costs in the suits on the 31st of October 1856. *Vide,* the files of the *Sandy Hill* (N. Y.) *Herald,* for 1874 and '75.

A VISIT TO THE STANDING ROCK AGENCY.[1]

BY DANIEL LEASURE, M.D.

On the morning of the 24th of July, 1875, I went on board of the steamer Josephine at Bismarck, bound for Standing Rock, one of the largest and most important of the Indian agencies on the Upper Missouri. Standing Rock is below Bismarck, about sixty miles overland, but more than double that distance by water. Our trip down was pleasant indeed. In the afternoon we passed Fort Rice, the point from which the Stanley-Custer expedition of two years ago started out. Fort Rice is an infantry post, though sometimes a company of cavalry is stationed there for a short time to look after marauding bands of roving Sioux. We stopped at the fort and I visited the commandant, an old army acquaintance, and an hour later left for Standing Rock.

After dark the steamer lay up for the night at a woodyard on the eastern shore, and the woodman came on board for late papers and news from the inside world. He was a rather well informed and intelligent man who had lived in that secluded spot for many years. He was a "squaw man," which is the name given to a white man who marries or cohabits with a squaw. His last wife before the one he has now was a Sioux, and they had two children, but one day, not long since, a band of Rees came along and killed and scalped her. On being asked if he did not feel her loss very much, he replied : "Of course I did; it cost me twenty good dollars to get another."

Next morning (Sunday) we arrived at the agency, and in company with a friend from Bismarck, I stopped off to await the return of the boat from below. I had imagined that the name Standing Rock was derived from some immense rock on the river shore, or some overhanging cliff constituting the main feature of the spot, and on inquiry, I was informed that the rock was some distance inland. Major Burke, the agent, was absent,

---

[1] Reprinted from the Pittsburgh (Pa.) *Evening Chronicle*, for August 21, 22, 1876, revised by the author for the *Indian Miscellany*.

but his son very kindly took us in an open spring wagon, through the various villages of the Indians, up to the lodge of Two Bears, head chief of the Yanktonnais, about four miles from the agency buildings. On our way up he stopped and told us that *there* was the Standing Rock. It was a little boulder about twenty-eight inches in height, by fifteen inches at the base, and eight inches at the top, and was painted over in various colors, and surrounded by pieces of gay colored ribbons, bead work and the ears and tails of small animals, and other tokens, indicating that the Indian women looked upon it as sacred, and came "to make medicine," in their domestic troubles, or in "white man's talk," to offer sacrifice.

The story or myth of Standing Rock is quite as respectable as many another found in the traditions of savage or semi-barbarian people. It is to the effect that "once upon a time," a young Arickaree woman, wife of a great brave, and who loved him dearly, was so mortified and spirit broken because her husband took a second wife, that she went out on the prairie and sat down and neither ate nor drank till she died, and the Great Spirit turned her into that standing stone. To this day, the women of a hostile tribe, the Sioux, who now occupy the country, hold it as a sacred thing, and offer to it their sacrifices to propitiate it, and secure its good offices for them in their no doubt sufficiently frequent little domestic difficulties. A man of ordinary strength could carry the stone away, but no one has ever molested it, and it remains a pillar of rock to mark the credulity of a simple and superstitious people.

On arriving at Two Bears village we found that he had gone to a sacrificial dance to the God of evil, at the village of the Blackfeet Sioux. His wives, four in number, all sisters (a fifth sister a wife also, being dead), were at home. His favorite daughter received us in state within her father's lodge, which is a double log cabin with sod roof and earthen floor. She was dressed in gay calico as plainly cut as an ordinary working woman's dress, with her hair carefully braided in two long plaits, and ornamented with narrow red ribbons hanging down behind her shoulders, her feet encased in very beautifully ornamented moccasins, and her face and the skin of the scalp, at the partings of her hair, painted vermillion. She was seated in state upon a buffalo robe, laid over a lounge bed, or divan, made of some empty candle boxes, with her hands folded in her lap, or playing with her ear ornaments, which consisted of a kind of shell called Iroquois, worked into a band about ten inches long by one inch at the part next the ear, and two inches at the most dependent part. This form of ear ornament is very much affected by both sexes, old Two Bears himself sporting an enormous length and breadth, so that they fall clear down over his breast. After talking awhile, through an interpreter, we found she wanted to marry a white man, who would be rich enough to support her in the style to which she has been accustomed, for she alone, of all her father's family, is relieved from the curse of squawdom — hard labor.

After the sacrifice at the Blackfeet village was over, Two Bears returned my call and invited me to call again, which I did, but the account of which I postpone for a description of the ceremony at the sacrifice to the God of evil, or Indian devil. This sacrifice is similar in its nature and objects to those offered by many savage tribes of men in all ages and all countries. The gods of nearly all primitive men are demons who delight in afflicting mankind, and are all supposed to be blood drinkers, and to be appeased by sacrifices of either men or animals, or, they are to be frightened or over-awed by self torture on the part of men, to convince them that no amount of injury or maiming can give them pain. Thus, they torture themselves and make no sign of distress in order to convince the demon that it is not worth his while to fool away his time tormenting them, for don't he see for himself, that they are insensible to pain, therefore he may spare himself unnecessary trouble in the vain effort to hurt them. With this explanation, the philosophy of that Sunday sacrifice at Standing Rock will be self-evident. A dog is killed by torture, and divided into four parts, which are put into four kettles and set on the fire till boiled tender, or till he is supposed to be as tender as a dog ought to be. A young squaw as near as possible to womanhood, but not quite a woman, supposed to represent chastity, then strips herself entirely nude, and to the sound of a low chant by her associates, and vigorous beating on a drum or tom-tom, performs a peculiar dance with a sidelong motion around the fire, on which are the kettles containing the pieces of dog, and all the time muttering some incantation. At a signal the young braves or old ones either, who wish to take part in the ceremony, in turn step up to one of the kettles, and, reaching in his bare hand and arm, takes out a piece of boiling meat, tears off a mouthful himself and swallows it, and passes it to his next neighbor, who must take it and eat of it in the same way, and so on they keep taking out the scalding mess and eating it till the skin of hands, lips and mouth hang loose in whitened shreds, and all this time no sign of pain or discomfort finds an expression on any face, and the seething morsels are slowly masticated and deliberately swallowed with a composure absolutely diabolical, and the miserable dupes feel themselves the better for it.

The sun dance is another sacrificial rite of torture, and is a form of sun worship in which that luminary is supposed to be a demon and highly pleased with the self-inflicted pains of his worshipers, and in return he gives them strong hearts to overcome their enemies, or bear with indifference the penalties of captivity. The young braves are admitted at once into the councils of the tribe after undergoing the terrible tortures of these ceremonies which are too horrible to bear description, and are falling into disrepute in proportion as the various bands of the wild tribes come under the influence of white men of the better sort.

There are three large bands of the Sioux at the Standing Rock agency, namely, the Yanktonnais, the Uncpapas and Blackfeet, numbering in all about eight to ten thousand, of all ages. The chief of the Yanktonnais, the noted Two Bears, is one of the most intelligent and fair men to be found among Indians. He is naturally a courteous gentleman, though but a few years ago he was a very " bad Injun," till General Sully defeated him and his band, and taught him the folly of contending against the mighty arm of the great father. Since that time he has been a peace man, and all his dealings with the whites have been honorable, though sometimes he has had sore provocation. But more of him hereafter. The other sub-chiefs of his band at the agency are Big Head, Black Eyes and Wolf's Necklace. The chiefs of the Uncpapas are Bear's Ribs, Running Antelope, Iron Horn, Thunder Hawk, and Belly Fat.

I had much talk, through an interpreter, with Running Antelope, who is constitutionally a blatherskite, and likes, above all things, to "shoot his mouth," as "talk making" is called on the border. He is now getting rather too old and fat to run very fast, but he has long been the mercury of the tribes, and has been admitted into the lodges of hostile bands as a messenger, when no other would dare venture into their power. His costume when he called on me was, in addition to the breech clout and leggins, a summer blanket made of four flour sacks, colored by prairie dust, worn negligently over his shoulders, and where the sweat struck through, seemed spotted with grease. At one time, a few years ago, he wanted the steamboatmen to pay his people for the use of the water to float their boats, and on being pressed for a reason, said, " they were wearing out the river,'' but he has gotten bravely over that now since he is an agency Indian, and gets his subsistence brought by the boats. He is a very shiftless individual and always wanting something. The principal chief of the Blackfeet band is Kill Eagle, and the next most noted is John Grass, whose Indian name signifies " the man who stops the bear." His wife is a half breed, and I believe it was at her desire that he accepted the white man's name of John Grass. I met all these chiefs and many of their soldiers or braves at the various villages or at the lodge of Two Bears.

While at Standing Rock some of the officers of the military post and attachés of the agency proposed that I should witness a "squaw dance." So about ten o'clock at night they loaded two barrels of hard tack, several boxes of raisins, a large box of candies, some webs of flashy calico and divers and sundry trinkets into a wagon, and we started for the village of Two Bears. The interpreter had gone before and given an intimation to the chief, who had sent out to the other villages for a reinforcement of young squaws. When we arrived, at midnight, they were all assembled to the number of about one hundred in their highest state of ornamentation of paint and feathers, though it is but fair to say that they were all modestly and becomingly dressed in plain calico dresses; many of them wearing over all, a dark blanket ornamented with large bands of handsome parti-colored beadwork. Though none of them were handsome, they all looked well, were neat and tidy and behaved with much decorum.

On our arrival the stores were taken out of the wagon and placed in Two Bears' lodge, and John Dillon, the agency farmer and contractor, himself a "squaw man," was master of ceremonies, and introduced me to the assembled chiefs as a big war chief and strong medicine man, a combination that strikes the Indian as something above the ordinary. Two Bears requested us all to be seated, my Bismarck friend and myself in the middle of the circle, and lighting his great pipe, he took a whiff and passed it to the "next gentleman," and after a whiff or two he handed it to the next, until it passed around and was refilled and passed again, all the while conversation going on; Dillon acting as interpreter. After our smoke a few strokes on the great drum called all hands to the council house which stood near at hand. It was a circular building of cottonwood logs, set perpendicularly, close to each other, and extending above the ground to a height of six feet, and covered with puncheons and sods, leaving an opening in the center for the escape of the smoke from the council fire. All the "bucks" (which is the term by which young male Indians are designated until they reach the honors of braveship) were excluded, and the soldiers of Two Bears formed a cordon of guards around the house to preserve order, permitting only the white men, the young squaws, with a few of the wives of the chiefs and the chiefs themselves, of whom there were about a dozen, to enter. The squaws and the white men formed a circle around the lodge; there being barely room enough for them all to get in. The great drum, composed of a hoop like an ordinary bass drum, with raw-hide heads, was swung on four forked sticks driven into the ground. Around the drum were squatted all the chiefs, each armed with a big drumstick, except Two Bears, who brought in an old candle box, and placing it beside the "band" seated me upon it, with my friend on my left and Two Bears on my right. At a signal the music burst forth, and such music! The chiefs chanted a song in a minor key at first, accompanying it by beating very good time on the drum. Presently the dancers started off in their part of the performance. Contrary to the commonly received idea of savage dances, there was no leaping or capering. Indeed the feet were not raised from the ground at all, but by alternate raising upon the toes and sinking upon the heel, with a queer dip at the knees and a side movement to the left so as to cause the whole circle to move around from right to left, they kept time to the music with great accuracy. The effect was most unique, and not by any means ungraceful.

As the dance went on, Two Bears got excited, and leaving my side on the candle box, squatted beside the drum, and seizing one of the sticks, gave a tremendous yell, and brought down his stick as though he was going to, as Dillon said, knock — out of it. Then raising the song into a higher key he infused new ardor into the dancers. One of his daughters, the princess, sprung out of the circle, and seizing my friend, pulled him off the candle box and into the ring, where he did some of the most astonishing things in the way of dancing to the great gratification of his dusky partner and her admiring friends. Momentarily I expected to be served in the same manner, but I suppose politeness and etiquette forbade, and I was unmolested.

It was a July night, and for want of a thermometer, we could only estimate the heat of that lodge by its effect upon the paint on the faces of the dancers and musicians, and it was determined to adjourn the dance to the outside. Soon a great fire was kindled, my candle box was installed alongside, the ring was again formed, and the word was, "on with the dance." But I now perceived that some of the white men had something in their souls more inspiring than music. Knowing that all were armed, and the bucks were jealous, I thought I had seen enough of the performance, and my friend and I retired with Two Bears into his lodge, where, after another smoke all around, we bade good bye to our host, and quietly stole away to our quarters at the agency at four o'clock in the morning. The rest of our party however, kept up the dance till sunrise, when the presents were distributed by Two Bears, and thus ended the squaw dance.

During my stay at Standing Rock, I had ample opportunities for observing the operations of the subsistence plan of pacifying the Indians and helping them toward civilization. A large portion of the adult males and able-bodied squaws were out on the annual antelope hunt, but daily coming and returning they exhibited a fair average of the whole population. They destroyed thousands of antelopes; Bear's Ribs having killed nine hundred himself, but very little of the meat was saved, those beautiful animals being mercilessly slaughtered for their skins, which are not worth more than an ordinary sheepskin. The killing taking place in July, with the mercury at more than a hundred degrees upon the blazing prairie, the preservation of the flesh could not be attempted, save as the squaws cut portions of it into slips and "jerked" it in the sunshine. Later in the season the skins would be worth more, and the flesh, which is delicious, could have been cured for winter use.

I visited the farm and gardens where white laborers had ploughed the ground and planted the crops, and depended upon the Indians to tend and keep them clean; but alas for the attention. The ground was smothered in weeds, and the poor crops were struggling against fearful odds, and yet, such was the fertility of the soil and the favors of the climate, that they would yield what in the east would be deemed a fair, average crop. The truth is, work is disgraceful, and no Indian of spirit would lower himself in the eyes of the squaws, for no squaw would respect a man who worked with his hands.

Standing Rock is a Sioux agency under charge of the Catholic church, and is, I think, as faithfully administered as is possible under the circumstances. The bands on the agency are no doubt of the better class of the large tribe or tribes designated Sioux. They do not call themselves Sioux, but *Dakota*, which means friends, and the other tribes, with whom they are always in a state of chronic unpleasantness, call them Sioux, which is a corruption of a French-Indian word meaning enemies, or cut-throats. They are no doubt a fair specimen of the best development of the Indians of the plains, who have made the first step towards civilization in acknowledging the right of private property. The men are rather above the average Indian in development and prowess, and the women are from necessity chaste. I say chaste from necessity, for although there are instances of unchastity, they are rare, because its punishment is terrible. If an Indian maiden of the Dakota tribe permits herself to receive unchaste advances from one of the bucks, he straightway boasts of it, and thinks it a merit to do so, in order that she may be "passed upon the prairie," which is equivalent to abandoning her to the unbidden lust of every man who meets her; and she can claim no protection. If she did, none would be given her, and the fear of hell has not more terror for civilized female sinners than the certainty of exposure and its swift penalty have upon their uncivilized sisters.

AMONG THE GUATUSOS; A NARRATIVE OF ADVENTURE AND DISCOVERY IN CENTRAL AMERICA.[1]

By O. J. PARKER.

[There are a few aboriginal or Indian tribes or families, scattered at intervals over the continent who, from their inaccessible position and other circumstances, have succeeded in maintaining an entire isolation from the rest of the world, and whose characters and habits are unknown, although probably little altered from what they were at the time of the discovery. An interesting example is afforded by the Guatusos, an Indian tribe occupying the basin of the Rio Frio, a considerable stream rising in the mountains of Costa Rica, and running northward into Lake Nicaragua, which it reaches at very nearly the point of debouchure of the Rio San Juan. Many attempts were made by the Spanish missionaries and others toward the close of the last century to penetrate into this region, but they all failed through the firm and unappeasable hostility of the Indians. An attempt was made by the Costa Ricans, during the war against Walker, in 1856, to send a body of troops down the Rio Frio, to surprise the fort of San Carlos, near its mouth, but they were met by the Guatusos and driven back. As might be expected the most extravagant stories prevail in Central America concerning these unknown and bellicose Indians. They are reported to be nearly white, with red hair, and to be as cruel as warlike. But these stories have recently been set at rest, and the secrets of the valley of the Rio Frio exposed by Captain Parker, who for several years was engaged on the steamers of the Nicaragua Transit Company, plying on the river San Juan and Lake Nicaragua. He undertook to ascend the river in 1867, in a canoe, and penetrated to the head of canoe navigation. We subjoin his simple and unadorned narrative of the expedition, which is now published for the first time.]

My curiosity to penetrate into the valley of the Rio Frio, explore its course and learn its capacities, as well as something of the strange people called the Guatusos, who live on its banks, was early greatly excited by the numberless stories I had heard concerning the Indians and their country, and I had not been long in Nicaragua before I resolved on the adventure. I, however, sought for companions in vain; everybody denounced the enterprise as hazardous and foolhardy in the extreme. Some years of service with the Texan Rangers, and my experience in river navigation, led me to think otherwise, and after a year or two of effort, I succeeded in raising a canoe party, consisting of three Europeans, named A. C. Roberts and José Pëlang, Franco-Californians, and C. Debbon, a German, long resident in Louisiana, to accompany me; all good canoemen and experienced shots. Of course we were well and heavily armed, and moreover furnished for a three months' journey. My canoe was of the

[1] Reprinted from Frank Leslie's *Illustrated Newspaper* (New York) for January 25, 1868.

ordinary kind in use upon the coast, twenty-two feet long, of a single cedar log, light and strong, capable of making six knots an hour with ease to three paddles, and drawing twelve inches of water with my party aboard.

Commencing our journey from San Juan del Norte, on arriving at Fort San Carlos, we were quite as agreeably as unexpectedly joined by Captain Hart, of the Transit Company's steamer, Granada, and two other Americans, William Hanger and William Godden, who offered to accompany us part of the distance on a hunting trip, game being very abundant near the mouth of the river. They brought a light double-oared boat with them.

Leaving Fort San Carlos at four o'clock A.M., August 8th, we reached a plantain patch eight miles up the river, belonging to the fort, at sunrise. So far, the banks and adjacent country were low and swampy. By climbing trees on the river side we were able to see numerous lagoons connected by channels with each other, and with the river. This being the height of the rainy season, many of these lagoons were deep lakes, miles in extent, around which the picturesque coyol palm and *gamalota* were fringed in the solitary but beautiful landscape, as far as the eye could reach, with here and there small clumps of larger timber pleasantly relieving the uniformity. The river itself at the mouth, and for many hundred yards into the lake, is much obstructed by sand banks and the alluvial deposit of the river, but there is a good though narrow channel to the westward, carrying four feet of water. A short distance from its mouth the stream becomes and continues of an average width of one hundred yards; depth five feet, with a current in general of one and a half miles per hour. The temperature of the water is at least ten degrees lower than that of the lake : it also is clearer, and of a bluish color. Game began to be very plentiful, particularly turkeys, ducks and water birds, and on the banks, deer, *guari* (wild-hog), and many varieties of the monkey-tribe. As we ascended the mouths of the creeks we frequently came across the remains of old fish-traps, and fish of many varieties were observed, especially the *guapote*, which is a fine-flavored, speckled fish, averaging five pounds in weight.

At four in the afternoon we reached a number of bends in the channel, and selecting a point in the left bank which we named Godden's bend, went ashore and built a camp, covering a frame of poles with swallowtail grass, known in the country as *sweety*, which began to be abundant. We adhered to a plan during the trip, which was put in practice the first night, to secure us from any surprise or attack, namely, that of building a large camp fire at fifty feet distance from our shelter, and stationing a guard thirty feet in an opposite direction, near whom the end of a long canoe line was made fast. Sand-flies and musquitos were numerous, but, having a large muslin bar, we slept soundly until daylight, having traveled thirty-five miles of deep water free from obstructions.

Early in the morning of the second day we discovered Indian signs, but not recent; and at nine A.M. entered Blue lake by a short, deep channel from the left bank. We did not cross it, but estimated its diameter at ten miles. It is fed by the river, through a channel at its south-eastern extremity, but two-thirds of the water thus received is discharged by a channel at the western side, which, possibly, is the Rio Negro, falling into Lake Nicaragua eighteen miles west of San Carlos.

Resuming our ascent of the river, we observed high banks of red clay, larger and greater varieties of timber, and a luxurious vegetation. About three P.M. we were much amused in passing an immense drove of large red monkeys (ringtails). They appeared for a while determined to ascend the river in our company, swinging along the highest branches with an indescribable amount of chattering and grimacing. Our lowest estimate numbered them at *fifteen hundred*. We camped at 4.30 P.M. on the right bank, distant from last camp twenty miles. At 9.30 P.M. heard Indians, and making a careful examination, could smell fire; however, passed the night undisturbed.

The third day we continued our course at daybreak. At nine A.M. arrived at the first obstruction in the river. This consisted in the accidental fall of an immense Balsa tree across the river, and through which we were compelled to cut a passage with axes. Close by the bank was tied a small raft, upon which had been a fire burning recently, and a quantity of freshly-cut plantains. Jumping ashore with Roberts, we struck into a well-worn path up the stream (in some places nearly a foot deep), but finding the trail cold, we returned to our party after an hour's absence.

At two P.M. saw another raft, upon which two Indians were cooking plantains. They jumped ashore immediately on perceiving us, taking with them their arms (bows and spears), and uttering the loudest cries. We hastened to follow them, but, encumbered and cramped as we were, no wonder without success. We had brought several articles of great value in Indian eyes to barter or give away. I had also a gay old uniform, which I was anxious to give to the chief, if we could only effect communications with the tribe. It was pretty evident that they possessed neither firearms nor cutlery — indeed, during our trip we saw no metal of any kind, manufactured or unmanufactured, in their possession. Their arrow-heads and axes are made of coyol (a hard black palm) and stone; their cooking and other utensils, of coarse red clay ware, similar to that used by the Indians of the lake, while the breech-cloth, which is their only covering, is simply a piece of *ule* (india-rubber) or *mahagua* bark, beaten into a kind of felt upon a smooth stone.

The trail upon the left bank is much better than the one upon the right bank of the river; the latter is perhaps solely used for hunting, or in passing along to the fishing-weirs, etc. We carefully selected our camping-ground, about four P.M., upon the left bank, on a high point, round which the river winds in a sudden curve, having made, by our estimate, twenty-five miles since morning.

Starting at daylight on the fourth day, we began to observe signs of cultivation, and after a while perceived on both sides of the river fair quantities of plantain, cassava, *kilisky*, papays, maize and cacao, the last remarkable fine, and the trees, from their great size, evidently old. At nine A.M. passed the entrance of a large sheet of water, Parker lake, which, however, we did not stop to explore, and an hour afterward came unexpectedly upon another Indian, who gave us a better opportunity of examining him, and I may as well take this opportunity of describing his appearance, and the characteristics of the tribe we encountered, so far as we could ascertain them. I can do so concisely, by stating that a Guatuso Indian, to the eye, in all respects, resembles a Comanche; but to those who may never have had the misfortune to meet this gentle specimen of humanity, I will add that in stature they average six feet, and in weight two hundred pounds, the females likewise being of large size. They are of a clear copper color, untainted, apparently, by admixture with either white or negro blood, and are perfect models of strength and muscular development. Their faces are somewhat broader, with higher cheek-bones than the Lake Indians, with coarse but not generally unpleasant features, whilst the long, straight black hair is allowed to fall around the body in both sexes until it sometimes trails on the ground. They were apparently without ornament, or rather disfigurement of any kind; and altogether, the appearance of us to the Guatusos fully justified the appellation of Wild Indians, in the strictest sense of the term, as applied by the natives of the country, who are, nevertheless, not a whit further advanced in the arts of horiculture, road-making, or in social progress than these Guatusos, and physically they are much inferior.

We arrived at a small island in the river at 11 A.M. (Hart's island); good channel along right bank. Constantly passed old rafts and deserted shanties, the latter being covered with *waha* leaf only, which is very perishable, and hence one would infer that the Guatusos villages are not located on the river; these buildings being merely used as occasion requires for visiting the plantations, collecting game, etc., and that the people permanently reside upon the slopes of the mountains, where they are not molested by musquitos and other troublesome insects, and where the position would be more open and agreeable.

From 11 A.M. to 4.30 P.M. passed great numbers of India-rubber trees on both banks, a belt fifteen miles long, and from one hundred to eight hundred yards wide. The most experienced rubber men of our party had never seen such an immense grove before. Several creeks likewise, which fell into the river on both banks, contained scarcely any other timber. The river here is less tortuous. We camped at 4.30 P.M. on the left bank, opposite Muddy creek, which some of the party declared contained more rubber than the river itself. We also saw several varieties of cedar of fine growth, and some mahogany. Estimated distance this day, thirty-five miles.

Finding plenty of fresh signs around our camp, I made the most of our position, which was naturally a good one, by cutting paths from it up and down the stream from camp, and remembering old times in Texas, I drove half a dozen stakes into the ground around the fire, upon which were hung the wet clothes of the party so as to somewhat resemble sitting figures. The guard was stationed near the point where the canoe was moored under a large chilimata tree. In the middle of the night I heard Indians down the stream, and rousing Roberts, heard them passing behind our camp, and soon afterward a slight crackling in the brands near the fire satisfied us of their immediate presence. Without disturbing the balance of the party, we lay waiting for "what would turn up," and shortly afterward an arrow flew with great force amongst the decoy stakes, striking one obliquely, and then glancing to the ground, where it firmly planted itself. Firing a couple of shots in the direction from which the arrow came, we heard no more of our visitors, and slept unmolested the rest of the night.

In reconnoitering the vicinity in the morning of the fifth day, we found a spot not half a mile up the river, where at least forty Indians had camped during the night. Fires were burning, and there were plentiful supplies of plaintains in every stage of ripeness ready for the morning's meal. We went ashore to examine the place, and tapped an immense India-rubber tree. At eight o'clock Captain Hart and his companions parted from us to join the steamer on the San Juan river.

Resuming our upward course alone at about 9.30 A.M., we reached the forks of the river and the head of steam navigation. At the mouth of the eastern fork, which appeared rapid, rocky and unnavigable, is a small island which would be of use as the site of the pioneer fort or depot. We therefore entered the western branch and with considerable labor ascended the channel, which is full of rocks, trees, bars and shoals, a distance of twelve miles, when we arrived at a broad gravel reach, about five hundred yards wide and nearly dry, over which it was impossible to pass the canoe, and referring to my log, found the distance from the mouth of the river to this point one hundred and thirty-five miles. Leaving the canoe, we proceeded a short distance up the channel, and sunk a hole on a bar in a favorable looking position for gold, but without finding a "color." However, while walking about the bars and adjacent banks, I picked up a piece of bluish quartz, which was subsequently assayed, and yielded very rich returns of both gold and silver.

The Marivalles mountains cross the head of this branch nearly at right angles, and at apparently a distance of two or three miles only. Their uniformity and general appearance would, however, lead one to suppose it next to impossible to find through them a pass for a practical road to the valley beyond. Toward the east, and most likely following the cañon of the eastern fork for many miles, is a great depression in the range, which would indicate this as the easiest, as it is the most direct route for a road of communication between the valley of the Rio Grande de Costa Rica and the head of navigation on the Rio Frio.

We cut marks upon several soto-cavalho trees with machetes, on the right bank, and commenced our return trip at three P.M. Between this point and the forks we saw in our ascent many groups of shanties, sometimes numbering a dozen together; but they were quickly vacated at our approach. Fires were left burning, and we saw the recent track of children's feet, heard dogs barking, and a great deal of noise made by the Indians in their flight. About four P.M., we came quietly within twenty-five feet of three Indians on a log at the riverside, shooting fish with arrows. Contemplating us for an instant with the most perplexed and curious air imaginable, they suddenly raised a great yell, and scrambled up the high bank with the most surprising agility. They, like all the rest, ran into the forest, screaming at the top of their voices.

Repassing the forks, we shortly after saw a man and woman landing from rafts tied to the right bank. On examination the ground showed unmistakable signs of at least three hundred persons having crossed quite recently from the left bank. Runing the canoe as quickly as possible alongside, we strenuously endeavored by words and signs to induce a parley. They were each armed with bows and spears, and "retreated in good order" to a plantain patch, making several stands meantime, as if to show us that fear had less to do with their movements than policy — and soon afterward commenced the usual yelling and screaming, which we unanimously agreed could not be outdone by any other tribe on earth.

Two miles below, and whilst regretting the futility of our efforts at communication with the Indians, we approached unobserved a raft tied to the right bank, upon which was seated an Indian busily engaged in plucking the feathers from a speckled bittern nearly the size of a turkey, which he had just shot with his bow, which lay beside him on the raft. When within a few feet of him, he first saw us, and instantly seizing his arms, ran ashore apparently in the greatest fury. He immediately fitted an arrow to his bow, but appeared to disapprove of it, changing it rapidly for another, we in the meantime by every means in our power endeavoring to arrest his movements and attract his attention, calling to him in the various Indian dialects with which we were acquainted — Spanish, French, and English — without any avail. Continuing his preparations amid the wildest cries and gestures, he at length drew the arrow full upon me as I sat in the stern of the canoe, and at the same moment dropped dead by a shot from our party. I very much regretted this unfortunate result, which I did my utmost to avert, strictly enjoining no shot to be fired in any event, unless we were surrounded by numbers, and I was willing to take the chance of the arrow-shot in hopes of securing the Indian afterward. He was about thirty years of age, fully six feet high, and of large, robust limbs. He had a large head, covered with hair reaching below the hips, which, combined with a savage expression of face, rendered his appearance and gestures somewhat more ferocious than fascinating.

After this unfortunate occurrence, we continued our descent of the river in heavy rain the whole night without stopping, passing Camp No. 2 about one A.M., and arriving at Fort San Carlos soon after daylight, or about fifteen hours after commencing our return. Captain Hart and party had arrived the previous night in safety. Allowing two miles per hour for the current, as the rain had raised the creeks considerably, and an average speed of six miles for the canoe, we have as the length of the river one hundred and twenty miles, of which distance one hundred and eight are capable of steamer navigation.

THE REV. JOHN ELIOT, AND HIS INDIAN CONVERTS.[1]

By Rev. Martin Moore.

No portion of history is more worthy of the careful study of the descendants of the Pilgrims, than that which relates to the life and character of the fathers of New England. We cannot indeed boast of a long line of illustrious ancestors, who have been distinguished by titles of nobility, or who figured in the days of chivalry. Our ancestors had a nobility, which many of the titled gentlemen of Europe never possessed. It was the nobility of high intellectual attainments, of stern integrity, and devoted piety. They were men of whom the world was not worthy. One of their own number, in the quaint language of those days, has given their true character. "God," said he, "sifted three kingdoms, that he might send over choice grain into this wilderness." The Pilgrims came to these shores to establish a church on the primitive foundation. Such men were Robinson, Carver, Bradford, Brewster and Winslow, the leaders of the Plymouth colony. Of the same spirit were Endicott, Higginson, and Skelton, who founded a plantation at Naumkeage, afterward called Salem, the town of peace. Winthrop, Cotton and Wilson, the leaders of the company that settled around Massachusetts bay, were men of the same cast. Davenport, of New Haven, Hooker and Stone of Hartford, partook largely of the same spirit. Men, who were so deeply embued with the spirit of Christ, could not be contented to see the Christian religion confined to their own infant settlements. The spirit of devoted Christianity has, in every age, been the spirit of missions. They looked upon the poor savages by whom they were surrounded, with compassion. They viewed them, as among that number whom Christ had died to redeem, and to whom he had commanded them to preach the gospel. Their sense of duty did not permit them to remain

---

[1] Reprinted from *The American Quarterly Register* (Boston) for February, 1843.

inactive. The Mayhews, on Martha's Vineyard, and Bourne, of Plymouth colony, labored successfully among these untutored sons of the forest.

But the most laborious and successful missionary to the Indians in the early days of New England, was the Rev. John Eliot, the first minister of Roxbury. He is commonly styled the apostle of the North American Indians. Mr. Eliot was born at Nasin, Essex county, England, in 1604. He received a strictly religious education, such as the Puritans uniformly gave their children. He was in after life grateful to his parents for their care of his education. They trained him up in the way in which he should go, and when he was old, he did not depart therefrom. "I do see," said he, "that it was a great favor of God that my early years were seasoned with the fear of God, the word, and prayer." After he left the university, he was engaged for several years in the instruction of youth. During this period, he sat under the ministry of Rev. Thomas Hooker, who afterwards founded Hartford, in Connecticut. Hooker exerted a salutary influence in the formation of his character. He came over to America in 1631, and was settled at Roxbury in 1632. The church in Boston was desirous to secure his services; but he had engaged himself to the company that came over with him, who formed the settlement at Roxbury. A young lady to whom he was pledged before he left England, came over the following year, and became his wife. He did not enter upon his missionary work until he had been located a number of years, at Roxbury.

Eliot commenced the study of the Indian language, when he was forty-two years old. It was an unwritten language, attended with great and peculiar difficulties. One word, for example, was expressed by thirty-two, and another by forty-three letters. He took a young Indian into his family, and by constant conversation, acquired the words, one by one, so that he reduced this spoken to a written language. At the close of his Indian grammar, he wrote the following sentence: "Prayers and pains through faith in Christ Jesus, will do any thing." He was greatly encouraged in his work by the neighboring ministers. They often supplied his pulpit while he was absent preaching among the natives. The Indians among whom Eliot labored, had a general belief in the existence of a great spirit, who created all things. They had also some vague traditions respecting the primitive state of man, the flood, etc. Their powows, or priests, had an entire control over them. If they were sick, they resorted to the powow to drive away the disease. They supposed that he, by performing certain incantations, could remove diseases, or deprive an individual of life. The first formal interview that Eliot had with the Indians, was at Nonantum, in the east part of Newton. The following is a partial account of this interview, in his own words:

"A little before we came to the wigwam, five or six of the chief men of them met us with English salutations, bidding us much welcome. Leading us into the principal wigwam belonging to Waban, we found many men, women and children, gathered together from all quarters, having been exported thereto by Waban, their chief minister of justice among them; who himself gave more hope of serious respect of the things of God, than any I have yet known of that forlorn generation. Being all there assembled, we began with prayer, which was now in English, we being not so acquainted with the Indian language, as to express our hearts therein before God, or them. When prayer was ended, it was an affecting, yet glorious spectacle, to see a company of perishing, forlorn outcasts, diligently attending to the words of salvation then delivered, and professing that they understood all that had been taught them in their own tongue. For about an hour and a quarter the sermon was continued; wherein one of our company ran through all the principal matters of religion; beginning first with the repetition of the commandments, and the brief explication of them; then showing the curse and dreadful wrath of God against all who break them, or the least of them; and so applying the whole unto the Indians then present, with much affection. He then preached Jesus Christ unto them as the only means of recovery from sin, wrath, and eternal death; he explained unto them who Christ was, and whither he is gone, and how he will, one day, come to judge the world. He spake to them of the blessed state of all those who believe in Jesus Christ and know him feelingly; and he spake to them also, observing his own method, as he was most fit to edify them, concerning the creation and fall of man — the greatness of God — the joys of heaven and the horrors of hell, and then urging them to repentance for every known sin wherein they live. On many things of the like nature he discoursed; not meddling with matters more difficult, until they had tasted more familiar and plainer truths. Having thus in a set discourse familiarly opened the principal matters of salvation to them, we next proposed certain questions to see what they would say to them, so that we by a variety of means, instructed them in things of religion."

Eliot sought to civilize as well as to Christianize the Indians. He had no hope of permanently benefitting them, unless they had settled habitations. Without this state of things, they could not be brought steadily under the influence of divine truth. He selected a tract of land in the east part of Newton, and called it Nonantum, which in their tongue signified *rejoicing*. This and other similar settlements that were afterwards formed, were denominated *praying towns*. The settlement at Nonantum was begun in 1646. It was removed to Natick in 1651. Eliot formed fourteen praying towns in Massachusetts. Natick still retains its original name. Nashobah is now called Littleton; Punkapag, Stoughton; Massanamissit, Grafton; Okommakamessit, Marlborough; Wamixit, Tewksbury; Magunkaquog, Hopkinton; Manchage, Oxford; Chabanakocumwomum, Dudley; Manexit, north part of Woodstock; Quintisset, south part of Woodstock; Wabquisset, south-east part of Woodstock.

Philip's war produced a disastrous effect upon these praying towns. He formed a confederacy among the natives for the purpose of exterminating the English. He used every possible art to draw the praying Indians into this league. The English on the other hand feared that they would turn traitors. The praying Indians stood between two fires. Both parties needed their assistance, and neither of them dared trust them. The number of praying Indians was about 3,000. The whole number of English was about 20,000. Philip's confederacy probably numbered less. It was quite an object with both parties, who were nearly balanced, to secure the praying Indians. The English were so fearful of them that at the commencement of the contest they dared not take them to the war. The general court finally removed them to Deer island in Boston harbor. In December, 1675, Gen. Gookin and Mr. Eliot visited them. "I observed in all my visit to them," says Gookin, " that they carried themselves patiently, humbly and piously, without murmuring or complaining against the English for their sufferings (which were not few), for they chiefly lived upon clams and shell fish, that they digged out of the sand at low water. The island was bleak and cold; their wigwams were poor and mean; their clothes few and thin. Some little corn they had of their own, which the court ordered to be fetched from their plantations, and conveyed to them by little and little; also a boat and man was appointed to look after them. I may say in the words of truth that there appeared much of practical Christianity in this time of their trial." One of their number thus bewailed his condition to Mr. Eliot: "Oh sir," said he, "I am greatly distressed, this day, on every side; the English have taken away some of my estate, my corn, my cattle, my plough, cart, chain, and other goods. The enemy Indians have taken part of what I had; and the wicked Indians mock and scoff at me, saying 'now what is come of your praying ot God?' The English also censure me and say I am a hypocrite. In this distress I have no where to look but up to God in the heavens to help me. Now my dear wife and eldest son (through the English threatening) run away, and I fear will perish in the woods for want of food; also my aged mother is lost, and all this doth aggravate my grief. Yet I desire to look up to God in Christ Jesus, in whom alone is help." Being asked whether he had not assisted the enemy in their wars when he was amongst them, he answered, "I never joined with them against the English. Indeed they often solicited me, but I utterly denied and refused them. I thought within myself, it is better to die than fight against the church of Christ." After the war had raged a while, the minds of the English were softened towards them. They let them go forth to the war under the command of English officers. General Gookin says that they took and destroyed not less than four hundred of Philip's men.

In 1686, a Mr. John Dunton, an English bookseller, visited Natick, the principal settlement of the praying Indians. He went out with a party to attend one of Mr. Eliot's lectures, and recorded the incidents of his visit as here follows:

"We had about twenty miles to Natick, where the best accommodations we could meet with, were very coarse. We ty'd up our horses in two old barns, that were almost laid in ruins. But there was no place where we could bestow ourselves, unless upon the green sward, till the lecture began. While we were making discoveries around the Indian village, we were informed that the sachem, or the Indian king and his queen were there. The place, it is true, did not look like the royal residence, however we could easily believe the report, and went immediately to visit their king and queen; and here my courage did not fail me, for I stept up and kissed the Indian queen, making her two very low bows, which she returned very civilly. The sachem was very tall and well limbed; but had no beard, and a sort of horse face. The queen was very well shaped, and her features might pass very well. She had eyes black as jet, and teeth white as ivory; her hair was very black and long; she was considerably up in years. Her dress was peculiar. She had sleeves of moose skin, very finely dressed, and drawn with lines of various colors, in arratic work, and her buskins were of the same sort; her mantle was of fine blue cloth, but very short and ty'd about the shoulders, and at the middle with a zone, curiously wrought with white and blue beads into pretty figures; her bracelets and necklace were of the same sort of beads, and she had a little tablet upon her breast very finely decked with jewels and precious stones. Her hair was combed back and tied up with a border which was neatly worked with gold and silver."

Tradition has handed down to us some anecdotes respecting individuals, which exhibit the shrewdness of the Indian character. Waban, at whose wigwam at Nonantum Mr. Eliot began to preach, was commissioned as a justice of the peace. Instead of having a long warrant, needlessly multiplying words, as legal instruments do at the present day, he was accustomed to issue his precepts in a very laconic form. When he directed his warrant to the constable, he simply wrote: "Quick you catch um, fast you hold um, and bring um before me, Justice Waban." On another occasion a young justice asked him what he should do with Indians after they had had a drunken fight, and entered a complaint against any of their number? His reply was, "Whip um plaintiff, whip um defendant, and whip um witnesses."

Mr. Eliot translated the Bible into the language of the Indians. He was often troubled to find words in the Indian language, owing to its poverty, to express the precise meaning. In translating the song of Deborah and Barak, where the mother of Sisera is represented as looking through the lattice to see her son return from the battle, he was at a great loss for an Indian word to express lattice; as they lived in wigwams, and had nothing about them that answered to this term. He called an Indian and described to him a lattice, as a wicker work, and wanted to know what word there was in their language that would convey the idea. The Indian could think of nothing but an eel-pot. The mother of Sisera looked through an eel-pot. He found that this word would not do; but what word he substituted I do not know.[1]

---

[1] Some facts respecting Eliot's *Indian Bible*, were published not long ago in the *Boston Recorder*, which it may be interesting for the reader to refer to in this connection.

Eliot's Bible was printed in Cambridge, in 1663, by Samuel Green and Marmaduke Johnson, under the immediate patronage of the society, which had been formed in England, for the propagation of the gospel among the Indians in New England, commonly called the Corporation. Johnson was sent over from England by the Corporation for the express purpose of assisting in this great work. Green had been connected with the press almost ever since it was first established in Cambridge. The Corporation, at first, had their printing done in England, but when Eliot had translated his catechism, etc., and eventually the Bible, into the Indian language, it became necessary that the printing should be done here.[1] The first materials for the work arrived in 1655. In 1658, it seems by the following record, Green petitioned, through the general court, for more types:

"At a General Court holden at Boston, 19th of May, 1658; in answer to the Petieon of Samuel Green, printer at Cambridge, The Court Judgeth it meto to commend the consideration to the Commissioners of the united colonies at their next meeting, that so if they see meete they may write to the Corporation in England for the procuring of 20 pounds worth more of letters for the vse of the Indian Colledg."

What is here called the Indian college, was the building used for the printing office. It had been erected by the Corporation, and designed as a college for Indian youth; but was afterwards taken for a printing office. The printing of the Indian Bible was considered — as it would be indeed at this day — a work of great magnitude. It excited the attention of the nobility in England, and the press of Harvard college became famous in consequence of it. Two editions of the Bible were printed. The first in 1663, which consisted of 1,000 copies. The whole cost of the edition, including 500 extra copies of the New Testament, and also an edition of Baxter's Call, the Psalter, and two editions of Eliot's Catechism, all in the Indian language, was about 1,200*l.* sterling. The second edition of the Bible of 2,000 copies, was completed in 1686, and cost considerably less than the first. Mr. Eliot gave a part salary of his towards it.

The Bible was printed in quarto, on paper of the pot size. It had marginal notes, and contained an Indian translation of the New England version of the Psalms. The title was as follows: "The Holy Bible: containing the Old Testament and the New. Translated into the Indian language, and ordered to be printed by the Commissioners of the United Colonies in New England, at the charge and with the consent of the Corporation in England for the Propagation of the Gospel amongst the Indians in New England." The title in the Indian language is as follows: "Mamusse Wunneetu-panatamwe Up-Biblum God naneeswe Nukkone-Testament kah wonk Wusku-Testament. Ne quosh-

---

[1] There was an Indian who had been instructed at the Charity school in Cambridge, to read and write the English language, who became a printer, and was called by the name of James Printer. He assisted in printing the Indian Bible. Within the last half century some of his descendants were living in Grafton.

A few of Eliot's converts entered Harvard College. A brick building was erected for their particular accommodation. Only one or two ever completed their collegiate course.

The work of converting the Indians was opposed, both by the powows and sachems. The people stood in awe of the sachems. Hiacoomes, a convert of the Mayhews on Martha's Vineyard, defied the power of the powows. In the midst of a great assembly on the island, the power of the powows was debated. One called

---

kinnumuk nashpe Wuttinnenmoh Christ noh osoowesit John Eliot. Nahohtoeu ontehetoe Printewoomuk. Cambridge: Printenoop nashpe Samuel Green kah Marmaduke Johnson."

It is impossible at this day to form any conception of the labor and patient industry which this work must have cost Mr. Eliot. To reduce to writing the rude language of the Indians, to translate into it the whole Bible, and then to superintend the printing by persons unacquainted with the language; and all this in the midst of unremitted efforts to bring the Indians to the knowledge of the truth, and in addition to his labors as pastor of the church in Roxbury — was an undertaking which might well have tired the strongest hand, and discouraged the stoutest heart.[1] It is striking illustration of the mutability of human affairs, that a book thus laboriously prepared, for enlightening a people then numerous, is now, in less than two centuries, a sealed book — the race of beings for whose benefit it was designed, is entirely extinct, and probably not a person on earth can read it.[2]

The Indian Bible was dedicated to King Charles the Second, who had encouraged the undertaking. The following extracts from the dedication, will interest the curious reader:

"*Most Dread Soveraign.*— We are bold to Present to Your Majesty the WHOLE BIBLE, Translated into the Language of the Natives of this country, by *A Painful Labourer in that Work*, and now *Printed* and *Finished*, by means of the Pious Beneficence of Your Majesties Subjects in England; which also by Your Special Favour hath been continued and confirmed to the intended Use and Advancement of so Great and Good Work, as is the *Propagation of the Gospel to these poor Barbarians* in this (Ere-while) Unknown World."

"And though there be in this Western World many colonies of other European nations, yet we humbly conceive no Prince hath had a return of such a Work as this. The Southern colonies of the *Spanish Nation* have sent home from this American Continent, much Gold and Silver, as the Fruit and End of their Discoveries and Transplantations: That (we confess) is a scarce commodity in this colder climate. But (suitable to the Ends of our Undertaking) we present the Fruit of our poor Endeavors to Plant and Propagate the Gospel here; which upon a true account, is as much better than Gold, as the Souls of men are worth more than the whole World. This is a nobler Fruit (and indeed in the Counsels of All-Disposing Providence, was an higher intended End) of *Columbus* his Adventure. And though by his Brother's being hindered from a seasonable Application, your Famous Predecessour and Ancestor, King Henry the Seventh, missed of being sole Owner of that first Discovery, and of the Riches thereof; yet if the Honour of first Discovering the True and Saving Knowledge of the Gospel unto the poor Americans, and of Erecting the Kingdome of JESUS CHRIST among them, be Reserved for, and do Redound unto your Majesty, and the English Nation, After ages will not reckon this Inferiour to the other. Religion is the End and Glory of Mankinde. And as it was the Professed End of this Plantation, so we desire ever to keep it in our Eye as our main design (both as to ourselves and the Natives about us) and that our Products may be answerable thereunto."

[1] There is a tradition — which we believe has the authority of Mather's *Magnalia* — that Mr. Eliot wrote the whole of his translation with one pen.

[2] "It remained for a scholar of our generation, Mr. J. Hammond Trumbull, of Hartford, Conn., to revive this extinct language, and he has found its study something more than the mere gratification of literary curiosity."— Field's *Indian Bibliography*, New York, 1873.

out, " Who is there that does not fear the power of the powows?" The powows were enraged with the praying Indians, and threatened them with immediate death; but Hiacoomes challenged them to do their worst. " Let all the powows on the island come together, I will venture myself in the midst of them all. Let them use all their witchcrafts, with the help of God, I will tread upon them all." The heathen Indians were astonished at the boldness of Hiacoomes. But they saw that no harm came nigh him, and they concluded that the God of the English was superior to the God of the powows. The gospel destroyed the tyranny that the sachems were accustomed to exercise over the common people. Hence they were all united in opposing its introduction. After a public lecture, a sachem used threatening and insulting language, and told Eliot that all the sachems in the country were opposed to the work. In giving an account of this interview, Mr. Eliot says, " I was alone and not any Englishman with me; but it pleased God to raise up my spirits; not to a passion, but to a bold resolution, so that I told him it was God's work in which I was engaged; that He was with me, and that I feared not him, nor all the sachems in the country; and that I was resolved to go on, do what they might." This bold reply caused the sachem to quail before the man of God.

King Philip felt the same hostility. After Mr. Eliot had presented to him the great truths of the gospel, he took hold of a button on Mr. Eliot's coat, and said, " I care for the gospel just as much as I care for that button."

The life of a missionary is not one of luxury and ease, but of toil and trial. He needs much of the spirit of Him that endured great contradiction of sinners, and came not to be ministered unto, but to minister. He is called to practice great self-denial. Eliot thus describes his own personal hardships on one occasion : " I was not dry, night nor day, from the third day to the sixth; but so traveled, and at night I pull off my boots, wring my stockings, and on with them again, and so continue, yet God helped. I considered that word 2 Timothy 2, 3. Endure hardness, as a good soldier of Jesus Christ."

In the times of Eliot there was no missionary periodical, through which he could communicate the results of his labors. He sent over to England an account of his success, and the hearts of Christians there were affected. Sir Robert Boyle and his friends formed an association to assist Mr. Eliot, which defrayed the expense of publishing two editions of his Bible.

Eliot lived to the advanced age of eighty-six. He brought forth fruit in his old age. After he was unable to preach publicly, he was accustomed to give instruction to the negroes, at his own house. Cotton Mather applies the words of Polycarp to Eliot. "These eighty-six years," said the holy man, "have I served the Lord Jesus Christ, and he has been such a good master unto me all the while, that I will not now forsake him." Eliot's last words were, "Welcome joy;" and he departed calling upon the bystanders, "Pray, pray, pray."

Mather applies to his death, what he was accustomed to apply to the death of others. When informed of the death of pious men, and asked what shall we do? he would answer, "Well, but God lives! Christ lives! the Saviour of New England yet lives! and he will reign till all his enemies are made his footstool."

The leading trait in Eliot's character was a desire to do good. This was indeed the secret spring of all his actions. He desired to do good in the best and highest sense. He wished to improve the temporal condition of the Indians, to break up their savage habits, and introduce among them the arts of civilized life. But his principal object was to bring them to be acquainted with the gospel. For this great and holy purpose of doing good, he reduced their speech to a written language; translated the Bible, and other religious books; made painful journeys in the wilderness; partook of coarse fare in their wigwams, and endured opposition from the powows and sachems. He was a true disciple of Him that went about doing good. He was equally ready to do good to his neighbors as to the sons of the forest. He was indeed sometimes guilty of overmuch generosity. So great was his charity that his salary was often distributed for the relief of his needy neighbors so soon after the period at which it was received, that before another period arrived, his own family were straitened for the comforts of life. One day the parish treasurer, on paying the money for the salary due, which he put into a handkerchief, in order to prevent Mr. Eliot's giving away the money before he got home, tied the end of the handkerchief in as many hard knots as he could. The good man received his handkerchief and took leave of the treasurer. He immediately went to the house of a sick and necessitous family. On entering he gave them his blessing, and told them that God had sent them some relief. The sufferers, with tears of gratitude, welcomed their pious benefactor, who, with moistened eyes, began to untie the knots in his handkerchief. After many efforts to get at his money, and impatient at the perplexity and delay, he gave the handkerchief and all the money to the mother of the family, saying, with a trembling accent, " Here, my dear, take it, I believe the Lord designs it all for you."

INDIAN LANGUAGES OF THE PACIFIC STATES AND TERRITORIES.[1]

By Albert S. Gatschet.

A few decenniums of research in our newly acquired western dominions have acquainted us with the singular fact that clusters of very numerous, and for the larger part narrowly circumscribed areas of languages exist in these vast and remote regions. In California, and north of it, one stock of language is generally represented by several, sometimes by a large number of dialects and sub-dialects; but there are instances, as in Shasta and in Klamath, where a stock is represented by one idiom only, which never had diverged into dialects, or the sub-dialects of which have become extinct in the course of time. Although certain resemblances between them may be traced in their phonological morphological character, they are totally distinct in their radicals, and by this criterion we are enabled to attempt their classification by stocks or families. Any other than a *genealogical* classification is at present impossible, for we do not possess even the most necessary grammatical data for the majority of the languages spoken along the Pacific coast.

For the western languages, and those of the great Interior Basin, our main sources of information are (and will be for many years to come) vocabularies of one hundred to two hundred terms each. Those obtained and published frequently bear the stamp of dilettantism, sometimes that of profound ignorance of linguistic science on the part of word-collectors, who wholly underrated the great difficulty of taking down a set of disconnected words in a totally unknown and phonetically unwieldy idiom. These word-gatherers would have fared much better, and collected more reliable material, if they had taken short sentences of popular import or texts containing no abstract ideas. For

---

[1] This paper was prepared especially for the *Indian Miscellany* in December, 1876, but was subsequently extended and published in *The Magazine of American History* (New York), for March, 1877, from which it is here reproduced.

an Indian is not accustomed to think of terms incoherent, or words disconnected from others, or of abstract ideas, but uses his words merely as integral parts of a whole sentence, or in connection with others. This is the true cause of the large incorporative power of the American tongues, which in many of them culminates in an extended polysynthetism, and embodies whole sentences in one single verbal form.

At a time when the principal languages and dialects of Asia, Africa and Australasia, the living as well as the extinct, are being investigated with uncommon ardor; myths, popular songs, dirges and speeches collected, published and commented upon with erudition and corresponding success, very few of the American languages, north and south, have been the object of thorough research. There is no scarcity of thorough linguists among us, but the reason for their want of activity in this direction simply lies in the want of proper encouragement from the authorities, the publishers, the press and the public. This is very discouraging, we confess; but it shall not hinder us from examining somewhat closer this topic, and from trying to get at the true facts.

The general public is very ignorant of languages and linguistics, and as a rule confounds linguistics with philology. Many people have a horror of philology because the Latin and Greek paradigms which they had to study in college classes, recall to them the dreariest days of compulsory education, juvenile misery and birch-rod executions. From these two languages they infer, superficially enough, that the study of all other foreign tongues must involve similar mental torments. Others believe that the Indian languages are not real tongues, deserving to be termed so; but only thwarted productions of the diseased heathen mind, because they do not agree with classical models, nor with the grammar of the primeval language of the world, the Hebrew, "which was spoken in paradise."

The majority, however, suppose that any Indian language is simply a gibberish not worth bothering about; they ought to remember that every language, even the most harmonious and perfect, is a gibberish to those who do not understand it, sounding unpleasantly to their ears, because they are unaccustomed to its cadences and phonetic laws. The mastering of a language is the only remedy against a certain repugnance to it on the side of the listener.

A further objection which is sometimes raised against studying the tongues of the red man, consists in the erroneous assertion that they have no literature of their own. This statement is founded on a profound ignorance of existing facts, and moreover, is only the expression of the old-fashioned, mistaken idea that languages should be studied only on account of their literatures, thus confounding philology with linguistics. Indians never did and do not write down their mental productions, simply because they do not trace their immediate origin from the Eastern races, from whom we have received the priceless gift of alphabetical writing; but that they really possess such productions, as well as the Malays, Polynesians and South Africans, no one can doubt who has read of Indian prophets, orators and story-tellers, with their fluency and oratorical powers, who has listened to their multiform, sometimes scurrilous mythological tales or yarns, heard their war-shouts, the words accompanying their dancing tunes, or in the darkness of the night overheard some of their lugubrious, heart-moving dirges sung by wailing women, as they slowly marched in file around the corpse of some relative, the whole scene lit up by the flickering flames of the lurid camp-fires. A volume of Schoolcraft's Indians contains a large number of Odjibway songs, and the author of this article has himself obtained over seventy most interesting and popular songs from the Cayuses, Warm Springs, Klamaths, Taos, Iroquois and Abnákis, in their original form. So the white race alone is to blame for its imperfect knowledge of the unwritten, often highly poetical productions of an illiterate race.

The science of linguistics is of so recent a date, that few men have yet grasped its real position among the other sciences. We must henceforth consider it as a *science of nature*, and reject the old conception of it as a science of the human mind. Stylistics and rhetorics of a language may be called the province of the human mind, but language itself is a product of nature, produced through human instrumentality. Man does not invent his language, any more than a bird does its twittering, or a tree its leaves. It requires a whole nation to produce a language, and even then such nation must start from phonetic elements already understood.

The innumerable agencies which give to a country its climate will also, by length of time, shape man and his language. Nothing is fortuitous or arbitrary in human speech and its historical developments; the most insignificant word or sound has its history, and the linguist's task is to investigate its record. Thus every language on this globe is perfect, but perfect only for the purpose it is intended to fulfill; Indian thought runs in another, more concrete direction than ours, and therefore Indian speech is shaped very differently from indogermanic models, which we, in our inherited and unjustified pride, are prone to regard as the only models of linguistic perfection. The Indian neglects to express with accuracy some relations which seem of paramount importance to us, as tense and sex, but his language is largely superior to ours in the variety of its personal pronouns, in many forms expressing the mode of action, or the idea of property and possession, and the relations of the person or persons addressed to the subject of the sentence.

Another prejudice against the Indian tongues is derived from the filthy or uninviting appearance of the red-skinned man himself. It is true that most Indians seem very miserable, disgusting, poor, silly, even grotesque and comical; yet this is partly due to the state of degradation to which he has been reduced by the land-grabbing Anglo-American settler, who has deprived him of his former, natural ways of subsistence; but it is also a characteristic of his cinnamon-complexioned race, and has been so for times immemorial. In the numerous settlements, where the condition of the Indian has undoubtedly undergone a great change for the better, through the advent of the white population, he seems just as miserable, shy, sad and filthy as before. To draw conclusions from the exterior appearance of a people on their language, and to suppose that a man not worth looking at cannot speak a language worth studying, would be the acme of superficiality, and worthy only of those who in their folly trust to appearances alone.

Pursuant to these intimations, I judge that the only means of bringing about a favorable change in public sentiment concerning the tongues of our aborigines, is a better understanding of the real object and purpose of linguistic science. Languages are living organisms, natural growths, genuine productions of race and country, and scientifically speaking, it is as important to investigate them as to describe minutely a curious tree, a rare plant, a strange insect or aquatic animal. But to gather information on them with success, a much more accurate method of transcription or transliteration than those generally used by word-collectors must be adopted. The old nonsensical method of using the English orthography, so utterly unscientific and unbearable to the sight of every instructed man, has at last been discarded almost universally. Only scientific alphabets must be here employed, and an alphabet can be considered as such only when *one* sound is constantly expressed by *one and the same* letter only. Such alphabets have been proposed by G. Gibbs, Professors Richard Lepsius, Haldeman, Alex. Ellis, and many others, and it would be a fitting subject for a congress of linguists to decide which system is the most appropriate for transcribing Indian tongues. Cursive Latin characters must be used, and in some cases, altered by diacritical marks, to convey peculiar meanings; the invention of new alphabetic systems or syllabaries like those of Sequoyah, and the hooks and crooks recently used for transcribing Cree and other northern tongues are not a help to science, because they are not *readily* legible or reducible to the accepted old-world systems of transcribing languages. A debate may also be started by a linguistic congress, what term should be employed instead of *Indian*, which is unsatisfactory in many respects; a thorough remodelling of the terminology used in Indian grammars would form another fruitful theme of discussion. Our indogermanic ideas of grammar must be entirely disregarded if we would write a correct grammatical sketch of some Indian language.

The vocabularies,[1] in the shape as we possess them now, are

---

[1] In 1875, the 29th year from its foundation, the Smithsonian Institution, in Washington, had collected texts, phraseology, and 771 vocabularies of about 200 words each, but for unknown reasons had published only a small portion of this enormous linguistic material.

useful in many respects. They do not give us much information about the structure of the languages, but serve at least for classifying purposes, and the small number of them which bear the stamp of accuracy in their notation of the accent and the use of a scientific alphabet, at least give a foothold for Indian phonology.

But men of science need a great deal more than this. Language is a living organism, and to study it, we must not only have the loose bones of its body, but the life-blood which is throbbing in its veins and forms the real essence of human speech. Not the stems or words alone, but the inflectional forms, the syntactical shaping of the spoken word and the sentence itself are desideratums mostly craved for. Linguists must therefore, as reliable grammars and full dictionaries (all the words properly accentuated!) cannot be expected at once, place their hopes in collections of *texts* illustrating the native customs and manners, the religious beliefs, superstitions, scraps of Indian history, speeches, dialogues, songs and dirges, descriptions of manufactured articles, and of the houses, tools, implements and dress of each nation and tribe visited.

These texts should be given *in the Indian language*, and accompanied by a very accurate, and if possible, an interlinear and verbal translation of the items. All the commentaries and remarks needed for a full understanding of the texts should be added to it. The more material is furnished in this way, the better our linguists will be enabled to disclose the hidden scientific treasures stored up in these curious, but now almost unknown, forms of human speech, and to present them to the world, in the shape of grammars, dictionaries and anthologies of aboriginal prose and poetry. To the ethnologist such texts will be just as valuable as to the historian and the linguist.

The Languages of the Western Slope.

A most singular fact disclosed by the topography of language-stocks all over the world is the enormous difference of the *areas* occupied by the various families. In the eastern hemisphere, we see the Uralo-Altaic, the Chinese, the Indogermanic, Semitic and Dravidian, the Pullo and the Congo-Kafrian or Ba'-ntu family of languages, extending over areas much wider or as wide as the Tinné, Shóshoni, Algónkin, Dakóta, Cháhta-Máskoki and Guaraní stock, while small areas are, perhaps, as numerous in the eastern hemisphere as in the western. Their size evidently depends on the configuration and surface-quality of the lands, which again determine the mode of the subsistence of their inhabitants.

The natives of a country, when not influenced by the civilization of the white race, will in barren plains, steppes, prairies and woodland, generally become hunters; on the shores of the sea and on the banks of the larger rivers, they will resort to fishing, and sometimes, when settled on the coast, turn pirates or form smaller maritime powers, while the inhabitants of table-lands will till the fields, plant fructiferous trees, or collect esculent roots for their sustenance. Of these three modes of sustenance we see frequently two combined in one tribe. The fishers live peacefully and in *small* hordes, because large settlements, on *one* spot of a river bank at least, could not be supplied at all seasons of the year with a sufficient supply of fish from the river. Hunters become, from their nomadic habits, accustomed to a restless, adventurous life, and in their thus acquired warlike disposition will constantly threaten their weaker neighbors; if opportunity offers itself will declare war, overwhelm and enslave or destroy them, and thereby extend the dominion of their own language over a wider area. Agricultural pursuits bear in themselves the germs of steadiness, of order and progress; countries settled and improved by agriculturists will gradually, when the population becomes more dense, consolidate into oligarchies or monarchies, generally of a despotic character. Such political bodies have frequently absorbed neighboring communities engaged in similar pursuits, and turned with them into powerful empires, as in the case of the Aztecs, Mayas, Chibchas and Quichhuas, in the western hemisphere. For obvious reasons pastoral pursuits were almost entirely unknown in America, but were powerful agents of culture in Asia and Europe, since they facilitated the transition from the hunter or nomadic state to the state of agriculturists.

Indian Languages of the Pacific States. 423

California and portions of the Columbia river basin, with their numerous rivers and the enormous quantity of salmon, trout and lamprey eel ascending annually their limpid waters, were essentially countries occupied by fisher-tribes, and before the advent of the white man, are supposed to have harbored a dense native population. Among these fisher-tribes we also find the smallest areas of languages; six of them are crowded on the two banks of the Klamath river and many more around the Sacramento, although these streams do not exceed in length, respectively, 250 and 400 miles. To produce or preserve so many small language families, totally distinct from each other in their radicals, these tribes must have lived during very long periods in a state of comparative isolation, and have remained almost untouched by foreign invaders, protected as they were by the sea coast, and by the high-towering wall of the snow-capped Sierra Nevada.

In the wide basin of the upper Columbia river several tribes hunting the bear, buffalo, elk, deer and antelope, roam over the thinly populated prairies, and occupy enormous tracts of barren and sage-brush plains. Hunting tribes need a wide extent of territory, and when it is refused to them they will fight for it. Thus originate the constant wars of extermination among many of these tribes, and their encroachments over others in regard to territory. Of this we find the most conspicuous instances among the nomadic tribes roving between the Rocky mountains and the Mississippi river.

In their morphological character the languages of America do not differ materially from the Asiatic tongues of agglutinative structure, except by their more developed power of polysynthetism. But in many of their number this faculty remains only in an embryonic state, and by dint of a far-going analysis, some of them approach the structure of our modern European analytic languages. Still, in a number of others, the incorporative tendency prevails in a high degree; they are synthetic as much as the Latin, Greek or Gothic — many of them superlatively so. They use not only prefixes and affixes, as we do, but also infixes, viz: particles, or particle-fragments, inserted into the stem. As a general thing, American languages are not sex-denoting, though we find a distinction of sex in the dual of the Iroquois *verb*, and in some Central American verb-inflections, where *he* is distinguished from *she* in the personal pronoun. A true substantive verb *to be* is not found in any American language,[1] and the word-stems have not undergone that process of thorough differention between noun and verb which we observe in German, English, and French. These three languages we call accentuating, since the quantity of their syllables is of relative importance only, the influence of the accentuation being paramount. In many American languages we observe, on the contrary, that accent shifts from syllable to syllable, though only in a restricted number of words, and that instead of the accent length and brevity of the syllables receive closer attention. Such idioms we may call quantitating languages, for their system of prosody does not seem to differ much from those of the classical languages.

No plausible cause can as yet be assigned for the frequent, perhaps universal, interchangeability of b with p, d with t and n, g with k, χ, and the lingual k, m with b and v (w), hh with k, χ; but as there is nothing fortuitous in nature or in language, a latent cause *must* exist for this peculiarity. No preceding or following sound seems to have any influence on this alternating process, and the vowels alternate in a quite similar manner.

From these general characteristics, to which many others could be added, we pass over to those peculiarities which are more or less specific to the languages of the Pacific slope. It is not possible to state any absolute, but only some relative and gradual differences between these western tongues and those of the east, of which we give the following:

The generic difference of animate, inanimate, and neuter nouns, is of little influence on the grammatical forms of the Pacific languages. A so-called *plural* form of the transitive and intransitive verb exists in Selish dialects, in Klamath, Mutsun, San Antonio (probably also in Santa Barbara), and in the Shóshoni dialects of Kauvuya and Gaitchin. Duplication of the entire

---

[1] Full and detailed information concerning the structure prevailing in American languages, will be found in Prof. J. H. Trumbull's article on *Indian Languages*, in Johnson's New Cyclopædia, vol. II. New York, 1875.

root, or of a portion of it, is extensively observed in the formation of frequentative and other derivative verbs, of augmentative and diminutive nouns, of adjectives (especially when designating colors), etc., in the Selish and Sahaptin dialects, in Cayuse, Yakon, Klamath, Pit River, Chokoyem, Cop-éh, Cushna, Santa Barbara, Pima, and is very frequent in the native idioms of the Mexican states. The root or, in its stead, the initial syllable, is redoubled regularly, or frequently, for the purpose of forming a (distributive) plural of nouns and verbs in Selish dialects, in Klamath, Kizh, Santa Barbara, and in the Mexican languages of the Pimas, Opatas (including Heve), Tarahumaras, Tepeguanas, and Aztecs.

A definite article *the*, or a particle corresponding to it in many respects, is appended to the noun, and imparts the idea of actuality to the verb in Sahaptin, Klamath, Kizh, Gaitchin, Kauvuya, Mohave. In San Antonio this article is placed *before* the noun. The practice of appending various classifiers or determinatives to the cardinal numerals, to point out the different qualities of the objects counted, seems to be general in the Pacific tongues, for it can be traced in the Selish proper, in the Nisqualli (a western Selish dialect), in Yákima, in Klamath, in Noce or Noze, and in Aztec. In De la Cuestas' Mutsun grammar, however, no mention is made of this synthetic feature.

The phonological facts, most generally observed throughout the coast lands, from Puget sound to San Diego, are as follows: Absence of the labial sound *F* and of our rolling *R* (the guttural *kh* or χ is often erroneously rendered by *r*): comparative scarcity of the medial or soft mutes as initial and final consonants of words; frequency of the *k*, or croaking, lingual *k*, identical with the *c castañuelas* of the south; sudden stops of the voice in the midst of a word or sentence; preponderance of clear and surd vowels over nasalized vowels. From all the information obtainable at present, we can properly infer that all the above mentioned peculiarities will by future investigators be discovered to exist also in many *other* tongues of our Pacific states. In the northern sections the consonantic elements predominate to an enormous degree, sometimes stifling the utterance of the vowels; many southern tongues, on the contrary, show a tendency towards vocalism, though the consonantic frame of the words is not in any instance disrupted or obliterated by the vocalic element, as we observe it in Polynesia. Languages, with a sonorous, sweet, soft, and vocalic utterance, and elementary vocalism, are the Mohave, Hualapai, Meewoc, Tuólumne and Wintoon (and Kalapupa further north), while the dialects of the Santa Barbara stock seem to occupy an intermediate position between the above and the northern languages.

Unnumbered tongues have in the course of centuries disappeared from the surface of these western lands, and no monuments speak to us of their extent, or give a glimpse at the tribes which used them. Many others are on the verge of extinction: they are doomed to expire under the overpowering influx of the white race. Other languages labor under the continued influence of linguistic corruption and intermixture with other stocks, and the Chinook jargon seems to make havoc among the tongues of the Columbia river. To transmit these languages to posterity in their unadulterated state, is not yet altogether impossible in the decennium in which we live, and would be a highly meritorious undertaking. It would be equivalent almost to rescuing these remarkable linguistic organisms from undeserved oblivion.

In the subsequent pages I attempt to give a synoptical survey of our Pacific language-stocks west of the Rocky mountains (excluding the pueblos of New Mexico and Arizona), based on the writings of such predecessors as George Gibbs, Latham, H. H. Bancroft, Stephen Powers, and I have taken pains to carefully compare their data with the linguistic material available. For obvious reasons, I have found myself frequently constrained to dissent from them, and I claim the decision of men of undoubted competency concerning the correctness of my classifications.

SHÓSHONI.— The Shóshoni family borders and encircles all the other stocks of the Pacific slope of the United States, on the *eastern side*, and my enumeration, therefore, commences with the dialects of this populous and widely-scattered inland nation. The natives belonging to this race occupy almost the whole surface of the great American inland basin, extending from the Rocky mountains to the Sierra Nevada. To the northeast, and all along the western border, they have crossed these towering land-marks, constructed by nature itself, but do not appear to have interfered considerably with the original distribution of the tribes in the Californian valleys and mountain recesses. The dispositions evinced by them are more of a passive and indolent than of an aggressive, offending or implacable nature, though they are savages in the truest sense of the word; some bands of Utahs, for instance, really seem too low-gifted ever to become a cause for dread to peaceful neighbors. We do not yet understand any of their numerous dialects thoroughly, but as far as the southern dialects are concerned, a preponderance of surd and nasalized *a*, *o* and *u* vowels over others is undoubted. They all possess a form for the plural of the noun; the Comanche, even one for the dual. Their dialects, are sketched in the rough, as follows:

Snake.—This dialect received its name from the Shóshoni, Lewis or Snake river, on whose shores one of the principal bands of Snake Indians was first seen. Granville Stuart, in his *Montana as it is* (New York, 1865), gives the following ethnological division: *Washakeeks*, or Green river Snakes, in Wyoming: *Tookarikkah*, or Salmon river Snakes (literally, Mountain-sheep eaters), in Idaho. These two bands he calls genuine Snakes. Smaller bands are those of the *Salt Lake Diggers* in Utah, the *Salmon Eaters* on Snake river, the root-digging *Bannocks* or *Panashl*, on Boisé, Malheur and Owyhee rivers, and a few others, all of whom differ somewhat in their mode of speech. Snakes of the *Yahooshkin* and *Walpahpe* bands were settled recently on Klamath reserve in Oregon, together with a few Piutes.

Utah (*Yutah, Eutaw, Ute;* Spanish, *Ayote*), is spoken in various dialects in parts of Utah, Wyoming and Arizona territories, and in the western desert regions of Colorado, where a reservation of Confederated Utes has been established, with an area of twelve millions of acres. To draw an accurate limit between the numerous bands of the Utahs, and those of the Snakes and Payutes seems to be impossible at present, since all of them show the same national characteristics; I give the names of some of the more important bands of Utah Indians, which no doubt differ to a certain degree in their sub-dialects: *Elk Mountain Utahs* in southeastern Utah; *Pah-Vants* on Sevier lake, southeast of Salt lake; *Sampitches*, on Sevier lake and in Sampitch valley; *Tash-Utah* in northern Arizona; *Uinta-Utahs* in Unitah valley reserve; *Weber-Utahs*, northeast of Salt lake; *Yampa-Utahs*, south of the Uinta-Utahs.

Payute — (*Pah-Utah*, *Pi-Ute* — literally, River-Utah; Utah, as spoken on Colorado river), a sonorous, vocalic dialect, spoken throughout Nevada, in parts of Arizona and California. The dialect of the Southern Payutes on Colorado river closely resembles that of the neighboring *Chemehuevis*, but differs materially from that spoken in northern Nevada, and from the dialect of Mono and Inyo counties, California. Other Payute tribes are the Washoes and Gosh-Utes.

Kauvuya — (*Cáwio*; Spanish, *Cahuillo*). This branch of the Shóshoni stock prevails from the Cabezon mountains and San Bernardino valley, California, down to the Pacific coast, and is at present known to us in four dialects: *Serrano*, or mountain dialect, spoken by Indians, who call themselves Takhtam, which means men, people. *Kauvuya*, in and around San Bernardino valley. *Gaitchin* or *Kechi*, a coast dialect in use near the missions of San Juan Capistrano and San Luis Rey de Francia. *Netéla* is another name for it. *Kizh*, spoken in the vicinity of the mission of San Gabriel by a tribe calling itself Tobikhar, or settlers, and of San Fernando mission, almost extinct. The two last mentioned dialects considerably differ among themselves, and from the mountain dialects of the Takhtam and Kauvuyas.

Comanche, formerly called *Hietan*, *Jétan*, *Na-uni*, in northern Texas, in New Mexico and in the Indian territory. They are divided into three principal sections, and their language resembles in a remarkable degree that of the Snakes.

Various Shóshoni dialects have largely influenced the stock of words of a few idioms, which otherwise are foreign to this family. We mean the Pueblo idioms of New Mexico, the Moqui of Arizona, and the Kiowa, spoken on Red river and its tributaries. There exists a deep-seated connection between the Shóshoni stock and several languages of northern Mexico in the radicals, as well as in the grammatical inflections, which has been pointed out and proved in many crudite treatises by Professor T. C. E. Buschmann, once the collaborator of the two brothers Alexander and William von Humboldt.

YUMA.— The Indians of the Yuma stock are scattered along the borders of the Lower Colorado and its affluents, the Gila river and the Bill Williams fork. Their name is derived from one of the tribes — the Yumas — whom their neighbors frequently call Cuchans or Ko-u-tchans. Some dialects, as the Mohave, possess a large number of sounds or phonetic elements, the English *th* amongst them, and are almost entirely built up of syllables, which contain but one consonant followed by a vowel. The verb possesses a plural form. At present we know of about seven dialects: *Mohave* (Spanish *Mojave*), on Mohave river and on Colorado river reservation; *Hualapai*, on Colorado river agency; *Maricopa*, formerly Cocomaricopa, on Pima reservation, Middle Gila river. *Tonto*, Tonto-Apaches or *Gohun*, on Gila river and north of it; *Cocopa*, near Fort Yuma and south of it; *Cuchan* or Yuma, on Colorado river; their former seats were around Fort Yuma; *Diegeño* and *Comoyei*, around San Diego, along the coast, on New river, etc.

Scattered tribes are the kóninos, and the Yavipais or Yampais, east of the Colorado river. The term *opa*, composing several of these tribal names, is taken from the Yuma, and means *man;* the definite article -*tch* joined to it forms the word *épach* or *Apache*, man, men, people.

PIMA.— Dialects of this stock are spoken on the middle course of the Gila river, and south of it on the elevated plains of southern Arizona and northern Sonora, (Pimería alta, Pimería bá ja). The Pima does not extend into California, unless the extinct, historical *Cajuenches*, mentioned in Mexican annals, spoke one of the Pima (or Pijmo, Pimo) dialects. *Pima*, on Pima reserve, Gila river, a sonorous, root-duplicating idiom; *Névome*, a dialect probably spoken in Sonora, of which we possess a reliable Spanish grammar, published in Shea's Linguistics; *Pápago*, on Pápago reserve in southwestern Arizona. The Pima language bears a close relationship to the various dialects of the Opata family and to a number of languages spoken in the interior Mexican states.

SANTA BARBARA.— We are not cognizant of any national name given to the race of Indians who spoke the intricate dialects of this language-family. Its northern dialects differ as much from the southern as Minitaree does from Santee-Dakota, or Scandinavian from the dialects of southern Germany.

The southern dialects are: *Santa Inez*, near Santa Inez mission; liturgic specimens, translations of parts of catechisms, etc., of this dialect, and of that of Santa Barbara mission, were forwarded to the Smithsonian Institution by Mr. Alex. S. Taylor, of Santa Barbara city; *Santa Barbara*, around Santa Barbara mission, closely related to *Kasud* or *Kashwdh*, Spanish Cieneguita, three miles from Santa Barbara mission; *Santa Cruz island*, this dialect reduplicated the root in forming the plural of nouns, and probably extended over the other islands in its vicinity; it is extinct now.

The northern dialects are: *San Louis Obispo;* stock of words largely mixed with Mutsun terms. The Indian name of the locality was Tixilini. *San Antonio*, spoken at or near San Antonio mission, known to us through Padre Sitjar's dictionary. The plural of nouns is formed in more than twelve different ways, and the phonology is quite intricate.

MUTSUN.— This name, of unknown signification, has been adopted to designate a family of dialects extending from the environs of San Juan Bautista, Cal., in a northwestern direction up to and beyond the bay of San Francisco and the straits of Karquines, in the east reaching probably to San Joaquin river. It is identical with the language called *Runsien* or *Rumsen*, and shows a great development of grammatical forms. Its alphabet lacks the sounds of *b, d, f* and of our rolling *r*. We can distinguish the following dialects: *San Juan Bautista;* Padre F. Felipe Arroyo de la Cuesta has left us a grammar and an extensive phraseological collection in this idiom, which were published by John G. Shea, in two volumes of his Linguistic Series. *Mission of Carmelo*, near the port of Monterey; the Eslenes inhabited its surroundings. *Santa Cruz*, north of the bay of Monterey; vocabulary in *New York Historical Magazine*, 1864 (Feb.), page 68. *La Soledad mission;* if this dialect, of whose grammatical structure we know nothing, really belongs to the Mutsun stock, it is at least largely intermixed with San Antonio elements. The tribe living around the mission was called Sakhones. *Costaño*, on the bay of San Francisco, spoken by the five extinct tribes of the Ahwastes, Olhones, Altahmos, Romonans, Tulomos. See Schoolcraft's Indians, vol. II, page 494.

Under the heading of "Mutsun" I subjoin here a series of dialects spoken north of the bay of San Francisco, which judging from the large number of Mutsun words, probably belong to this stock, but show also a large amount of Chocuyem words, which dialect is perhaps not, according to our present information, a Mutsun dialect. This point can be decided only when its grammatical elements, as verbal inflection, etc., will be ascertained.

The dialects, showing affinities with Mutsun, are as follows: *Olamentke*, spoken on the former Russian colony about Bodega bay, Marin Co.; vocabulary in Wrangell, Nachrichten, etc., St. Petersburg, 1839, and reprinted by Prof. Buschmann. *San Rafael mission*, Marin Co. Vocabulary taken by Mr. Dana; printed in Hale's Report of Exploring Expedition, and in *Transactions of American Ethnological Society*, II, page 128; the words are almost identical with those of Chocuyem. *Talatui* or *Talantui*, on Kassima river, an eastern tributary of the Sacramento, is clearly a dialect of Chocuyem; vocabulary by Dana, *Tr. Am. Ethn. Soc.*, vol. II. *Chokuyem* or *Tchokoyem* was the name of a small tribe once inhabiting Marin county, north of the Golden Gate. Their language extended across San Antonio creek into Sonoma valley, Sonoma Co. G. Gibbs's vocabulary published in Schoolcraft, III, 428-sq, discloses the singular fact that almost all Chocuyem words are *dissyllabic*, and frequently begin and termi nate in vowels. A Lord's prayer in Chocuyem was published in Duflot de Mofras' Explorations, II, 390, and reproduced by Bancroft; the name of the tribe living around the mission of San Rafael was Youkiousmé, which does not sound very alike, nor very different from Chocuyem. Some of the more important terms agreeing in the Chocuyem and in the Mutsun of San Bautista, are as follows:

ENGLISH.	CHOCUYEM.	MUTSUN.
head	móloh	mogel
teeth	ki-iht	sit, si-it
foot	coyok	coro
house	kotchâ	kuka, ruca
white	pahkiss	palcasmin
black	mūlūtá	humulusmin
I, myself	kani	can
thou	mī	men
two	osha	utsgin
father	api	appa
mother	enu	anan

The supposition that the Chocuyem belongs to the Mutsun stock is greatly strengthened by the mutual correspondence of these terms, but cannot be stated yet as existing on this ground alone, for the terms for most numerals, parts of human body, and those for fire, water, earth, sun, moon and star disagree entirely.

The Chocuyem stock probably included also the Petaluma or Yolhios, as well as the Tomalo and other dialects spoken beyond the northern limit of Marin county. From a notice published by Alex. S. Taylor, Esq., we learn that Padre Quijas, in charge of Sonoma mission from 1835 to 1842, composed an extensive dictionary of the idiom spoken in the vicinity of this religious establishment.

YOCUT.— This tribe lives in the Kern and Tulare basins, and on the middle course of the San Joaquin river. Consolidated in 1860 into one coherent body by their chief, Pascual, the Yocuts show more national solidarity than any other California nation. In the *Overland Monthly*, Mr. Stephen Powers gave a sketch of this remarkable tribe, and described at length one of their terrific nocturnal weeping dances, called Kotéwachil. The following tribes and settlements may be mentioned here: *Taches* (*Tatches*), around Kingston; *Chewenee*, in Squaw valley; *Watooga*, on King's river; *Chookchancies*, in several villages; a *King's river tribe*, whose vocabulary is mentioned in Schoolcraft's Indians, vol. IV, 413–414; *Coconoons*, on Merced river; their vocabulary in Schoolcraft, IV, 413; a tribe formerly living at Dent's Ferry, on Stanislaus river, in the Sierra Nevada of Calaveras county, vocabulary given by Alex. S. Taylor in his *California Farmer*. In former years many individuals of the Yocut nation were carried as captives to San Luis Obispo, on the coast, and were put to work in the service of the mission.

MEEWOC.—Stephen Powers (*Overland Monthly*, April, 1873), calls the Meewoc tribe the largest in California in population, and in extent. " Their ancient dominion reached from the snow-line of the Sierra Nevada to the San Joaquin river, and from the Cósumnes to the Fresno: mountains, valleys and plains were thickly peopled." Bands of this tribe lived in a perfectly naked state in the Yosemite valley, when this spot first came into notice. The language is very homogeneous for a stretch of one hundred and fifty miles, and the radicals and words are remarkably vocalic. Meewoc, mi-ua, mivie, is the word for Indian, and *osoamit*, whence Yosemite, which means the grizzly bear ; *wakdlumni* is a river, hence Mokélumne was formed by corruption ; *kossumi* a salmon, hence Cósumnes river. Some of the Meewoc bands were called by the following names, which probably represent as many dialects or sub-dialects: *Choomteyas*, on middle Merced river; *Cawnees*, on Cósumne river; *Yulónees*, on Sutter creek: *Awnaees* in Yosemite valley; *Chowchillas*, on middle Chowchilla river; *Tuólumne*, on Tuólumne river. Their vocabulary was taken by Adam Johnson, and published in Schoolcraft's Indians, IV, 413. *Four Creek Indians;* vocabulary published in the San Francisco *Wide West* in July, 1856, under the name of Kahwéyah, but differing considerably in the words given by Mr. Powers. Some further Meewoc bands are called after the cardinal points of the compass.

MEIDOO.—The Meidoo nation formerly extended from Sacramento river to the snow-line, and from Big Chico creek to Bear river, the cognate Neeshenams from Bear river to the Cósumnes, where the language changed abruptly. The Meidoos are a joyful, merry and dance-loving race. Their language is largely made up of vocalic elements ; vowels and n's terminate more than one-half of their words. We possess vocabularies of the following bands : *Yuba*, opposite the mouth of Yuba river, a tributary of

Feather river. A collection of some forty words was made by Lieut. Edward Ross, and published in *Historical Magazine* of New York, 1863, page 123. *Cushna*, on mountains of South Yuba river, Nevada county. Vocabulary by Adam Johnson, an Indian agent, published in Schoolcraft, II, page 494. *Pujuni*, or Bushumnes, on western bank of Sacramento river; *Secumnes*, also west of Sacramento river. Short vocabularies of both dialects were collected by Mr. Dana, and reprinted in *Tr. Am. Ethnol. Soc.*, vol. II. *Neeshenam*, south of Bear river; Powers separates them as a distinct nation from the Meidoos: but from the words given, it appears that both speak dialects of the same language. Their bands are partly called after the points of the compass. Of other Meidoo tribes or bands, we mention the *Otdkumne* in the Otakey settlement; the *Ollas*, opposite mouth of Bear river, and the *Concows* or Cancows, in Concow valley. Mr. Powers gives the names of about a dozen more. Perhaps the little tribe of the undersized *Noces* or *Nozes*, in Round mountain, Oak run and vicinity, should be classified here, because a few of their numerals, which almost all end in *mona*, agree with those of the Cushnas. Mr. Powers supposes these and the ferocious *Mill Creek Indians* to be of foreign origin.

WINTOON.—The timid, superstitious, and grossly sensual race of the Wintoons is settled on both sides of upper Sacramento and upper Trinity rivers, and is found also on the lower course of Pit river. Stephen Powers calls their language rich in forms and synonyms; the dialect studied by Oscar Loew forms the plurals of its nouns by means of a final -*t* preceded by a reduplicated vowel of the root. Loew's vocabulary, published with one of the Uinta-Utah and thirteen others by the author of this article in his recent publication, *Zwölf Sprachen aus dem Südwesten Nord-Amerikas;* Weimar, 1876 (150 pages), offers a few words of very difficult guttural pronunciation; but in general the language (called Digger in that vocabulary) is of a soft and sonorous character.

Some of the more noteworthy Wintoon tribes are as follows: *Dowpum Wintoons*, on Cottonwood creek, the nucleus of this race: *Noemocs* or southern people; *Poomeocs* or eastern people;

Nome Lakees or western talkers; *Wikainmocs*, on extreme upper Trinity river and Scott mountain; *Normocs*, on Hay Fork: *Tehdmas*, near Teháma Town; *Mag Reading Wintoons*: vocabulary taken about 1852, by Adam Johnson, and published in Schoolcraft, IV, p. 414. *Cop-éh*. A tribe of this name was found at the head of Putos creek, the words of which are mostly dissyllabic, and partake of the vocalic nature of southern languages.

Stephen Powers calls by the name *Patween* a race inhabiting the west side of the middle and lower Sacramento, Caché and Putos creek, and Napa valley. Physically, the Patweens do not differ from the Wintoons. Their complexion varies from brassy bronze to almost jet-black, they walk pigeon-toed, and have very small and depressed heads, the arch over their eyes forming sometimes a sharp ridge. They are socially disconnected and have no common name; but their language does not differ much in its dialects, and belongs, as far as we are acquainted with it, to the Wintoón stock. Powers (*Overland Monthly*, December, 1874, p. 542, sqq.) classes under this heading a number of clans or bands, of which we mention: — *Suisuns*, in Suisun valley, Solano Co.; *Ululatos*, in Ulatus creek, near Vacaville: *Lewytos* and *Putos*, in Putos creek; *Napas*, in Napa valley; *Lolsels*, east of Clear lake; *Corusies*, near Colusa, on Sacramento river; *Chenposels*, on Caché creek. *Noyukies*, inter-married with Wintoons, on Stony creek. *Guilulos* or *Guillilas*, in Sonora valley. A Lord's prayer given in their dialect, by Duflot de Mofras, II, p. 391, differs entirely from the Chocuyem, hence the Guilulo may belong to the Patween stock. The words of the *Napa* root-diggers, collected by Major Bartlett, and another vocabulary of the Napa have not yet been published by the Smithsonian Institution.

YUKA.— The Yuka or Uka language extends over a long and narrow strip of territory parallel for a hundred miles to the Pomo dialects and the coast, in and along the coast range. The area of the Pomo language, however, breaks across that of the Yuka from the west at Ukiah and surrounds Clear lake. The revengeful race of the Yukas, who are conspicuous by very large heads placed on smallish bodies, originally dwelt in Round valley, east of Upper Eel river. Nome Cult, meaning western tribe, is the Wintoon name for this solitary and fertile valley, which has become the seat of an Indian reservation. Of the Yuka we have a short vocabulary by Lieut. Edward Ross in *New York Historical Magazine* for April, 1863. Surd vowels, perhaps nasalized, are frequent; also the ending *-um, -un*, which is probably the plural termination of nouns. No connection with the Chokuyen is perceptible, but a faint resemblance with the Cushna can be traced in a few words. Other tribes speaking Yuka are the *Ashochemies* or *Wappos*, formerly inhabiting the mountain tract from the Geysers down to Calistoga Hot springs; the *Shumeias*, at the head of Eel river; and the *Tahtoos*, on the middle and south forks of Eel river, and at the head of Potter valley.

POMO.— The populous, unoffending Pomo race is settled along the coast, on Clear lake and on the heads of Eel and Russian rivers; a portion of them now inhabit the reservation of Round valley, together with their former tormentors, the Yukas. Those of the interior show more intelligence and a stronger physical constitution than the coast Pomos. The Cahto Pomos and the Ki Pomos, on Eel river, have adopted the Tinné dialect of the Wi Lakee, which is closely allied to the Hoopa. Powers considers as the nucleus of the numerous Pomo tribes the Pome Pomos, living in Potter valley, a short distance northwest of Clear lake. The language rapidly changes from valley to valley; but the majority of the dialects are sonorous, and the vocalic element preponderates.

We enumerate the following bands : — *Pome Pomos*, earth people, in Potter valley. *Ballo Ki Pomos*, Wild Oat valley people, in Potter valley. *Choan Chadéla Pomos*, Pine-pitch people, in Redwood valley. *Matomey Ki Pomos*, Wooded valley people, around Little lake. *Usáls* or *Camalèl Pomas*, on Usal creek. *Shebalne Pomos*, neighbor people, in Sherwood valley. *Gallinomeros*, below Healdsburg; a few grammatical informations given in H. H. Bancroft's Native Races, vol. III, part second. *Yuka-i* or *Ukiah*, on Russian river (not to be confounded with Yuka in Round valley); vocabulary by G. Gibbs in Schoolcraft, vol. III (1853). *Choweshak*, at the head of Eel river ; Gibbs's vocabulary in Schoolcraft, III, pp. 434, sqq. *Batemdikaie*, at the head of Eel river, called after the valley in which they live: vocabulary in Schoolcraft, III, 434, sqq. *Kulanapo*, on southwest shore of Clear lake; vocabulary in Schoolcraft, III, 428. Bancroft has called attention to the fact that many words of this and other dialects, spoken south of it, correspond to Polynesian and Malay terms, but on account of the uncertain nature of Oceanic consonantism, he is unwilling to draw any ethnological deductions from this coincidence. Kulanapo agrees pretty closely with Choweshah and Batemdikaie, but differs somewhat from Chwachamaju. *Chwachamaju*, to the north of Bodega bay. The words in Wrangell's vocabulary (see Olamentke, *mutsun*) appear to agree more closely with Yuka-i than with any other Pomo dialect.

WISHOSK.—Spoken on a very small area around the mouth of the Eel river, on the seacoast, and called so from the Indian name for Eel river. We know of two sub-dialects almost entirely identical, and showing a rather consonantic word-structure. Vocabularies were collected with care by George Gibbs, and published in Schoolcraft, III, p. 422. *Weeyot*, or *Veeard*, on mouth of Eel river; *Wishosk* on northern part of Humboldt bay, near mouth of Mad river; *Patawat*, identical with G. Gibbs's Kowilth, or Koquilth; and about a dozen other settlements speaking dialects of the same language.— Proceeding through the basin of the Klamath river, we meet with a number of small, socially incoherent, bands of natives engaged in salmon or trout fishing on the shores of this stream and of its tributaries. Some do not possess any tribal name, or name for their common language, and were in a bulk called Klamath river Indians, in contradistinction to the Klamath lake Indians, E-ukshiknit on the head of Klamath river. These latter I call here Klamaths.

EUROK.— The Euroc tribe inhabits both banks of the Klamath river, from its mouth up to the Great bend at the influx of the Trinity river. The name simply means down (down the river), and another name given them by their neighbors, Pohlik, means nearly the same. Their settlements frequently have three or four names. Requa is the village at the mouth of the Klamath river, from which they set out when fishing at sea. The language sounds rough and guttural; the vowels are surd, and often lost between the consonants, as in mrpr, *nose;* chlh, chlec, *earth;* wrh-yenex, *child.* In conversation, the Euroes terminate many words by catching sound (-h'-) with a grunt; with other Indians we observe this less frequently. They are of darker complexion than the Cahroks, and in 1870 numbered 2,700 individuals in the short stretch of forty miles along the river.

WEITS-PEK.— In Schoolcraft we find a vocabulary named after the Indian encampment at Weits-pek, a few miles above the great bend of Klamath river, on the north shore, whose words totally disagree from Eurok, Cahrok, Shasta, or any other neighboring tongue.

CAHROK.— *Cahrok,* or *Carrook,* is not a tribal, but simply a conventional name, meaning above, upwards (up the Klamath river, as Eurok means down, and Modoc — probably — at the head of the river). The Cahrok tribe extends along Klamath river from Bluff creek, near Weits-pek, to Indian creek, a distance of eighty miles. Pehtsik is a local name for a part of the Cahroks; another section of them, living at the junction of Klamath and Salmon (or Quoratem) rivers, go by the name of Ehnek. Stephen Powers thinks that the Cahroks are probably the finest tribe in California; that their language much resembles the Spanish in utterance, and is not so guttural as the Euroc. In Schoolcraft we find vocabularies from both tribes.

TOLEWA.— The few words of the Tolewa, or Tahlewah language on Smith river, between Klamath and Rogue rivers, which were given to G. Gibbs by an unreliable Indian from another tribe, show a rough and guttural character, and differ entirely in their radicals from any other language spoken in the neighborhood.

SHASTA.— At the time of the Rogue river war the Shastas, or Shasteecas, became involved in the rebellion of their neighbors, and after their defeat the warriors of both tribes were removed, with their families, to the Grand Ronde and Siletz reserves in Oregon. Hence, they almost entirely disappeared from their old homes in the Shasta and Scott valleys, which are drained by affluents of the Klamath river, and also from their homes on Klamath river, from Clear creek upwards. Nouns form their plurals by adding oggára, ukára, *many*, and the language does not sound disagreeably to our ears. We know this vocalic tongue only through a few words, collected by Dana; the Smithsonian Institution owns three vocabularies. The Scott's valley band was called Watsahéwa; the names of other bands were T-ka, Iddoa, Hoteday, We-ohow.

PIT RIVER.— The Pit river Indians, a poor and very abject-looking lot of natives, live on upper Pit river and its side creeks. In former years they suffered exceedingly from the raids of the Modocs and Klamath lakes, who kidnapped and kept them as slaves, or sold them at the slave-market at Yánex in southern Oregon. Like the Pomos and most other Californians, they regard and worship the coyote-wolf as the creator and benefactor of mankind. Powers calls their language "hopelessly consonantal, harsh and sesquipedalian, very unlike the sweet and simple tongues of the Sacramento river." Redoubling of the root seems to prevail here to a large extent. A few words from a sub-dialect are given by Mr. Bancroft, which do not differ materially from the Palaik (or mountaineer) vocabulary printed in *Transactions of Am. Ethnol. Soc.*, vol. II, p. 98. After a military expedition to their country, General Crook ordered a removal of many individuals of this tribe to the Round valley reserve, where they are now settled. *Pú-su, Pú-isu* is the Wintoon name of the Pit river Indians, meaning eastern people. According to Mr. Powers's statement (*Overland Monthly*, 1874, pp. 412, sgg.), the Pit river Indians are sub-divided in: *Achomdwes* in the Fall river basin; from *achoma* river, meaning Pit river. *Hamefcuttelies*, in Big valley. *Astakaywas* or *Astakywich*, in Hot spring valley; from *astakáy*, hot spring. *Illmawes*, opposite Fort Crook, south side of Pit river. *Pácamallies*, on Hat creek.

KLAMATH.— The watershed between the Sacramento and Columbia river basin consists of a broad and mountainous tableland rising to an average height of four to five thousand feet, and embellished by beautiful sheets of fresh water. The central part of this plateau is occupied by the Klamath reservation, which includes lakes, prairies, volcanic ledges, and is the home of the Klamath stock of Indians, who inhabit it together with the two Shóshoni tribes mentioned above. The nation calls itself (and other Indians) *Máklaks*, the encamped, the settlers, a term which has been transcribed into English *Múckalucks*, and ought to include all the four divisions given below. About 145 Modocs were, after the Modoc war of 1873, removed to Quápaw agency, Indian territory. The language is rich in words and synonyms, only slightly polysynthetic, and lacks the sounds *f* and *r*. They divide themselves into: *Klamaths* or *Klamath Lakes*, *E-ukshikni*, from e-ush, *lake*; on Big Klamath lake. *Modocs* originally inhabiting the shores of Little Klamath lake, now at Yánex. The Pit Rivers call them Lútuam; and they call the Pit Rivers, *Móatuash* or southern dwellers. *Kómbatuash*, grotto or cave dwellers, from their abode in the Lava Bed caves—a medley of different races. Some *Mólele* or Molále, renegades of the Cayuse tribe, have recently become mixed with Rogue Rivers and Klamaths, and have adopted the Klamath language in consequence. No Klamath sub-dialects exist, the idioms of all these tribes being almost identical. Klamaths and other southern Oregonians communicate with other tribes by means of the Chinook jargon.

THE TINNÉ FAMIY.—The Tinné family of languages, which extends from the inhospitable shores of the Yukon and Mackenzie rivers to Fraser river, and almost to Hudson's bay, sent in by-gone centuries a powerful offshoot to the Rio Grande del Norte and the Gila rivers, now represented by the Apache, Lipan and Návajo. Other fragments of the Tinné stock, represented by less populous tribes, wandered south of the Columbia river, and settled on the coast of the Pacific ocean; they were the Kwalhioqua, Tlatskanai, Umpqua, Rogue Rivers (or Rascal Indians) and the Hoopa. Following them up in the direction from south to north, we begin with the Hoopa.

Hoopa.—The populous and compact Hoopa (or better, Húpô) tribe has its habitation on the Trinity, near its influx into Klamath river, California, and for long years kept in awe and submission the weaker part of the surrounding tribes and clans, exacting tributes, and even forcing their language upon some of them, as upon the Chimalaquays on New river, the Kailtas on Redwood creek, and upon the two Pomo bands above mentioned. Powers holds their language to be copious in words, robust, strong in utterance, and of martial simplicity and rudeness. The *Wylakies*, or, *Wi Lakees*, near the western base of Shasta butte, speak a Hoopa dialect. No information is at hand to decide whether the *Lassics* on Mad river, the *Tahahteens* on Smith river, and a few other tribes, speak, as the assumption is, Tinné dialects or not.

Rogue River.— The *Tototen, Tootooten,* or *Tututamys* tribe, living on Rogue river and its numerous side creeks, Oregon, speaks a language which is, like the majority of Oregonian and northern tongues, replete of guttural and croaking sounds. According to Dr. Hubbard, whose vocabulary is published in Taylor's *California Farmer*, this nation comprised in 1856 thirteen bands, consisting in all of 1,205 individuals. (See article *Shasta*.) The appearance of the numerals, the terms for the parts of the human frame, many other nouns and the pronoun, *mine, my* (ho, hwo, hu), induced me to compare them with the Tinné languages. They differ considerably from Hoopa and Taculli, but singularly agree with Apache and Návajo, and Tototen has, therefore, to be introduced as a new offshoot of the coast branch into the great Tinné or Athapascan family of languages. The Smithsonian Institution owns two vocabularies, inscribed "Rogue River," two "Tootooten," and one "Toutouten."

Umpqua.— The Umpquas live in and around Alsea sub-agency, on the sea coast, together with the Alsea, Sayústkla and Coos Indians. Their idiom is softer than the other branches of the Tinné stock. Further north we find two other small tribes of the same origin, whose languages were studied only by Horatio Hale, of Wilkes's exploring expedition. One of them was the *Tlatskanai*, south of Columbia river; the other, the *Kwalhioqua*, at the outlet of this stream, both extremely guttural. On account of the smallness of the tribes speaking them, these idioms have probably become extinct; their owners merged into other tribes, and were identified with them beyond recognition. They roved in the mountains at some distance from the coast and the Columbia, living on game, berries and esculent roots.

YAKON.— Before 1848, the Yakon tribe was settled on the

Oregon coast, south of the Tillamuks, numbering then about seven hundred individuals. In the collection of fifty Yakon words, given in *Transactions of Am. Ethn. Soc.*, II, part 2d, pp. 99 sqq., we discover very few monosyllables, but many clusters of consonants, not easily pronounced by English speaking people, as kwotχl, *fingers;* pusuntχlχa, *three.*

CAYUSE.— The national appellation of the Cayuses, whose home is in the valley of Des Chutes river, Oregon, is *Wayíletpu*, the plural form of *Wa-ílet*, one Cayuse man. The Wayíletpu formerly were divided into Cayuses and Moléles, but the latter separated, went south and joined other tribes (see Klamath), or were removed to the Grande Ronde reserve. The Cayuses are rapidly assimilating, or identifying themselves, with the Wala-walas on and around Umatilla agency, about seventy miles east of Des Chutes river outlet, and a majority of them has forgotten already their paternal idiom. Judging from the Cayuse words printed in the *Transactions of Am. Ethn. Society*, II, p. 97, this language prefers consonantic to vocalic endings, and possesses the aspirates *th* and *f*. The occurrence of both sounds, especially of *f*, is not uncommon in Oregonian languages.

KALAPUYA.— The original seats of this tribe were in the upper Willamette valley. The laws of euphony are numerous in this language, whose utterance is soft and harmonious; thus it forms a remarkable contrast with all the surrounding languages, the sounds of which are uttered with considerable pectoral exertion. The personal pronoun is used also as a possessive; no special termination exists for the dual or plural of nouns. *Yamkalli*, on head of Willamette river, is a dialect of Kalapuya.

CHINOOK.— The populous, Mongol-featured nation of the Chinooks once dwelt on both sides of the Lower Columbia; but after the destruction of four-fifths of their number in 1823 by a terrible fever-epidemy, a part of the survivors settled north, and now gradually disappear among the Chehalis. The pronunciation is very indistinct, the croakings in lower part of the throat frequent, the syntaxis is represented as being a model of intricacy. To confer with the Lower, the Upper Chinooks had to use interpreters, although the language of both is of the same lineage. The dialects and tribes were distributed as follows: *Lower Chinook*, from mouth of Columbia river up to Multnomah island, Clatsop; *Chinook proper;* Wakiakum; Katlámat. *Middle Chinook*— Multnomah, Skilloot. *Upper Chinook*— Watlála or Watχlála, showing a dual and a plural form in the inflection of the noun; Klakamat, south-east of Portland, a tribe once dispossessed of its homes by the Moléles; the idiom of the Cascade Indians, and of the extinct Waccanessisi. Following the authority of George Gibbs, I mention also as an Upper Chinook dialect the Wasco or Cathlasco language. From their original homes east of the Dalles, the Wascoes were removed to the Warm Spring agency.

CHINOOK JARGON.— The location of the Chinooks in the central region of western border commerce, and on the outlet of the international roadway of Columbia river, rendered the acquisition of the Chinook, or Tsinúk language very desirable for the surrounding tribes. But the nature of this language made this a rather difficult task, and so a trade language gradually formed itself out of Chinook, Chehali, Selish, Nootka and other terms, which, on the advent of the whites, were largely increased by French, and in a less degree by English words. The French words were derived from the Canadian and Missouri patois of the fur traders. Two-fifths of the jargon terms, were taken from Chinook dialects, and as the inflectional forms, prefixes and affixes of these unwieldy idioms were dropped altogether, and replaced by particles or auxiliaries, the acquisition of the jargon became easy. A comprehensive sketch of this idiom will be found in the preface to George Gibbs's *Dictionary of the Chinook Jargon*, New York, 1863 (in Shea's Linguistics).

We have similar instances of medley jargons from very disparate languages in the Lingua Franca of the Mediterranean ports, in the Pidgin English of Canton, the Negro-English-Dutch of Surinam, the Slavé on the Upper Yukon river, in a Sahaptin slave-jargon, and in the numerous women-languages of South America.

SAHAPTIN.— This name belongs to a small affluent of the Koos-

kooskie or Clearwater river, and has been adopted to designate the stock of languages spoken in an extensive territory on the middle and lower Columbia river, and on its tributaries, Yákima, Paluse, Clearwater and Snake rivers. The morphological part of the Sahaptin grammar is rich and well developed, and polysynthetism is carried up to a high degree. The exterior of the race recalls the bodily structure, not the complexion, of the Mongolian type of mankind. The easternmost tribe is:

Nez-Percés, the most numerous and powerful Sahaptin tribe, settled on a reserve in northern Idaho (about 2,800 Indians), or roaming in the neighborhood. A sketch of their grammar was published in *Transactions of American Ethn. Society*. The western and northern Sahaptin tribes are the following: *Wálawálá* (rivermen), on Umatilla agency, in northeastern Oregon; *Palús* or Paloose, on Palús river and Yákima reservation; *Yákama* or Yákima, on Yákima reserve, Washington territory. Rev. Pandosy wrote a Grammar, Texts and Dictionary of this dialect, which were published in Mr. Shea's Linguistic Series. From their habitat they are called Pshuanwappum, dwellers in the stony country. *Klikitat*, on Yákima reserve and vicinity, formerly roaming through the woodlands around Mount St. Helens. *Umatilla*, on Oregon side of Columbia river and on Umatilla agency. No vocabularies. *Warm Spring Indians* on west side of Middle Des Chutes river. They call themselves Tishχáni-hhláma, after a locality on that water-course, or Milli-hhláma, from the thermal sources surging on the territory of their reservation (*milli*, bubbling, or tepid, *hhláma* " belonging to, pertaining). A slave jargon exists among the Nez-Percé Indians, which originated through their intercourse with prisoners of war, and contains expressions for *eye, horse, man, woman* and other most common terms, which are entirely foreign to Sahaptin.

SELISH.— The Selish family extends from the Pacific ocean and the straits of Fuca, through America and partly through British territory to the Rocky mountains and the 113. meridian. This race is most densely settled around Puget sound, and its main bulk resides north of Columbia river. By joining into one name their westernmost and easternmost dialect, their language has been called also Tsihaili-Selish, or Chehali-Selish. A large number of words of this truly northern and superlatively jaw-breaking language are quite unpronounceable to Anglo-Americans and Europeans — i. e., tsatχlsh, *shoes;* skaiχlentχl, *woman* in Tsihaili; shitχltso, *shoes* in Atnah. This stock abounds in inflectional and syntactical forms, and redoubles the root or part of it extensively, but always in a *distributive* sense. It divides itself into a large number of dialects and subdialects, among which we point out the subsequent ones as probably the most important, going from west to north, and then to the east: *Nsietshawus* or *Tillamuk* (Killamuk), on Pacific coast, south of Columbia river; *Tsihaili, Chehdli;* on or near Pacific coast Washington territory: has three subdialects; *Tsihaili* proper on Chehali river and in Puyallup agency; *Quiantl, Quaiantl* or *Kwantlen; Quéniauitl.* A few *Chehalis* and Chinooks inhabit Shoalwater bay. *Cowlitz* or *Kd-ualitsk,* spoken on Puyallup agency. Their ancient home is the valley of the Cowlitz river, a northern tributary of the Lower Columbia river. *Soaiatlpi,* west of Olympia city. This tribe once included the Kettlefalls Indians. *Nisqualli, N'skwdli;* east of Olympia, on Nisqualli river, settled there in company with the Squaxins, on Puyallup agency. *Clallam, (S' Clallum)* on S'Kokomish agency, northwest of Olympia city. Twana, in same locality. *Dwamish,* partly settled on Tulalip sub-agency. *Lummi,* on Nootsak or Lummi river, near the British boundary. This dialect is largely impregnated with Nootka and other foreign elements. The *Shushwap, Suwapamuck* or *Southern Atnah* belongs to the Selish stock, but does not extend from middle course of Fraser river and its affluents so far south as to reach American territory. It closely resembles Selish proper. The eastern Selish dialects are: *O'Kinakane (Okanagan),* with the subdialect *St'lakam,* on Okanagan river, a northern tributary of Upper Columbia river and on Colville reserve, which is located in the northeastern angle of Washington territory. *Kullespelm, Kallispelm,* or Pend d'Oreille of Washington territory, on Pend d'Oreille river and Lake Callispelm. The Upper Pend d'Oreille are settled on Flathead or Jocko reservation, Montana. *Spokane,* on Colville reserve and vicinity; three subdialects; Sngomenei, Snpoilschi, Syk'eszilni. *Skitsuish* or Coeur d'Alène; on a reservation in northern Idaho. *Selish* proper or Flathead. The tribe speaking it resides on Flathead reservation, and is called so without any apparent deformity of the head. The dialect lacks the sounds b, d, f, r; it has been studied by a missionary, Rev. Gregory Mengarini, who at present is writing a second edition of his *Grammatical linguae Selicae;* the first edition was published in New York, 1861 (in Shea's Linguistics). *Piskwaus* or *Piskwas,* on middle Columbia river and on Yákima reservation, Washington territory.

NOOTKA.— The only dialect of this stock spoken within the limits of the United States is that of the *Makah,* Classet or Klaizzaht tribe in Neah bay, near Cape Flattery. The Smithsonian Institution published in 1869 a very elaborate ethnological sketch of this fisher-tribe, written by James G. Swan. Nootka dialects are mainly in use on Vancouver's island, which is divided in four areas of totally different families of languages.

KOOTENAI.— The Kootenai, Kitunaha, or Flatbow language is spoken on Kootenay river, an important tributary of Upper Columbia river, draining some remote portions of Idaho, Montana and the British possessions. A Lord's prayer in Kootenai is given in Bancroft's *Native Races,* vol. III, p. 620.

In bestowing the greatest care and accuracy on the composition of this topographical survey of Pacific languages, my principal purpose was to give a *correct division,* of the idioms into stocks, and their dialects and subdialects, and I shall be very grateful for suggestions correcting my statements, if any should be found erroneous. To have given another location for a tribe than the one it occupies at present, cannot be considered as a grave error, for many American tribes are nomadic, and shift constantly from one prairie, pasture or fishing place to another, or are removed to distant reservations by government agents. For want of information, I was unable to classify the Hhána in Sacramento valley, the Hagnaggi on Smith river, California, the Chitwout or Similkameen on the British-American border, and a few other tongues; but, in spite of this, I presume that the survey will be useful for orientation on this linguistic field, where confusion has reigned supreme for so many generations.

For the better guidance of students in ethnology and linguistics, I propose to classify all the Indian dialects in a very simple and clear manner, by adding to their dialect name that of the stock or family, as it is done in zoölogy and botany with the genera and species. In the same manner as the Mescaleros and Lipans are called Mescalero-Apaches and Lipan-Apaches, we can form compound names, as: Warm-Spring Sahaptin Piskwaus Selish, Watχlála Chinook, Kwalhioqua Tinné, Hoopa Tinné, Dowpum Wintoon, Gallinomero Pomo, Coconoon Yocut, Kizh Shoshoni (or Kizh Kauvuya), Comoyei Yuma, Ottare Cherokee, Séneca Iroquois, Abnáki Algónkin, Delaware Algonkin, and so forth. The help afforded to linguistic topography by this method would be as important as the introduction of Linnean terminology was to descriptive natural science, for genera and species exist in human speech as well as among animals and plants.

The *thorough* study of *one* Indian tongue is the most powerful incentive to instructive and capable travelers for collecting as much linguistic material as possible, and as accurately as possible, chiefly in the shape of texts and their translations. It is better to collect little information accurately, than much information of an unreliable nature. The signs used for emphasizing syllables, for nasal and softened vowels, for explosive, lingual, croaking, and other consonantic sounds, must be noted and explained carefully; and the whole has to be committed to such publishers or scientific societies as are *not in the habit* of procrastinating publications. Stocks and dialects become rapidly extinct in the west, or get hopelessly mixed, through increased inter-tribal commerce, so that the original shape, pronunciation and inflection can no longer be recognized with certainty. The work must be undertaken in no distant time by zealous men, for after "the last of the Mohicans" will have departed this life, there will be no means left for us to study the most important feature of a tribe — its language — if it has not been secured in time by alphabetical notation.

CHASTISEMENT OF THE YAMASEES.
AN INCIDENT OF THE EARLY INDIAN WARS IN GEORGIA.[1]

[*To the Author of the London Magazine.*

SIR: We have received many accounts of the barbarous ravages and massacres of the Indians, in America, during the course of the present war, owing to our impolitick treatment of them for many years past, and the tame and corrupt measures pursued by a late ministry, or rather confederacy against the honour and interest of their country. Perhaps an occurrence that happened, in the last war, in that part of the world, may be amusing to your readers: Sure I am, that it contains a striking instance of the righteous judgments Providence inflicts, for wise ends and purposes, sometimes even in this life, on the cruel, the base, and the treacherous. In the latter part of the transaction I myself was an actor; and therefore you may depend upon it as a fact not to be disputed.—I am, your constant reader,

June, 8, 1760.   AMERICUS.]

About the year 1740, and, I think, towards the close of the year, General Oglethorpe, then commanding in Georgia, had erected a small fort at a place called Mount Venture, about 96 miles from Savannah, capital of that province, to protect the Indian traders, and keep the communication open for the friendly savages. One Mr. Francis, a brave and honest officer of Rangers, commanded the garrison, consisting of but a few men, though strength sufficient for a defence against the attacks of a considerable party of Indians, whilst within the fort, and able to manage their swivels and small arms. Mr. Francis had also with him his wife and an infant son; and some circumstances had happened in their union, that made them a fond, endeared, and happy pair. It was necessary, now and then, for the commander to repair with a party of his men to Savannah, or Fort Argyle, for provisions and ammunition; and, as the Yamasee Indians, then the most troublesome nation attached to the Spaniards, had been severely handled in the preceding year, he ventured now to leave the fort, and his beloved family, with fewer protecting hands than usual.

He had scarce been set out a day before a scouting party of these Indians discovered themselves, and, to the great terror of Mrs. Francis and the two or three Rangers with her, surrounded the palisade, and soon, notwithstanding a smart fire from the

---
[1] Reprinted from *The London* (England) *Magazine*, for June, 1760.

fort, made themselves masters of it. The Rangers they killed and scalped before the poor woman's eyes, whose fears operated even to distraction, whilst she held the tender infant clasped in her arms, and besought the barbarians to spare them. It shall suffice to say, that, after many shocking insults and brutalities, (too gross and too affecting, for your readers' ears) they shot the child in its mother's arms, and soon after also dispatched the frantic matron in the same manner. One Creek Indian, named Notoway, had the good fortune to escape to a neighboring creek, where a canoe lying, he, unobserved, got from them, and arrived at Savannah with the dreadful tidings.

The husband, overwhelmed by a blow that at once reduced him to the utmost misery and distress, soon returned with proper assistance to take revenge upon the savage monsters; but they were gone, and in vain he pursued their tracks; so far, however, he pursued, that it would have been the greatest rashness to proceed farther. As they had burnt the fort to the ground, he had then opportunity only of paying his last duties to the mangled remains of his family. He missed no occasions of engaging the Indians of this tribe, who felt, in bloody traits, the power of his arm. Yet never had he met with any of those concerned in the tragedy above related; for the Indian who escaped had taken such notice of them, that, from his report, he was able to distinguish those most active in the dreadful deed, from any other.

At the latter end of the year 1743, a large body of these Yamasees fell upon a remote part of Captain Kerr's plantation, and, after doing considerable mischief, carried off fifteen of his company of marines, and set off with them for St. Augustine. It was two days before this fresh irruption was known to Captain Horton, then commanding officer at Frederica; but then he ordered out a select party of the regiment, a number of friendly Indians, who then happened to be there, and about twenty Rangers under Lieutenant Francis, to pursue them. Francis, with unwearied diligence, reached the lake de Poupa, which he knew they must cross in their way to St. Augustine, and imagined they would make such a compass to elude pursuit, as would permit him to arrive there before them. As no tracks were perceived, we imagined we had luckily got the start of them; and therefore, crossing the lake upon rafts, we lay in ambush for them, well defended from immediate view by the thick-spreading shrubs and palmettoes behind which we prepared to receive our expected visitants.

The detachment of the regiment was posted in front; and on one flank, the Indians under the famous Tonnahowi, son of Tomo Chichi, king of Yamacraw, both well remembered by the people of London; on the other, Mr. Francis with his Rangers were concealed. Thus we continued, constantly lying upon our arms for near forty-eight hours, pretty well harrassed by the usual tortures of the climate, heat, musquitoes, wood-ticks, sand-flies, and other insects and vermin. At length one of our Indian scouts discovered them passing the lake, and seemingly in great consternation at the tracks they discovered in their way. Soon after, one of their party, upon the same errand, by an indiscreet and eager discovery of our Indians, returned back to his body with the relation of what he had seen. It was, however, too late to retreat, had they known our real number, which, notwithstanding, was much inferior to theirs, who were near one hundred. They then resolutely came up, with their infernal war-whoop, and pushed into the very defile, but were so warmly received, and such a number of them dropped by our first discharge, that, though they fired briskly for a few minutes, yet our Indians and Rangers then running in upon them, as many as escaped their fury fled in the utmost consternation. It was then the gallant Indian chief received his death-wound, valiantly fighting in the cause of his beloved English. Our other loss was very trifling; but near forty of the Yamasees were killed, many made prisoners, and, perhaps, many more died of their wounds in the woods and marshes to which they fled; so that it was the greatest blow they had received since the commencement of the war.

Amongst the prisoners the faithful Notoway discovered the very villain that shot poor Mrs. Francis; and, in the first emotions of grief and rage, Francis would have shot him thro' the head; but, recollecting it was improper for him to show an example of this sort, he called some of the young Indians, who scalped him in our presence, whilst he neither changed countenance, nor faltered in the song he chanted, importing how many of the English Indians he had served in the same manner, what blood he had shed, and particularly boasting of his murder of Mrs. Francis. Enraged as we were, none of us could steadily face this horrid scene; and his tormentors were ordered to put him to no further torture; upon which they shot him to death. Thus ended our expedition. But I must remember to tell you, that we rescued our fifteen captives, who had the presence of mind to fling themselves flat on the earth at the beginning of the engagement, and received no hurt; though by little but their language could they be distinguished from their late masters, being stripped, and scorched by the rays of the sun to nearly the same hue. One prisoner we brought to Frederica, who was given up to the Indians, and burnt by them for the loss of their chief, as we afterwards understood. The brave Tonnahowi we buried with military honors at Fort William, in the island of Cumberland; a respect truly due to his fidelity and bravery.

THE LAST OF THE PEQUODS.[1]

BY BENSON J. LOSSING.

In the vestibule of the library of the New York Historical Society is the figure of a North American Indian, in purest marble, wrought by the hand of Thomas Crawford. The man is sitting, with his head low bent and resting upon his palm, and his expression is that of one entirely absorbed in deep and sad contemplation. That fine work of art is called The Last of his Race. Art, history, and romance have touchingly depicted that rare, melancholy person, the last of *his* race or nation, but have yet failed to portray that rare, melancholy being, the last of *her* race or nation.

A dozen years ago I visited that rare woman, the last living survivor of *her* nation. She was then just one hundred years old, and blessed with a liberal share of bodily and mental vigor. She was undoubtedly the last of the Pequods, a powerful nation (in the limited sense of the term) of Indians, who occupied an extensive region of country along the borders of Long Island sound, in eastern Connecticut. They had come, nobody knew when, from the more vigorous north — a hardy people, inured to the chase and war — and driven away the weaker ichthyophagists of the seaboard. They exercised wide authority, by right of conquest, over the continent tribes in their vicinity and a greater portion of Long Island; and they were so aggressive that they won the fear and hatred of all around them. Their national seat was at the mouth of the Thames, and their chief sagamore, when the white people first settled in Connecticut, was Sassacus. He was a sort of emperor, having under his control between the Thames and the Hudson rivers, along the sound, twenty-six chiefs and almost four thousand warriors. His royal residence was upon a hill a little southward of the present village of Groton, then covered with the primeval forest. Upon the Mystic river,

---

[1] Reprinted from *Scribner's Monthly* (New York) for October, 1871.

eastward, not far from Stonington, he had a strong fort, and around him stood seven hundred young warriors ready to obey his every command. Haughty and insolent, he spurned every overture of the white people, and looked with contempt upon the rebellious doings of Uncas, of the royal blood, then in armed insurrection against him. The English were but a handful compared to his people, and he scorned their friendship. What had he to fear? Much, very much, as a brief campaign against him in May, 1637, proved.

The outrages of Sassacus and his followers had made his name so terrible, that white and dusky mothers alike drew their babes closer to their bosoms whenever it was uttered. It was evident that he aspired to be master of all New England, and that his first business toward the accomplishment of that end would be the extermination of the English. Imminent danger caused quick and energetic action. Captain John Mason was sent, with less than one hundred men, to land on the shores of and penetrate the Pequod country, and bring the haughty savages under subjection. His little army sailed in pinnaces down Narraganset bay. Two hundred Narraganset warriors, under Miantonomoh, their principal chief, joined the English; so also did many brave Niantics, and the Pequod rebels under Uncas. When, early in June, Mason approached the fort of Sassacus, on the Mystic, he had full five hundred light and dark warriors following him.

At early dawn that little army from the east stealthily crawled up the thick wooded hill crowned by the Pequod fort. The whole garrison were in deep slumber, excepting a solitary sentinel; and at the same moment when he shouted into dull ears, "The English! The English!" the invaders scaled the mounds, beat down the palisades, and swarmed into the fort with gun, sword, and tomahawk. The mattings of the wigwams and the dry bushes and timbers of the fort were fired, when seven hundred men, women, and children perished by the flames and steel! The strong, the beautiful, and the innocent were mercilessly slaughtered; and the impious leader in his account said, "God is above us! He laughs his enemies and the enemies of the English to scorn, making them as a fiery oven. Thus does the Lord judge among the heathen, filling the place with dead bodies."

Swift couriers flew to Sassacus with the sad news. Close upon the steps of the bearers of evil tidings followed the remnant of his warriors who escaped the massacre, and were excited to madness by the dreadful calamity. The sagamore sat, stately and sullen, under a canopy of boughs, while they boldly charged the disasters of the morning to his haughtiness and misconduct. With violent gestures and frequent yells, they threatened him with death; and they would doubtless have pushed the threat to action had they not been startled by the blast of a trumpet near by. Another foe was upon them. From the head of the Mystic came two hundred armed settlers from Massachusetts and Plymouth, to seal the doom of the Pequod nation. Their advent brought despair to Sassacus and his followers, and these instantly set fire to their wigwams and palisades, and crossing the Thames, fled westward, closely pursued by the English, with great slaughter. These spread utter desolation over the beautiful land of the Pequods. Wigwams and gardens disappeared before them, and men, women, and children met the fate of the Canaanites before the sword of the son of Nun. With a few followers Sassacus took refuge in Sasco swamp, near the present Fairfield, where all surrendered but the Sagamore and half a dozen warriors, who escaped to the Mohawks and met death by murder among them. And so it was that a nation was destroyed in a day. None of all that once powerful people remained but the few captives and their families, and the surviving rebels under Uncas himself the last of the Mohegans of the royal line of the Pequods.

Almost a hundred years later, a descendant of one of these Pequod captives was a man of energy and wisdom, named Mahwee, or Mahweesum, whose family lived in western Connecticut. With a party of hunters (he was then quite young), he chased a buck to the summit of a range of high hills beyond the usual limits of their hunting. At near sunset they looked down into a beautiful valley flooded with golden light, through which flowed a winding stream. In the morning they descended to the plain and there discovered rich corn-lands. Bringing their families over the hills, they made their homes there, near the mouth of a little tributary to the river. The corn-lands and the little stream they called Pish-gach-ti-gock — the *meeting of the waters* — and the river they named Hoo'-sa-tah-nook', *the stream over the mountains*. Their place of settlement was near the present village of Kent, in Litchfield county, Connecticut. Such was the origin of the name of the Housatonic river, and the tribal one of the remnants of the Pequod, Narraganset, and other New England Indians who settled there, which has been corrupted into Schaghticook. Of this mixed tribe, so formed, Mahwee, about the year 1728, became sachem or civil ruler, and held the scepter until his death.

One day, before he became sachem, Mahwee was hunting on the mountains westward of Schaghticook, and from their tops he looked down into a lovely valley covered with rich grass, and broken into little rocky and wooded hills that appeared like islands in a green sea. Through it flowed a sparkling stream that received many a brook from the mountains. It was the valley of the Weebetuck or Ten Mile river, in the town of Dover, N. Y. The mountain sides of the valley were full of game, and the river abounded with fish. There Mahwee built a wigwam for his family, gathered about him an Indian settlement, and became its sachem. He afterward dwelt in one or two other places, and finally went back to Schaghticook, where he drew around him the other settlements, and became sachem over all.

Several years after that general gathering, Moravian missionaries had penetrated that region. A station was planted, in 1741, at Shekomeko, in the eastern part of Duchess county, N. Y., and not many miles from the valley of the Weebetuck. The labors of the missionaries among the Indians were extended to Schaghticook, and the first convert among the tribe there was sachem or King Mahwee, to whom they gave the baptismal name of Gideon. He was baptized by Martin Mack, on the 13th of February, 1743, and to the end of his life he was faithful to his profession. For a long time he was an exhorter among his people. Believing it would add to the dignity of his household, he was married to another wife from among the Stockbridge Indians, farther up the Housatonic river, and took her to Pishgachtigock. But his people were so offended by the act that he felt compelled to reside, for a time, in the valley of the Weebetuck, his old home. There he lived until convinced that he had done wrong, when he sent his second wife back to her people, and returned to his own.

Eunice Mahwee, grand-daughter of Sachem Gideon, and who was descended in unmixed blood from her Pequod ancestors, the unfortunate contemporaries of Sassacus, was "the last of *her* nation" to whom I have alluded. I visited her under circumstances of peculiar interest.

The fact that one of their missionary stations had been planted in the province of New York, near the borders of Connecticut, more than a hundred years before, had almost faded from the Moravian mind, and was known only to a few students. A farmer plowed up, on the site of Shekomeko, a fragment of a stone bearing an inscription in the German language. It was an impenetrable enigma until records pointed to the spot as the site of the settlement of the praying Indians. The Moravian Historical Society of Bethlehem, Pennsylvania, became interested in the matter. A delegation from it visited the spot as explorers in June, 1859, and it was found that the fragment was part of a monument erected there at the grave and to the memory of Gottlieb Büttner, one of the two earliest missionaries at Shekomeko. The writer accompanied the explorers, and a few months afterward he participated with the Moravian bishop and other clergy and laymen of the United Brethren, in the dedication of a monument erected at the grave of Büttner, and another near Sharon, Connecticut, where the Moravians had a missionary station. From these interesting places we rode through a most picturesque region southward, passing on the way the upper borders of the Weebetuck valley, and arrived at Kent, on the Housatonic, at sunset. The next morning the whole party rode a short distance down the western side of the river to the Schaghticook reservation, and visited Eunice Mahwee, the chief subject of this paper. At that time only about fifty persons composed the remnant of the mixed tribe over which Sachem Gideon had ruled; and Aunt Eunice, as her friends and neighbors called her, was the only one in whose veins then ran the pure blood of the Pequods.

As we approached the reservation we found the valley very

narrow and more picturesque, with the Pisgachtigock or Schaghticook mountain overlooking it. Some of the houses were of logs, and others were framed; and around each was a patch of cultivated land. Some of the dwellings were adorned with flowers, shrubbery, and vines. Thus beautified, was the house in which Eunice dwelt with her grand-daughter Lavinia, who was in the yard when we drew up. She was tidily dressed in faded calico, and had a man's straw hat upon her head, and an implement of labor in her hand. Undisturbed by the sudden arrival of so many strangers, she led us quietly into the house, where, at an open fire-place, before some glowing embers, sat upon a rush-bottomed chair the venerable object of our visit, with a half-finished basket on which she had been working by her side. In an open doorway, connecting with another room, stood Lavinia's pretty, bright-eyed daughter, a young married woman, with a babe in her arms. So the eye rested upon living members of the same family born a hundred years apart! Glancing around the room we saw evidences of poverty, but not of want. Three chairs, a deal table, a small cracked looking glass, a faded paper window-shade, and a pair of bellows composed the furniture.

EUNICE MAHWEE.

On the table was a wooden dish nearly filled with lamprey eels, a fish which one of the Moravians of the company said was often mentioned in the records of the mission there as a wholesome and abundant article of food in the settlement.

Eunice had evidently been a stout, thick-set woman in her prime, a little below the ordinary height of her sex. She had strongly-marked Indian features, evidently lighted in earlier life by brilliant black eyes. Age had now made its furrows everywhere upon her face, and somewhat dimmed her vision; but her voice, low and clear, had all the force and melody of that of her young womanhood. Her mind was strong, but a little sluggish; and when, by questions, we tried to draw from her the salient points in the story of her long life, she would sit a moment, with her eyes fixed upon the fire, to summon tardy memory to give us answers. She never failed; and by patient questioning and more patient waiting our curiosity was satisfied.

Eunice was born in Derby, Connecticut, between the Naugatuck and Housatonic rivers, in the year 1759. Her father, Gideon Mahwee's second son, was named Joseph, and wore the costume of the white people. She remembered a visit made to him by her grandfather and a few friends, when she was a little child. They were dressed in the Indian manner, and were entertained at dinner, of which they partook with their fingers out of a huge kettle of meat and vegetables, all sitting around it on the ground. Their wild appearance frightened her and she hid in the bushes for fear of being eaten up by them. She lived in Derby until she was married to a Narraganset Indian named John Sutnux, who, almost immediately afterward, went to the north with Connecticut troops, and was engaged in the short campaign that ended in the capture of Burgoyne and his army at Saratoga.

At that time there were only five Indians in Derby, and soon after her husband's return from camp they settled among the Schaghticooks at Kent, where there was then no sachem, her grandfather being dead, and no person of unmixed blood remaining who might bear the honor. His memory was dear to the people, for he had been a father to them, telling them where and when to plant and sow, and reap and gather. He allowed no drinking of fermented liquors; and while he lived the tribe flourished and increased. They were so numerous when Eunice first went among them that she was timid for a long time, they seemed so wild. After Gideon's death the tribal bonds became weakened.

Intemperance and idleness marred their prosperity, and the community began to scatter. At the opening of the revolution there were yet a sufficient number to send one hundred warriors to the field. In that war many of them perished.

Eunice's husband died at Kent, and she afterward married Peter Sherman. She had borne nine children, and had outlived them all. Skillful in basket making, many years of her womanhood in the early part of this century were spent in that business. She often wandered over the mountains into the Weebetuck valley (now Dover plains), selling her wares, and was made welcome by everybody. Many a night was spent by her in the hospitable mansion of the estate on which the writer now resides, when the young people of the family would listen during a long evening to her marvelous stories of the past. One of these, now almost four-score years of age, and other old residents of this region, have a vivid recollection of the vigorous and wandering Eunice, the basket-woman, and also of her contemporary and friend of the Stockbridge Indians, John Konkepot, who was educated at Nazareth Hall, in Bethlehem, by the Moravians. He was better known as Doctor Konkepot, because he was famous for his certain cures of the bite of the rattlesnake, as well as of almost every other disease, by the use of Indian medicines. Strong drink became his enemy. He had no cure for *that* serpent which "stingeth like an adder," and he died its victim.

Somewhat late in life Eunice again became a widow; and when, in 1844, at the age of eighty-five years, she was baptized and received into the Congregational church at Kent, she took her maiden name of Mahwee, by which she was ever afterward known. In fact, she had assumed it on the death of her second husband, many years before.

The Schaghticook reservation was originally more extended than when we visited it. It was bounded on the north by the creek which gave it its name, on the south by the Weebetuck, on the east by the Housatonic river, and on the west by a line on the mountains. Sachem Gideon laid out this tract into oblong strips extending from the river to the mountain, and assigned one to each family. This partition gave to each the right to hunt in the mountains and to fish in the river. He compelled each family to till their land and live off of the products, and thereby discouraged laziness.

Eunice was still living on land assigned to her family, and she was so much attached to it that she did not want to leave it, even for an hour. She spoke sadly of the decay of her people, and almost contemptuously of those whose blood was mixed with other than that of the Indian race. She remembered when there was a fair degree of prosperity in the settlement, the inhabitants quite numerous and the pappooses in the fields as plentiful as squirrels. Alas! at the time of our visit not more than thirty persons with the Indian purple in their veins were inhabitants of the reservation, and these were of almost every shade of brown. Eunice spoke with honest pride of her own pure blood, and said she was the very last one of the Pequods whose pedigree was free from the taint of amalgamation.

Our questions concerning the past excited Eunice's memory of her youthful days. She told us that even so late as in her young womanhood she had heard her people declare how much they loved the Moravians, and delighted to relate the manner and incidents of their visits.

Those faithful missionaries came first one and then another, singly, stayed a while, and returned; and then they came again, with their women. During the few years that they ministered in Eastern Duchess they baptized no less than one hundred and fifty Indians in the Schaghticook settlement.

Perceiving signs of weariness in the face of the venerable centenarian, we bade her farewell and continued our journey, satisfied that we had been face to face with the last survivor of a once powerful nation, whose race inhabited our continent ages, perhaps, before Europeans discovered it — a race now rapidly fading away, there remaining not more than three hundred thousand within the broad domain of our republic of the vast multitude who were here when De Soto and his fellow-invaders, a little more than three hundred years ago, swept over the gulf region from the peninsula of Flowers to the eastern slopes of the Rocky mountains. Crawford's grand figure of The Last of his Race is a prophecy soon to be fulfilled.

THE TRADITION OF AN INDIAN ATTACK ON HADLEY, MASS., IN 1675.[1]

[Read before the Pocomtuck Valley (Mass.) Memorial Association, Feb. 24, 1874, and before the New England Historical Genealogical Society, May 6, 1874.]

BY GEORGE SHELDON.

There is probably not one before me, who has not heard the thrilling story of the regicides, Edward Whalley and William Goffe, two of the English judges who sent king Charles I. to the executioner's block in 1649; of their flight to New-England on the restoration of the Stuarts to the throne in 1660; of their successful concealment at New Haven and other places, while the minions of Charles II. hunted them through every town in the colonies; of their final haven of refuge in the house of the Rev. John Russell in Hadley; and more especially of the angel who appeared Sept. 1, 1675, in the person of General Goffe, to deliver Hadley from the power of the enemy, for this story has been repeated in one form or another all over the civilized world.

The alleged appearance of Goffe at Hadley, whether considered in connection with the supposed miracle or as the heroic act of a brave man, has been a fruitful theme for historians and an inspiration for poets. Divines have seen in it a special interposition of Providence; the champions of liberty have pointed to it as new evidence of the valor of that strong defender of the rights of man; and the mighty "Wizard of the North" has woven it into the pages of delightful romance. Notwithstanding all this, I make bold to ask your attention while the story of the guardian angel of Hadley is examined from a new point of view, which it is but fair to say, in the beginning, is that of a skeptic. The origin of the story, with its growth and development under the hands of the leading historians, will be shown, and such conclusions drawn as the premises may seem to warrant.

The Rev. Increase Mather, in his history of the war with the

---

[1] Reprinted from the *New England Historical and Genealogical Register* (Boston), for October, 1874.

Indians, published at the close of Philip's war in 1677, makes this statement: "On the 1st of September, 1675, one of the churches in Boston was seeking the face of God, by fasting and prayer before him ; also that very day the church in Hadley was before the Lord in the same way, but were driven from the holy service they were attending by a most sudden and violent alarm which routed them the whole day after."

Nothing more is heard of this affair for eighty-nine years, when, in 1764, Gov. Hutchinson published his valuable history of Massachusetts. In the text of this work he says: "Sept. the first, 1675, Hadley was attacked upon a fast day, while the people were at church, which broke up the service and obliged them to spend the day in a very different exercise." The story has here advanced one step: Mather having spoken only of an *alarm*, which with Hutchinson has become an *attack*.

When Hutchinson wrote he was in possession of a diary kept by Goffe for many years, from which he gives an account of the wanderings and concealments of the regicides. In a marginal note he adds: "I am loth to omit an anecdote handed down through Gov. Leverett's family." Then follows this anecdote: "The town of Hadley was alarmed by Indians in 1675 in the time of public worship. The people were in the utmost confusion. Suddenly a grave elderly person appeared in the midst of them. In his mien and dress he differed from the rest of the people. He not only encouraged them to defend themselves, but put himself at their head, rallied, instructed and led them on to encounter the enemy, who by this means were repulsed. As suddenly, the deliverer of Hadley disappeared. The people were left in consternation, utterly unable to account for this phenomenon. It is not probable that they were ever able to explain it." It will be perceived that this is a great advance in the story, but as yet there is no angel, only a mystery.

President Stiles, of Yale College, in his History of the Judges, published thirty years later, writes as follows:

"Though told with some variation in various parts of New-England, the true story of the angel is this. * * * * * That pious congregation were observing a fast at Hadley on the occasion of this war; and being at public worship in the meeting house there on a fast day, Sept. 1, 1675, were suddenly surrounded and surprised by a body of Indians. It was the usage in the frontier towns, and even at New Haven, in those Indian wars, for a select number of the congregation to go armed to public worship. It was so at Hadley at this time. The people immediately took to their arms, but were thrown into great consternation and confusion. Had Hadley been taken, the discovery of the judges had been inevitable. Suddenly, and in the midst of the people, there appeared a man of a very venerable aspect, and different from the inhabitants in his apparel, who took the command, arrayed and ordered them in the best military manner, and, under his direction, they repelled and routed the Indians, and the town was saved. He immediately vanished, and the inhabitants could not account for the phenomenon, but by considering that person as an angel sent of God upon that special occasion for their deliverance; and for some time after, said and believed that they had been delivered and saved by an angel. Nor did they know or conceive otherwise till fifteen or twenty years after, when it at length became known at Hadley that the two judges had been secreted there; which probably they did not know till after Mr. Russell's death in 1692. This story, however, of the angel at Hadley was before this universally diffused through New England, by means of the memorable Indian war of 1675. The mystery was unriddled after the revolution [of 1688 in England], when it became not so very dangerous to have it known that the judges had received an asylum here, and that Goffe was actually in Hadley at that time. The angel was certainly General Goffe, for Whalley was superannuated in 1675." In the above account the angel is full-fledged, and the outline of the battle is given for the first time in print.

In 1824, General Epaphras Hoyt, of Deerfield, Mass., published some result of his studies in his *Antiquarian Researches*. In this work, after a detailed account of an attack on Hadley by Indians, June 12, 1676, he adds : " A curious circumstance occurred in this attack. When the people were in great consternation and rallying to oppose the Indians, a man of venerable aspect, differing from the inhabitants in his apparel, appeared, and assuming command, arrayed them in the best manner for defence, evincing much knowledge of military tactics; and by his advice and example continued to animate the men throughout the attack. When the Indians drew off, the stranger disappeared, and nothing further was heard of him. Who the deliverer was, none could inform or conjecture, but by supposing, as was common at that day, that Hadley had been saved by its guardian angel. It will be recollected that, at this time, the two judges, Whalley and Goffe, were secreted in the village, at the house of the Rev. Mr. Russell. The supposed angel was then no other than General Goffe, who, seeing the village in imminent danger, put all at risk, left his concealment, mixed with the inhabitants, and animated them to a vigorous defence." Observe that the assault has now become a dangerous one, a more particular account of the principal actor is given, but the whole affair is dated nine or ten months later: June, 1676, instead of Sept., 1675.

Holmes, in his *Annals of America*, quotes Mather, Hutchinson, Stiles and Hoyt. He fully credits the story, but doubts whether Hoyt is justified in placing the appearance of Goffe at a later date.

In his address, at the bi-centennial celebration at Hadley, June 8, 1859, the Rev. Dr. Huntington, with unquestioning faith, says: "It was, as everybody knows, in the attack of the Indians, Sept. 1, 1675, a day of fasting, while the people were assembled in their meeting-house, that Goffe, willing to incur the sacrifice of exposing his own life to the double enemy, one here in the bushes, and another on the British throne, came suddenly forth from his hiding place, and by valor and skill, arraying the affrighted worshipers in ranks, and putting himself at their head, drove the assailants back."

He does not believe that the meeting-house was surrounded, but that the engagement occurred east of the village, adding: "this accords with a traditional feature of the story which I heard for the first time last winter. An aged woman, in a remote part of the town, says she had heard that Goffe saw the Indians entering the town from the mountains at a distance." As if the subtle red man, who was *never seen* till he struck his blow, could have been discovered coming over the hills at a distance like an army with baggage and banners!

Dr. Holland, in his *History of Western Massachusetts*, with no apology for a change of time and circumstance, and with no apparent misgivings as to the fact of the attack, fixes the date as June 12, 1676, and gives this circumstantial account of the event in question. "The attack was made with the desperate determination to succeed. On the preceding night they had laid an ambuscade at the southern extremity of the town, calculating to sweep the place from the north, and by driving the inhabitants southward to force them into the snare there set for them. The enemy were warmly received at the palisades. At one point on the north the palisades were pierced, and the Indians succeeded in gaining possession of a house, but were at last forced out of it and beaten back with loss. At this moment of extreme confusion and alarm, the course of events was under the keen survey of a pair of eyes that were strangers to all but one or two families in the town. They were eyes practiced in military affairs, and belonged to a man who held the stake of life on the issue of the conflict. Unable longer to remain an idle spectator of the struggle, he resolved to issue forth. Suddenly he stood in the midst of the affrighted villagers, a man marked in his dress, noble in carriage and venerable in appearance. Self-appointed, he in a measure assumed the command, arranged and ordered the English forces in the best military manner, encouraged here, commanded there, rallied the men everywhere, filled them with hope and firmness on every hand, and at last succeeded in repelling the overwhelming numbers that swarmed on all sides. The discharge of a piece of ordnance put them to flight, and Major Talcott, going over from Northampton with his forces, joined the victorious villagers and soldiers of Hadley in chasing the enemy into the woods. This feat was accomplished with the loss of only two or three men on the part of the English. But the mysterious stranger, who had been partly if not mainly instrumental in effecting this thorough rout, had retired from sight as suddenly as he had made his advent. Who he was, none knew. That such a man could live upon a plantation and not be known was not deemed possible ; and it is not strange that in the superstitious spirit of the times he should have been regarded by the people as ' an angel sent of God upon this special occasion for their deliverance.' "

Sylvester Judd, the most noted antiquary of the Connecticut valley, writing one hundred years later than Hutchinson, can find no new evidence in support of the oft-repeated tale. He quotes Mather and Hutchinson, criticizes sharply the account by Stiles, thinks Hoyt mistook the date of the occurrence, and says : " The attack was undoubtedly upon the outskirts of the town, probably at the north end. The approach of the Indians may have been observed by Goffe from his chamber, which had a window toward the east. There is no reason to believe there was a large body of Indians, but the people being unaccustomed to war, needed Goffe to arrange and order them. The Indians appear to have fled after a short skirmish." Thus the proportions of the story are reduced by Judd. The meeting-house was not surrounded, the attack was at the north end of the town, and there was but a slight skirmish after all.

However, this matter is not to rest here. Palfrey's *History of New England*, published in 1865, contains so vivid and graphic a picture of the encounter, that we can almost see the wily foe stealing down upon the quiet village, the confusion and dismay when their savage war-whoop burst upon the astounded congregation of worshipers, the awe-struck look but ready obedience of the soldiers and citizens as the old hero, Goffe, appeared among them and gave the word of command. We can almost hear the tramp of the steadied line, the sharp crash of musketry, and the final rush of victory. I cannot forbear quoting him at length :
" At the end of another week separate attacks were made upon two of the settlements on the Connecticut. At Deerfield, several houses and barns were burned, and two men killed. At Hadley, from which place the Indians had observed most of the garrison to be absent, the inhabitants were keeping a fast, when their devotion was disturbed by the outcries of a furious enemy. Seiz-

ing the muskets which stood by their sides, the men rushed out of their meeting-house and hastily fell into line; but the suddenness of the assault from a foe now enclosing them all around, was bewildering, and they seemed about to give way, when it is said an unknown man, of advanced years and ancient garb, appeared among them, and abruptly assumed the direction with the bearing and tone of one used to battles. His sharp word of command instantly restored order, musket and pike were handled with nerve, the invaders were driven in headlong flight out of the town. When the pursuers collected again, their deliverer had disappeared, nor could any man get an answer by what instrument Providence had interposed for their rescue. It was the regicide Colonel Goffe. Sitting at a window of Mr. Russell's house, while his neighbors were at worship, he had seen the stealthy savages coming down over the hills. The old ardor took possession of him once more; he rushed out to win one more victory for God's people and then went back to the retirement from which no man knows that he emerged again."

The story has now attained full stature. Mather's alarm has become a furious battle, victory wavering for awhile between the combatants.

I now quote from the Rev. Chandler Robbins's *Regicides Sheltered in New England.* "In the summer of 1676, while Philip's war was raging, a powerful force of Indians made a sudden assault upon Hadley. The inhabitants at the time were assembled in their meeting-house, observing a day of fasting and prayer, but, in apprehension of an attack, they had taken their muskets with them to the house of God. While they were engaged in their devotions, the younger of the solitary captives, who perhaps taking advantage of the absence of observers, to enjoy a brief interval of comparative freedom, may have been seated at an open window, or walking near the house, discovered the approach of the wily foe, and hastened to give the alarm. With the air of one accustomed to command, he hastly drew up the little band of villagers in the most approved military order, put himself at their head, and by his own ardor and energy inspired them with such confidence, that rushing upon the swarming savages, they succeeded, with the loss of only two or three men, in driving them back into the wilderness." Here again the details of the affair are essentially changed. Goffe discovers the Indians, gives the alarm, and leads the attack, which is made by the whites. Their loss is given, and I do not despair of yet seeing a list of the names of the killed, wounded and missing.

I will lastly quote John Farmer, secretary of the New Hampshire Historical Society, who gives, as his authority, the Rev. Phineas Cooke, a native of Hadley. With such endorsement this extract should receive especial attention, and have due weight.

It was while the regicides resided with Mr. Russell, "and while his people were observing a fast on account of the Philip's war, Sept. 1, 1675, that a party of Indians collected and were about to attack the inhabitants while assembled in the meeting-house. Some accounts represent the scene to have occurred on the Sabbath, but all agree that it happened during a time of public worship, and while almost the entire population were collected. The party approached the town from the north, with the manifest design to surprise the people at meeting, before they could be prepared to make any effectual resistance. Gen. Goffe and Gen. Whalley . . . . . were the only persons remaining at home at Mr. Russell's. Goffe saw from his chamber window the enemy collecting, and approaching towards the meeting-house, and knowing the peril of the congregation, felt himself constrained to give them notice, although it might lead to the discovery of his character and his place of concealment. He went in haste to the house of God, apprised the assembly that the enemy were near, and preparation must be immediately made for the defence. All was alarm and trepidation. 'What shall we do, who will lead us?' was the cry from every quarter. In the confusion the stranger said, 'I will lead, follow me.' Immediately all obeyed their unknown general and prepared to march against the enemy. Though some of them were armed, yet their principal weapon of defence was an old iron cannon, sent there sometime before by the government; but no one of the inhabitants was sufficiently skilled in military tactics to manage it to much purpose. The marvellous stranger knew, and having loaded it proceeded to the attack. Beholding this formidable array, the Indians retreated a short distance, and took refuge in a deserted house on Connecticut river. The cannon was so directed, that when discharged, the contents threw down the top of the stone chimney about the heads of the Indians, who took fright, and fled with great terror and dismay. The commander ordered his company to pursue, take and destroy as many of the enemy as they could, and while they were in pursuit of the Indians, he retreated unobserved, and soon rejoined Whalley in their private chamber. When the pursuers returned he was gone, and nothing was heard of him for years afterward. The good people supposed their deliverer was an angel, who having completed his business, had returned to celestial quarters. And when we consider his venerable appearance, his silvery locks, and his pale visage, together with the disposition of the pious of that period to see a special providence in events which they could not comprehend, and the sudden manner of his disappearance, it is not surprising they supposed their deliverer came from another world."

Let us try to imagine the gentle savages considerately delaying their attack until the confusion had subsided, and the silverhaired leader had loaded to his mind this new instrument for bush fighting, and then retreating in a body to a deserted house! The absurdity of this account is only equalled by the credulity of the writer.

We will now review in an inverse order these successive accounts of the affair at Hadley, that we may discover their basis and historical value.

Nothing more need be said of the Farmer and Cooke version of the story.

Confused by the conflicting accounts of the local historians (Hoyt, Judd, Huntington and Holland), not satisfied of the truth of either, but seeing no ground for their rejection, Dr. Robbins seems to have compromised with himself by endorsing the leading points of each. He makes no claim to new sources of information; his only references being Dr. Holland's *History of Western Massachusetts*, Dr. Huntington's address, before referred to, and Sir Walter Scott's *Peveril of the Peak*.

While Dr. Palfrey gives such a glowing description of the assault, he not only fails to bring any evidence to support it, but throws a shadow over what have been considered the best authorities. In reference to the story he remarks, in a marginal note, "I am sorry to say that I can find no other authority than Hutchinson," and " am disappointed in the hope of finding confirmation of it in the Connecticut river records or traditions. I can hear of no traditions that are not traceable to Hutchinson's history.

Dr. Holland, though giving us fuller particulars than preceding writers, quotes no more recent authority to justify his interpretation of the story.

As Dr. Huntington, with few exceptions, gives Judd credit for the historical facts of his address, his account and Judd's will be treated as one. The latter, in his careful and minute search after materials for a history of Hadley, has found absolutely nothing to confirm the Leverett family tradition, and after his severe scrutiny it seems safe to assert that nothing ever will be found. Both were believers in the whole story as given by Hutchinson. They attempt to account for the silence of Hubbard and other historians on the ground, says Judd, that "It was necessary at that time and long after to throw a veil over the transactions of that day," or, as Huntington expresses it, "considerations of policy fully account for the obscure allusions in the contemporaneous records " — these considerations being, of course, to prevent the betrayal of the secret of the concealment of the judges at Mr. Russell's.

Were it only a question as to the silence of *such* men, on the *appearance of General Goffe*, the argument would be conclusive; but when made to cover their silence in regard to the *attack upon Hadley*, as well, it fails to convince. On the contrary, the omission in Hubbard's history of so important a fact as the first attack of the Indians upon a village in the Connecticut valley, must have provoked inquiry as to the cause of such an omission, and inquiry at Hadley under the circumstances must have resulted in the discovery of the fugitives. Suspicion had already been directed here, and their very house of refuge had been searched by zealous agents of the crown. Hubbard was undoubtedly acquainted with these facts. Hadley, at the time in question, probably contained about five hundred inhabitants, every man, woman and child of whom, save those in the secret, must have been filled with awe and amazement at their supernatural deliverance. Signs and wonders were familiar to the people of those days, but no event of such significance had occurred in the history of New England, and the news of such a marvellous providence must soon have spread over all the colonies; especially as Hadley became the head quarters of military operations, and within that same week hundreds of soldiers were collected there from all parts of Massachusetts and Connecticut. Silence as to this event *might* perhaps have been imposed upon the historians and ministers, who were the chief letter-writers of that period, but it is inconceivable that the lips of this great multitude could have been closed, while from the very nature of the case no good reason could be given for silence. Well might the people say, "Jehovah hath bared His arm in our defence. Let us proclaim from the house-tops his wonderful interposition for our deliverance, and spread the glorious tidings throughout the length and breadth of the land, that we may thereby encourage the armies of the Lord, and strike terror to the hearts of our superstitious foe." To such an argument there could have been no opposition without betraying the fugitives.

If the appearance of Goffe were a fact, it would be strange indeed that so imposing an event should have been entirely lost sight of save in the traditions of one family, that of Governor Leverett Why have we no trace of it as well in the traditions of the Russell family, the families of Nash, Wells, Hawks or Dickinson, of Hoyt or Barnard? for the ancestors of those bearing these names now among us, were living in Hadley at this period, and must have been eye-witnesses of the events; or in the families of Catlin, Stebbins, Clesson or Sheldon, whose ancestors lived hard by in Northampton? And it is well nigh impossible, that a secret in the keeping of so many people could by any means escape the keen scent of that subservient and untiring spy on New England, Edward Randolph, backed as he was by a royal commission and the power of Charles the Second.

Hoyt, while relating what he believed the facts of the story, but dating it later, says in a marginal note that he "finds no evidence of any attack Sept. 1," and "that Hubbard, who wrote his narrative from facts collected during the war and published immediately after, should have wholly omitted to notice an attack at the time mentioned by Hutchinson, would be extraordinary." He might have added, that Capt. Appleton, who was in command of the troops at Hadley certainly within five days after the alleged attack if not on the very day, was an inhabitant of Ipswich and a parishioner of Mr. Hubbard, which fact renders such an omission still more " extraordinary."

A careful examination of the work of President Stiles shows that he made no *investigation* of the angel story. After copying what was to be found in Hutchinson, *including* the traditional anecdote, he says: " *Hitherto* we have proceeded upon *accurate* and *authentic* documents, I shall now collect and exhibit other scattered lights and traditionary information, preserved partly in public fame, and partly in traditions in families whose ancestors were privy to the secrets of these men."

Considering the *anecdote* "accurate and authentic," he seeks only to concentrate the scattered rays of light that may be found elsewhere. Accordingly he visits the scene of the wonder and corresponded with aged people in the vicinity, and says he finds the story is preserved in the traditions at Hadley and New Haven, giving as the best evidence to be found a letter from the Rev. Samuel Hopkins, of Hadley, dated March 26, 1793. In this letter the writer records particular traditions which he found in several families as to the fact of the regicides having been concealed in Hadley, likewise about the places of their burial, disagreeing, to be sure, but containing evidence that they were founded in fact; but only *general* traditions as to the *appearance* of Goffe. This we must bear in mind was thirty years after the Leverett anecdote was published by Hutchinson; time enough for the romance to have become naturalized and wedded to the tradition of their residence and death in Hadley above mentioned. Mr. Hopkins's testimony, so satisfactory to President Stiles, would have more value had it appeared before Hutchinson wrote.

Stiles took the angel story for granted, making no independent investigation. His statements are vague and careless; consequently his conclusions should have little weight with historians.

In compiling his history, Hutchinson had access to Mather's papers and library, from which great depository of historical matter he drew largely, often quoting from Mather's history of the war as authority. There seems therefore no room for doubt, that Hutchinson's story of the *attack*, Sept. 1, was his version of Mather's account of the *alarm* quoted at the beginning of this paper, and that he had no other source of information relating to that event. Nothing in Hutchinson then remains to be examined but the anecdote of the tradition in Governor Leverett's family, before given.

After the death of the regicides, their papers came into the possession of the Mather family. Among them was Goffe's diary, containing a record of their adventures for six or seven years. Hutchinson, from this diary, gives a full account of the wanderings, escapes and concealments of the judges, but not one word from that in support of the story of Goffe's sudden appearance at Hadley. In a marginal note, at the close of this narrative, he thus introduces the tradition: "I am loth to omit an anecdote handed down through Governor Leverett's family." All accounts of Goffe's appearance at Hadley, Sept. 1, 1675, can be traced directly to this anecdote, and there is no pretence of any other authority.

The interpretation given to Mather's account by Hutchinson, seems to have been hitherto accepted without question, by all succeeding historians; and upon this slender foundation they have builded and enlarged. Let me repeat Mather's statement:

"One of the churches in Boston was seeking the face of the Lord by fasting and prayer before him. Also that very day the church in Hadley was before the Lord in the same way, but were driven from the holy sanctuary by a sudden and violent *alarm* which routed them the whole day after." We have here no particulars of a fight, no indications of the point or method of an attack, no account of arrangement for defence, no result of battle, no list of losses — all these details are added by subsequent writers; in fact he does not assert or hint that there was an *attack;* yet this paragraph is literally *all* the evidence that has been given of an attack on Hadley Sept. 1, 1675. Is it sufficient?

Let me give briefly further reasons which lead me to a different conclusion, namely:

First, that there was no attack on Hadley Sept. 1, 1675.

Second, that the story of General Goffe's appearance either as man or angel, at *any* attack on that town, is a pure romance.

An *alarm* is not necessarily an *attack*, and we may find an explanation of Mather's language in a letter from the Rev. Solomon Stoddard, of Northampton, to Mather, dated Sept. 15, 1675, in which he gives a long and minute account of the events which had occurred during the three preceding weeks; events the most important that had transpired in the valley settlements. After describing the pursuit of the Hatfield Indians when they fled from their fort to join the Pocomtucks in the interest of King Philip, and the fight with them in the swamp, south of Wequamps or Sugar Loaf mountain, Aug. 25, he continues: "After this fight we hear no more from them till the first of September, when they shot down a garrison soldier of Pocomtuck (now Deerfield), that was looking after his horse, and ran violently up into the town, many people having scarcely time to get into their garrisons. That day, they burned most of their houses and barns, the garrison not being strong enough to sally out upon them, but killed two of them from their forts."

When Deerfield was attacked on Feb. 29, 1704, the alarm was given in Hadley so quickly, that men from that town reached the scene of carnage in about three or four hours from the time the attack was made. Can any one doubt that the news of this earlier assault upon Deerfield, described by Stoddard, might soon have reached the inhabitants of Hadley?—and remembering that this was the first attack by the savages upon any white settlement in the valley, we can conceive the consternation and *alarm* it must have created among the settlers, and can readily believe that the people of Hadley were "violently alarmed and routed the whole day after."

This seems to be a reasonable solution of the whole matter, in which I am confirmed by recorded events of a similar character.

Colonel John Pynchon, writing from Springfield to the governor at Boston, says: "It is troublesome times here; we have had two *alarms* lately, which in mercy prove nothing in reality. But the same with other disquiets, takes up my time and prove hard for me."

Again, in a letter from Boston to London, dated Sept. 28, 1675, the writer says: "An *alarm* was made in Boston about ten in the morning, 1200 men were in arms before eleven, ... One that was on guard at Mendon, thirty miles off, got drunk, and fired his gun, the noise of which alarmed the next neighbors and soon spread to Boston."

Governor Hutchinson himself records another event from which he might have taken a hint of Mather's meaning, the language being so similar. "The 23d of February, 1676, being a fast with the first church in Boston, they were disturbed by an *alarm* from the report that the Indians were within fifteen miles of Boston." Similar examples might be multiplied. I quote one more. Major Savage, writing from Hadley to Governor Leverett, March 16, 1676, says: "This morning about 2 o'clock we were *alarmed* from Northampton which was occasioned by Indians being seen on two sides of the town." Doubtless Mather intended to record only a similar *alarm* at Hadley, Sept. 1, 1675.

Hubbard's narrative of the war, before referred to, was published under the patronage of the general court only about eighteen months after the supposed attack. A committee from that body examined his manuscript, and pronounced the work "faithfully and truly performed." Yet this book contains no allusion to any disturbance at Hadley, Sept. 1, while it gives full accounts of all the movements thereabouts, in those eventful weeks of Sept., 1675. Truly, as Hoyt remarks, "an extraordinary omission."

Cotton Mather wrote a history of Philip's war, detailing the principal events which occurred in the Connecticut valley, without *hinting* at an attack upon Hadley in 1675. Can we account for the omissions of these writers, except on the grounds I have assumed?

Stronger evidence yet remains to be considered. The letter before quoted, from the Rev. Solomon Stoddard, of Northampton, to Mather, contained a long and circumstantial narrative of the breaking out of Philip's war in the valley; of the attempt to disarm the Indians at Hatfield fort, Aug. 24; the fight that followed the next morning near Wequamps; the attack on Deerfield, Sept. 1; the slaughter of the eight men at Northfield, Sept. 2; the defeat and death of Capt. Beers, Sept. 4; the march of Major Treat to Northfield, Sept. 6; the second attack on Deerfield, Sept. 12; the expedition to Pine Hill, Sept. 14, in pursuit of the party which made this last attack; but not a *single word* to indicate trouble at Hadley, Sept. 1.

On Friday, Sept. 3, 1675, Major Treat came into Hadley with a hundred or more Connecticut troops. The ill-fated Capt. Lothrop was there with "the Flower of Essex;" Capt. Appleton was also there, and it is to be supposed his company was with him; and Capt. Beers, with his company. Yet on that very day, says Hubbard, Capt. Beers "with thirty-six men was sent to Squakeag with supplies both of men and provision to secure the small garrison there, but before they came very near to the town, they were set upon by many hundreds of Indians out of the bushes by the swamp side, of whom Capt. Beers, with about twenty of his men, were by this sudden surprisal there slain, the rest flying back to Hadley."

Is it reasonable to suppose, that the only two days after a terrible assault on Hadley, in which the town was barely saved by the interposition of an angel, and while several hundred soldiers under arms were there, a supply train of ox carts should have been sent a distance of thirty miles through the wilderness with a guard of only thirty-six men? Capt. Beers's expedition, an unpardonable blunder at the best, is only to be accounted for on the supposition that the authorities believed Philip's forces had crossed the Connecticut river, joined the Hatfield tribe and the Pocomtucks in the attack on Deerfield, Sept. 1, and that the hostile Indians were then all on the west side of the river. They had not then heard of the assault on Northfield the day before. With a suggestion of the intrinsic improbability of the soldiers at Hadley putting themseves under the lead of a stranger while their veteran commanders were present, I leave this division of my subject.

In regard to my second point, namely, that Goffe's appearance at *any time* is a pure romance, it may be asked, admitting that we have proved that there was no attack on Hadley Sept. 1, 1675, what evidence is there that Hoyt and Dr. Robbins were not right in their statements that Goffe's appearance was on the 12th of June, the next year, when the Indians really did fall upon that town?

To this the following facts are a sufficient reply. There is no correspondence between the well-known events of this day, and those of the Leverett tradition. 1st. The 12th of June, 1676, *was not a fast day.* 2d. The inhabitants were not assembled in the meeting-house. 3d. The attack was made upon a small party who had fallen into an ambuscade. 4th. It was made early in the morning. 5th. The town was not then in a defenceless condition; for besides the soldiers of Capt. Turner's company who had survived the Falls fight some three weeks previous, and were now under Capt. Swain, nearly five hundred Connecticut men were in Hadley under Major Talcott, two hundred of whom were friendly Indians under Oneko, son of Uncas, the famous sachem of the Mohegans. The Connecticut forces had but recently arrived, and doubtless Philip's Indians expected to attack a defenceless town, but at no time during Philip's war had Hadley been in so good a condition to repel an attack.

The spirit which, some years later, caused the arrest and execution in England of Lady Alicia Lisle, for concealing Mr. Hicks and Mr. Nelthorpe, two persons obnoxious to the crown, sent that subtle spy and informer, Edward Randolph, to New England in March, 1676, to seek matter of accusation against the inhabitants preparatory to abrogating their charters. Special instructions were given him to search for the regicides. Active and crafty, as he was zealous and malicious, he lost no opportunity of serving his master. The fugitives must have been fully informed of his mission and purpose, and fully aware of the consequences of their discovery. General Goffe knew that Hadley was in no danger of capture, and that there was no occasion for leaving his hiding place, thereby exposing himself, his companion in exile and his generous protectors to certain destruction.

THE END.

ERRATA.

Page 105, Line 35 and elsewhere — For *Allonez* read *Allouez*.
" 149, " 35 — (In note) For *mississanga* read *mississauga*.
" 155, " 22 — For *sixty-seven* read *seventy-six*.
" 158, " 34 — (In note) For October, 1868 read October, 1869.
" 252, " 4 — Omit *and a preceding*.
" 254, " 20 — For *these articles* read *this article*.
" 285, " 21 — Omit *populating*.
" " " 22 — After *purpose of* insert *populating*.
" 333, " 33 — (In note) For *Reprinted* read *Printed*.
" 335, " 26 — For *Carantonannis* read *Carantouanais*.
" 342, " 20 — For *Levallos* read *Zevallos*.
" 350, " 28 — For *beat* read *beating*.
" 352, " 33 — (In note) For *Commission* read *Commissioner*.
" 361, " 3 — For *Prof. 1. 1. Ducatel* read *Prof. J. J. Ducatel*.
" 400, " 16 — For *of us to* read *to us of*.
" 411, " 38 — (In note) For *part salary of his* read *part of his salary*.
" 416, " 11 — Insert *and* after *phonological*.
" 424, " 5 — For *differention* read *differentiation*.
" 426, " 6 — For *Kalapupa* read *Kalapuya*.
" 433, " 22 — For *Awnaves* read *Awanees*.
" 434, " 37 — For *Poomeocs* read *Pooemocs*.
" 436, " 8 — For *Chokuyen* read *Chokuyem*.
" 437, " 28 — For *E-ukshiknit* read *E-ukshikni*.

Errors in uniformity of orthography not noted.

INDEX.

Abnakis, 418; their locality, 211.
Aborigines, ignorant of the use of iron, 161; of one family, 378; origin of, 285, 286, 287; characteristics of, 287—802.
Absarokas, 222.
Acequias, Mexican, 201
Acheotennes, 234.
Adair's North Am. Indians, 280.
Adobe houses, 189.
African dialects, 417, 423; origin, no evidence of, 223.
Agriculture, Indian, 197, 198.
Ahahnelins, 218.
Ahyouwaeghs (John Brant), 149.
Alabamas conquered, 120.
Alaska nations, 234.
Alaska peninsula, 255.
Alaskan mummies, 344, 349.
Aleut Eskimo, 346; customs, 348.
Aleutian island, source of migration, 255, 256; burials, 344.
Alfred, Prince, among the Mohawks, 153.
Algonkin, migrations, 211, 212, 218; population, 285; residence, 225; settlements, 176; notion of the turtle, 26; spoken by Allouez, 111, 115.
Algonkins, religious influences upon, 104; their locality, 218; historical and mythological traditions of, 9; numerous, 280; territory of, 280, 281; similarity of stock, 42.
Alligewi, see Tallegwi, 40.
Allouez, Claude Jean, 105, 110, 112; met Dakotas, 213; visits Kickapoos, 115.
Alphabets suggested, 420, 424.
Amaknak island mummies, 347.
America, accessible from Asia, 256; effects of its discovery, 9.
American fur company, 81; trading post 361, 372.
American Horse, chief, 265.
American Quarterly Register, 405.
American Whig Review, 9.
Amoukhta pass, 255.
Anbury's Travels, 386.
Animals unknown to the aborigines, 199; west of Rocky mountains, 180.
Annuities, Indian, 361.

Anonymous conqueror of Mexico, 193.
Antelope, native of the prairies, 170.
Apache language, 46; spinners, 352.
Apaches, a ride with, 43; styles of dress, 43; assault Village Indians, 190; obtained the horse, 234.
Apalaches, 120.
Apalachicola villages, 120.
Appleton, Capt., at Hadley attack, 472.
Appleton's Journal, 65.
Arapahoes, 216, 261, 262.
Araucanians, 10.
Arickarees, 223, 230, 231.
Arickaree woman turned to stone, 388.
Arizona idioms, 428.
Arkansas river, 104, 114.
Asiatic origin of Indians, 287; indications of, 224; considered, 254; dialects, 417, 423; stocks, affinity of, 256.
Asiniboines, their locality, 220; Mountain alphabet of, 76.
Athapasca lake, 166, 173.
Athapascans, fish eaters, 164.
Athapasco, Apache migration, 233.
Atka island mummies, 347.
Atlantic Monthly Magazine, 74; nations, 211; origin, no evidence of, 223.
Attou island, 256.
Australasian dialects, 417.
Axacan settlement, 336; abandoned 343.
Axe of copper, used by Mexicans, 199, 200;
Aztec civilization, 196; confederacy, power of, 246; origin of, 250; migrations, 238, 241; government, 208; pueblo, its plaza, 206.
Aztecs, 422, 425; agriculturists, 164; as cultivators, 204; held table land of Mexico, 191, 192; their houses, 193; picture writing of, 162; their location, 10.
Aztlan, migration from, 240, 241.

Bad lands, fossils, 259.
Balsam Tree, his speech, 365.
Banana, Indian plant, 198, 202.
Bancroft's Hist. U. S., 166, 280.
Barren region, 172.
Bartlett, John R., his theory, 242; personal narrative, 166, 203.
Bartram, W., historian, 41.

Bates, Lieut., battle with Indians, 262.
Bean, Indian plant, 198, 199, 202.
Bear's Ribs, chief, 391.
Beavers, 234.
Beers, Capt., killed, 476.
Behring's island, 255; strait, 256.
Belle Isle, straits of, 65.
Benettau, Julien, died, 119.
Bergier, Jean, died, 118, 119; M., missionary, 105.
Beucher, Philip, 118; died, 119.
Bible, Eliot's translation, 411.
Big Head, chief, 391.
Büttner, Gotlieb, 456.
Bill Williams fork dialects, 429.
Bismarck, steamer from, 387.
Black Eyes, chief, 391.
Blackfeet, 217; Sioux, 388, 390.
Blackfoot Dakotas, 219; dirge, 84; Indians, 74, 81.
Blackhill fossils, 259, 262.
Blackhills of Nebraska, 226; map of, 265.
Blacksnake, Gov., 153.
Black Snake medicine man, 76, 80.
Blood band of the Blackfeet, 81.
Blue lake, 398.
Blue mountain surveys, 88, 89.
Blue river (Mississippi), 221.
Bone-hunters, 259, 263, 269.
Bourmont, Sieur, 270, 271, 273.
Boyle, Sir Robert, assisted Eliot, 414.
Bradford on Indian origin, 287.
Bradford, Wm., marine artist, 65.
Bradley, Gen. L. P., 260.
Brantford, church yard at, 150; residence of Mohawks, 151.
Brant, John, 149, 153; Joseph, portrait of, 155; his posterity, 145; Mollie, 149; house, 145, 153, 154.
Brants, last of the, 157.
Bread roots, 181.
Brebeuf, missionary, 107; to the Hurons, 108.
Brest, French trading post, 335.
British America, native population, 188.
Brontotherium, skull of, 259, 268.
Browne, John Mason, 74; J. Ross, 303.
Brulés, 219.
Brulé, Stephen, 335.
Buffalo, his speech, 364.
Buffalo of the prairies, 170, 178.
Burials, 300; at Behring's strait, 345.
Burns, John, 35.
Butler, Walter, 150.
Bryant, William C., 145.
Byrd, Col., 51.

Cabot's map, 133.
Cahokias 104, 105, 106; mission, 118, 119.
Cahorok dialect, 438.

California, 112, 114; Indian dialects, 416; Indian population, 189, 303; Indian reservations, 303; government aid to, 305; abuses of, 306; Indians, depopulated, 321; shortest route to, 172.
Calvin, religious influences of, 104.
Calvinists, French, 107.
Camanche spinners, 352, 357.
Camp Robinson, 264.
Canaanite origin of Indians, 285.
Canada, ceded to the French 1632, 107; Louis XIII in, 106; unfavorable to Indian sustenance, 178.
Captain Jacobs, reward for, 94.
Carantouanais, 335.
Cards introduced among Indians, 368.
Carignan, regiment of, 110.
Cawios, 231.
Carolina Indians, whence they came, 41.
Carpenter, Lieut. W. L., 266.
Carver visited Dakotas, 219.
Casey, Captain, 120.
Cass, Lewis, 221, 270.
Castaneda, estimate of population, 190.
Catawbas, 230; their vocabulary, 230.
Cathay, Smith's voyage for, 334.
Cathead Sioux, his vision, 80.
Catlin on the Indian songs, 16.
Cawtantowit, Indian God, 42.
Cayugas, 226.
Cayuse tribe, 418, 442.
Central America, navigations to, 53; adventure in, 396.
Chagouamigon, 111, 113.
Chalcans, 193.
Chalco, cultivation at, 205; lake, diked, 202, 203.
Champlain, in command at Quebec, 106, 107; founder of Quebec, 335.
Charlevoix, 22, 26, 107, 114, 115; on Indian origin, 285.
Charms as medicine, 83.
Chat, Nation du, 110; see *Heries*.
Chatahooche river, 120.
Chegoimegon, 213.
Chelaqui vocabulary, 120.
Chelokee dialect, 121.
Cheppeyans, 104.
Cherokees, 230; traditions, 41; have a written language, 76; susceptible of industry, 377.
Chesapeake, first mission colony, 333.
Cheyenne river, 216.
Cheyennes, 262.
Chibchas, 422.
Chicago, Marquette leaves, 114; Miamis visited at, 111; prairie touching at, 164; river route, 105.
Chickahominy, Smith's voyage up, 334.
Chichemecas, 104.
Chihuahua, 46; irruptions on, 353.

INDEX. 481

Chillicothe, council at, 58.
Chica, voyage to, 334; vicar of, 106.
Chinantecas, 195.
Chinook tribe, 442; seat of, 182; jargon, 426, 443.
Chippeway, tradition of the mother of the human race, 26; migration, 29; metāi song, 16.
Chippeways, 273; a fortnight among, 361; efforts to Christianize, 377; invite Jesuits, 104, of Canada, 151.
Chisel of stone in use, 199.
Chocot-harjo, 120.
Choctas, 223.
Chocuyem dialect, 432.
Cholula, cultivation at, 205.
Cholulan confederacy, 192, 195.
Chontal language, 197.
Chronicle, song of, 30, 35.
Chukchee peninsula, 344.
Cincinnati Miscellany, 323.
Circe, Augustine Meulande, 106.
Civilization problem to be solved, 105.
Clark, Geo. Rogers, hero of Kaskaskia, 51.
Clarke, the traveler, 12.
Clarke's river salmon, 185.
Clavigero, estimate of Mexican population, 193, 194.
Cletart, chief, 275.
Clifford, Hank, guide, 260.
Climate, dryness on the prairies, 168; of Columbia river, 180.
Clothing, 371.
Cooandas, 120.
Coatl, a Mexican copper implement, 199.
Cocoa, Indian plant, 198, 202.
Cohuicas, 195.
Colorado, Indian houses, 180; parks of, 170.
Columbia river, climate genial, 180, 187; migrations from, 158; salmon, 184, 185; Indians, 186; first inhabited, 187; valley, its advantages, 252, 253; migration from possible, 224, 226.
Comanches, 231, 232, 233; dialects of, 428.
Conjurations, effect of, how accounted for, 80.
Connecticut, aborigines of, 280; number of, 285; valley Indians, 282, 283.
Conquering Bear, 265.
Cooke, Phineas, on attack of Hadley, 468.
Copan monuments, 162.
Copper implements, 199.
Coppermine river, 81.
Copway, George, 17.
Corn, Indian, the only cereal, 196, 202, 205; discovery of, 251.
Cornplanter, 153.
Coronado, expedition of, 190, 232.
Cortez, Don Jose, 234.
Cotton, Indian plant, 198, 202.
Council house described, 325.
Courcelles, governor, 110.

Coyoteros, 234.
Crane Indian legend, 174, 175.
Crawford, Col. Wm., 57; executed, 57; Lieut., 261; Thomas, sculptor, 452.
Creation, the song of, 18.
Creator, idea of indicated, 21.
Cree, characters, 420; war party, 81; union, 212, 213, 217.
Creeks, 41, 223, 230.
Cross, the symbol of, among the Indians, 104.
Crows, or Upsaraukas, 83, 222; their locality, 231; medicine man, 78.
Crowell, Samuel, 323.
Cuesta's Grammar, 430.
Culinary art, 372.
Cumberland island, burial at, 451.
Custer, Gen., 261.
Cut-off band, 261.
Cuvier on extinct quadrupeds, 258.

Dablon, missionary to Sault St. Marie, 111; visits Kickapoos, 115.
Dakotah confederacy, 83; location, 178; migrations, 218, 219; signification of name, 394; territory, 127, 213, 216, 220, 223; stock, of western origin, 224, 226, 227.
Dall, W. H., his paper, 344.
Dance, at dog sacrifice, 327; customs, 366.
Daniel, early missionary to the Hurons, 108.
Darion, missionary, 119.
Dear, J. W., 264.
Death chant, 451.
Debbon, C., 396.
De la Foret, Sieur, 273.
Deed to Wm. Penn, 87.
Deerfield burned, 466, 476.
Delawares, on White river, 14; chastised by Six Nations, 91; they strike the whites, 94; migration of, 212; their locality, 212.
Deluge, the song of, 23.
Democratic Review, 102.
Dequerre, Jean, 105; slain in 1661, 105.
Derby, Indians at, 458.
De Smet, describes fisheries, 183.
De Soto, 221, 224; his march, 121; invader, 400; visited Florida, 41.
De Tonty, Sieur, 273.
Detroit, Indian affairs around, 270.
Dialects on Pacific coast, 416, 425.
Diaz, Bernal, 200, 206.
Dickinson, Obed, 325.
Diggers of California, 304, 320.
Dillon, John, squaw-man, 392.
Dog-Ribs, a tribe, 234.
Dog, meat relished, 374; sacrifice, 389, 390; of the Senecas, 323, 329.
Donna Marina, interpreter, 195.
Dorr, Herbert C., a ride with the Apaches, 48.

32

Dover, Indian settlement at, 455.
Dream of Hard Hickory, 328.
Dreaming, 375.
Drocoux, Jean Charles, 105.
Du Chesnau, memoir of, 213.
Ducatel, J. J., 361.
Dunton, John, 409.
Du Sable nation, 270.
Dyes, Indian, 352.

Ear-ornament, 389.
Earthworks, an insoluble problem, 176.
Ecclesiastics who followed the conquerors, their superstition and intolerance, 11.
Eliot, Rev. John, 405; first minister of Roxbury, 406; translates Bible, 410; his converts, 412; died, 414.
Elk of the prairies, 170, 178.
Enatzas, 223.
England and France, war between, 106.
English population 1675, 408.
Eries, or Lynx, 28, 226, 227; natives on Lake Erie, 110.
Eskimos, 179, 244; burials, 346, 348, 350; see *Esquimaux*.
Espiritu Santo, 336.
Esquimaux, discovery of, 9; of Labrador, 65; pilot, 66; natives flesh eaters, 73; being depopulated, 73; wars with Indians ceased, 69.
Etchimons, their locality, 211.
Eunice, last of the Pequods, 457, 458.
Eurok tribe, 437.
European origin, no evidence of, 223; settlement, first in Virginia, 333.
Evil spirits, 283.

Farmer, John, on Hadley attack, 468.
Fast, Christian, his captivity, 51; died, 64.
Fasts, long continued, 374.
Favré, Florentin, 119.
Feasts, numerous, 374.
Females, overtaxed with labor, 200, 372.
Fire fiend, 332.
Fish, basis of Indian subsistence, 164; drying scaffolds, 183; baskets for catching, 184.
Fisheries west of Rocky mountains, 181.
Flatheads, 83.
Flint river, 120.
Flora, arctic, 70.
Florida, French colony destroyed, 334.
Floridian tribes, 10.
Foos-harjo, educated Indian, 120.
Fort Levi, 110.
Forest area, 167, 171.
Fort Benton, 81; Laramie, 260; Rice, 387.
Fossil, perilous hunt, 258, 260; region, 265; remains, 258.
Four Mountain island mummies, 347.
Fox river ascended, 105, 113.

Foxes, arctic, 70; country of, 115.
Francis, Lieut., commands rangers, 449.
Frank Leslie's Illustrated Newspaper, 396.
Frazier's river Indians, 188.
Frederica, commanding officer at, 449.
French vessels captured, 106; Calvinist, 107; Indian subjection to, 112.
Fresno agency, 318, 319; expenses of, 321.
Friday, chief of Arapahoes, 261, 265.
Fulton, 115.
Funerals, 300.

Gakwas, 227.
Galaxy, the, 379
Gallatin, Mr., linguist, 120.
Gamblers, Indian, 367.
Gamelin, missionary, 119.
Ganowanian family, 210, 211, 217, 228, 229, 231, 235, 243, 257.
Garreau, sufferings of, 110.
Gatschet, Albert S., his paper, 416.
Georgia, early Indian wars of, 448.
Gibbs. George, 126, 420, 426.
Gibson, John, on the Tallegwi, 39.
Gideon, sachem, 455, 456.
Gila river, irrigation on, 201; dialects, 429.
Girty, Simon, 57, 58.
God of evil, Sioux, 388.
Godden, William, 307.
Goffe, William, regicide, 461; his defence of Hadley controverted, 462-478; his diary and papers, 473.
Gomara on Indian origin, 285; estimate of Mexican population, 193.
Gomez, Gabriel, massacred, 342.
Gonzales, Vincent, missionary, 342.
Good Hunter, chief, 324; his speech, 331.
Good spirit, feast to appease, 328.
Gookin on Indian origin, 286; account of praying Indians, 409; Hist. Coll. of Indians, 280.
Goreloi island, 255.
Government abuses in California, 321.
Grass, John, chief, 391.
Grasses, growth how affected, 168.
Great lake nations, 212.
Green Bay, Jesuit relics found at, 117; mission to, 102.
Gros-ventres, 218.
Grotius on Indian origin, 285.
Groton, residence of Sassacus, 452.
Guatemala, languages of, 197.
Guatusos, 396; their stature, etc., 400.
Gulf nations, migrations of, 229.
Gymnastics, 369.

Hadley, attack on, 461.
Hamilton inlet, 65, 70.
Hamor, Raphe, 343.
Hand, chief, 265.

INDEX. 483

Hanger, William, 397.
Hardcastle, Lieut., his map, 206.
Hard Hickory, chief, 324; his dream, 328.
Hares, a tribe, 234.
Harney's peak, 266.
Harper's Magazine, 303.
Hart, Captain, 397.
Hartford Indians, 283.
Hay, Judge, his testimony, 381,384; Lieut., 260.
Hazard's Register of Pennsylvania, 86.
Heckewelder, 57; on Indian picture writing, 15, 38.
Hennepin, prejudices of, 116; his return, 118.
Herera, 199, 206.
Heries destroyed by Iroquois, 110, 116.
Heve dialect, 425.
Hiacoomes, Indian convert, 412.
Hill, Capt. Aaron, 148; George W., account of captivity of Christian Fast, 51.
Historical Magazine, 125, 430, 434, 436.
Hitchitee vocabulary, 121.
Hobbamock, 297, 298.
Hodenosaunian nations, 226, 227, 229.
Holland, Dr., on attack of Hadley, 465.
Holmes, Abiel, on attack of Hadley, 464.
Hoopa tribe, 440.
Hoopahs, 234.
Hoosatahnook (Hoosatonic), 455
Hopedale, narwhal at, 70; sail to, 65, 66.
Hopkins, Rev. Samuel, on attack of Hadley, 472.
Horse, among the Indians, 74; his use in hunting, 163, 178.
Horses, expensive trappings of Apache, 43.
Horton, Captain, pursues Yamasees, 449.
Hoyt, Epaphras, on attack of Hadley, 463.
Huastecas, 194.
Huaxtepec garden, 205.
Hubbard's narrative, 475.
Hudson bay region, 170; unfavorable to Indian sustenance, 178.
Huecos, 231.
Huehuetoca outlet, 203.
Humboldt bay massacres, 319.
Hunting-grounds, the Indian paradise described, 79.
Huntington, Rev. Dr., on attack of Hadley, 465.
Huron fort, 270.
Huron-Iroquois, 234.
Hurons, a missionary field, 107, 108; contest with, 28; indifferent to religion of Jesuits, 108; introduced agriculture, 198; of Georgian bay,175; Talmatan,? 41; their locality, 226, 227.
Hutchinson, Gov., on attack of Hadley, 462; Hist. Mass., 280.

Ice floe, extent of, 65.

Illinois Indians, 111, 114; mission to the, 105, 106; river, 113; first visited by the Jesuits, 117, 118; route, 105.
Incas, conquerors of, 10.
India rubber trees, 400, 401.
Indian, converts of John Eliot, 405; council at Chillicothe, 58; expedition against the border settlements of Virginia and Pennsylvania, 58; medicine, 74, 80; memoranda, 76; migrations, 158; nations, homogeneity of, 159; physique, 287; justice, 288; gratitude, 289; hospitality, 290; population, estimate of Bancroft, 177; by Simpson, 170; walk in 1682; do, in 1692, 88; in 1735, 89; in 1756, 94.
Indiana, mission in, 113.
Indians, alienated from the French, 107; finest specimens where found, 272; knowledge of their extent acquired, 209; origin of, 12.
Industrial arts, 362.
Infant baptism, importance of, 103.
Inland Magazine, 127.
Intoxication of both sexes, 374.
Invoctoke bay, 65.
Iowas, definition of, 241; their locality, 220, 224.
Iron Horn, chief, 391.
Iroquois, 418; change of location, 186; descent of sachemships, 147; transplanted to Canada, 148; Christianized, 152; differ from Talamatan, 41; early locality of, 226, 237; expedition against, 110; families, 10; forced Otawas westward, 213; in New York, 211, 212; killed Father Jogues, 109; attacked Hurons, 110; destroy the nation du Chat, 110; league with Sioux, 115; their fisheries, 175; tradition of migration, 238.
Irrigation, Indian, 200, 201, 202.
Isauntie dialect, 219.
Israelitish origin of Indians, 285, 286
Itazipcos, 219.
Istapalapan causeway, 205.

James on the Indian songs, 16.
Japan, vicar in, 106.
Jemison, Mary, 153.
Jesuit accounts unsatisfactory, 11; early, missionaries, in Wisconsin, 102; missionaries of the northwest, 102.
Jicarillos, 234.
Jogues. Isaac, 104; slain, 109.
Johns, Catharine Brant, 150, 156.
Johnson, Myskoke speaker, 120; Peter, chief, 154.
Johnstown, Indian trail to, 58.
Joliet, his return to Quebec, 114; his route, 105, 113.
Jones, Calvin, trapper, 127.

Judd, Sylvester, on attack of Hadley, 466.

Kadiak archipelago, 344, 350, 351.
Kagâmil island, 347.
Kahgegagahbowh, 17.
Kaime of the Blackfeet, 81.
Kalapny, a tribe, 442.
Kalispelm Indians, missionary among, 77.
Kamash root, 180, 181.
Kamtchatka cape, 255, 256.
Kaning Eskimo, 346.
Kankiki, 105.
Kansas, its landscape, 168.
Kuskaskia, 104; mission, 118, 119.
Kathayakutchak, chief, 347.
Kaws their locality, 221.
Kauvuya dialects, 428.
Keechies, 231.
Kenistennux, 212, 213.
Kent, residence of the last of Schaghticooks, 455.
Kentucky, invasion of, 51.
Kerr, Wm. Johnson, 149; Elizabeth, 150; W. J. Simcoe, portrait of, 151; notice of, 153; died, 156; plantation, capture at, 449
Kettle falls fisheries, 183.
Kewassa, Indian, 55.
Kickapoos, 112, 115, 216.
Kill Eagle, chief, 391.
King's river farm, 318.
Kiowa idioms of Red river, 428.
Kitchelus lake, fish weirs, 183.
Kichtan, 297, 300.
Klamath, agency expenses, 321; Indians, 439; language, 416; reserve, 418, 422, 427.
Konkepot, John, Stockbridge Indian, 459.
Kootenai Indian, singular power of, 77, 80; fisheries, 184; language, 446.
Knight, captive, 57.
Kruth, superintendent, death of, 66.
Kutchin Indians, 188, 234.

La Belle Riviere, 104.
Labrador climate, 170; hunting in, 71; religious services, 71; Kyak races, 72; fishing at, 73.
Lachine, visited by La Salle, 334.
Lac Tracy, 104.
Lacustrine region, 178.
Lake Erie, first Jesuit mission west of, 109.
Lake Michigan, Jesuit routes from, 105.
Lake Omaxeen, 81.
Lakes, the first white men on, 102.
Lake, Superior Chippewas, 361; tropical, 269.
Lambronde, Jesuit missionary, 118.
La Mothe, Sieur, 270, 278.
Lampreys, abundant food, 457.

Language, number of dialects, 209; diversity of, 238; of the western slope, 421.
Lapointe, trading post, 361.
La Salle, voyage for China, 334.
Las Casas, estimate of Aztecs, 196.
Last of his race, statue of, 452.
Latrobe, death of, 66.
Lawson, John, historian, 41.
Leasure, Daniel, his paper, 387.
LeBlanc, Jean, 270, 273, 274, 276, 277; Maxime, missionary, 118.
LeJeune, his boast, 104.
Lenape migration, 38, 39; bark record of, 9, 14, 39.
Lewis and Clarke, 185; their estimate of population, 188; Isaac, tekarihogea, 151; Morgan, his testimony, 384.
Linares, Peter de, massacred, 342.
Linguistics, 418; confounded with philology, 417.
Linklater, Mr., 67.
Lipans, 234.
Little Wound, 261, 265.
Llama of the Andes, 170.
Lobsters unknown at Labrador, 70.
Lodges, how constructed, 362.
London Magazine, 448.
Long Walk, narrative of, 86, 97, 98.
Los Angeles, 303.
Loskiel on Indian picture writing, 15, 34,38.
Lossing, Benson J., his paper, 452.
Louchoux Indians, 188.
Louisville, attack on, 51.
Loyola, influences of, 104.
Lynn, John, spy, 59.
Lyon, Thomas, Indian leader, 53, 63.

Mack, Martin, missionary, 455.
Mackenzie river, 81.
Mackina, mission to, 102.
Mackinaw, isle of, 114, 115.
Magazine of Am. History, 416.
Magdalen islands, walrus exterminated in, 70.
Maguey, Indian plant, 198, 202.
Mahwee, Eunice, last of the Pequods, 456; Joseph, 458; Pequod captive, 454, 455.
Maine salmon fisheries, 186.
Mambre, Zenobe, missionary, 118.
Manabozho, the demi-god, 23.
Manatoulin islands, 213.
Mandans, 83; of Welsh descent, 85; their location, 222.
Manitou, 104, 297; the bad spirit, 22.
Manitouwock, 298.
Manoir Menard, 270.
Mansolia, emissary of Iroquois, 116.
Manufactures, 370.
Maquèapos, medicine man, his extraordinary predictions, 80, 82, 83.
Marest, Gabriel, died, 119; Jesuit, 279.
Maret, Jesuit missionary, 110.

INDEX. 485

Marines captured, 449.
Marivalles mountains, 402.
Marquette, 225; charged to explore Mississippi, 112, 113; his route, 105; died 114; mission to Sault St. Marie, 111, 112, 114; riviere du, 114, 115; remains taken to Mackinaw, 115; his successors, 118.
Marriages among Apaches and Zunis, 87.
Marsh, O. C., fossil student, 258, 262.
Marshall, Edward, concerned in the long walk, 98; Moses, his testimony of the long walk, 97, 98, 99, 100, 101.
Martyr, Peter, on Indian origin, 285.
Masconteuec, 115, 116.
Mascontins, 105, 112, 115.
Mason, Capt. John, 453.
Massachusetts nations, locality of, 211.
Massasoit, anecdote of, 289.
Massé Evremond, 107.
Matagorda bay, 166.
Mather, Cotton, his notion of the origin of the aborigines, 11; history of Phillps war, 475; his confidence, 414; increase, his account of the delivery of Hadley, 462; Magnalia, 280; theory of Indian origin, 286.
Matlatzincas, 194.
Mattabesets, their locality, 283.
Mattole station, 319.
Mayas, 422; language, 197.
Mayhews of Martha's Vineyard, 406.
Mazatecas, 195.
McCrea, Jane, tragedy of, 379.
Mechassippi, unknown course of, 112, 113.
Medicine men below contempt, 75; extraordinary acts of, 76, 77, 78, 79, 80.
Meewoc dialects, 433.
Migrations, song of, 28.
Meidoo nation, 433.
Meldrum, his snow medicine, 78.
Melendez, Don Pedro, 334, 343.
Mendivil, Jose, 48.
Mendocino agency expenses, 321; reservation, 319.
Mengwi, the, 39, 40, 41.
Menominees, 216.
Mesnard, sufferings of, 110.
Mexican causeways, 203; migrations, 239, 240; population, estimates of, 193; languages, 194; records burnt, 11; saddles, expensively ornamented, 43.
Mexico founded, 240, 241; gulf of, 112, 114; lake of, 204, 206; floating garders, 205; migrations from the north, 253; petty nations of, 191, 195; pueblo villages, 193. *
Meztitlans, 194.
Miamis, 104, 106, 111; kill Ottawas, 270, 271.

Miantonimoh, chief of Narragansetts, 453.
Michassippa river, 104, 105.
Michel, Jaques, 107.
Michigan lake, voyageurs of, 115; purchase of, 361; see *Lake Michigan*.
Michilimakinak (the great turtle), 26.
Michuacan confederacy, 192, 194.
Micmacs, their locality, 211.
Migrations, traditions of from the west, 41; routes of, 169, 170, 171, 173, 324; 230, 231, 232, 233, 235, 239, 242, 245, 253; considered, 210, 212.
Mikasuke vocabulary, 129, 125.
Mines of California, 305.
Minikanyes, 219.
Minneconjous, 261, 265.
Minnesota, Dakotan occupation of, 229; Dakotas located in, 219.
Minnitarees, 198, 222.
Minsi tribe, 40; their locality, 212.
Miscaleros, 234.
Miskaouki, speech of, 270, 277.
Mission of the Rappahannock, 339; destroyed, 342.
Missions established, 16, 68, 111; system a failure, 322.
Missisagas, their locality, 212, 273.
Mississippi, 104, 105, 114, see *Michassippa*; missions, 106; passage of, 26, 27; passed by migrations, 41; the blue river, 221.
Missouri nations, 220; river, 113; unfavorable to Indian sustenance, 178; the muddy river, 221.
Missouri, definition of, 241; their locality, 220, 222 see *Upper Missouri*; nations, 222.
Mix, Capt., 260.
Mixtecas, 195.
Mobile, Jesuits at, 119.
Modocs, 439, 440.
Moqui idioms of Arizona, 428.
Mohave dialect, 429.
Mohawks, 226; cast their fortunes with the British, 145; reside on the Grand river, 151; territory, 284; prowess, 284; massacred last of the Pequods, 454.
Mohegans, or Wolves, 28; their locality, 211, 212.
Molunthe, Indian name of Fast, 55.
Mongolian resemblance of Seneca, 224.
Monseys, see Minsi, 40.
Montaks, their locality, 211.
Montezuma, conquerors of, 10.
Montigney, missionary, 119.
Moore, Martin, his paper, 405.
Moravian, missionaries, 455, 456; ruins, on the Tuscarawas, 59; supply ship, 66; agent, 60.
Morgan, Lewis H., on Indian migrations, 158.

Moss, edible, 181.
Mound-builders, 176, 216, 243.
Mount Venture fort, 448.
Mountain areas, 170.
Mountaineers, 234.
Muddy river (Missouri), 221.
Mummies, Alaskan, 344, 349.
Muscogulges, 41.
Musical traits, 339.
Mutsun dialect, 422, 425, 430, 431.
Mvskokes, 120, 121.
Mystic river, Indian fort on, 452; destroyed, 454.
Mythological history, importance of, 12.

Nanticokes, their locality, 212.
Narragansetts join English, 453; last remnant of, 455; their locality, 211.
Narwhal at Labrador, 70.
Natches, 120, 236; assimilated to the Toltecans, 41.
Natches 104, Favrè at, 119.
Natick, praying Indian settlement, 409.
Nation du Chat destroyed, 110; de Feu (Mascoutins), 115.
Naumkeage, plantation of, 405.
Navijoes, 234; assault Village Indians, 190; spinners, 352, 359.
Neblaska, definition of, 167.
Nebraska, its landscape, 168.
Nehantics, their locality, 283.
Netelas, 231.
Neutral nation, their locality, 227.
Nevome dialect, 429.
New England, Indians, their fisheries, 175; Hist. and Gen. Register, 461.
New Englander, 280.
New France company, vessels captured, 106.
New Mexican Indians, 189; dialects, 233; Indian spinners, 352.
New York Historical Society, paper read before, 9.
Nez-perces, 444; mission to, 111.
Niantics, join English, 453.
Nicaragua, language of, 197, 249.
Nicholas, missionary to Nez Percés, 111.
Nicollet, 13.
Niobarra expedition, 260.
Nipmuck territory, 282.
Niza, Marcos de, 246.
Nome Cult agency, expenses, 321; outrages, 318.
Nome Lackee agency, expenses of, 321.
Nonantum, Eliot at, 407, 408.
Nootka dialect, 446.
North American Indians, origin of, 253; Indian, Crawford's statue of, 452; Review, 159, 161.
Northampton county destroyed, 94.
Northern Blackfeet, 81.
Northfield, Treat's march to, 476.

North western territory, early Jesuit missions to, 102, 103.
Nattowas, 226, 228; extinct, 227; escape of, 449, 450.
Nouvelle France, viceroy of, 110.
Nowikakhat Indians, 345.
Nueces river, 166.

Odjibway songs, 418.
Ogallahs, 219.
Ogallallahs, 261.
Oglethorpe, General, 448.
Ohenonpas, 219.
Ohio, falls of, 51; Indian sacrifice, 323; river, 104; poor for subsistence, 175; woodlands, 166.
Ojibwas, 212, 213, 217; fish eaters, 164; of Lake Superior, 174; paths blazed, 15.
Okames, their locality, 221.
Old Man Afraid of his Horses, chief, 265.
Omahas, 220.
Oneidas, 226.
Oneko, son of Uncas, 477.
Onion, Indian plant, 198.
Onondaga, definition of, 241.
Onondagas, 226; enemies of the Hurons, 110.
Ontonagon, 213.
Ord, Gen. O. C., 259.
Osages, their locality, 221, 224, 225.
Otawas, 212; forced westward, 213; of Mackinaw, 174, 175; see Ottawas.
Otoes, their locality, 220.
Otomies, 194.
Ottawas, 113; their location, 110; deputation to Quebec, 110; mission to, 110; coasts Lake Superior, 111.
Oviedo, 333; on Nicaragua languages, 197.
Ouyatanons, 270.

Pacific Indian languages, 416, 424, 426, 446; migrations to, 253.
Pacification of the Indians, 394.
Packard, A. S. Jr., 65.
Palfrey, on attack of Hadley, 466.
Palmer, Lieut., killed, 380.
Pamakona, 272.
Pampticos, their locality, 212.
Panama Indians, 189.
Parker, O. J., his paper, 396.
Parker lake, 399.
Parks of the Colorado, 170.
Patagonia, Esquimaux of, 10.
Patween race, 435.
Pawnees, 230, 231.
Pawnee Killer, chief, 265.
Payutes, 427, 428.
Peabody, W. O. B., 102.
Peace between French and Six Nations, 111.

INDEX.

Peace river plateau, 167.
Peel river Indians, 189.
Pelang, Jose, 396.
Penn, Wm., his arrival, 86.
Pennsbury manor, 88.
Pennsylvania Indians, first murder by, 101; purchase of, 86, 87.
Pepper, Indian plant, 198, 202, 205.
Pequod fort destroyed, 1637, 453; nation destroyed, 454; their location, 452; their number, 452; last of the, 452, 456.
Pekitanoni, 114.
Perrot, 111. 112.
Peruvian Indians, 41, 162.
Pesant, chief, 270, 271, 273, 278.
Peters, Henry, his paper, 352.
Peoria, 105.
Philip, his contempt for the gospel, 413; his war, effect upon the Indians, 408; history by Cotton Mather, 475.
Picture writing of aborigines, 15.
Pilgrims prompted by religious motives, 104.
Pima dialects, 429.
Pinart, Alphonse, 344; M., 351.
Pinet, Hugues, 105; successor of, 118.
Pinols, 234
Pish-gagh-ti-gock, original of Schaghticock, 455.
Pit river Indians, 439.
Pit river massacre, 320.
Pittsburgh Evening Chronicle, 387.
Platte river, poorly supplied with fish, 178; occupied by Dakotahs, 226, 231.
Plow unknown to the aborigines, 199.
Plymouth colony, 406.
Pocahontas, Velasco a kinsman of, 343.
Pocomtuck Valley Association, 461.
Poconchi language, 197.
Poduncks, their locality, 283.
Pomo race, 436.
Popolocas, 195.
Population, centre of, 173.
Porter, Hist. Discourse, 283.
Potomac, Spanish standard planted on, 343; the Espiritu Santo, 336.
Pottawatomies, 104, 106, 111, 113, 114, 115, 212, 213, 273.
Poupa, lake, 449.
Powder river, battle on, 262.
Powow, 299.
Powhatan confederacy Algonquins, 343.
Powhattans, their locality, 212.
Prairie area, 165, 168, 169; line, 167, 170, 171; nations, migrations of, 230, 231, 232; never occupied by Indians, 169; nurseries of the antelope, 170; solitudes, 177.
Praying Indians, 456; number of, 408.
Prehistoric immigration, 223.
Prescott's Conquest of Mexico, 193.

Pretty Crow, chief, 264, 265.
Prophets, Indian, 418.
Protestants prohibited in Canada, 107.
Provision of Chippewas, 369, 371.
Puants (Winnebagoes), 221.
Pueblo idioms, 428; Indians, 235.
Puget sound, dialects, 425; estimate of Indian population, 188; region, 180.
Punkas, 220.
Pynchon, John, 475.

Quamash, 186.
Quappas, their locality, 221, 224.
Quarante Sous, chief, 270, 275, 276.
Quebec, 105, 106; famine at, 106; deputation to, 111; records, 117; surrendered to the English, 107.
Queen Charlotte's island, 182; Indians of, 188.
Quetzalcoatl, 11.
Quiche language, 197.
Quichhuas, 422.
Quinnipiacks, their location, 283.
Quintè, bay of, 151.

Rafinesque, characteristics of, 13, 37.
Raguenaw, father, 109.
Rainy lake, 220.
Raleigh, Sir Walter, 333.
Randolph, Edward, pursues regicides, 471, 477.
Rappahannock, Spanish mission, 333.
Rattlesnake doctor, 459.
Ray, Luzerne, 280.
Raymbault, Charles, 104, 109.
Red Cloud, 265; agency, 260, 261; map of, 265.
Red Dog, 265.
Red Jacket, 153.
Red Knives, 234.
Red Leaf, chief, 265.
Redondo, Christopher, massacred, 342.
Red river, dreaming at, 375.
Rees Indians, 387.
Religion of the Indian, 296-99.
Religion the motive of the Jesuit missionaries, 103; also of the Pilgrims, 104.
Religious belief of Indians, 77, 78.
Rice, fort, attacked, 60.
Richardson's boat voyage, 172.
Richelieu, Cardinal, 106.
Riggs, Dakotan lexicon, 219.
Rio Frio Indians, 396.
Rio Grande, 166; Indians, 189, 190.
Rising Head, noted war chief, 82.
River Indians, 218, 283.
Roanoke island, 333.
Robbins, Chandler, on Hadley attack, 467.
Robe Noire, riviere du, 115.
Roberts, A. C., 396.
Rocky Bear, chief, 265.

Rocky mountain, bands, 234; nations, 217; languages, extinct, 253; scenery, 81.
Rocky mountains, barriers to emigration, 173.
Rogue river Indians, 441.
Roman Catholic missionaries, success of, 377.
Roquemont, M. de, 106; captured, 107.
Roving Indians, 189, 194; stone, age of, 163; avoided Ohio, 220.
Roxboro, duke of, 149.
Running Antelope, chief, 391.
Rupert's land, voyage through, 172.
Russell, Rev. Mr., conceals regicides, 461-78.
Russian America, cession of, 255.

Sabianism, 10.
Sacramento valley Indians, 304.
Sacrificial dance, 388, 390.
Sacs, 273.
Sagamon, bay of, 110.
Sahaptin, 425; stock, 443.
Salmon, fisheries, 181, 182; habits, 183, 184, 186.
Salt river, 335.
Saltillo blankets, 45.
San Carlos, fort, 397.
San Joaquin, 319; Indians, 304.
San Juan del Norte, ascension of, 397.
Sans arcs, 219, 261.
Santa Barbara dialects, 426, 430.
Sassacus, Pequod chief, 452; massacred, 454.
Saskatchewan, 81, 220, 224; a route of migration, 169, 173; migration, 233; river, 75.
Susquehannocks, 226; extinct, 227.
Saukies, 273.
Sauks, 111, 113, 213.
Sault St. Marie, 104, 115; mission to, 109, 111, 112, 113, 114.
Sauteurs, 273.
Sawks, their locality, 213.
Schaghticooks, how composed, 455, 458; reservation, 450; baptisms among, 460.
Schoolcraft, 15, 18, 22; Indians, 418.
Scoffies, their locality, 211.
Scott, Walter, on attack of Hadley, 460.
Sea trout taken at Labrador, 70.
Segura, John Baptist, massacred, 342.
Selish dialects, 422; family, 444.
Seminoles, 223; in Alabama, 120, 121; vocabulary, 120, 125.
Semisopochnoi island, 255.
Semitchi island, 255.
Seneca, definition of, 241.
Seneca-Iroquois system, 257; resemblance to Mongolian, 224.
Senecas, 226, 227.
Sequoyah, alphabet suggested, 420.
Serpent, a symbol of evil, 20, 23.

Seven council fires, 220.
Sharon, Moravian missionary station, 456.
Shasta, dialect. 438; language at, 416.
Shawnees, 216; area, 221.
Shauanos, 120.
Shea, John Gilmary, his paper, 333; Linguistics, 429.
Shekomeko monument, 456.
Sheldon, George, his paper, 461.
Sherman, John, 459.
Sheshatapoosh locality, 211.
Shingask, reward for, 94.
Shiyans, 198; of Algonkin lineage, 225; their locality, 216.
Shoshonee migrations, 231, 232, 233, 234, 248; dialects, 422, 426, 428.
Shovels of the Mexicans, 199.
Shumagin island mummies, 347.
Siam, missionary to, 106.
Sickness, despondency in, 376.
Sierra Madre, 46; sheep herds, 383.
Sierra Nevada, 120; effect upon the winds, 168; Indians, 304.
Simcoe lake, 226.
Simon, Louis Hyacinth, 119.
Simpson, Sir George, estimate of Indian population, 170.
Sinago, Ottawa chief, 273.
Sinagoes, 270.
Sioux, league with Iroquois, 115; mission among, 110; origin of name, 228; roving, 387; sacrificial dance, 389; their location, 178, 213; treaty, 1868, 260; vision, 127.
Sissetons, 219.
Sitjar's Dictionary, 430.
Sitting Bull, 261, 263, 265.
Six Nations destroy Hurons, 109; in treaty at Phila., 91; peace with French, 111.
Slaughter, Col., 51.
Slover, captive, 57.
Smith, Buckingham, 120, 338; Capt. John, his voyage for Cathay, 334.
Snake dialects, 427; Indians, 231; river salmon, 186.
Snakes, expelled, 27.
Snow medicine, 78.
Songs of the Indians, 16.
Sonora, irruptions on, 353.
Sonoma mission, 432.
Southern dialects, 430.
Spanish, mission colony in Virginia, 333; priests in California, 300, 313.
Spider, chief, 265, 267.
Spinners, Indian, 352.
Spirituous liquors, 373; prohibited, 374.
Square island, 65.
Squash, Indian plant, 198.
Squaw dance, 391.
Squaw-man, definition of, 387.
Squier, E. G., his paper on the Walum-olum, 9.

St. Augustine, founder of, 343; Yamasees flee to, 449.
St. Francis Xavier, mission, 102.
St. Helena sound, 336.
St. Ignace, mission at Mackina, 102.
St. John's cape, 333.
St. Joseph, 104, 105, 113. 114.
St. Louis, mission of, 105; Peoria, 119.
St. Marie, sault, fishing place, 213; sault, white fish, 183.
St. Martha, bishop of, 147.
St. Mary, mission, 102.
St. Mary's bay mission, 333, 334.
St. Michael, chapel at, 111.
Stabber, chief, 265.
Standing Rock, original of, 388; agency, 388; under the Catholic church, 394.
Stanley-Custer expedition, 387.
Stanton, Col., 260.
Stiles, Ezra, on Hadley attack, 462.
Stockbridge Indians, 455.
Stoddard, Solomon, on Philip's war, 476.
Stone age, 253.
Stone, Wm. L., his life of Brant, 145; his paper, 379.
Stuart Granville, 427.
Subsistence, means of, 173, 174, 175.
Sugar manufacture. 370.
Sukley, Dr., 182.
Sulley, Gen., defeated Two Bears, 390.
Sun, the symbol of the good spirit, 23.
Superior, mission on, 105; coasted by Allouez, 111.
Susquehanna palisaded towns, 340.
Sutnux, John, 438.
Swain, Capt., at Hadley, 477.
Swan, Caleb, 120.
Swearinger, Col., 62.
Sword, chief, 265, 267.
Sylleri, plains of, 110.

Tacullies, 234.
Talamatan, not Iroquois, 41.
Talcott, Major, 477.
Tall chief, 324.
Tallegwi, contest with, 26, 38.
Talocan valley, 194.
Talon, intendant, 110.
Taltecs, of Mexico, 191.
Tamarois, 104, 105; mission, 118, 119.
Tamil people, 257.
Tampa, 120.
Tampico, natives of, 194.
Tanner on the Indian songs, 16; narrative, 378.
Taos, 418.
Tarasca language, 194.
Teakiki, 105.
Tecumseh, prediction of, 85.
Teedyuskung, treaty with, 80; talk with, 95, attacked the whites, 99.
Teeton dialect, 219, 220.

Tejon agency, expenses of, 321; reservation, 307.
Tekarihogea of the Mohawks, 150.
Ten Mile river, 455.
Tenochtitlan, Mexico, 203.
Tepanecans, 192.
Tepejacac causeway, 203.
Tetenchoua, chief of Miamas, 111, 115.
Texas, forests of, 166; Indian spinners, 352.
Tezcuco lake, its elevation, 203, 204, 206.
Tezcucans, 192.
Thayendanegea (Joseph Brant), 145.
Thick-headed-horse's dream, 127.
Three Bears, chief, 265.
Tinné Indians, 440.
Tlacopans, 192; causeway, 203.
Tlahuicas, 195.
Tlascalan, confederacy, 192, 195; agriculturists, 164.
Tobacco, Indian plant, 198, 202.
Tolewa language, 438.
Toltecans, 41.
Toltecs, original seat of, 240, 247, 249.
Tomochichi, chief, 450.
Tonnahowi, chief, 450; buried, 451.
Tonti, his Relation, 115; lieutenant of La Salle, 116.
Torquemada, estimate of Mexican population, 193.
Torn Belly, chief, 265.
Totonacs, 195.
Tototen, tribe, 441.
Towaches, 231.
Tracey, Marquis, viceroy, 110.
Traders, villainy of, 373.
Trapper, keen scent on a trail, 81.
Treat, Major, march of, 476.
Treaty at Philadelphia, 1742, 90.
Trout, varieties, 183.
Trumbull, J. Hammond, 412.
Trumbull's Hist. Connecticut, 280.
Tuckabatchee, prediction of, 85.
Tunicas, mission to the, 119.
Turanian system, 257.
Turner, W. W., linguist, 234.
Turner's falls fight, 477.
Turtle, mythology of, 26.
Tuscaroras, 226; removal of, 227.
Two Bears' lodge, 388.
Tymochtee river, 55, 57.

Uchees, 120, 230.
Ulpius's map, 333.
Umkwas, 234.
Umpquas of Alsea, agency, 441.
Unalashka, 347.
Uncas, 282; Pequod rebel, 453; last of the Mohegans, 454.
Uncpapas, 219, 261, 390.
Unga caves, mummies of, 347, 350.
United States Catholic magazine, 361.

Upper Missouri nations, 222.
Utah dialects, 427, 428.

Vancouver Indians, 188.
Vaudreuil, speech to, 270, 277.
Velasco, Don Luis de, 334, 343.
Vermont, without Indian population, 285.
Village Indians, 161; arts among, 162, 163; migrations, 235, 236, 242, 243; mound builders, 176; of Mexico, 191, 195, 207; abuses of, 197; of New Mexico, 189, 190; their power, 209; their system, 210.
Vincennes, 104, 110; Francois Morgan, 110.
Virginia, first European settlement, 333; Spanish standard planted in, 343.
Visit to the Standing Rock agency, 387.
Visscher, Matthew, letter to, 148.
Vocabularies collected by Smithsonian Inst., 420.
Voltaire on Indian origin, 286.
Voyages, account of the first, 197.

Waban, praying Indian, 410.
Wabash, 104, 105, 110.
Walrus exterminated at Labrador, 70.
Wulum-olum, with translation of, 9, 14, 18.
Wanawanda, Sioux chief, 128.
War between France and England, 106.
Warm Springs, 418.
Warner, Benj. F., 324.
War-trail, how detected, 81.
Washington, Mount, flora, 70.
Watson, John, narrative of, 86.
Weathersfield Indians, 283.
Weavers, Indian, 352, 360.
Weebetuck river, 455, 456.
Weeping dances, 432.
Weiser, Conrad, his testimony of the long walk, 96.
Weits-pek dialect, 138.
Welsh descent of the Mandans, 85.
Wequamps fight, 474, 476.
Western Reserve and Ohio Hist. Society, 270.
Western slope, languages of, 421.
Whalley, Edward, regicide, 461.
Wheat, Indian, 199.
Wheeling, Va., attack on, 59.
Whirlwind's village, 27.
White river, 263; bonefield, 260.

White Tail, chief, 262, 265.
Whittlesey, Col. Charles, his paper, 270.
Wild Indians of California, 304.
Williams, Roger, 42.
Wilson, Daniel, his theory, 160.
Winds, effected by the mountains, 168.
Windsor Indians, 283.
Winnebagoes, 211; their locality, 213; their location, 221.
Winnipeg lake, 220.
Winslow's Relation, 280.
Wintoon tribes, 434.
Wisconsin, its discovery, 102; purchase of, 361; river, 104, 105.
Wishkosk dialects, 437.
Witchitas, 231.
Withlacoochc, signification of, 125.
Wolf's Necklace, chief, 391.
Wolverine found at Labrador, 70.
Wongungs, their, locality, 283.
Wyandots, 275; ancient Hurons, 226.
Wyckoff, Wm. C., 258.

Xalisco villages burned, 197.
Xochimilco lake, dikes of, 202, 203.

Yakima salmon fisheries, 183.
Yakon tribe, 441.
Yale college, fossils at, 258.
Yamacraw chief, Tomochichi, 450.
Yanktons, 219.
Yellowstone expedition, 261.
Yamasees, chastisement of, 448.
Yanktonnais, 388, 390.
Yendats, true name of the Hurons, 107.
Yocuts of California, 432, 433.
Young Man Afraid of his Horses, chief, 265.
Yucatan, languages of, 194, 197; population of, 196.
Yuka language, 435.
Yukon Indians, 188; valley burials, 345.
Yuma dialects, of Colorado, 429.

Zane, Col. Silas, 59; Elizabeth, 60.
Zapotecas, 195.
Zeisberger's Dictionary, 14.
Zevallos, Sancho, massacred, 342.
Zuazo, estimate of Mexican population, 193.
Zuni Indians, visits to, 43; Indian houses, 190; language, 46.

www.ingramcontent.com/pod-product-compliance
Lightning Source LLC
Chambersburg PA
CBHW051232300426
44114CB00011B/702